JAMES MCENANEY is a former secondary school English teacher turned lecturer and journalist. With a focus on education, transparency and freedom of information, he writes regularly for publications including *The Herald*, *The Guardian* and the *Times Educational Supplement Scotland*. In 2017, he contributed a chapter on Scotland's school system to *A Nation Changed? The SNP and Scotland Ten Years On*. He lives near Glasgow with his wife, son, dog and rabbit, and still can't quite believe that he was lucky enough to get the chance to write about this Scottish journey.

A Scottish Journey

Personal impressions of modern Scotland

JAMES McENANEY

Luath Press Limited

EDINBURGH

www.luath.co.uk

First published 2018

ISBN: 978-1-912147-42-7

The paper used in this book is recyclable.
It is made from low chlorine pulps produced in a low energy,
low emission manner from renewable forests.

Printed and bound by Bell & Bain Ltd, Glasgow

Typeset in 11 point Sabon by Main Point Books, Edinburgh

Contents

For Ruth and Ciaran,
the most important people in Scotland.

Acknowledgements

IT IS IMPORTANT at this stage to thank the many people without whom this book would never have happened, but I am unable to list all of those whose assistance and encouragement has been invaluable. The most important of these is my wonderful (and very tolerant) wife, Ruth, whose support means everything to me, and whose opinion I value more than any other, as well as my mum and dad who both supported and encouraged me throughout this process. Then there are the people who welcomed me into their homes all around the country and gave me a glimpse, albeit a brief and fleeting one, of their lives. I can never repay their generosity so instead offer unreserved gratitude for their kindness.

To everyone else who played a part – the people who have given me opportunities to write in recent years; the friends who read numerous drafts of this or that chapter; those who simply took a few minutes out of their day to talk to me along the way; and to all at Luath Press – I wish to say thank you for being a part of my Scottish journey.

Introduction

IT ALL STARTED back in 2012. I was an English teacher at Arran High School and in my first year of being fully qualified was given the opportunity to teach Advanced Higher to a class of three brilliant students. One of the options for the literature component of the course was the great Scottish writer and poet, Edwin Muir, whose work I had first encountered as a teenager.

It was through teaching Muir's poetry that I first discovered *Scottish Journey*, a record of his impressions as he travelled through the country in the mid-'30s, from Edinburgh to Orkney via the south, Glasgow and the Highlands. Unheralded at the time of publication and unappreciated, even by the author himself, it is nonetheless a fascinating, insightful and beautifully written account which, in the words of the historian TC Smout – who penned introductions to both the 1979 and 1996 editions – 'held up a mirror to the face of Scotland all those years ago'. It is, Smout added, 'frightening to see so many recognisable features in its glass', an observation which remains true even into the 21st century.

It occurred to me at the time that a modern version of Muir's book, examining both the striking similarities and profound differences between his Scotland and ours, could be something worth pursuing. In the 1930s, the country was struggling to recover from the Great Depression whereas now it is trying to cope with the consequences of the 2008 financial crash, the resulting worldwide recession and the devastating decision to impose austerity economics. While three generations ago Muir saw the emergence of what would become the SNP, today that party has been in government in Scotland for more than a decade, holds a majority of Scottish seats in Westminster and even managed to deliver not just a historic majority government to Holyrood, but also a referendum on Scottish independence. The twin shadows of deindustrialisation and depopulation loomed large in Muir's Scotland, destroying the lives of countless people, and they still darken the skies of ours.

Although I could perceive all of these connections, I never expected to have the chance to explore them further. Surely, I thought, such opportunities are only available to the Lesley Riddochs and Neal Aschersons of the world, not an unpublished, 20-something high school English teacher whose most extensive work to date had been an undergraduate dissertation on Frankenstein? So I put the whole idea to the back of my mind and went about my business as a teacher. A few years later, I reluctantly left Arran and returned to Glasgow, taking up a position as a college lecturer while also drifting into journalism, first writing opinion columns for new media sites such as *CommonSpace* and *Bella Caledonia*, then building a bit of a reputation as a specialist in Scottish education and Freedom of Information.

All the while, the idea for my own Scottish journey had been bubbling away. In 2017, five years after it had first occurred to me – and after a push from a friend who pointed out the hypocrisy of telling students never to hold themselves back while refusing to have a bit of faith in myself – I started to make tentative plans, trying to figure out what the whole process would involve and whether I might be up to it after all. I was fortunate – and grateful – to be directed to Luath Press, who supported the idea from the start.

When I finally decided to go ahead and attempt to write this book, the idea was very simple: I would retrace the route of Muir's original journey, following the same roads and making the same stops wherever possible, reporting on the ways in which the nation had changed in the 80-odd years between our respective trips. I spent days trying to plot Muir's tyre tracks from Edinburgh to Orkney, transposing that original trip onto modern roads as far as possible – but soon realised that I was wasting my time.

One of the most obvious issues I encountered was that Muir's journey ended in Orkney, whereas mine could not. There are two reasons for this. First, and most obvious, is the fact that I live in Glasgow and would have to return to the Central Belt regardless of how the story in my book ended. Even if the final chapter featured a beautiful Orcadian sunset framing a series of profound, ground-breaking reflections, the next morning I would still be getting back on my bike and heading south. My journey, in a physical sense, would not be over.

Beyond this simple matter of geography, however, lay a more fundamental problem, which also explains why I eventually decided that I would not bind myself to Muir's long-lost tyre tracks. In travelling to Orkney, Muir was returning to his childhood home for a summer holiday with his family. For those familiar with his work – and especially his poetry – there is a pleasing circularity to this conclusion of his own personal journey around Scotland: he was, in a very real sense, going back to where it all started and using that experience to frame his reflections on the country as a whole. Though my book could conceivably have found some sort of conclusion on Orkney, it would never have felt quite right. It therefore seemed to make sense to incorporate my inevitable travels back to the Central Belt into the whole project. By abandoning the idea of a simple A to B approach, as well as the plan to stick slavishly to the route Muir laid out, and instead setting off on what would ultimately become a circumnavigation of Scotland, I could open up a whole new section of the country as part of my adventure. Crucially, I would also be able to complete my own, personal, Scottish Journey.

That settled, all I needed was a jumping-off point, a start-and-finish location fit for the modern nation through which I would be travelling. As a Glaswegian, I would have liked this to have been somewhere in my home city but, in truth, there was only ever one serious contender: the Scottish Parliament. Founded in 1999 following a landslide referendum two years earlier, and moving into its current home in 2004, it is now the undoubted centre of gravity for Scottish political and civic life; it seemed only natural that any attempt to paint a picture – however flawed, personal and incomplete – of 21st century Scotland had to begin and end in front of the building that has come to symbolise so much of the country. This is especially true for a millennial, 'post-devolution Scot' like myself who, having been born in 1986, has never really known a Scotland without its own, distinct voice, even if it does often struggle to tell its own story.

Of course – like any worthwhile journey – not everything went to plan. Days before setting off my motorbike failed its MOT due to issues with the headlights and the throttle cable, while both tyres also had to be replaced; then a forecast for snow and ice across the middle of the country forced me to head to Edinburgh a day earlier than expected, disrupting my preparation. During the first two days of the journey, the weather was so bad – at points dangerously so – that the whole project looked at risk of having to be abandoned. Yet for every unexpected roadblock there were a dozen highlights, from chance conversations to glorious views, from sites reaching into the ancient past to tantalising glimpses of the future.

Like Muir, however, I feel that I should also warn readers of what they will not find in these pages. In his introduction he explained that he was not offering 'a survey of Scotland but a bundle of impressions' and insisted that his was 'not *the* Scottish Journey, but *a* Scottish Journey'. The same is true now. This book is by no means an attempt to resolve the endless contradictions of this country – which Muir accurately described as a 'confusing conglomeration' – into any sort of definition of either the nation or its people. It is merely a pile of imperfect snapshots, arranged and presented in an attempt to reflect my impressions of the Scotland I encountered in the spring of 2018.

I would also advise readers not to expect a travel guide to the towns and villages through which I passed, few of which could be done justice by the limited time I was able to spend in them. My travels took me in and out of many of these places at random, with rarely any effort made to visit the 'must see' attractions that dotted my path. Instead I tried to follow Muir's advice, taking this road or that depending upon my feelings at the time and, as far as possible, gathering up my impressions as casually as a 'collection of shells picked up on a sea-shore'.

Finally, I wish to be clear about one thing above all else: despite the assumptions of many of those to whom I spoke in the months leading up to my journey, as well as some of those I met along the way, this is not a book about Scottish independence.

Readers expecting a treatise on the constitutional future of

Scotland, or a polemical deconstruction of one or other side of that particular debate, will be disappointed. In fact, if there is a central thesis to this project, a core idea buried beneath the simple joy of spending time on the road and becoming better acquainted with one's home country, it is that the increasingly obsessive attempts to view Scotland through a narrow constitutional lens are doomed to failure. The unresolved issue of Scottish independence is an important one, but I do not believe that it is necessarily core to most people's sense of self or, indeed, their sense of Scotland; my experience of travelling through the country, away from the bubbles of both traditional and social media, has only served to sharpen this opinion.

Scotland is as endlessly, wonderfully varied as the people who live here; in the spring of 2018 I was fortunate enough to be able to explore a few fragments of that diversity, gathering my experiences – those snapshots of modern Scotland – together in my own subjective, flawed and deeply personal account of the country I call home.

James McEnaney
Glasgow
August 2018

Edinburgh to Gatehouse of Fleet

'This is a forgotten corner of Scotland'

I AWOKE ON the first morning of my journey with a sense of dread. The day before, the weather had been awful and by the time I went to bed, incessant rain had turned into thick, slushy snow. I had gone to sleep with no real idea of what I would do if, as expected, the roads were not safely rideable the following day. Moving the trip back by a few days was not an option, not least because I had already arranged to stay with some incredibly generous people around the country and couldn't expect them to just rearrange their plans to accommodate my delay.

The threat of a serious snowstorm had already changed my plans once – forcing me to come to Edinburgh a day early – and there was no way I'd be able to safely make my way through the 150-or-so miles to Scotland's south west coast if it finally struck now. My best hope, it seemed, was that any snow would clear by early afternoon, giving me time to get to the parliament and then on to my first overnight stop at Gatehouse of Fleet, even if I would have to take a far more direct route than I had anticipated or desired. It wouldn't be the ideal start, but it would be a start nonetheless.

When I opened the curtains, however, I felt an immediate sense of relief. The temperature had evidently crept up just enough overnight, replacing the snow that had been falling a few hours previous with heavy rain. It felt strange to be so excited about the prospect of setting off on my journey in the midst of a downpour, but you don't ride motorcycles in Scotland for more than a decade without becoming extremely well versed in the art of coaxing the bike over soaking-wet, slippery roads. I had never expected to get through the trip without getting drenched anyway, so why not just get it out of the way? An hour later I was off, heading towards the city centre and, beyond that, the starting point of the journey: the Scottish Parliament.

Being a good Glaswegian I am obviously required to dislike Edinburgh. In fact, one of my earliest memories of my grandfather is his response to someone (I can't remember who) asking if he wanted to go through to the capital for the day:

'Edinburgh? Don't be daft. Nothin' in Edinburgh.'

I certainly couldn't claim to possess an intimate knowledge of the city, but it is also true that I have never warmed to the place during my visits over the years. Having arrived in Edinburgh a day earlier than expected I had taken the opportunity to explore. My cousin and her husband were away for a few days and had kindly allowed me to borrow their home near Murrayfield, so on my first evening I spent some time wandering alongside the Water of Leith as the sun hovered above, and then dropped beyond, the treelines and rooftops. The next day I walked into the city centre and back in order to meet my wife and son, who had come through for a short visit, but relentless, icy rain made it feel once more that Edinburgh was simply a place to be endured.

On a bike things are even worse. Glasgow's roads are far from perfect but the grid system on which the city centre is based at least makes it easy to navigate; in contrast, Edinburgh's incomprehensible junctions, tramlines and occasional cobbled streets (to name just a few challenges) are a nightmare. Even after my desperation led me to use sat nav I still managed to make a few wrong turns as I weaved through the city before the distinctive outline of the parliament building finally came into view.

Delivered three years late and comically over-budget, the Scottish Parliament is one of the most recognisable buildings in the country. It is a staggeringly complex blend of modernism and abstract inspiration, all curves and angles and disparate shapes brought together on a single canvas which, like a magic eye painting, changes as you move around it, each step subtly shifting the angles of light and perspective as the brain struggles to take it all in. It is not, I must confess, entirely to my taste either inside or out (with the exception of the stunning debating chamber, which is superb) and the public reaction to it also remains mixed, even if critics, most notably the judges for the 2005 Stirling Prize, tend to love it.

Of course, the Scottish Parliament is much more than a building and it is what it represents that had really brought me here to start my journey. Although I was born 13 years before the restoration of the parliament in 1999 I am, without a doubt, part of the generation of post-devolution Scots whose whole view of the country has been unavoidably, inextricably shaped by the existence of a national legislature. By the time I went to university, the parliament had been in existence for five years and had already shifted the national consciousness. Now, 14 years on, its absence is simply unthinkable. I cannot say what impact devolution had on older generations but it is clear to me that, for Scots of my generation and presumably those to come, it has secured the *idea* of Scotland as a nation in its own right, and not one whose existence depends upon the paternalistic generosity of the other parliament in London, the seat of what the poet, Norman MacCaig, in his tour-de-force 'A Man in Assynt',

The bike outside the Scottish Parliament building

called a 'remote and ignorant government'.

I wanted a few photographs of the bike with the parliament in the background so I bumped it up on to the kerb near some traffic lights and got off, diving underneath the building's huge, umbrella-like overhang before taking off my helmet. It was then that I was approached by one of the police officers stationed at the entrance.

'Hi there, sir. About the motorbike...'

Let us look at the situation from her perspective: I, an unidentified man in a balaclava and lots of loose-fitting, armoured clothing, had arrived unannounced and placed a motorbike (with a bright orange package strapped to the seat) on the pavement between the Scottish Parliament and the Palace of Holyrood House, the latter being the Queen's official residence in Edinburgh. In retrospect, it is a wonder that I even made it as far as the building.

Promising that I would only be a few minutes, I explained that I was about to set off a ten-day trip for a book I was writing, and that I was just waiting for someone from the publisher's office to come and take a few photos before departing. She was, to my great relief, very understanding and even talked to me about the project for a few moments until the photographer arrived.

After a few photos and a quick chat, it was time to really get started. I switched on the sat nav – which I would only be using to find my way back out of Edinburgh – and rolled off onto the road, skirting around the north of Holyrood Park and Portobello before eventually reaching the A7 headed south. As I rode out of Edinburgh and into Midlothian, the whole environment through which I passed began to change but as the landscape opened up, the rain became progressively heavier, magnified by a headwind gusting towards me. Barely half an hour down the road I could already feel my gear struggling to keep me dry and had entirely given up on the prospect of staying warm. I was in for a slog, and I knew it.

By the time I passed a sign welcoming me to the Scottish Borders I was surrounded by the snow that I had feared the night before. The fields and hills on both sides of me were painted a tired, greyish-white which matched the low, heavy clouds, blurring the boundary between ground and sky. The road was mercifully clear but was still very cold and slippery, and I was never sure whether I would swing around the next bend to be confronted by a mound of sludgy snow or a patch of half-melted ice. Minute by minute and mile by mile, the near-freezing rain just kept on falling.

I had initially planned to have my first stop of the trip in Galashiels but, conscious of the worsening weather when I arrived, decided to push on to Hawick while the going was bearable. On the way I passed through Selkirk and various little roadside villages, all of which are, I'm sure, far more pleasant and interesting than they appeared amidst the shivering, unrelenting gloom of that particular morning.

As I arrived in Hawick just before midday, the rain, until now utterly incessant, had begun to ease ever so slightly and the clouds ahead were looking marginally less threatening, so I decided to park the bike and find a place where I might be able to spend an hour warming up and, if I was really lucky, drying out a little. By then, I hoped, the weather might have improved enough to make the rest of the day more enjoyable than the first stretch had been.

I had lunch in the Heart of Hawick, a multi-purpose community space housing a heritage hub, a textile museum, a cinema and a café, part of which sits within a little glass-walled annex hanging over the Slitrig Water, just before it joins with the River Teviot in the middle of town. The café itself is bright and welcoming, far more so than is often the case in facilities attached to this sort of enterprise, and, even on a thoroughly miserable day like this one, the space was busy with families out for lunch, friends meeting for coffee and a few individuals simply reading the newspaper with a cup of tea. After ordering a bowl of soup I sat down in the annex (in a seat chosen largely because of its proximity to a radiator) and watched as the falling rain crashed into the glass roof above me, while the river raced by in a swollen, swirling torrent below.

Hawick is, if not quite pretty (at least not in the rain), certainly a rather fine-looking, resolute sort of place, the type of town its people are probably proud to call home. Even with a few empty shop-fronts, it still feels more substantial and alive than many similar-sized towns further north where it is increasingly common to walk down deserted high streets populated by little more than takeaways, charity shops and bookies. This might be down to simple geography – there are, for example, no motorways in this part of the country carrying huge numbers of people to the out-of-town shopping centres so prevalent in the Central Belt – but I suspected that some other factors might also be at play. Either way, the result is a town which I would have liked to have explored with the benefit of a bit more time and a little sunshine.

By the time I had finished my excellent lunch, the weather had noticeably eased and the sky seemed to be clearing, with patches of lighter grey slowly displacing the dark mass smeared overhead. As I got back onto the bike the rain had faded into little more than a light shower, which seemed like a good omen for the rest of the day. Even if the weather didn't get any better, I reasoned, it would at least be a marked improvement on what I had ridden through to get this far, and so I set off south hoping that the conditions would continue to improve. They did not.

Moments after I departed Hawick, the sky burst in the most spectacular fashion and I found myself riding through a staggering, merciless downpour all the way to the border. Although the road I followed was relatively straight and well-surfaced, the rain had become so heavy that around almost every bend I was faced with water, either pooled on the road or, in the worst cases, actually running across it. Even at relatively slow speeds I found myself aquaplaning – a uniquely unsettling experience on two wheels – as my tyres struggled to cope with the conditions. On several downhill sections I ended up afraid to use the front brake for fear of the bike skidding out from under me, instead depending upon a combination of engine-braking, gear changes and conservative cornering lines to keep the machine, and myself, the right way up.

The weather became so bad it seemed to be affecting the bike's electronics. Just north of Langholm – a 'muckle toun' not far from the border with England – I noticed that the display showing the engine oil temperature, which usually sits at around 80 degrees during normal riding, had gone blank. I presumed that this was a result of the weather, and worried about the rain affecting more of the bike's electronics, but when the wind eased a little the numbers reappeared, slowly creeping up from 35 degrees, which is the temperate at which the system activates when the bike is first turned on. The electronics, I realised, were fine. I was simply riding through weather so hostile, with such an enormous quantity of water constantly ploughing into me, that it had almost entirely cooled the engine and was now preventing it from properly warming back up.

I had already been riding cautiously but was now forced to slow down even more to protect the bike, thus extending the time I would have to spend exposed to the very conditions which were causing the problem in the first place.

All of this gave me very little opportunity to really see, never mind explore, this part of Scotland. I would like to be able to describe the way in which the hills around me rolled through these beautiful borderlands, tumbling down towards the north east of England where they are welcomed by the Cheviot, or the way the light seemed to wash down from the slopes and soak into the fertile farmland below, radiating promise of new life and a good harvest. Maybe it's all true but, on this occasion, I was not fortunate enough to find out. I did enjoy a very brief gap in the rain as I passed a 'Welcome to England' sign – the irony of which was not lost on me – before the road tilted back into Scotland, but by the time I made it through Gretna on my way west it came roaring back, as heavy as ever. I saw little alternative but to get my head down and keep pushing through, past Dumfries and Kirkcudbright (which I had been looking forward to visiting) all the way to Gatehouse of Fleet, where I had been offered a bed for the night by the author, Karen Campbell.

When I arrived the streets seemed largely deserted, my only company the gorgeous, turreted, granite clock tower standing proudly in the centre of town. Muir had briefly passed through here and described it as a 'pleasant little secluded town with holiday-makers wandering about the streets' but I saw no sign of such activity. It would be nice to believe that the foul weather was the sole culprit for my apparent isolation but something in the air – other than the water – suggested that there were other, more persistent factors at play. I later discovered that I was right.

By the time I reached Karen's home (where I also met their lovely old Collie named Sam) I was utterly soaked, every single item of clothing on my body clinging to the layers above and beneath, with the whole mass of fabric stuck to my skin as though I were in the process of being embalmed. I was keen to stretch my legs after the first day on the bike, especially as I had only stopped once since leaving Edinburgh, so was grateful for the recommendation of a walk around the road running behind the house where, I was assured, I would find something well worth the effort.

With my gear hanging up to dry, I borrowed a pair of boots and a light jacket and set off, frustrated to find that, finally, the rain had stopped completely and the sky was beginning to clear. I walked for about a mile, past some farmhouses, a little body of water known as Woodend Loch (not much more than a large pond with tree-covered hills sloping away on the far side, a small wooden jetty and a little dinghy beached on the bank – but strangely pleasant all the same) and a flooded bog overflowing with water-lilies just on the cusp of bursting into life. And then, as promised, and I simply couldn't miss it: Anwoth Old Kirk.

Best known for its use as a location in *The Wicker Man* (in the Maypole scene, for those familiar with the film) the ruined, roofless chapel was, according to a carving in the archway above the entrance, 'BUILT AD 1627'. These words stand frozen in time, below a modern plaque providing brief details of the life of Samuel Rutherford, the minister here from 1627 until 1638; a 'preacher of permanent renown' and 'reformer and defender of the faith', now buried in the grounds of St Andrew's Cathedral. A monument to him, erected in the mid-19th century, apparently stands 'on the near-by hill'.

The building itself is surrounded by a graveyard penned in by a solid, drystane wall, with the whole site resting in a quiet, shallow glen which somehow manages to belie its relative proximity both to

The entrance to Anwoth Old Kirk

Gatehouse itself and, a few miles beyond, the main road through this area. It is as soothing and tranquil a location as any I have ever encountered – exactly the sort of place to rest for a while after a long, hard, cold and wet day on the road.

Many of the graves are, obviously, ancient, with some of the best preserved actually located within the walls of the kirk building. The most striking of these stands in the centre of the place, a huge, ornate monument of dark, lichen-speckled stone. One of the narrow ends is decorated with carvings of a skull and cross-bones and an hourglass, with the words MEMENTO MORI clearly framing the former; the remaining three sides are covered in inscription which, though mostly still legible, is written in a tongue which I could not properly understand. As such I could only grasp snippets of the information, such as: 'LIVED LONG A VIRGINE NOW A SPOTLES WIFE'.

I have always enjoyed exploring burial grounds and found Anwoth so engaging that I soon lost track of time – it was only when I finally noticed the rapidly fading light that I realised I should head back. I considered going via a small footpath running alongside the kirk and over the hill before me, thinking that I might be able to catch a decent glimpse of the surrounding area on the way. Once again, however, I was foiled by the day's weather, which had turned the path into little more than a strip of thick mud stretching into the trees. I decided I had already been through enough for one day, so ignored the road less travelled and ambled back the way I had come.

When I got there, Karen's husband – whose boots I was wearing – had arrived home. Dougie, a recently retired police office from Glasgow and now a local councillor for the SNP, welcomed me in and offered me a glass of wine, insisting that I choose my preference of red or white when I offered to take whichever was already open. The

Grey skies above the fields behind Gatehouse of Fleet

three of us soon sat down to a lovely dinner, talking about their move from Glasgow, his (unexpected) step into local government, and the challenges of life in Scotland's south-western corner, a conversation which continued when a few of their friends – who had agreed to come and talk to me – arrived a short time later.

The most common theme of these discussions was that Dumfries and Galloway is, in the words of one woman, a 'forgotten corner of Scotland', one which policymakers and politicians don't know or care enough about, and where the problems affecting communities are both long-standing and, all too often, entirely ignored. In short, they felt that their part of Scotland has suffered from major neglect and a consequently inevitable decline, and there seemed limited real hope that its fortunes would be substantially reversed by those in power at any level of government. Dougie was, as would be expected given both his position and obvious commitment to the role, more optimistic on this point, but he was also admirably realistic about the barriers – geographic, economic and attitudinal – to serious progress.

The lack of 'connectivity' is a serious problem in the area. I heard one story of someone who had secured a job in a nearby town only to then face a struggle for transport because existing bus services did not run early enough to allow her to be in work on time. The reaction from the rest of the group told me that this was not an isolated incident. It was even suggested that I should complete the first version of my trip on the motorbike and then come back and try to do the same thing on public transport, a point made on a number of occasions as I travelled round some of the outer reaches of Scotland.

Housing is also an issue, with a large volume of poor quality, run-down buildings still in use, often by vulnerable people and young families due to a lack of investment. Opportunities for young people also seem to be limited, with many feeling that they have to leave to continue their education or careers – like in other parts of the country, the reality is that once they are gone they are unlikely to return, either because they do not want to or because it becomes a practical impossibility. For those who do stay, the work available is often low paid, insecure or seasonal. To make matters worse, poverty in this area is partially hidden from national, postcode-based statistics because it does not occur in high enough densities to show up properly, meaning that the problems doing such damage to people's lives are, frankly, too easy for the powerful to ignore. Deprivation in the Central Belt, one woman explained, is 'right in your face' and demands attention whereas here it is more subtle.

All of these concerns were brought into particularly sharp relief by the fact that just a few hours earlier local people had learned that a fish processing factory in nearby Annan was to be closed, a decision which would result in 450 jobs disappearing from the area. In a town with fewer than 10,000 residents, the loss of employment on that sort of scale would be 'devastating'. Significant, cross-party attempts were naturally made to rescue the facility but, at the time of writing, they have proven to be unsuccessful; however, even if the plant and associated jobs had been saved the incident was still a particularly stark example of the pressures facing vulnerable communities in this part of Scotland.

At 6,426 km², Dumfries & Galloway is the third largest council area in Scotland, sandwiched between Aberdeenshire and Argyll & Bute (though a very, very long way short of Highland council, which is effectively four times the size). It stretches across the entirety of Scotland's southern coastal edge, from Gretna in the east all the way to the Rhins of Galloway in the west, and is home to around 150,000 people, roughly the same as the population of Dundee. A normal car journey from Stranraer to Dumfries, where the council headquarters are located, takes at least 90 minutes; depending on the time of day, the same journey on public transport might take another hour. As was made clear to me several times – both on this particular evening and later on in my journey – it is somewhere between optimistic and downright insulting to consider such distances, which would take more than two days for even a brisk walker to cover, an appropriate use of the term 'local'. Even the individual wards of which the local authority area is comprised seem enormous. Dee and Glenkens, which Dougie represents, reaches from Kirkcudbright all the way inland, past New Galloway and St John's Town of Daly, and up to the border with East Ayrshire between Dalmellington and New Cumnock. In a typical week, he told me, he might drive hundreds of miles just to hold regular surgeries. There was universal agreement that the problems being experienced in this area are at least partly related to the sheer size of what is, at least in theory, the local government.

But the problem doesn't seem to be limited to a matter of simple mileage – there is a much more important issue around individual and collective identity, and the associated connections to a particular place, at play here. For the people I spoke to, the problem was far deeper than the apparent remoteness of Dumfries and was summed up in simple, striking terms: 'Dumfries and Galloway isn't a real thing'. Again and again I heard about the damage done by 'regionalisation', a programme of local government reform in the 1970s which amalgamated smaller council areas – such as Wigtownshire and Kirkcudbrightshire – into what is now Dumfries and Galloway. This did not just group people into areas which were too large to ever feel local and responsive, it also undermined the sense of identity that, in this part of the country at least, appears to have been very strong. I was told that many people here still write Kirkcudbrightshire when giving their address and, when talking about 'home', will be referring to Galloway. For someone born in the mid-'80s, this is a difficult thing to fully understand: the only configuration of Scotland that I have ever really known is the current one, with the country broken up into 32 council areas, which was implemented when I was ten years old and mercifully unaware of the fascinating intricacies of local government. I am also from a part of the country – East Dunbartonshire – to which I doubt a single human being has ever attached any sense of identity whatsoever.

Jimmy Reid identified this very issue in his famous 'Alienation' address, delivered in 1972 during his inauguration as Rector of the University of Glasgow. He described the reorganisation of local government as a 'blue-print for bureaucracy, not democracy' and asked of those driving the proposals:

'Where and how in your calculations did you quantify the value of a community? Of community life? Of a sense of belonging? Of the feeling of identification?'

In this part of Scotland those questions are still being asked.

2

Gatehouse of Fleet to Glasgow

'So this isn't exactly ideal, is it?'

EDWIN MUIR DESCRIBED the scenery 'in a line from Kirkcudbright to Girvan', as being 'so beautiful and varied' that he was unable to fully describe it without his impressions of the environment overwhelming the entire chapter. It had been my intention to follow the same route, riding northwest towards the Ayrshire coast at Girvan – a former holiday town left behind by the emergence of package holidays and budget airlines – just as he had, from which point I could follow the road north past Turnberry, Maidens and Culzean on the way into Ayr. Here I had been invited to stop at Unity Grill – a new social café tackling food poverty in the area – for lunch and a chat. In the afternoon I would be riding up through Prestwick, Troon, Irvine and Ardrossan until I reached Portencross Castle, a 14th century fortress by the sea near West Kilbride. This underappreciated gem of the west coast, which has a history dating back to the Battle of Bannockburn, also happens to be where I got married. The ancient rectangular tower is accessed by a narrow, twisting staircase climbing past a restored main chamber and up to a rooftop platform with stunning views over the whole Firth of Clyde where, on a good hot day with just the right amount of sunshine, Bute, Arran, the two Cumbraes and Kintyre seem to hover on the aura of a living, sparkling sea. From there I would probably go up over Fairlie Moor – which itself affords some truly spectacular vistas over Scotland's south-west coast – towards

Dalry before continuing to Glasgow. If there was time I might be able to visit the Whitelees Wind Farm or the Cathkin Braes for a look over the city; ideally, I'd even have time to stop for a cup of tea and a cake, and maybe even a walk through the city centre.

I didn't get to do any of that.

In what became a daily ritual throughout my journey, I awoke on the second day and immediately checked the weather forecast on my phone. That morning I was confronted with the image of a thick band of heavy snow careering down through the country and threatening to strand me somewhere between the Solway Coast and the Central Belt. It was immediately clear that my grand plans for the day would have to be abandoned. Like all bikers, especially those with families, I am aware that people often worry about me when I am riding in wet weather, but I've never considered rain to be a massive issue. On top of that, anything short of actually riding into a loch was unlikely to match the experience I'd had the previous day. Ridden properly, even road bikes like mine are perfectly capable of continuing on through heavy rain, wind and, within limits, even hail. But not snow.

There are two reasons for this. The first is that it is obviously dangerous to be riding something with two wheels across a near grip-free surface. Having already experienced - as all bikers inevitably must - the sensation of sliding down a road, face down and feet first, I have absolutely no desire to ever do so again. The second reason is even more straightforward: even if you are able to follow perfectly in a car's tyre tracks and, by some miracle, keep the bike upright, there is nothing you can do about the snow coating your visor – riding blind, whatever the meteorological conditions, is clearly a bad situation in which to find oneself. Under normal circumstances I wouldn't have even considered getting on a motorbike in the face of such a hostile forecast but these were not normal circumstances. It was risky, and there was a very good chance of everything going horribly wrong, but I had to at least try to keep going. Having decided to make an attempt to reach Glasgow I had a quick breakfast with Karen (and Sam), loaded my gear onto the bike and headed off, unsure of how far I'd make it or where I'd end up.

The rain was almost as heavy as it had been the previous afternoon, and even the 20-minute ride to a petrol station in Castle Douglas was enough to leave me intensely aware of water once again penetrating my theoretically waterproof jacket and boots. Even so, I was still considering an attempt to stick to my original route, going back past Gatehouse and then over the road to Girvan, reasoning that if I made it to the coast then the weather probably wouldn't be so hostile as further inland. Having lived and worked in Ayrshire for several years in my 20s I had been looking forward to spending the day there, meandering along the coast and visiting towns which, in contrast to those I had passed the day before, I knew well, but ultimately I decided that bloody-mindedness wasn't a good enough excuse to take the risk, which seemed considerable, of crashing a motorbike on an isolated road in the middle of a snow storm. Instead I reluctantly settled on the most direct route available and began riding north, intending to join the A77 at Ayr and then reassess the situation, but acutely aware of the fact that I might end up forced to simply blast back to Glasgow as quickly as possible. If I was really lucky, I might even manage to dodge the worst of the weather and, assuming that the snow didn't last too long or lie too widely, I just might be able to keep going onwards to Oban the next day.

The road from Castle Douglas to Ayr cuts straight through the south-western corner of Scotland, skirting the eastern edge of the

Galloway Forest Park as it passes by, or through, places like New Galloway, St John's Town of Dalry, Carsphairn and Dalmellington. It's a road which I have travelled, and enjoyed, several times: my first significant journey on motorcycle (a little 125cc Honda with a top speed, down hill, of around 70mph) took from me Glasgow to the Wickerman Festival near Kirkcudbright, and I even bought my first 'big' motorbike in Patna, a decidedly strange little village which, when travelling from the south, marks the starting point for the 'classical' Ayrshire landscape of farms painted in a million shades of green (at least in the sunshine) rolling gently over the hills in all directions.

Just like the day before, however, I wasn't really able to appreciate any of it due to the weather, my only lasting impression of that section of my journey being the relentless grey misery within which I seemed to find myself permanently enveloped. Although the rain was not as heavy as it had been for the previous 24 hours, it was significantly colder, a sure sign that the promised wall of snow was indeed on the way, and as I crossed what felt like an endless stretch of dreich moorland I found myself wondering whether the whole trip might have been a bad idea. I doubted whether I would really be able to endure a full ten days of this sort of punishment and, even if I could, asked myself whether there would really be any point in doing so?

But while this internal debate continued I was still making progress and, despite the rain, I was able to keep up a decent speed. The signs I passed told me that the distance to Ayr was declining in spirit-lifting, double-figured jumps and there was very little traffic holding me up (because few people were stupid enough to be out in these conditions). As I finally reached the outskirts of Ayr the rain lightened and I enjoyed a little wave of optimism that I might just get away with this after all.

Then came the snow. It started with a single, sleety blob on my visor as I banked to the right on a roundabout just before the A77; a few second later, there was another, and then another. I soon found myself doing the very thing I'd been desperate to avoid: trying to keep my wheels in one of the grey stripes left by the cars in front of me, keeping the gears high, the throttle smooth and the bike straight to give the tyres the best possible chance of maintaining some grip. The weather alternated rapidly through a seemingly random cycle of rain, sleet and snow. Two or three times I felt the back wheel hesitate a little in response to a miscalculation on my part but it was just about possible to keep going. It was not ideal, but I was still moving in the right direction.

But then, just north of Kilmarnock, it all went wrong. The cycle of rain, sleet and snow through which I had been pushing changed suddenly into a thick, white, seemingly impenetrable barrier. I could not see never mind ride and I accepted that I had no choice but to stop. In a stroke of immense good fortune – to which, after my experiences over the previous few days, I felt entitled – I was approaching the exit for Stewarton, my wife's home town and the location of my first home after moving out at the age of 22. Crucially, my in-laws still live there so I gingerly peeled off the motorway and began the short, normally routine ride into town.

In recent years Stewarton has grown quite significantly, stretching out into the fields which, when I lived there, marked the edge of town. It seems as though hundreds of new houses have been built to satisfy demand in this ideal, aspirational, semi-rural commuter town with its own rail link and within easy reach of Kilmarnock, Irvine and

Glasgow. Most are ridiculously overpriced but this has proved to be no barrier to sales. Despite this, the atmosphere hasn't much changed in the time I've known it and the place still feels like a small Scottish town in the middle of the Ayrshire countryside.

The road into Stewarton from the A77 winds between low hills (usually green but on this occasion already dusted white) with farms on both sides until it finally crosses the Annick Water before dropping into the south-eastern corner of town. It's a road I know well, and one I must have ridden on hundreds of times, although it also happens to be the only road on which I've ever had a serious crash on a motorbike. I rode slowly and oh-so-carefully, being desperately careful to keep the bike upright and moving smoothly. Despite a few minor wobbles and one distinctly less minor slide, I eventually made it to my in-laws house in the middle of town, parking on their driveway before seeking shelter, largely in vain, beneath a small overhang partly covering the steps to their kitchen door. After a couple of phone calls and a short wait (which admittedly seemed never-ending) my mother-in-law, who fortunately had been nearby, came back to let me in before going off to work.

'So this isn't exactly ideal, is it?' she asked, looking to the sky, as she opened the door.

I decided to go for a shower to warm up but found that, although my arms, legs and torso were glad of the hot water, I had to keep my hands and feet, which had turned a deep and concerning crimson, out of the way due to the pain. And so I stood, essentially trapped in the semi-circular shower cubicle, hands pressed against the sliding glass door and feet as far apart as possible, waiting for the effects of the weather to fully wear off. I once again began to think about the trip, wondering whether I'd ended up thoroughly out of my depth.

Outside the snow has eased slightly but still continued to fall

Bob, unimpressed by the snow outside

and, although the ground was too wet for it to lie properly, there was still no chance of me making it through it and reaching Glasgow. The one sliver of light in the whole situation was a slight change in the weather forecast which hinted at a window in the weather a few hours later. With no option but to wait, I covered almost every radiator in the house with soaking wet bike gear, made myself a cup of tea and sat by the window with the family cat, Bob, for company.

It was not until early evening that the forecast came true: the snow turned to sleet and eventually rain before finally stopping altogether. By this point I had no time for exploring and would have to head straight up the motorway; although disappointed, I had at least been given the chance to rescue my journey and would just have to hope that things improved from here on. In a final stroke of luck, my father-in-law arrived home just as I was leaving and, taking pity on me, produced a waterproof jacket and trousers which I could wear over my existing gear. Aside from a small panic when I plunged into a brief but terrifying white out where the motorway crosses Eaglesham, the ride back to Glasgow was uneventful; I spent most of my time observing the skies away to the north, my spirits lifting as clouds slowly parted and a fragile patchwork of blue began to appear while, despite the time of day, the temperature even managed to creep up a few degrees.

At the end of most days during the trip, I would be staying with people I had never met. There were two exceptions to this: Orkney, where I would be staying with a friend who had recently moved there, and Glasgow, where I would be going home for the night, despite the fact that it would have been easier to secure an offer of a bed in Scotland's largest city than any other part of the country. Although I had considered doing so I decided that, having grown up just outside Glasgow, studied there and, on returning from Arran, taken on a job in one of the city's colleges, a third-party impression was a less pressing concern here than elsewhere. More than anything else, however, I wanted to see my wife and young son before setting off for a week on the road.

As I came along the motorway and over the Kingston bridge, the clouds had parted enough to illuminate buildings ahead. I think that this is perhaps the best vantage point from which to view the architectural patchwork of central Glasgow, as the carriageway crosses the River Clyde and then, thanks to what is surely one of the most bizarre decisions in the history of city planning, ploughs straight through the heart of the city. Heading north on the bridge, as I was, opens up views of the redeveloped riverfront on the left, with the famous Titan crane, that great symbol of the city's shipbuilding heritage, standing resolutely alongside the new, spaceship-like concert venue and, across the water, the cavernous BBC headquarters. Ahead and to the right, however, one is confronted with a remarkable mishmash of sandstone and steel, glass and concrete, all of which seems to have been glued together at random as the city has stumbled through the decades. Alongside the motorway, the gorgeous copper-domed masterpiece that is The Mitchell Library is juxtaposed with a bizarre, horizontal office block which seems to float above the carriageway before coming to an end so abrupt that it looks for all the world as through the builders just got fed up during the construction process and gave up, hoping nobody would notice.

Without doubt the biggest change to the Glasgow skyline in recent years has been the demolition of the Red Road Flats, a fortress of high-rise homes which towered over the motorway in the north-east of the city. Built in the 1960s to tackle the city's (apparently unending) housing crisis, at their peak they were home to nearly 5,000 people. My mum grew up in the single yellow block that stood on the hill just beyond the others. I remember visiting my gran there as a small boy – the clunk of the lift as the door closed, or the sight of her living room light swinging pendulously during bad weather. Years later a very close friend lived in one of the long, multi-tower slabs, and I was a regular visitor during my late teens and early 20s until he was moved in 2006 as part of the process to allow the site to be torn down. Although this was the right decision it was handled in a characteristically catastrophic manner, with the original plans – to blow up the towers as part of the opening ceremony for the 2014 Commonwealth Games being held in the city – abandoned after an entirely justifiable outcry from people whose former homes, and lives, were about to disappear forever.

Ongoing questions about Glasgow's commitment to its built environment were brought into particularly sharp relief in 2014 when a fire devastated part of the internationally recognised Glasgow School of Art, regarded as the great Charles Rennie Mackintosh's masterpiece. An enormous – and enormously expensive – restoration project was undertaken in order to bring the destroyed sections, which included the world-famous library, back to their former glory; sadly, as I write this, the building is once more in ashes after another fire, this one far more devastating than the last, ripped through the The Mack. Also badly damaged was the neighbouring ABC venue which, though not held in the same regard as the Art School, is absolutely central to the cultural life of the city. Both the Scottish and UK governments have already pledged to do whatever they can but there is a widespread fear that both of these icons might now disappear, and the council has already confirmed that much of the Art School will have to be demolished one way or another. If this does prove to be the case, it seems obvious that the whole block on which the buildings stand should be levelled and something new, reflecting the spirit of what has been lost and the Glasgow we want to see in the future, allowed to rise up in its place.

Whatever happens next, this catastrophe feels like a test of Glasgow's spirit but it should also, surely, be recognised as an opportunity to finally confront the appalling, short-sighted but long-term neglect of Glasgow's historic built environment. It is no secret that the city of Glasgow has a terrible track record for respecting or protecting its considerable architectural heritage. Huge numbers of historic buildings stand abandoned and derelict across the city, with far too many already lost to neglect and the pursuit of profit. The people who make Glasgow are, rightly, proud if it – but the city doesn't seem to be proud of itself.

Glaswegians are also profoundly, probably even deleteriously, attached to their home town's reputation as a tough city, an impression which is more than borne out by the available data for a city which is, perversely, both prosperous and poverty-stricken. According to the Glasgow Centre for Population Health, half of the city's residents live within the 20% of areas in Scotland regarded as being most deprived; both men and women from Glasgow have shorter lives than the national average; and around a third of children grow up in poverty. Overall employment levels in Glasgow are also lower than the national average and around a quarter of households have no working adults in them. Although Glasgow has a large amount of green, public space – the council lists a total of 22 parks and gardens within the city boundaries – 60% of people also live within 500m of land which has been left derelict. Around 1 in 4 adults have no formal educational qualifications. Voter turnout is invariably lower than the figures for both Scotland and the UK as a whole.

All of these issues are magnified by the fact that some of the areas immediately surrounding Glasgow, like East Dunbartonshire to the north and East Renfrewshire to the west, are some of Scotland's most affluent. Worst of all, by any reasonable measure they are also part of the city: people living in these areas identify, undoubtedly, as Glaswegians and almost all make use of services funded by the council tax of people living within the city itself. Having grown up in Kirkintilloch, for example, I am expected to live several years longer, gain more qualifications, earn more, and generally enjoy a superior quality of life compared to someone brought up just a few miles away within the boundaries of Scotland's largest city.

The whole picture becomes even worse when the variations across the city itself are properly acknowledged: there is a 15 year difference in life expectancy between men from the richest and poorest areas and child poverty levels vary wildly, with nearly half of children in some areas living in poverty while the figure for other parts of the city drops as low as 5%. Inequality blights all of society, but in Glasgow

The Talisman, Springburn

its impact is particularly profound, a fact highlighted particularly effectively by a recent explosion in the number of rough sleepers one encounters on Buchanan Street, the most expensive area in which to rent retail space anywhere in the UK outside of London.

Another particularly good, tangible example of this inequality is found in Springburn, a relatively deprived, profoundly working-class area to the north of the city, where the ruined shell of an old pub called The Talisman stands, blackened, broken and abandoned. The building is extremely dangerous, having been gutted by fire and long abandoned by its private owners, and counts as its neighbours numerous blocks of flats, a collection of shops and a children's play park. Were it found in some of the more affluent areas of Glasgow (or neighbouring East Dunbartonshire) it would have been demolished and redeveloped years ago – but here, where developers' potential profits are limited and residents generally lack the social capital of some of their middle-class city neighbours, no such action has been taken. In 2017 the local community council launched a petition calling for the building to be demolished but, of course, nothing much seems to have happened. In fact, the only noticeable change over the past few months – even years – has been the very brief appearance of the world's most optimistic To Let sign.

Yet, for all the bleakness of the data and the innumerable injustices standing in plain sight, it is also the case that Glasgow doesn't feel like the same city it was 20 or even ten years ago. In all sorts of subtle ways, Glasgow feels like a better place than it did when I was growing up. Take this example: when I was a teenager it was entirely normal, even routine, to see football shirts (either green and white hoops or dark blue, of course), bouquets of flowers and weather-beaten teddies tied to lamp-posts and railings, left there in memory of yet another young man stabbed to death, a victim of a culture of violence which claimed far too many lives.

Today, however, such tributes stand out because of their rarity. Crime rates, including violent crimes, have dropped dramatically, a phenomenon which, though identifiable in other parts of the country as well as internationally, is naturally most apparent in the places where the problem was most prevalent. This is not to say that the progress has been experienced uniformly by all residents, or that the fundamental inequalities eating away at the fabric of the city itself has been addressed, but the overall impression of Glasgow is, without doubt, an improved one.

The mood has also changed in the last few years, a process which predates the 2014 Independence Referendum (in which Glasgow voted Yes) but found its fullest expression in the subsequent city-wide victories for the SNP in the General, Scottish and Local elections which followed in 2015, 2016 and 2017 respectively. Less than a generation ago any one of these results would have seemed unthinkable in a city where monkeys with red rosettes could win elections for the Labour party. That all three could take place in consecutive years is a sign of just how significant the shift in the Glasgow psyche could be. Whether or not the SNP turns out to be the vehicle to deliver it, the people who make Glasgow have made their demand for change perfectly clear.

The sun held on as I passed through the city and out the other side, finally reaching home after one of the worst days I could remember. But I had no time to relax. Over the first two days of the journey I had been depending upon a trusty rucksack, wrapping it in its bright orange waterproof cover and strapping it to the back of the bike, but it had become clear something larger and much more waterproof would be required for the eight days still ahead of me. I also inspected my boots and found that some of the seams had started to come apart, which of course explained their complete inability to keep my feet dry over the previous two days. With no time to buy replacements, I attempted to repair them instead, mixing vaseline and superglue and using the resulting substance to seal the gaps where the stitching had failed or where the sole had begun to peel away from the leather. I had no idea if it would work and no alternative if it didn't.

From the top floor of my house you can see all the way out to the Campsie Hills, with their western tip pointing out towards Loch Lomond and on to the Highlands. Everyone here knows that if you can't see that little hill to the left of the range then it is certainly going to rain; now the hills were capped with snow and being bathed in inviting, late-evening sunlight with the hillside underneath just beginning to glow.

Tomorrow would be another day – hopefully a better one.

3

Glasgow to Oban

'We've really loved being in this place.'

IT WAS IN LEAVING Glasgow that my path first seriously diverged from Muir's. For the first two days of the journey, even without Muir's tyre tracks to guide me, I'd have followed a very similar path to the one which he had chosen. From there on, however, I had a problem. He had travelled east, through Motherwell and Carfin (writing at considerable length about the Grotto) before turning north towards Stirling, Perth, Inverness and, having crossed the country, Ullapool. I didn't want to miss out so much of the west coast, which has always been my favourite place to ride, and as this was supposed to be my Scottish journey I eventually decided on a coastal route which would take me past Loch Lomond, through Argyll, on to the Isle of Skye and then all the way along the coast of Wester Ross via Applecross and Gairloch, finally rejoining Muir's original route at Ullapool a couple of days later.

I said goodbye to my wife, son and dog and set off early, grateful for significantly better weather overhead and a favourable forecast for the rest of the day, as well as the opportunity for a good run to Oban, a particularly pleasant town which I had not had the chance to visit for several years. My usual route from my home to Loch Lomond would take me over the back roads from Lennoxtown, passing by Strathblane and the Whangie – a brilliant hill just outside Glasgow with spectacular views of the loch and on into the Highlands

– before reaching the beautiful little village of Balmaha on the loch's south-eastern shoreline. On this occasion, however, I changed tack, deciding instead that, as I had missed it all the day before, I would at least go back through Glasgow on my way out of the Central Belt. This meant cutting through Bishopbriggs and Maryhill before joining Great Western Road. Although this was a far less entertaining route – especially on a motorbike – than the combination of roads and views available further north, it meant I'd have a chance to see one of the more obvious contrasts in the city and one which I've always felt sums up the inequality of the Glasgow experience particularly well. According to the Scottish Index of Multiple Deprivation (SIMD) the area around Ruchhill Park in the north-west of the city is one of the 10% most deprived in the entire country, while those living around the Botanic Gardens – a stunning landmark of the wealthy, tourist-friendly West End just a mile away but a world apart – reside in one of the 10% least deprived zones in Scotland. Even without the SIMD data or the benefit of a long-term knowledge of the city, a visitor following my route, passing each park within minutes of one another, would likely have little difficulty differentiating between the two communities and the contrasting life experiences available to those living – especially growing up – within them.

The A82 begins life as Great Western Road and runs from the northern edge of Glasgow city centre all the way up to Loch Lomond. It initially passes through desirable areas such as Hillhead, Hyndland and Kelvinside where it is lined with smart little side-streets filled with grand sandstone homes, all separated from the main road by lines of mature, protective trees. Affluence isn't just visible in this part of Glasgow, it is unmissable, insistent, demanding your attention whether you want to give it or not. Really – who on earth needs a porch supported by faux-Grecian pillars?

A few miles further on, the surroundings shift as the road cuts through Anniesland, where rows of earthen-red tenements eventually give way to two-storey terraced houses which, though once probably white, have been beaten into a grim, grey-yellow submission by exposure to decades of Scottish weather and ever increasing levels of traffic on one of the busiest roads in the country. It then continues past Knightswood, Drumchapel, Parkhall and Duntocher before finally escaping the western limits of Glasgow's creeping urban sprawl while passing the Erskine Bridge, the final road-crossing over the Clyde before the river spills out into the firth between Gourock and Dunoon.

The road then turns inland and meets Loch Lomond at its southern shore before following it north on the western side, eventually reaching all the way to Inverness. Like much of Scotland, Loch Lomond always looks its best with a combination of snow on the hills and sunlight on the water, which was exactly what I saw as I rode north alongside it. Although the road was busy, my two-wheeled mode of transport meant that I was able to make good progress and stay on track for a mid-afternoon appointment near Oban. The hills opposite me were dusted white from their peaks down to the edge of the tree line, like icing sugar sprinkled over a patchwork cake.I have always preferred the quieter eastern shore of the loch but, either way, the proximity of all of this to Scotland largest, loudest, busiest city remains something of a minor miracle.

As I approached Tarbert I had a decision to make, with two competing roads before me: one continued north, following the A82 through Crianlarach and Tyndrum on the way to my next overnight stop near Oban; the other took me west, through Arrochar and eventually onto the coast. Had the weather been less co-operative

I'd have had little choice but to stick to the first, far simpler option, but with the temperature climbing and the clouds continuing to part, and with grim, shivering memories of the previous two days very much still fresh in my mind, I decided to head into Argyll. I had been particularly keen to take this route because I knew it would keep me on quieter roads, allowing me to enjoy the journey more than would be possible if I were constantly calculating whether or not I could overtake the car, van, bus or lorry in front of me. It also meant that I would be able to complete a single run around the Argyll Coast Road, a route I had only ever partly completed at any one time (not counting the occasion when I was a passenger in my wife's car and, to her justified displeasure, slept through at least half of the trip).

With that in mind, I turned west and soon found myself climbing up towards the Rest and Be Thankful. Just before the viewpoint, where travellers can pause and look over the landscape below, I was slowed down and then stopped by a short stretch of extensive roadworks which seemed connected to the installation of huge nets on the rock face. These, I presumed, were intended to prevent the sort of landslips known to occur here and which can lead to enormous detours for people living in or travelling through the area. A few minutes beyond the viewpoint which marks the road's highest point it turns left via a long, sweeping, downhill bend, crossing the Kinglas Water – a pleasant enough little burn which ambles down the nearby slope and through the glen – over a small road bridge. It was here that I had my first near miss of the trip when the driver of the car in front of me suddenly slowed – almost to a complete halt – in order to allow their passenger to lean out of the window, phone in hand, and take a photograph. Fortunately the open landscape here affords a good view along the road and I had already seen that no vehicles were coming in the opposite direction; I was therefore able to swerve around the sudden obstruction rather than risk hard braking and, having admittedly broadcasted a few choice words towards the vehicle, continued on my way and never saw the car or its occupants again.

I reached Inveraray around a quarter of an hour later, stopping briefly in the little car park by the waterfront to stretch my legs and enjoy the view over the loch, with bright, mostly blue skies bouncing off the surface while the grand stone bridge to my left glowed in the intermittent sunshine. The hills were still in the intermediate stage between winter and spring, with remnants of snow clinging to the tops and the signs and shades of new life creeping up the steep slopes. The scene was made all the better by the fact that Inveraray Castle – a grotesque, soulless tribute to feudal opulence and precisely the sort of 'must see' visitor attraction which visitors would be well advised to avoid – was hidden behind the tree line.

The road from Inveraray to Lochgilphead follows Loch Fyne, often clinging to the shoreline, and offers travellers a seemingly endless selection of picture-postcard views across the water in which, on this particular day, the brooding hills of Argyll were reflected. Though perhaps lacking the overt, towering drama of other sections of the west coast, this has always seemed to me to be a part of the country very much at ease with itself; it is less insistent on its own beauty, and subsequently manages to be even more charming. As I arrived in Lochgilphead, the sun, which had been a welcome but rather unreliable companion throughout the morning, finally escaped from behind the clouds, drenching the town in a wave of warm, springtime light, which I enjoyed while I sat on the grass looking out over the loch and drank a cup of tea. An 18th century planned town,

Lochgilphead manages to be attractive without being particularly beautiful, a quality likely enhanced by the fact that, as the official and administrative centre of the region, it does not feel as though it is so deeply engaged in the desperate, self-perpetuating scramble for tourist cash.

From Lochgilphead, I headed north and over the next hour or so was rewarded with an uplifting run to Oban spent gliding along in the sunshine, twisting and turning and rising and falling for mile after mile, through impossibly attractive little villages set amidst the remarkable canvas of the Argyll landscape. I didn't even mind when I found myself caught behind a little blue and white tour bus which I was unable to pass; instead it was an opportunity to slow down and turn even more of my attention to what lay beyond the tarmac – fields and burns and bogs and peaks, moorland and woodland and forest, all set beneath a fresh spring sky.

I arrived in Oban in mid-afternoon, continuing on through the town as the road bent around the coast, passing a handful of tiny golden beaches before finally coming to my destination: Stramash Outdoor Nursery. The site is accessed via a short but steep path from the roadside car park and is split into two sections, the first of which, on the right hand side, is an open field sprinkled with tractor tyres and wooden pallets, a willow tunnel and garden maze, wheelbarrows and spades and rope and all manner of imaginative accessories. And, most importantly of all, children learning, growing and having fun outside. Sheep wander through the neighbouring field, and the only sound competing with the children is the combined chorus of birds and, briefly, the sound of the little prop-plane coming into the local airport from a nearby island. By the perimeter fence is a huge fallen tree, the sort of thing which would have been removed by safety-

Stramash Outdoor Nursery

obsessed council workers in other places; here, it is a climbing frame.

The path then continues to the left and up the slope to a beautiful, sunlight-dappled pocket of woodland on the crest of the hill. From this vantage point the kids can see out across the bright blue water towards Lismore, Morvern and Mull, beneath which a ferry was creeping serenely through the water, headed north. Amongst the tyre swings, climbing ropes and tunnels there are also two wooden huts, each with a little wood burning stove and various craft and reading materials, as well as three individual outdoor toilets, all of which are a significant upgrade on the sort of facilities with which festival-goers will be familiar.

More than 60 local children come here for their time at nursery, their parents understandably attracted to both the setting and the ethos. The kids spend the overwhelming majority of their time outdoors, no matter the weather, making use of both their own site and the surrounding area, often walking down to one of the nearby beaches to explore, and learn, and play. If such a thing as an idyllic childhood exists, then it must surely look a lot like this. Having shown me around the staff left me to take another walk through the site, so I went back to the top of the hill, next to a tyre-swing looking out over the sound, and thought about how much my own son would have loved an environment like this one, and how good it would be for all children to have the opportunity to experience it.

After my visit I followed the road down to its end beside the beautiful, white-sand beach at Ganavan. Though once a caravan park and campsite, the land here now features a collection of private properties offering premium views (at premium prices) over the bay. I parked the bike, took a few photographs and sat down on the warm white sand.

A good deal of all recent debate in Scottish politics has centred, directly or otherwise, around education. This is a natural phenomenon given the limitations of the Scottish Parliament but it has also been magnified in recent years by the current First Minister's decision to demand that she be judged on her record of improving the educational experiences of Scotland's children. Specifically, her government has focused on tackling something called the 'attainment gap', a clumsy and ultimately unhelpful term used in an attempt to describe the variations in school performance between children from affluent backgrounds and those who have grown up in poverty. This is a noble aim but it is also a far more complicated issue than most people – certainly most of those debating it in the parliament or in the comment pages of newspapers – seem to understand.

Numerous policies have been pursued in recent years, including standardised testing, targeted funding, a First Minister's Reading Challenge and a raft of structural changes to the education system. None of it is coherent, and too much of it is driven by political, not educational, needs – but the problem is that the whole approach simply misses the point. Though people tend, and desperately want, to believe that schools have an enormous impact on children's achievement levels, the truth is different. At the Spectator's 'Schools Revolution' conference in 2010, renowned educationalist Dylan Wiliam pointed out that in England:

> Some schools get all their students five good grades at GCSE including English and mathematics, and some get hardly any, but only 7% of the variation between schools on this standard benchmark is due to the effect of the school. The other 93% is due to factors over which the school has no control.

Critically, schools are already heavily focused on leveraging what influence they do have, to the extent that the wider system depends on teachers giving up their own time to help pupils during lunchtimes or run after school clubs. As a result, they simply do not have the ability or capacity to effect the sort of miraculous transformation that people now feel they have been promised. The problem, it turns out, isn't schools – it's poverty. In the end, a brutally unequal society like ours will always subject its children to unequal educational experiences.

But this doesn't mean that nothing can be done. There is a very strong argument to say that we send children to school too early in Scotland, while in 2014 research by the Joseph Rowntree Foundation found that even by the age of three there is a measurable developmental gap between rich and poor children. Research by the campaign group Upstart Scotland shows that only 12% of countries around the world send their children to school aged four or five as we do, all of them former territories of the British Empire. 66% of countries do not send their children to school until the age of six and the final 22% wait until seven. International comparisons also show that, contrary to many assumptions, 'top performing' countries tend to have later starting ages.

If there is a structural, system-level change worth pursuing in the hope of tackling inequality then it must be a vehicle for a levelling of the playing field in the early years stages. Recently introduced 'Baby Boxes' – a range of essential items like babygrows, a thermometer and books, provided to all new mothers free of charge – are an example of this type of policy and a largely positive development; another, far more transformative one would be the creation of a nationwide, universal kindergarten system, free at the point of use just like primary and secondary schools, for all children aged 3–6/7, staffed by highly paid professionals and supported by both financial resources and a step change in the importance with which we view Early Years education. There is no doubt in my mind that Scotland would be much improved as a result of such a change.

After half an hour at the beach I rode back in to Oban, parking the bike right down at the front next to an information board informing me that, over the centuries, the town has been visited by the likes of Boswell and Johnson, Wordsworth, Turner and even Mendelssohn. There's something about this little town which I have always found particularly appealing, an ultimately ineffable impression which I nonetheless suspect may find its origins in the way in which Oban

Parked up at Ganavan Sands, Oban

seems to be able to mix what should be competing features: the past and the present, the mainland and the islands, isolation and activity. With the sun still shining – and who knew for how long? – and some time to spare I treated myself to a superb fish supper, which I ate at a little picnic bench outside looking onto the water and out to the islands crowding round the horizon.

No day out in Oban would be complete without at least a mention for McCaig's Tower, a bizarre monument conceived by a local banker as a means of commemorating his family and, naturally, himself. The huge, circular construction is obviously inspired by Greek and Roman architecture and looms over the town from the hill behind. It offers wonderful views over the bay to the isles beyond and, although I was unable to test this myself, is likely one of the best spots in the whole country from which to watch a sunset. It should feel out of place, overwhelming, ridiculous, or simply irrelevant but somehow – quite possibly because it is so wonderfully eccentric – it seems to belong.

I departed at around half past four and set out on the hunt for a place called Fasnacloich, a tiny collection of homes near Appin which I had been told was around a 30-minute ride north of Oban. The route took me over the Connel Bridge – a grim, grey, steel-latticed monstrosity which, aside from being single track, is horribly at odds with the environment in which it stands – past Ardmucknish Bay and then along the southern coast of Loch Creran before crossing over on another, much smaller and more appropriate bridge. I had been told to turn right here and head into the glen along a tight and twisty road which weaves through the trees and by the water. It all felt extremely familiar but I had no idea why – until a memory suddenly sparked into life.

It was Halloween in, I think, 2005, and my now-wife and I had gone away for the night. Before we were married we did this most years to celebrate our 'anniversary', generally picking somewhere a few hours from Glasgow, staying in nice accommodation and going out for dinner. This time we had decided to eat at a well-known seafood restaurant in Oban, so had booked a B&B a short drive away – the same short drive I had just completed. The B&B, I realised, was on this very road. After checking in and quickly changing our clothes we headed back along the lochside road for Oban. The sun was long gone and the blackness beyond the range of our headlights was near total as we wound along the tarmac when suddenly, apparently out of nowhere, there it was: a child's teddy, soaked and tattered, with sandy-coloured fur and pitch-black eyes, hovering four feet off the ground in the middle of the road. It waited there, staring at us, for ten or 20 seconds, the whole experience like the opening scene of a mid-budget horror film where someone makes the mistake of getting out to investigate. And then, without warning, whatever spell was holding the bear off the ground was broken and it dropped onto the road surface, its face still turned towards us. We drove on, silently, for Oban.

I had received an offer of a bed for the night in a cottage a little further along this road, having been furnished with directions, a description and instructions to go inside and make myself at home if nobody was there. As it turned out the house was empty when I arrived so I manoeuvred the bike into the driveway then went inside, where I was welcomed by an impressively aloof little black and white cat which seemed to have been expecting its owners. Disappointed to see me instead, it simply turned around and strolled off. I changed quickly, replacing my heavy bike gear with jeans and a fleece, and then went back outside to take a look around. The house itself was a long, low, stone construction, surrounded by trees and slopes on three sides and separated from the road by a bright rectangular garden on the fourth. I later discovered that it was originally two separate homes which had been combined many years before. Opposite, the great, snow-capped hulk of Beinn Sgulaird dominated the sky, although a wave of cloud had begun to roll in, lapping against the monochrome peak.

A few minutes later I thought I heard some people approaching from above and soon a party of walkers appeared from the trees covering the hill behind the house, accompanied by a sprightly little Westie and an absolutely gorgeous Pointer. My hosts, Pat and Fedor, were among the group, and their friends stayed to chat for a few minutes, discussing the merits of different styles of motorbikes, asking me about my journey so far and listening to my plans for the day ahead, before returning to their own homes.

Pat is originally from Ireland but came to Scotland to train as a midwife and has, in her own words, 'been here ever since'. She and Fedor have lived all over Scotland, from Orkney to Applecross to Leith, but it is here that they seem to have been most settled. 'We've really loved being in this place,' Pat tells me, but this doesn't stop her from being honest about the problems facing the area. There is, I heard, a crisis in social care, with the council facing financial problems which are making it increasingly difficult for people to access appropriate support and protection. This has also put huge pressure on remaining staff, damaging the quality of what care is available and restricting service users' quality of life. Having had personal experience of these problems in the Central Belt I could well imagine that things would be even more stretched out here.

One of the reasons for this, I was told, is the lack of public transport which, as in the south-west of the country, has a constrictive effect on small communities and the people living within them. I heard about a group of local people looking to form a community transport group to try to address the problem, but there was only so much that they would be able to achieve. More than that, there is a justifiable sense of injustice that volunteers should have to try to solve a problem which they – rightly – believe should be the responsibility of the state. If areas like this are to be truly liveable, sustainable communities in the 21st century then a proper network of public transport has to be one of the very top priorities. Yet, just like in Dumfries & Galloway (and, as I later discovered, many other parts of the country) it is simply an afterthought. The obvious problem is that the geography and low population density of parts of Scotland makes it difficult for private companies to make a profit without also offering a limited, expensive or inconvenient service. Where volunteers feel the need to come together just to establish a basic transport system for their area then it is clear that the market has failed to provide and the state has failed to protect – the former is inevitable, the latter unacceptable. One possible solution for this problem is to subsidise private companies to run unprofitable services; another, far better option is to have publicly owned companies operate all routes not for profit but instead for the – far more valuable – common good.

The three of us spent the evening discussing our backgrounds, the book, Brexit, independence and, best of all, their extended trip on the Trans-Siberian railway. They also talked about their plan to leave Scotland. Pat's sister had bought land in Ireland and it included a house that she didn't intend to use, which was an opportunity they had felt compelled to accept. For Pat it means going back to her first home and Fedor has always wanted to live there some day, but it clearly had not been an easy decision to leave Scotland. Did it have anything to do with Brexit? 'No. I mean, not really. But I think maybe now is the right time all the same.' Both Pat and Fedor are retired community nurses who had spent their working lives helping other people, as well as two of the warmest people I have every had the privilege of spending time with, and it is clear that they care deeply about not just their part of the country but also Scotland as a whole. Our loss will undoubtedly be Ireland's gain.

4

Oban to Skye

'It's a different country up here.'

I SET OFF the next day from Fasnacloich after a lovely breakfast of poached eggs and toast and some more very welcome conversation with Pat and Fedor. By the time I got on the bike it was just after 10am and a blanket of grimy cloud had settled over the hills around me, so I began this leg of my journey riding through an intermittent sprinkling of mercifully light – and surprisingly warm – rain showers. I was initially aiming for Mallaig from where I would catch the ferry to Skye a few hours later before continuing all the way to Geary, a tiny settlement near the northern tip of the remote Waternish peninsula. This section of the trip included a treat that I had been particularly looking forward to: a first ever ride along the Road to the Isles, a famously beautiful ribbon of tarmac weaving its way from Fort William – from memory a grim, dull town which sits in the shadow of Ben Nevis – out to the west coast. The most direct route north from Appin is to cross the bridge at Ballachulish and then follow the A82, which I had left by the side of Loch Lomond the day before, all the way along the beautiful eastern edge of Loch Linnhe, enjoying an endless panorama of marvellous views across the water to the hills and mountains beyond.

But there's also the Corran Ferry, a tiny, open decked vessel carrying people and vehicles across the narrow channel to Sunart, with Morvern, Moidart and Ardnamurchan waiting beyond. It would certainly be a more interesting journey but it would also take longer and, with the skies looking increasingly threatening, might result in yet another drenching. I still hadn't decided which route to take until I came over the hill at Corran and, looking out across the loch, saw the little vessel setting off from the jetty on the far side. Acting purely on impulse I slowed the bike and swung it to the left, rolling down towards the short queue of cars waiting for the boat to arrive. We were soon on our way across the loch and, within a few minutes, I was rolling off the folding deck at the far side.

I had used this crossing once before en route to a family holiday in Strontian but on that occasion had ridden south, straight into the most incredible storm I had ever witnessed in Scotland. This time I would be heading in the opposite direction, following a small, single-track road along the shoreline before eventually joining the Road to the Isles west of Loch Eil and continuing to Mallaig. Some of Scotland's most rugged and beautiful locations are to be found amidst those hills, coves and hidden beaches, like Castle Tioram on its tidal island and the lighthouse at the most westerly point on the UK mainland, and I wished – already for the umpteenth time – that I'd had time to really explore those areas once again.

As if in partial compensation for my disappointment, however, I was presented with 20 miles of simple, relaxing and, best of all, dry riding. I spent the next half hour gliding left and right around the twists and kinks of the shore-side road, passing only three vehicles travelling in the opposite direction as I followed the western edge of Loch Linnhe before turning onto the southern shore of the adjoining Loch Eil. When I joined the Road to the Isles just beyond Kinlocheil, a light rain had started to fall but it did nothing to dampen my spirits as I rode west, passing between the Glenfinnan Viaduct and

A mural at Mallaig harbour

Monument, and alongside the paradisiacal (even in this weather) beaches of Arisaig.

I arrived in Mallaig at the same time as the *The Jacobite*, a beautiful steam locomotive running between here and Fort William. By the time I had collected my ferry tickets and returned to the main part of the town the streets had filled with tourists brought here by the train, many wearing scarves, hats, bags and, in a couple of cases, presumably decorative glasses marking them out as Harry Potter fans, for whom the rail journey is something of a pilgrimage after it featured in the blockbuster film franchise. Every café in town seemed to be suddenly full as I wandered from door to door, hoping to find somewhere for a quick lunch before the ferry departed. I was about to give up, resigning myself to a supermarket sandwich to keep me going, when a waitress in one of these establishments took pity on me and very kindly managed to find me a single seat by the bar, squeezed between the wall and another solo customer – a man around my age presently engaged as a private tour guide for a Spanish family visiting Scotland for the first time. We talked for a while about his job and my journey and the timeless question of what one actually does with the English degree that we both possess, when it was time for both of us to get going.

With the bike safely secured to the deck below me I took out my phone and checked the weather forecast for the rest of the day – it warned of heavy rain for the whole afternoon but, so far, the skies looked relatively clear. As the ferry pulled out of Mallaig harbour I climbed the stairs to the upper deck and looked out across the water, with the unmistakable, snow-capped silhouette of Skye waiting on the horizon. Though the sea appeared choppy – warning of the conditions ahead – the vessel seemed unaffected and we sailed gently over the sound. I even allowed myself a little optimism that maybe, just maybe, I'd make it to my destination on this famously wet island before the situation changed.

The rain began in almost the same instant that the rubber of my front tyre made contact with the ground and did not relent the whole way to Geary, more than an hour and a half away. Within minutes of disembarking from the ferry I was drenched and by the time I passed Broadford, one of the more substantial settlements on the island, what had begun as a heavy shower had become a downpour. When I stopped for petrol in Portree I found it difficult to get my gloves back on and, having taken my attention from the road, become hyper-aware of the damp, cold patches which, despite my upgraded gear, were spreading. Despite this, I actually enjoyed the journey, especially the points where the road ran close to the water and I was able to watch the shifting light skimming across the surface. Even with the famous mountains hidden away, Skye is an effortlessly beautiful and endlessly dramatic environment and, more than almost any other place I have visited, does a remarkable job of reminding us just how small, transient and insignificant our lives really are; it feels as though people are permitted to live here at the discretion of the island itself, and that this privilege could be rescinded at any time.

Waternish is the middle of three rugged peninsulas reaching out from the north of Skye into the Lower Minch and towards the Hebrides, the others being Trotternish to the east and Duirinish to the west. Geary, where I would be staying on the fourth night of my journey, lies on north-eastern side of the peninsula at the end of a very old and particularly narrow single-track road. Along the way it passes numerous tiny, sporadic settlements – mostly old crofting communities – where low, white-washed houses rest, calm and content, amidst the grand canvas of the Skye landscape. The little road snakes across the land, eventually falling down towards Geary, passing an isolated school building with views out over Loch Snizort towards Uig on the opposite side.

I finally arrived, a little soaked but in good spirits, at Mint Croft, a B&B run by Shaz and Ali, incomers from very different lives further south who are now totally committed to this community. The light was fading into the late afternoon gloom as the loch below soaked up the inky shadows of the thickening clouds, and the whole scene was overwhelmingly peaceful. There are three main buildings on the croft: the main house, which was where I would be staying and where guests have breakfast each morning; an old, single storey blackhouse with a sloping roof which, because it has been turfed from the surrounding fields, would be covered in beautiful wildflowers in the summertime; and a striking, two store building with a high pointed roof and, presumably, the most spectacular morning views out over the water.

'It's a different country up here,' Shaz told me, bright-eyed and smiling as she looked out of the kitchen window and across the loch 500ft below. 'And it's weird but living here has just changed my whole perception of time and distance – even weather.' She was right, of course – in any number of ways this beautiful corner of a beautiful corner of Scotland feels like an entirely different country from the heavily populated, polluted and urbanised Central Belt. I experienced this phenomenon during my time on Arran – measuring the intensity of the weather by its likely effect on the ferry, or going out for a short walk and getting home six hours later. I remember feeling intensely stressed for the first few weeks after I moved back to Glasgow but now realise that this was simply a side-effect of me gradually readjusting to a very different pace of life.

Shaz explained to me the complicated logistics of running their business, a B&B which focuses on highlighting local, organic produce, in this gorgeous but intensely isolated location. The food deliveries do not come straight to the house; instead they are deposited at several 'drop off points' – behind a restaurant, or in a friend's porch – around the area, all because there's no other way to get a regular supply of the best that the Highlands and islands have to offer.

They rejected the idea that Skye is being damaged by too much tourism, a claim which had become a nationwide topic of conversation after inaccurate reports in the media that the police had 'closed' the island to visitors. They were actually just asking if people had booked accommodation, she told me, because, if not, they wouldn't be able to find any on the island that night: 'it was a sensible thing to do'. Yes, the island can become very busy during the holidays, especially during a run of particularly good weather, but they insisted that the issue is not the people coming here but rather the neglect of important infrastructure that has come about as a result of cuts to local government funding. A friend of theirs with a nearby hotel had become so frustrated with the state of the road to his property – which was preventing some customers from gaining access – and the council's lack of urgency in repairing it that he asked them for the tar and offered to do the work himself. Once again, there were the signs of communities being expected to cover for the increasing withdrawal of the state, a process which inevitably presents an existential threat to countless remote towns, villages and settlements.

For dinner that night, Shaz had made kedgeree with locally smoked haddock, which I watched her cook with great care and to absolute perfection, in their long, open-plan kitchen, and the three of us sat by the window, sharing a meal and our perspectives on Scotland. With fish already literally on the table, Ali talked about the threat of what he called the 'next great ecological disaster' – the industrial fish farming industry which, he argued, threatens to do immense damage to Scotland's coastal habitats. It's another matter I remember from my time on Arran, where the Community of Arran Seabed Trust (COAST), which helps to maintain the local No Take Zone and Marine Protected Area, has been a prominent opponent of proposals to significantly increase salmon production in Lamlash Bay, fearing that the resulting facility will do significant damage to this fragile, recovering habitat.

One certainly could not fail to notice the near-constant presence of the huge, circular, sub-aquatic cages lurking in sheltered lochs and inlets all along the west coast, each containing thousands of developing fish. The high concentrations of fish produces commensurately high concentrations of sea lice, which then escape from the cages and infest the local eco-system. The chemicals used to prevent this are also damaging to the environment and past investigations have found areas around fish farms to be massively in breach of recommended safe levels of such pesticides. And of course there is the huge quantity of biological waste produced by such a large number of animals.

There are serious welfare concerns for the fish as well, with the investigative website 'The Ferret' recently revealing a collection of hundreds of photographs 'taken since 2015 by fish health inspectors investigating mass deaths at salmon farms along the west coast and on islands' which revealed in horrifying detail the dark side of the industry: 'eight diseases, bloody lesions, eye damage, deformed organs, plagues of flesh-eating sea lice and much else'. A licence application has been submitted for a new venture nearby which claims to be an 'organic' salmon farm, but Shaz and Ali are not impressed and will not be serving it in the B&B. Despite the 'organic' tagline they insist that it is nothing of the sort, pointing to the fact that their operators may still end up depending upon chemicals to tackle lice infestations at which point they can simply switch to non-organic status. Furthermore, if they sell the facility, the new owners will not be required to continue operating on the same terms and with the same methods.

'Marine Harvest or one of the other Norwegian companies will buy it like they always do and it'll be just like all the others,' lamented Ali. His concerns seem well-founded, with *The Guardian* reporting at the time:

The UK chief operating officer of Norwegian fish farming company Villa Seafood is among the fish farm's five directors, as is Highland councillor Alister Mackinnon. In 2017, three of the five largest salmon producers in Scotland were Norwegian-owned.

A few days after my visit, Highland Council approved the application.

Salmon is a massively successful export for Scotland – in fact, it is the largest food export for the whole of the UK, with 2017 seeing a 35% increase and a total value of £600m. Nonetheless – or perhaps unsurprisingly, depending upon your point of view – there seems to be a real risk that whether it takes 10, 20 or 50 years, we will one day look back and wonder why we ever allowed the current situation – with such a poorly regulated system dominated by overseas corporations, widespread suffering of the creatures being farmed and significant environmental consequences – to become the status quo.

A similar question is already being asked, albeit far too late, in relation to another feature of life here: Gaelic. Though still spoken by several local people, the majority are of the older generation. The population of the area itself has also been progressively aging over the years as families and young people leave, sometimes by choice, but often in response to the pressures, many of them unnecessary, of living in such an isolated location. The tiny primary school I had passed on the way into Geary once educated 70 pupils – now there are just four.

And the loss of Gaelic would, she argued, mean more than just the disappearance of a language, it would also sever precious links to our past – a point quickly reinforced by the production of a pile of A4 printed paper entitled *Waternish: Place Names and Associated Lore*. It was a dissertation written by a local woman named Kathleen MacLeod, whose family had returned to their croft in Geary when she was two years old, continuing a link which has endured for four generations, and who had attempted to catalogue the fascinating stories scattered across near-forgotten parts of this little peninsula.

I took the papers with me when I retired to bed, planning to spend five or ten minutes reading before going to sleep – but an hour later I was still awake, utterly immersed in the history of Waternish. MacLeod's research is an attempt to map, record and analyse the incredible number of specific place names on the Waternish peninsula. She brings together information from academic and cartographic sources, blending it with the folk memories of local men and women, including the enigmaticall named Captain John Macleod (CptnJML), to produce a fascinating insight into the human history of the area:

> For several years, I have been encouraged to undertake a project like this to record the place names, as many of the older people who knew all the local names have passed away. They were of a generation of people who were heavily involved in agriculture and fishing and there were few cars, so all the travelling that they did by foot meant that they were far more familiar with the land and the coastline than the following generations.

'Many of the names have already been lost,' she warns, 'and there is no way of reclaiming them.'

That choice of verb, with its implications of ownership, belonging and identity, seems particularly apposite. I am keen to share some of these stories with a wider audience and Kathleen MacLeod has kindly given me permission to reproduce some of her work here, a privilege for which I am most grateful.

Dùn Geàrraidh Mòr – (CptnJML) Gaelic and Norse
The fort of the big enclosure

There are the remains of three prehistoric forts in Waternish, Dùn Geàrraidh Mòr, Dùn Borrafiach and Dùn Hàllain. Captain MacLeod says that this is the only place on the island or on the mainland which has three brochs within 5 miles, which shows that there must have been frequent attacks on the peninsula due to the ease of landing boats there. It is believed that the livestock was gathered up onto the hill and the women and children were put inside the brochs whilst one person secured the small door and the men would stay out and fight. Ellie buildings were certainly styled for defence as they could not be set alight because of the solid rock they were made of; they could not be scaled as they flared out at the top and the thick walls were very secure (Captain MacLeod). It is also believed that fires were lit at the top of the buildings as a warning signal and the warning was delivered much faster than a messenger.

An Talamh Fhuar – (CptnJML) Gaelic
The cold ground

When Waternish estate began to bring in guests for hunting and fishing, they would travel between Fasach and Ardmore. The landlord did not want these gentlemen to see the local people's accommodation incase it lowered their opinion of the estate. Therefore, the people were moved to sites behind the hills and by the shore so that they would not be seen. The land that they were moved to was not very far away from their old homes, but it took a lot of work to bring the ground to arable land, it was cold ground to them (Captain MacLeod).

Carn a' Ghille – (1750s map) Gaelic
The boy's cairn

This little cairn is to be found on a bend of the road just a short distance past Fairy Bridge. It is under a metre tall and it is unlikely to get much bigger as the majority of people pass it in their cars and are unlikely to add to it. Swire calls it by an English name, 'The Cat's Cairn' (1952:95) because of the story attached to it. She tells the story of a boy, about 12 years old, from Dunvegan who is sent to Watemish to take a message to his Granny. This he does and is on his return journey when a thunderstorm begins overhead. He takes shelter in a nearby ruin to wait for the storm to pass. He falls asleep there, tired after his journey, until he is woken by a scrabbling noise. He sees a black cat on the floor of the ruin looking up at two other black cats making their way in through the chimney. When they had all landed on the ground, they immediately turned into Women. The boy could tell that they were witches.

When the witches saw him, they threatened him with death if he told anyone of what he had seen. The first witch made a sign with her hands and put 'the Fear' on him. After they had left, and the boy had calmed down enough, he carried on his journey home. When he arrived, his mother knew that there was something wrong with her son, He seemed completely exhausted, had no appetite, was not able to settle to sleep and was terrified of leaving the house. Eventually, the mother was able to persuade him to tell her what was wrong (there is a local variant where the mother persuades the boy to tell the stove, as it is not a living person, and she goes outside to the vent to listen). She was shocked and went on her way to find the minister straight away. The minister was away from his house so the woman, in desperation, told a neighbour in confidence. Soon the whole village had heard about it as had the witches. The boy, having been unburdened, soon forgot about what had happened and was back to his former self.

The next summer, he was asked to take something to his Granny in Waternish again and once again he was caught in a storm on his way home to Dunvegan. He took shelter in the same ruin and his scratched and mauled body was found where the cairn is now (1952:95-96). Swire dates the story from 200 years before she published her book, So perhaps approximately 1750 (1952:95). She also thinks that this could be how the people of Waternish got their nickname of 'Na Cait' — the cats (1952:95). Forbes confirms the nickname and also gives 'Na Sgalaich, being ready to raise a hue and cry against their neighbours' (Forbes 1923:445).

The depth of the stories hidden behind these ancient names is awe-inspiring and acts as a reminder of what we stand to lose if Gaelic, and the history it contains, is allowed to disappear: a living, breathing link to our past and, with it, a huge chunk of the Scottish nation. Sadly the problems faced by Gaelic are not entirely demographic – they are also attitudinal. Attempts to rescue the language, such as the mainstream availability of Gaelic-medium schooling, are the subject of endless, mindless whining from a small but loud section of Scottish society, one which revels in this particular ignorance like a dog in a muddy pond. Part of this animosity has, predictably, become bound up in the ongoing debate over independence.

This is no doubt at least in part a hangover from the historical division between highlanders and lowlanders – according to Muir, 'no two sets of people could be more temperamentally incompatible', a description is which there is still plenty of truth – and manifests in all sorts of ridiculous ways: complaints that Gaelic names on street signs are a waste of money or, in some particularly myopic quarters, a dangerous distraction; performative outrage at the apparent extravagance of public funding for organisations established to secure the future of a language; articles in the national press decrying the language as a potential 'division in Scotland' and complaining about a Gaelic TV channel showing football matches in, unsurprisingly, Gaelic. This bizarre form of historical and cultural loathing is exacerbated by an impoverished and strictly transactional view of language, one where communication is merely a tool for buying food in the shops or '*dos cervezas*' on holiday – and it is entirely wrong.

My journey up the west coast and then Skye (where many of the street signs give the Gaelic first with the English translation below) reminded me of a basic reality: that there are endless pages of Scotland's story – told in words I cannot read and sounds I cannot form – that I am, at least as yet, unable to properly understand.

I went to sleep thinking about the boy from Dunvegan and wishing for some brighter weather the next day, during which I would be tackling some of the best roads from the whole journey.

Once again, I was also left wishing that I had much more time to explore the place in which I had stopped, and would have very much liked to have been able to spend a whole day, on foot, walking through the expansive history of this tiny land. Next time.

5

Skye to Ullapool

'They call it empowering communities
but it's about saving money.'

I WOKE UP early again on day five of my journey, in time to see the light wash up against the hills of Trotternish before pouring over the crest and down into the bay, flooding into Loch Snizort beneath a blanket of low, grey-blue clouds. The sea was calm and clear as it soaked up the emerging colours of the new day. Scottish weather is famously unpredictable but years of riding motorbikes and wild camping gives you a decent feel for the ebb and flow of its moods and today, with the clouds already starting to lift when I set off at half past eight, felt like it might be a good day.

I certainly hoped so as it was the leg of the journey which, from a biking perspective, I was most looking forward to, with the journey from Waternish to Ullapool to be punctuated by stops in Applecross and Gairloch. This would mean I'd be riding round an incredible coastal road but also over the famous Bealach na Ba, which I'd only tackled once before (and, like the Argyll Coast Road, I had been a passenger in my wife's car at the time).

Having covered the east of Skye on the way to Geary I decided to explore the west on the way back out, and I enjoyed a gentle, relaxing ride back down the island. The clouds were still trying to unpick themselves from the jagged hills and I repeatedly found myself climbing into little pockets of thick white mist before plunging back

Looking back to the mountains from Sligachan, Isle of Skye

out again a few seconds later. Eventually, however, the sun cleaved through, illuminating the road ahead of me – a good omen, if one believes in such things – as I rejoined the main road once again at Sligachan.

Returning to the mainland via the Skye Bridge, my next stop was in Lochcarron, a pretty little strip of a village clinging to a couple of miles of shoreline along the water from which it takes its name. Many years ago I had spent a week here with my wife's family and have particularly strong memories of clambering around the ruins of nearby Strome Castle. A few of us also had to abandon the ascent of a nearby mountain when a furious storm came crashing in, dumping so much rain on the mountainside that the stone path became a flowing burn, this in turn prompting the sudden appearance of dozens and

The road ahead from the back of the bike

dozens of frogs. I stopped briefly for a cup of tea while a band of rain passed by, then topped up my fuel and my tyre pressure and set out for Scotland's most famous road.

The sign as you turn off towards the Bealach Na Ba is absolutely explicit about what is coming:

> This road rises to a height of 2,053 ft with gradients of 1 in 5 and hairpin bends. Not advised for learner drivers, very large vehicles or caravans after first mile.

I found myself wondering whether anyone has ever driven all the way here, been confronted by that sign and then decided to heed the warnings and either turn around or take the alternative route. I suspect not.

The road itself feels thoroughly European in design, with the promised hairpin bends and steep slopes all stacked up on top of one another as the tarmac bounds excitedly skywards. The early twists and inclines presented no problems but each time I turned I caught a glimpse of the mist and cloud coating the pass up ahead. From around half-way up the hill my visibility started to sharply decline until I couldn't see much more than 10–20m in front of me, with the prospect of a view over the landscape below entirely out of the question. Fortunately this didn't affect my ability to see the hairpins which, though very tight, are actually very easy on a motorbike (especially if, like me, you don't encounter any vehicles going in the opposite direction whilst negotiating them). How anyone gets a motor home round these obstacles I'll never know but on two wheels with a good engine they are a lot of fun, even if you can't see much more around you. At the highest point I realised that the whiteness around me was not just fog and clouds – there was also snow, piled nearly two metres high on the left hand side of the road and carved by the wind into the shape of a breaking wave, a most unsettling thing to have suddenly appear in your peripheral vision.

I was close to the village of Applecross before I eventually emerged from the mist and saw the sun breaking through the cloud cover in sporadic, diagonal beams of springtime light, illuminating the waters of the bay and the inner sound beyond. As I swung around the tight bends where the road enters the village I passed a large stag standing opposite me, apparently unimpressed at the interruption to his day. I turned left on Shore Street and parked outside the Applecross Inn where I had arranged to meet someone qualified to help me learn about life in this isolated corner of the country.

Alison Macleod is a community activist and local development officer for the area. Along with her late husband Alasdair – who sadly died in a fishing accident earlier this year and is greatly missed both in Applecross and beyond – she has been a driving force behind a range of projects to support, improve or protect the village over the years.

Alison took her time to explain some of the various challenges of life here, such as the broadband that has to be bounced off several satellite dishes on the islands of Raasay and Rona, as well as another on the far side of Loch Torridon, with the whole thing largely maintained by volunteers. Then there is the community hydro scheme, now up and running but only after a long-running saga over the amount of power they could theoretically generate had threatened the entire project. In fact, the burn now being harnessed could generate twice as much energy as is currently produced by the system, much of which could then be sold on or turned to other uses, such as a community heating scheme, but a series of restrictions (some financial, others technological) mean that this potential is currently lost. Continuing the theme of insufficient infrastructure, I was particularly stunned to learn that the entire inn, containing a kitchen feeding hundreds of people a day, uses domestic appliances because it, like the vast majority of buildings here, is not connected to the modern (or 'three-phase') electricity systems that most of us take entirely for granted. Another problem – by no means unique to Applecross but pressing nonetheless – is the extortionate housing costs driving young people and families away from the area altogether.

Our conversation then moved on to something I had been hoping to discuss: the North Coast 500. As the name suggests, this 'Ultimate Road Trip' covers roughly 500 miles around the northernmost reaches of the Scottish mainland and is marketed as the country's answer to America's Route 66, guiding travellers through some of the most extraordinary landscapes in the world. Roadside advertising and merchandise in the shop and pub in Lochcarron had marked the point at which I had joined the route and, with the exception of a pause on Orkney, I would in fact be following it all the way to Inverness. It has been praised by travel publications from around the world and is credited with increasing the number of visitors to this part of the country. The official website sells t-shirts, tour guides and three different tiers of spurious 'membership', the most expensive of which will cost the gullible traveller £300. Behind the scheme are the North Highland Initiative, a business group set up in 2005 by the Prince of Wales focused on 'Food & Drink, Tourism and Community support and leadership' in areas of Caithness, Sutherland and Ross & Cromarty. It has, it seems, been a roaring success.

'It's been awful,' Alison says grimly. 'The whole thing has been a nightmare.' Her brow darkens a little as she describes the whole scheme having been 'imposed' upon communities by 'north Highlands businessmen' with no consultation or discussion. She laughs as she remembers those responsible describing the project as having been driven by the 'grassroots': 'None of those roots are in the ground around here. It's been brilliant for them further north but we have really struggled at times.'

The problem, Alison insists, is not tourism itself. She, and those who share her concerns, are not motivated by a NIMBY mentality and certainly have no desire to keep people away from Applecross – quite the reverse. They would love to welcome more visitors but face a severe lack of the sort of infrastructure necessary to sustain major increases in numbers. It is a simple matter of capacity, resources and, therefore, money. Applecross was already doing very well before the NC500 appeared, so much so that they had already approached the limits of what they would be able to handle in the summer months.

Now, those limits have been breached, putting huge pressure on facilities (such as the public toilets which are already operated by the community themselves) and, of course, roads: the Bealach na Ba – which brings the vast majority of people here – translates as Pass of the Cattle, and this precipitous, contorted, 200-year-old road was never designed to cope with the volume, or type, of traffic now seen here. Alison told me about inexperienced motor home drivers causing problems on the pass, or stopping to empty their toilet tanks and, finding no facilities for doing so, spilling the chemical waste on the floor as they try to pour it down a toilet.

The concern is simple really: that people will come to see Applecross as too busy, too touristy, too normal and, in the end, too much bother, so that the end result of the NC500 initiative is a reduction in people able to fully appreciate what this gorgeous little peninsula has to offer.

What became obvious to me was that the sense of isolation from decision-making and power structures, which I had already encountered in Galloway, Oban and Skye, is felt keenly in Applecross, and that this tiny community, as innovative and forward-thinking as it is isolated, is an especially good example of the challenges facing so many towns and villages along this coast. Alison argued that the problems faced by communities like hers have been exacerbated by a noticeable withdrawal of the state, with more and more responsibility being handed to – or imposed upon – volunteers.

'They call it empowering communities,' she says with a wry smile, 'but it's about saving money. The thing is, volunteering is good and a really important part of developing communities – but when it starts to incorporate infrastructure, a line is being crossed. Facilities like proper electricity and communication should be a right to which everyone is equally entitled – we shouldn't have to fight for basic things.'

It is no secret that Scottish councils have faced severe budget cuts in recent years, brought about by a combination of austerity economics from the Westminster government and further funding reductions, and a failure to reform local taxation, from the SNP government at Holyrood. Though these cuts have affected *almost* every level of Scottish society – the notable exception being the highest echelons in which those with most wealth and power reside – they have undoubtedly done the most damage to those who bear least responsibility for the disastrous financial crash in 2008, which threatened to collapse the entire framework of our economic system and was then used as justification to pursue the political goal of shrinking the state.

At an individual level it is those on the edges of a society who are most susceptible to negative shifts in the role of the state in their lives. Look at benefit reform agenda, where people who are, by definition, already struggling have been made subject to a grotesquely inhuman system which has made their lives far more difficult and stressful, while those of us who are relatively comfortable are insulated from the worst of the consequences. Communities are affected by a similar process, with the most isolated groups of people often most vulnerable to decisions being taken hundreds of miles away.

Twice in recent weeks, Alison told me, the community had found it necessary to come out in force to protect themselves, once to stop the Bealach na Ba being closed through the day during this very holiday, and before that to fight serious cuts to local healthcare services. Though these battles were won the larger war – between the needs, and rights, of living communities and the demands of both corporate and public balance sheets – is one in which communities will always be manifestly outgunned, at least without a major shift in the structures and patters of power and ownership in Scotland.

A few days ago I had set out on this journey from the steps of the Scottish parliament, an institution which was supposed to bring power closer to the people of Scotland and, as a consequence, give them more control over their lives and communities; but looking out across the sound to Raasay, Rona and Skye beyond, I wondered whether those who live in places like Applecross really feel that Holyrood is, in a day-to-day sense, any closer or more accessible than Westminster. I had chosen the parliament building as the starting point for my trip because, to me, it is the clearest symbol of modern Scotland's sense of itself – I'm not sure I would feel the same if I had grown up in Geary or Gairloch instead of Glasgow.

There is perhaps a risk that readers will take from these pages an impression of Applecross as somewhere to be avoided, which is categorically not true: it is a genuinely special place of rare beauty and character, an undoubted jewel in Scotland's considerable crown, and if you haven't visited it before now then you absolutely should. Nonetheless, thanks to Alison's honesty and patience, I learned a great deal about the challenges of life in this incredible location.

I so enjoyed my conversation with Alison that I ended up staying in Applecross quite a bit longer than I had planned and, though I could have happily stayed for much longer, I had to get going if I was going to reach Ullapool by evening. Rather than go back over the pass to the main road north I decided instead to follow the coast route which loops all the way around the perimeter of the Applecross peninsula. I had no real idea of what to expect from the next 25 miles of tarmac hugging the coastline almost the entire way to Shieldaig; what I found was one of the absolute highlights not just of this journey, but of any I've ever undertaken.

Not far round the coast I came across a rock daubed in yellow paint with the words 'ELF GOVERNMENT' (for which I would be happy to be furnished with an explanation), and stopped for a quick photo – before continuing along what turned out to be perhaps the best road along which I have travelled. It is not especially fast or technical, and isn't a place for the sort of full-on, knee-down, attention-seeking riding that some enjoy. It is simply a road which feels like it will get you where you're going, but one which you can only appreciate if you travel in the spirit of the landscape through which you are being guided: just take it easy and take it all in.

For mile after mile I rolled along, not concentrating on going particularly quickly but making little use of the brakes, relying on the engine and the gyroscopic sweep of the bike to keep me on the road as I passed places with beautiful names like Fearnbeg and Arinacrinachd

The 'Elf Government' rock near Applecross

– sounds that seem to lift off the tongue rather then roll from it – as well as single homes standing firm on isolated patches of land keeping watch over the sound to the west or across Loch Shieldaig and out to the peaks of Torridon in the east. I had overtaken a couple of cars as I made my way along the road but had not met an obstruction of any kind from the opposite direction, my average speed gradually creeping up as I became more familiar with the character of the road itself – but as I came to the crest of a steep, right-handed incline I was forced to brake suddenly and bring the bike to a juddering halt.

All across the road in front of me, and covering the ground on both sides, was a flock, dozens strong, of sheep and tiny lambs only weeks, perhaps even days, old. The adults ignored me but some of their offspring were curious about this strange new object in their world. A couple started inching towards me from the right hand side, where the exhaust system runs into a very hot silencer, and I began to panic at the prospect of a tiny lamb being horribly burned. I shooed the pair away with a wave of my boot and then, just as I was about to switch off the bike, another vehicle –the sort of 4x4 often used by farmers or forestry workers – appeared on the other side of the flock. I watched as it came to a gentle halt before a single whistle pierced through the scene; an instant later there was a flash of black and white as a collie leapt through the open passenger window and into a shallow ditch at the side of the road, hunching down on its shoulders, hind and forelegs as only their breed can. It paused, sizing up the situation before it and then, as the car started to inch forward, sprang into action, darting efficiently back and forth to herd the bleating white mass beyond me and down the road.

The gorgeous road, beautiful bends and outrageous views kept on coming as I worked my way north, with highlights including the gorgeous views of Loch Shieldaig and the route from Torridon to Kinlochewe where a relaxed, single-lane road ambles through the glen amidst spectacular, ululating mountains on both sides. I eventually reached the little harbour on Loch Gairloch where I stopped for half an hour to stretch my legs and rest my wrists by the 'Wildlife Observation Garden' (which, according to the little wooden sign alongside, is affectionately known as 'the Sit-oot-erie') overlooking the loch and the stacked peaks beyond. In the small shop nearby a young man behind the counter felt the need to warn me that most of the petrol stations in the area would be closed the following day – a Sunday. I supposed that he had probably recognised my accent and reckoned that an ignorant Weegie wouldn't have stopped to think about such a thing. He was right.

The harbour itself is still in use, although the collection of a dozen or so small fishing vessels and pleasure craft I saw, though a decent showing compared to similar locations along the coast, is undoubtedly a far cry from the size of the local fleet at its historic heights. In fact, the signage around the site strongly suggests that the main business here is not built around taking animals from the water but rather allowing humans to see a range of aquatic creatures in their own environment. In its own way this shift in focus represents a wider change that has taken place in this part of the country, with local economies reorienting towards the pursuit of the tourist pound.

The last stretch of my journey for the day would take me to Leckmelm on the outskirts of Ullapool, which I expected would take about an hour. On the other side of the headland protecting the harbour lies Gairloch Beach, after which the road rises as it turns east, carrying travellers through the beautiful villages of Poolewe, Altbea and Laide, all the while negotiating smooth, sweeping roads

The bike at Gairloch Harbour

as the miles continued to stack up.

It was only when I reached Leckmelm that I realised I didn't actually know where to find the house in which I would be staying for the night. The village is mostly a collection of houses built on either side of the main road passing through to Ullapool and, so far as I could tell, does not include actual streets or other means of navigation. I rode up and down the length of it looking for a sign matching the name of the house I had been given but, unable to find anything helpful, decided to ask for directions in one of the houses by the roadside.

'Oh aye, I know where you are son… just back along the road and up to the left. You can't miss it.'

I could, and did, miss it, initially going all the way 'up to the left' on a short but devilishly steep and – thanks to the carpet of dead pine needles – slippery slope which became the driveway for an empty holiday cabin. Fortunately I belatedly remembered that I had a phone number for my host for that night. One quick phone call ('I thought that was you we just saw going by...'), a few minutes and a nervous descent of the slope later I finally arrived outside a striking, bright blue house with huge sliding windows looking down towards the glassy waters of Loch Broom. Here I met Ailsa and Joe and their sons, Hamish and Archie, as well as their lodger called Jack (up from the West Country to work on a boat, I was told), friend Edel (who 'came here years ago' from Ireland and 'just never left') and two very good, and very friendly dogs.

Ailsa showed me where I would be staying, leading me across the driveway towards a small, barn-like building at the edge of their plot. I followed her to the rear of the building and up a few stone steps jutting out from the drystane wall behind (very similar to the construction style of the wall around Anwoth Old Kirk at Gatehouse of Fleet) then alongside a large enclosure full of chickens. Here a short wooden bridge a couple of metres long reaches back across to a door under the pointed eaves of the gable end of the little wooden building. Inside, in a cosy little room above a workshop below, I found a huge, comfy bed, a small wood-burning stove (already lit) and, at the opposite end from the door, a single, vertical window with a view out over water, all huddled beneath a low, sloped roof. It was affectionately called the 'Shed Bed', and though Ailsa kept apologising for not having a room available inside the house, I *loved* it. 'If things all get a bit crazy inside I sometimes come and sleep here,' Ailsa told me, and I could easily understand why.

I got changed out of my gear, carefully arranging various

A room with a view in Leckmelm

components – boots, waterproof(ish) socks, gloves – around the deceptively powerful stove and hanging the larger items around the room and then, after a brief conversation with two especially curious hens, went back to the house.

Ailsa is a marine scientist working 'with fish and fishy people'. With bright, energetic eyes and a warm smile, she is the sort of person who makes one feel instantly welcome and at ease, qualities which I imagine go a long way when working for conservation alongside the fishing industry. Her partner Joe, who built the house and the Shed Bed, runs a small oyster farm for part of the year while working in forestry the rest. They are, quite obviously, not the sort of people who would be satisfied spending their working lives at a desk in a climate-controlled, time-managed office.

Although unable to understand the language themselves, they have chosen to have their school-aged son educated in one of the Gaelic-medium classes at the local primary, having been convinced of the benefits of bilingualism for children but also in the hope of allowing him to develop greater connections to the Scottish landscape and history through the language. Ailsa has also, slowly and informally, been developing her own knowledge of Gaelic and its links to the land around them by translating names from maps of the local area into English.

The topic of the NC500, which passes straight by the house, also re-emerged when I was asked if I would be completing the whole route. I'd be covering three quarters of it, I explained, but only because it happened to cover the roads I would be using anyway. Joe used the same word to describe the route as Alison had, calling it a 'nightmare'. The roads, he explained, are already incredibly busy in the summer months and it looks as though things could get much worse in the coming years: 'If you'd been doing this trip in the summer instead of now you wouldn't believe the difference.' Once again the main problem did not seem to be visitors themselves, but a staggering lack of proper investment in the infrastructure needed to make such a scheme sustainable. Just like Alison had done a few hours earlier, he specifically mentioned people driving large motor homes, sometimes for the first time and often without proper preparation, as a particular concern; just like Alison, he also scoffed at the notion that the development of the route had been 'grassroots' or 'community led':

'Yeah that's what they say...'

As the night swirled on we sat around the table with music playing, delicious food and full glasses, swapping stories about our own pasts and presents, and sharing ideas about the future. Joe – who had to be up early to attend to his oysters – was first to call it a night, and it was into the early hours before I left the other three and returned to the shed bed, where I placed a few logs in the wood burner before sinking into a deep and rejuvenating sleep.

estHotChocola

6

Ullapool to Kirkwall

'Make sure you stop for hot chocolate!'

I LEFT LECKMELM just after 10am on day six of the journey, stopping briefly for a few photos in Ullapool before continuing on up the hill, out of the town and into the moorland and mountains of the north west. By the end of the day I would be on Orkney (for the first time ever) but I was determined to do more than simply rush to the harbour and wait; in fact, I had chosen the ferry from Gills Bay, just outside John O'Groats and 20 miles further on than the larger boat from Scrabster, precisely because its later departure time would allow me more of an opportunity to explore Caithness and Sutherland. I wanted to start by following the coast road past Achmelvich (which has one of the best beaches and campsites in the country) and Drumbeg but decided to first make a quick stop in Lochinver, a village with strong links to another of the great Scottish poets – Norman MacCaig. His masterpiece, 'A Man in Assynt', is an epic love letter to the area, the sort of poem that demands to be read periodically, and which is always at the front of my mind whenever I am lucky enough to visit this astonishing place.

The road to Lochinver passes directly by Loch Assynt, over which the ruin of Ardvreck Castle presides. Built at the end of the 16th century by the MacLeods, the castle rises from the sloped body of a promontory at the eastern end of the loch, looking out towards the massed ranks of the mountains of Assynt. It has been a ruin since burning down in 1737 and now all that remains are the vague edges of a single tower and tumbling, empty walls reverberating back through time. This is the sort of place, like Portencross in Ayrshire, Machrie Moor on Arran or St Blane's Chapel on Bute, in which it sometimes feels possible to snatch, however fleetingly, a vision of a world long past.

MacCaig's great poem asked if this is a place that 'belongs to the dead' and it is impossible to ignore the most consistent impression of the scene: the insistent, overwhelming emptiness which seems to repeatedly tap the traveller's shoulder and point out grimly into the silence all around. It is more than just a lack of human life but rather a pronounced absence of it, a feeling made stronger by the regular echoes of that past which ones hears in passing the tumbling walls and broken homes which still, despite everything, cling on to the landscape. Imagine that someone were trying to convince you that they had completed a jigsaw even though you could see that there are pieces missing – all too often, that is how it feels to experience places like Assynt.

I had just arrived at the shoreline at Lochinver when a patch of inky cloud spilled over the bay, bringing with it a sudden flurry of swirling rain. I decided to go looking for better weather further north, and changed into my thicker, wet weather gloves before setting off once more. The road skirted glorious beaches at Achmelvich, Clachtoll and Clashnessie which, though not quite at their sparkling, sun-drenched best as I passed, are nonetheless a match for any in the country. Although I saw the first two under an overcast sky, on reaching the third I was gifted a brief explosion of golden sunshine which briefly illuminated the white sands and turquoise water. From here the road approaches Drumbeg along the edge of a small lochan, with tiny tree-

Drumbeg viewpoint

covered islands dotted across the middle, a scattering of homes on the opposite slopes and the mighty, prehistoric outline of the Quinag rising up in the background. I stopped the bike by the side of the road for no other reason than to look out over the most idyllic, dare I even say romantic, scene which I had encountered on my journey, and wondered how people who live here ever get anything done.

The Drumbeg viewpoint itself is found at the top of the next hill and looks out in the opposite direction, across the island-filled waters of Eddrachillis Bay and on to the shorelines of Scourie More and Handa, above which the grey ceiling of clouds seemed to have come to rest on a narrow band of blue and white sky. The effect of these competing contrasts was to transform the scene below into another world, one isolated within a disorientating, back-lit bubble – a little imaginary land from some voluminous fantasy novel, filled with kings and swords and sex and monsters, where the inhabitants of one of those pretty loch-side houses finds themselves swept along on a life-changing adventure.

After a short rest I was about to continue on my way when the door of a nearby campervan flicked open and a woman leaned out to ask if I would like a cup of tea, which is the sort of offer that one travelling by motorbike should never refuse. Her husband was in the driver's seat, from where he chatted to me about the weather, the view and their drive up from Hampshire. Over a hot, sweet and very welcome drink I heard about their experience of being snowed in near Inverness, their connection to family in Scotland and their repeated visits to the area: 'We're up here a lot – love it here really.' They also told me about the son whom they had recently almost lost in a horrendous motorcycle crash. This is naturally not the sort of conversation one necessarily wants to have in the middle of a biking tour of the country, but I was glad to hear that he was recovering.

I encountered another patch of heavy rain as I rejoined the main road and headed towards Unapool and, unable to outrun it, decided instead to take a quick break in Kylesku to give it a chance to pass. I stopped the bike by the old jetty, where Edwin Muir would have caught a ferry 84 years before, his journey bringing him here a full half century before the opening of the bridge that I would use to cross the narrow channel between Loch Gleann Dubh in the east and Loch a' Chairn Bhain to the west. I imagined Muir, standing next to his borrowed Standard Car, cigarette in hand, waiting patiently for the little boat to arrive, but my concentration was broken by the appearance of two scuba divers who, having suddenly emerged from the water in front of the jetty, soon – and with no explanation

– plunged backwards and disappeared below the surface. The rain slowly began to ease as brighter skies emerged up ahead, so I climbed back onto the bike and rolled off up the hill. Unlike the Connell Bridge which I had so disliked, the Kylesku crossing is a legitimately beautiful piece of engineering and a wonderful example of thoughtful architecture displaying real sensitivity for the environment in which the final construction will stand. Its gentle sweep as it reaches across the water, supported on two pairs of v-shaped struts which subtly soften the bridge's hard edges, helps the whole entity to blend into the lines and frames of the landscape around and the flow of the water below. It was only opened in 1984, very nearly within my own lifetime, and must surely have transformed the pace of life here, replacing the ebb and flow of ferry crossings with immediate access – it probably encouraged more people to visit the area but it also enables them to do so without stopping. The bridge certainly represents progress (of a sort, at least) but, like everything else, there is also a clear downside.

It was after two o'clock by the time I reached Durness in the far north-west. It is, in its own way, a rather fascinating place with a strong 'end of the earth' vibe, and in the depths of winter is probably as bleak a spot as any other in the world. The entirely unremarkable buildings all seem to huddle together by the roadsides, as if fearful of the next inevitable storm – but by the time I arrived the rain had passed and the sky was showing tentative signs of co-operating with me. I expect that there is a very particular type of personality which makes one well-suited to living here and am absolutely sure that the overwhelming majority of the general population, like me, simply do not possess it. There seemed little reason to stay long and I would simply have continued on along the road had I not received two very enthusiastic, and entirely independent, recommendations to visit somewhere called Cocoa Mountain for what I was assured would be the best hot chocolate I had ever tasted. I had made good progress and had time to spare, but also had a further 90 miles of riding in front of me and, during the final ten miles leading into Durness, my right knee had started to ache badly, a sure sign of fatigue finally setting in. I decided that an allegedly life-changing hot chocolate would be a good idea after all and set about tracking it down.

On my first attempt to find this mythical drink I accidently drove straight past my target, following the road from Durness all the way down to the golf course next to Balnakeil Beach. After retracing my tyre tracks I eventually found what I was looking for inside Balnakeil Craft Village, an old MOD base converted into an arts community in the 1960s. I finally found what I was looking for and there, dear reader, I did indeed encounter the best hot chocolate I had ever tasted. More than just a café, this is also an artisan chocolatier, with a small factory in the other part of the building, and the beverage on offer tasted and felt as though that freshly made chocolate has simply been melted into a mug, mixed with a splash of milk and handed, uncorrupted, to me. It should be too thick, cloying and overwhelming, but instead this dark, velvety alchemy warms the heart and soothes the soul just like it is supposed to. It was the perfect fuel for the next leg of the journey, along almost the full length of the north coast to catch a ferry for Orkney.

I left the café at 3pm on the dot, allowing myself two hours to reach Gills Bay on the other side of the country, and rode off with the sea on my left while the mountains to the south hung over the flat, expansive landscape of Scotland's northernmost mainland edge. After days on roads which refused to sit still I found the long straights on which I now travelled equal parts intoxicating and disorientating,

Waiting for the rain to pass at Kylesku

and I struggled to calculate the time required or the distances that I still had to cover as I worked my way along the coast. By the time I reached the crossing at the Kyle of Tongue – a quite beautiful blend of bridge and causeway – the threat of rain had disappeared and a patchwork of rolling, lightly coloured clouds was even permitting the occasional burst of sunlight to pass through its fabric.

Then, not long after, I caught a glimpse of something that has been a part of my consciousness for as long as I can remember. Although Hunterston is far closer to where I grew up and Chernobyl literally exploded into the international consciousness, and despite not looking anything like the one in The Simpsons, Dounrey has always been what I have imagined when I think of a nuclear plant. yet now here it lay, a futuristic, decommissioned echo of the past, its shell sharing this vast, calming landscape with a sweep of wind turbines striding inland. Tiny Scotland's wind energy potential accounts for around a quarter of the figure for the whole of Europe, and current government targets call for renewable energy to meet 100% of the country's electricity demand by 2020 – Dounreay may have been the future once, but not any more.

I finally arrived at Gills Bay with some time to spare. The terminal here is little more than a huge, flat concrete slab poking out into the sea with the hunched shadows of Orkney hovering beyond. With just a few alterations it could conceivably make an excellent shooting location for some post-apocalyptic film. As I waited by the water's edge for the boat to arrive, the sun burst through the clouds once more, engulfing the whole cove and transforming the water from grey to a vibrant turquoise as the ferry – a low, sleek catamaran slicing through the sea – came into view.

Within half an hour the deck was full, with my bike the last vehicle to roll aboard, and as the boat pulled back out into the Pentland Firth I stood on the top deck looking out across one mainland while heading to another. The light was beginning to bleed from the sky, and in the interwoven waves of the ship's wake the water seemed to thicken as it swirled together, as if the colours drawn from above had mixed with the sea itself. The ferry passed the island of Stroma, once a crofting and fishing community but now empty, abandoned by the last of its residents in the 1960s. The ruins of their homes still stand atop the sheer cliffs, with an ephemeral blue-grey fog clinging on as we sailed by. At this point the sun, already well on its way to sinking into the west, slipped behind a great wave of cloud rolling in from the horizon; the temperature noticeably dropped so I went inside and bought a cup of Cullen Skink from the tiny cafe aboard,

Important information on the way to Orkney

and sat down to watch the water wobble by.

My introduction to Orkney took place at St Margaret's Hope where I disembarked the ferry and headed north for Kirkwall, the island's capital. Darkness was just beginning to settle and it had, once again, started to rain, but the showers were light and the roads, though unfamiliar, largely travel in long, straight, well-surfaced lines across this profoundly agricultural island. This final stretch of Day 7 took me over the Churchill Barriers for the first time – albeit in the near-dark – and then north, along Scapa Bay, and down the hill into Kirkwall to be reunited with a very important friend.

In 2011, I completed my PGDE qualification which allowed me to become a secondary school English teacher. One of the great strengths of the Scottish system is the probationary programme where newly qualified teachers are guaranteed one year of paid placement, during which time they are fully responsible for classes but are allocated a reduced timetable, providing valuable time and space to get to grips with the demands of the first year of an extraordinarily challenging job. There are two methods by which new teachers can be allocated a placement: the majority of applicants elect to rank five of their preferred local authorities and then hope to be posted to a school in an area nearer to the top of their list than the bottom; the rest, including myself, 'tick the box' to waive a preference, accepting the possibility of being sent anywhere in the country in exchange for a one-off, four-figure bonus.

And that is how I ended up on the Isle of Arran, living above the Pier Head Tavern in Lamlash with Marianne, a box-ticking chemistry teacher from Glasgow whom I had met, once or twice, during my PGDE course. That year I learned a great deal, most of all that living above a pub with your new friend in a completely unfamiliar village can simultaneously be a great idea (because you quickly find yourself in the proximity of other people, mingling and drinking and enjoying themselves, and it is easier to form connections in your new home) and a terrible one (because you end up with a tab at the bar by the end of your first night and the pattern continues from that point). Having left Arran – also reluctantly – the year before me, Marianne had since moved to Kirkwall to take up a post in nearby Stromness Academy, and had kindly offered to let me stay in her flat for a couple of nights.

I arrived just as the last of the light was seeping from the sky, following the road down to the harbour and then along the shoreline before arriving, finally, at Marianne's home. And then we did what we had always done: ate dinner, drank a few beers and talked. My best intentions of an early night melted away as I heard about life on Orkney: how her Glaswegian accent makes her stand out as the 'scary' teacher in the school (if any of her students are reading this then I assure you she's actually very nice) or how much she was enjoying being back on an island again.

Orkney is, however, very different from Arran. Kirkwall, for example, is 'a proper, good-sized wee town' far removed from Brodick or Lamlash and even has enormous supermarkets that would not be out of place in a Glasgow suburb. There is also, she noted, less of a sense that, in educating the young people, you are also all-but ensuring that they leave the island and never come back, a problem we had both noted during our time at Arran High. This is partly to do with the fact that there seems to be more opportunities for people here, with the archipelago presumably more self-sufficient than an island just an hour from the Ayrshire coast – but it is also deeply rooted in questions of identity. 'The people here are Orcadians first,' Marianne told me, echoing the view of Muir himself who, in a letter written in 1926, declared:

> I'm not Scotch, I'm an Orkneyman, a good Scandinavian, and my country is Norway, or Denmark, or Iceland, or some place like that. But this is nonsense, I'm afraid, though there's some sense in it.

I went to bed far later – and less clear-headed – than I had planned, excited for the day ahead and, as ever, hoping that the weather would co-operate. Most of all, I was glad to have been able to spend time with my friend.

7

Orkney Mainland and Wyre

'He said there's nothing on Wyre.'

FROM THE BEDROOM window I looked out over Kirkwall Bay to see deep, grey clouds covering the sky and melting into the dark haze of the horizon; I knew immediately that I would be getting wet, but it was going to take something extraordinary to keep me off the bike today, not least after surviving the weather in the first two days of the trip. I was excited by the prospect of seeing a bit more of Orkney and, above all, finally making it to the island of Wyre, where Edwin Muir had lived as a boy.

Marianne was heading off for an early ferry back to the mainland while I had a different, far smaller boat to catch later in the afternoon, so we said our goodbyes as we both packed up our gear. I would be staying in the flat myself that night.

'Oh by the way a friend of mine lives in Evie,' she told me as she prepared to leave. 'It's next to the ferry at Tingwall. I was telling him where you were going today and he said there's nothing on Wyre.'

I set off around half an hour later into the sort of smirry and persistent rain for which Scotland is famous. The day was ultimately all about Wyre but it still seemed a shame to come all this way and not see any of the rest of the island, especially since I'd be departing the next morning for the ferry back to Gills Bay. My first stop was Stromness, where Marianne teaches and which she had assured me was a beautiful little town well worth at least a quick visit. Even in less than perfect conditions it was immediately clear that she was right, and I was particularly taken with the narrow, paved, twisting streets in the old part of town next to the harbour, where an older Orkney seemed to merge effortlessly with the new.

I needed something to eat to keep me going for the rest of the day so parked the bike and strolled through the little lanes, eventually returning to the waterside where I was sure I'd find a cafe of some description. It was here that I came across a statue of a bearded man with a rifle slung over his shoulder, a hunting knife by his side and winter boots on his feet – he was a regular, perhaps even slight-looking man who, from the existence of such a fine memorial, had clearly achieved something extraordinary. The man I was looking at was Dr John McRae. Born on Orkney in 1813 he grew up to join the Hudson's Bay Company, learning to use native techniques to survive

Kirkwall

in and explore the Canadian wilderness and opening up huge areas including, in 1854, the final section of the North-west Passage. Dr Rae also solved the mystery of the Franklin expedition the same year after native people traded evidence and information about the gruesome fate of a wrecked crew which starved to death on the ice and, before the end, had turned to cannibalism. He died in London in 1893 but was buried in the graveyard of St Magnus Cathedral in Kirkwall.

Settling on a modern café in front of the harbour, I sat down next to a window with a radiator beneath and ordered scrambled eggs and a large pot of tea. When it arrived a few minutes later my plate was piled high with a mound of eggs so bright and yellow they looked as though they had been made from only the yolks. I enjoyed watching the gentle comings and goings of the harbour side while I ate, though I couldn't help paying particular attention to the rhythm of the puddles and the movement on the flags on the boats. The rain had barely relented by the time I left but I couldn't wait around all day, especially with an important ferry to catch in a couple of hours.

While consulting a map the night before, Marianne had assured me that I had plenty of time to spare, 'nothing is actually as far away as it seems,' and so I had quickly planned a rough, whistle-stop tour of a few of Mainland Orkney's most famous sites. I began at the Ring of Brodgar, an imposing circle of standing stones dating back thousands of years and built on the rise of a narrow strip separating a pair of low, small lochs. Worryingly, this already fragile site is now being threatened by factors including climate change, and work is underway to try to protect it for future generations. It is, of course, a hugely impressive sight but with the rain stubbornly refusing to abate and a sharp, sporadic wind racing in from the sea I decided not to hang about too long. Nonetheless, the stones are a fantastic, physical anchor point to the archipelago's past – with better weather, and under different circumstances, I would certainly have stayed longer, although I suspect that the whole site is at its best on a clear, dark winter night with the great sweep of the galaxy sparkling overhead, a spectacle which might begin to do justice to such an ancient, but also intensely human, place.

Though there weren't many people about I did encounter endless, enormous flocks of geese all across the landscape, working their way through the fields until they were startled by the sound of the bike and took off; on more than one occasion I found myself riding along the arrow-straight roads between dozens of these huge, beautiful birds flying, at roughly head-height, alongside me to my left and right, an unexpected privilege for which I was particularly grateful.

The more I saw of the landscape, the more the whole island seemed like one big, continuous farm parcelled up and shared out amongst the inhabitants at some point in the distant past. At the edge of many of the fields farmers have even used standing stones as part of their fences, wrapping the barbed wire around the rugged, ancient rocks scattered all around. I became even more interested in these fragments of the past than the grand set piece back at Brodgar, coming to regard them as tangible examples of the link between Orkney's prehistoric past and prosperous present as well as a sign of the innate practicality required of life on these and other islands.

I decided not to stop at Skara Brae, the Neolithic village which has somehow survived the ravages of time on the edge of the Bay of Skaill, as I had never visited before and did not want my first experience to be rushed and unsatisfying, although I admit that the entrance to the modern visitor centre, with its gleaming glass doors and prominent gift shop, all carefully constructed for the comfort of tourists, also put me off a little. Instead I continued along the coast until I reached Birsay, a tiny disparate little settlement on the island's north-western edge looking onto a tidal island which is periodically connected to the mainland via a narrow causeway. On the near side of the island stands the remains of the Brough of Birsay while, on the other, a lighthouse keeps watch over the endless expanse of the Atlantic ocean – unbroken between here and the eastern coast of north America – from the cliff tops above. Once again, however, the conditions conspired to block my path – I was unable to make it across to visit either of these sites up close as the tide had started rise, by now lapping over the centre of the concrete walkway before me and well on its way to covering it completely. I could certainly have gotten across but a one-way journey was no use to me, and photographs I had previously seen of the waves here at high tide served to obliterate any lingering thoughts of wading back across. Worst of all, I worried about having to make a humiliating emergency call for the nearest lifeboat, not least because friends who volunteer with the RNLI would inevitably have found out and, rightly, never let me forget about it. Even without getting all the way across, though, it was easy to appreciate the atmosphere of the place. I was the only person in sight and, with the bike's engine silenced and the road behind me, it was easy to imagine this imposing, isolated lump of land looking, and feeling, much the same way as it had done for millennia.

A little further inland, Birsay also boasts the dramatic ruins of the Earl's Palace, built in the 16th century and serving as the residence of Robert Stewart, Earl of Orkney, illegitimate child of King James V and half-brother of Mary Queen of Scots. The building seems to exist in a bizarre, suspended state somewhere between dereliction and preservation, for although the roof and several whole walls have

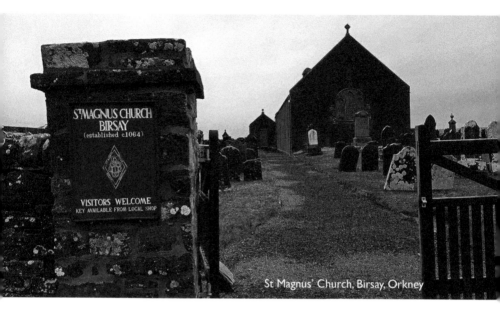

St Magnus' Church, Birsay, Orkney

been lost, enough remains to provide a sort of conceptual scaffolding, allowing visitors to partly rebuild in their mind's eye the structure which once stood here and the sort of lives that would have been lived within and around it. A few metres away from the palace stands a near-featureless rectangular church with a high, pointed roof, surrounded by an ancient graveyard and all contained within a low, drystane perimeter wall. From the roadside it appears entirely unremarkable, as though it could be lifted from this place and casually dropped in any number of others with minimal disruption to the old or new surroundings, but a small sign on the gate names it as St Magnus Church, a precursor to the cathedral in Kirkwall on a site at which people have worshipped since 1064, two years before the Battle of Hastings took place at the opposite end of the British Isles.

I set off from Birsay for Tingwall, from where I would catch my fourth ferry of the trip so far and, all being well, finally make it to Wyre. By now the rain had entirely ceased but the wind – though calmer than before – still regularly reasserted itself in brief and erratic gusts. The water between the north-eastern coast of Mainland and the little island of Rousay was also noticeably more animated than the calmer seas to the south and as I passed through the beautiful village of Evie I began to worry about the chances of the boat being unable to carry me to my destination.

There is very little to see at Tingwall – a few cars, a bus stop, the single-story ticket office, a short stone jetty lined with lobster pots and a couple of boats, one of which was in the process of being unloaded as I stepped off the bike. Like so much of Orkney it clearly exists with a purpose in mind, a charming triumph of function which generates form, and although tourists like myself are of course welcome this feels very much like a place which they happen to pass through, not one that has been conceived with us in mind.

Expecting to complete the next stage of my journey on foot I entered the ticket office. Bikes have to be strapped down on ferries which take any more than a few minutes to complete their crossing and I would not have felt aggrieved had it turned out that this boat did not routinely carry them on board. Fortunately the attendant noticed my helmet and asked if I wanted a ticket for the bike as well. This was obviously a rare occurrence – he couldn't remember another motorbike making the crossing – and it took some time to coax the computer system through an unfamiliar routine, but I was soon back outside, sitting, ticket in hand, watching the wind ripple across the water and through fields as I waited for the ferry, a diminutive little vessel just a few metres wide with a hinged bow and deck mostly open to the elements, to dock. As it edged to a halt on the concrete slipway one of the crew walked up off the deck and gestured to me to head aboard, her expression a mixture of surprise and amusement as I rolled past. I watched as a strap was indeed pulled over the seat and secured to the deck, then stepped into the tiny sheltered section to the rear of the vessel and sat down.

I was joined by three others – a group of Australians on their way to Rousay, the larger neighbour of Wyre – for a holiday, although when I asked where they were from they said 'Tasmania', a response which hinted at the sense of island identity in their own island home. The ferry ploughs back and forth between Rousay, Egilsay and Wyre each day and on this run would be stopping at the former first before dropping me off. As we left the shelter of the harbour and passed into the sound the little boat began to swing and pitch pendulously , the proportions of sea and sky visible from the side windows shifting wildly with each dip and climb. I do not suffer from sea-sickness but did find myself worrying about the bike and sat nervously, half-expecting to hear a crunching, grinding, catastrophic soundtrack as the machine broke free of its restraints and was hurled across the deck. Fortunately this did not last more than a few minutes, with the water calming as we passed by the western tip of Wyre and entered the narrow strip of water between it and Rousay, where the other passengers were soon deposited on the slipway. Ten minutes later, and after a week on the road, I finally was on Wyre.

To be clear, this is not some ethereal island paradise that seems to have emerged, fully formed, from the pages of a story book, and even on the very best of days nobody would mistake the scene for one from the Caribbean: there were no dazzling white beaches and turquoise waters welcoming me to the island, nor flower-filled fields rolling out before me in a dazzling array of colours and shades. Like Tingwall, the harbour on Wyre has a strictly functional feel, as if the only things to have ever moved through it in large numbers are the sheep (the tallest I've ever seen) wandering through the surrounding fields. Being so far north it seemed that spring had only recently started to chip away at the hard edges of winter here, with the landscape still dominated by earthen shades of deep brown and muddy, mottled yellow over a base-coat of drained and sickly green. Even bathed in brilliant sunshine this is probably not the sort of scene one would choose for a postcard or an advertising campaign yet, despite all this, there is a definite, immediate but ineffable appeal to the place.

The island apes the appearance of its dominant mainland neighbour, with a single, straight line of tarmac cutting through flat, fertile fields meeting the sea on either side. I followed this 'main' road – from which tracks to the handful of farms on the island branch off – to its highest point, parking next to a low, long, modern building with a blue and white sign on its gable end pointing the way to 'Cubbie Roo's Castle'.

From here I continued on foot and, following the path along the edge of a field, soon came to the gate of a ruined chapel, known as St Mary's, at the bottom of the mound on which the ancient castle rests. Like the fortification above it this place of worship dates back to the 12th century when the Norsemen controlled these lands. The now roofless, rectangular construction is surrounded by a graveyard, with some headstones illegible after a generations-long battle with the Orcadian weather, though others are so fresh that they suggest the ground might still be used for burials. The whole site is protected by a thick, straight wall constructed in the same style, and with the same materials, as the chapel itself, with a metal gate across the gap meeting the path at one side and a grand, stone stile – allegedly only there because the man paid to build a second gate had instead drank all his funds and had no other options – providing access towards the slope, and ruin, behind.

The castle itself is fascinating and remarkably well-preserved, a testament to its original construction but also the way in which the resilience of the past seems to be heightened here. Built by Kolbein Hruga (Cubbie Roo), the Norse chieftain of these islands, it is the earliest documented stone castle in the whole of Scotland. Historical records suggest that Hruga was a huge but peaceful man, a merchant and farmer, rather than a violent Viking invader (unlike his relatives). The *Orkneyinga Saga* refers to him as 'the most outstanding of all men', while his son Bjarni Kolbeinsson became a renowned poet and the bishop of St Magnus Cathedral. The castle is also mentioned in *Haakon's Saga*, described as 'an unhandy place of attack' in connection with a siege following the murder of Earl Jon Haraldson in Thurso in 1231.

With no admission booths or entry fees, and not a single human being in sight, I crossed the narrow moat and began to walk around inside the old walls of the castle, which are incredibly thick and solid at their base and rose well above my head at the highest remaining point. The entire fortification is comprised of stacked slabs of utterly imperious, lichen-coated rock placed here before Genghis Khan led the Mongol Empire and with Wallace's victory at Stirling Bridge still more than a century away. So many of Scotland's castles have become such sophisticated, well-developed tourist attractions that it is almost impossible for a visitor to truly locate them within their historic and geographic context – but here, where one can rest their hand on a wall which has stood for nearly 900 years, built by a culture far removed from our own, really does come alive in a truly special way.

When Muir lived here the building had not been excavated from the grassy hill which had partially consumed it over the centuries, although the site was nonetheless still called The Castle. Sitting atop the hill with a view of Wyre, Rousay and Egilsay, the opening lines of Muir's poem 'Childhood' came to mind, and so I sat down on the wet grass, removed a book – *Edwin Muir: Collected Works* – from my bag and began to read:

> Long time he lay upon the sunny hill,
> > To his father's house below securely bound.
> Far off the silent, changing sound was still,
> > With the black islands lying thick around.
>
> He saw each separate height, each vaguer hue,
> > Where the massed islands rolled in mist away,
> And though all ran together in his view
> > He knew that unseen straits between them lay.

Anyone familiar with Muir's poetry will know that at the heart of it lies the loss of Eden: the motif is repeated and revisited again and again, and is rooted in the loss of his own paradise right here when his family were forced – by bad landlords, economic forces and his father's limited farming abilities – first from their home and, ultimately, from Orkney itself. I found myself trying to imagine what it would be like, even now, to be ripped away from a childhood here and plunged into Glasgow, exchanging the view before me for the scene I witnessed crossing the Kingston Bridge a few days earlier. In Muir's time, at the dawn of the 20th century, the contrast would

The bike with the Bu in the backgroun

have been even more stark with Glasgow – a city 'burning in its pit' – dominated by the roaring fires and black plumes of the industrialised world. It is difficult to imagine a set of circumstances in which such a profound change would not have a major and, very likely, negative impact on anyone unfortunate enough to have to go through it.

Down below the little ferry was once again diligently passing over the sound. Between us, across what Muir described as a 'damp green meadow' lay the Bu – the farmhouse in which Edwin Muir had lived and my main reason for travelling to Wyre. Rather than cross the boggy ground beneath me I returned to the bike and rode down to where the track to the Bu meets the road, hoping that I might be able to take the bike all the way up to the farm house itself, but when I saw the condition of the track I realised that this wouldn't be an option. Instead I left it beside the road and began picking my

way along towards the house, avoiding particularly thick and sticky patches of mud by bouncing from rock to rock or, where possible, trying to balance along the verge at the side. As I approached the Bu, it became increasingly clear to me that much of it is now effectively abandoned; although the large, relatively modern barn still seemed to be in use, the little house next to it – the one in which Muir had lived – was dilapidated. Between the two buildings spent gas canisters lay scattered, accompanied by a range of general agricultural detritus, so that the area seemed to have been very much neglected over the years. This impression, however, was naturally coloured by my feelings about Muir and it would be unfair to judge those running a farm by the sentimental standards of an English teacher from the Central Belt visiting the childhood home of one his favourite poets.

Having seen the state of the building from the outside I briefly considered turning around, worried about the physical risks of going inside but also the disappointment I would feel at having come all this way only to find no remaining trace of Muir. But I was also determined – even desperate – to at least take one brief and necessarily cautious look inside. I entered through a gap at the back, nervously watching the roof and being careful not to do anything that might result in me being stuck in a ruined building on a tiny Scottish island on which I had thus far not seen a single other person. In one room I found a collection of small, white plaster statues on the floor, table and shelves; others contained what looked like decades worth of discarded furniture. There seemed, as I had feared, to be nothing left connecting me to Muir's time here, save for the frustratingly silent walls themselves, but just as I was about to leave an oval-shaped plaque on a narrow window sill caught my attention. It was difficult to read in the gloom of the farmhouse but when I tilted it towards the light it confirmed that I had indeed found what I was looking for. In the centre stood a young man, one hand holding a traditional plough while the other grasped the reins of a pair of horses, one brown and the other black and white, and around the outside it read: 'EDWIN MUIR'S BOYHOOD HOME – THE BU'.

Part of me felt then, and still feels now, that it is a shame that Muir's 'boyhood home' is not better recognised and preserved. And yet the idea of some sort of museum, a sterile, sentimental attempt to trap the past of this special little place in historical aspic, would feel equally wrong. In fact, the only appropriate tribute to Muir's happy, formative years here would be the continuation of life through further generations.

A mouldering tractor on Wyre

As I turned to leave, I toyed with the idea of leaving the little plaque outside for people to see but worried that it would simply fade away into the wind and wet, so instead returned it to the windowsill on which it had been resting when I arrived. I then left the house and walked back towards the bike where I met a woman with her young daughter and, to my particular delight, a very friendly border collie. They were, she told me, on their way back to the farm at the end of the road which was owned by her husband's family, whom they were visiting. The little girl seemed very happy on her near-private island and, with infectious enthusiasm, told me that she had been down to the beach exploring and collecting shells. As I said goodbye to the trio and got back on my bike I thought about my own son, soon to turn four, and resolved that I would bring him back here the next time I visited.

I continued down the slope towards the jetty but after just a few metres saw something which made me come to a sudden, unexpected halt. In the field to my left lay the remains not of a castle, or a kirk, or the boyhood home of one of Scotland's great poets – but rather a tractor, abandoned and in the process of being consumed by the earth below it. The drivers cab was long gone, so that what remained was the red-brown metal frame, tyres (those at the rear still attached to the axel) sinking into the mud and the steering wheel. It immediately brought to mind one of the strongest images of perhaps Muir's best-known poem, 'The Horses'.

In it, Muir tells the story of a tiny community clinging on to existence a year after an apocalyptic 'seven days war that put the world to sleep'. They rebuild their lives around a rejection of the 'old bad world', eschewing the technologies which symbolised it and reforging their ancient connection to horses and the way of life they represent. It ends simply: 'Our life is changed; their coming our beginning'.

That change is symbolised by the abandonment of the very machine which had replaced horses in their 'fathers' lands':

> *The tractors lie about our fields; at evening*
> *They look like dank sea-monsters couched and waiting.*
> *We leave them where they are and let them rust:*
> *'They'll moulder away and be like other loam.'*

I couldn't have imagined a more appropriate way to say goodbye, for now, to Wyre. Soon I was back aboard the tiny ferry to Tingwall and, from there, on the road back to Kirkwall. I had been asked to stop off at BBC Radio Orkney where I recorded a quick interview for their next day's programming before returning to Marianne's flat, changing out of my gear and going for a walk through the streets of the town. My first and only full day on Orkney ended down by the harbour, eating fish and chips as I watched the light change while the still, glassy water soaked up and magnified whatever colour was left in the sky as the night closed in. I thought I had gotten used to wishing I had more time available to me but the feeling was especially acute here, and I went to bed thinking that these islands deserve a whole journey of their own. Perhaps one day I might even have the chance to make it happen.

THE EMIGRANTS

COMMEMORATES THE PEOPLE OF THE HIGHLANDS AND ISLANDS OF SCOTLAND WHO, IN THE FACE OF GREAT ADVERSITY, SOUGHT FREEDOM, HOPE AND JUSTICE BEYOND THESE SHORES. THEY AND THEIR DESCENDANTS WENT FORTH AND EXPLORED CONTINENTS, BUILT GREAT COUNTRIES AND CITIES AND GAVE THEIR ENTERPRISE AND CULTURE TO THE WORLD. THIS IS THEIR LEGACY.

THEIR VOICES WILL ECHO FOREVER THRO' THE EMPTY STRATHS AND GLENS OF THEIR HOMELAND.

UNVEILED BY THE FIRST MINISTER OF SCOTLAND, RT HON ALEX SALMOND MSP, 23 JULY 2007

THE EMIGRANTS

COMMISSIONED BY CLEARANCES CENTRE LTD 2004

8

Kirkwall to Inverness

'I have no regrets about coming to Scotland.'

ON THE EIGHTH DAY of my journey I awoke to find myself utterly exhausted, even struggling to get out of bed to make a badly needed cup of tea. I sat on the couch and stared at the mug, willing my mind and body into gear. Reaching Wyre had been such a big focus for the trip, and a personal ambition for so long, that finally achieving it had felt like the end of something. The feeling I had experienced strolling through the streets of Kirkwall the previous night, as the light soaked away into the night sky and the breeze passed through, had been like a thousand tiny knots inside me untangling themselves and I was now feeling the full effects of this process. Had it been possible to stop and rest for a day I would have gratefully accepted the opportunity. Ironically my initial plan had indeed been to finish on Orkney – just as Muir had done – and I could certainly have constructed a fine ending to the whole tale around a scene on Wyre, standing on the jetty as the light began to fade, with the ferry before me and the Bu behind.

But I had already rejected this idea and it was time to get going so after another – stronger – cup of tea and some breakfast I loaded my bag back onto the bike. I knew that it would take less than half an hour to travel directly to the ferry at St Margaret's Hope which afforded me some time for the two final stops I wanted to make. The first was St Magnus' Cathedral, a spectacular 12th century masterpiece of the island's Nordic past located in the heart of Kirkwall. It had been closed when I passed the previous evening so I was eager to fit in a brief visit before I left, not least because I had been told of the presence of a little memorial to Muir somewhere within. The exterior is staggering, a genuinely gigantic, centuries-old mass of weather-beaten yet resolute red and yellow sandstone. Entry is gained through the middle of three doors on the west side of the building, each with tight rows of pillared stone on either side and a contoured archway of alternating colours above. At every point it is simply beautiful.

On setting foot inside the building, visitors are met with a full view of the long, cavernous interior, its immense roof held aloft by two parallel rows of towering sandstone columns. The whole thing exudes the sort of stoic, resolute certainty that seems to characterise life in this part of the country, and manages to achieve that very rare thing for any building – a sense of belonging, and the feel of real, timeless permanence. I wandered all the way around the edge of the exterior wall, taking in the various statues, tributes and artefacts until, in the rear right corner, I found a small collection of plaques dedicated to notable Orcadians. There, alongside the likes of George Mackay Brown and Eric Linklater, I found what I'd come looking for:

EDWIN MUIR

POET. 1887–1959

I left Kirkwall by heading south, past Scapa and towards the Churchill Barriers, a series of causeways constructed during the Second World War in order to protect the British fleet from German u-boats. Here I would be making my final stop on Orkney at the Italian Chapel on Lamb Holm. This, like Portencross, had been one of the few specific sites I had wanted to visit when I set out on my journey, the sort of

Looking out over the Churchill Barriers, Orkney

thing I've always felt that one would have to see to really believe, and I appreciated the little window of sunshine which greeted me as I crossed Barrier 1 and rolled into the car park.

The chapel stands on a gentle slope a few hundred metres from road, with a view from the entrance back across the bay and the barrier to the shadows of the mainland and the hills of Hoy behind. On this day, in the centre of all this, an enormous platform, presumably linked to the oil industry, sheltered in Scapa Flow.

From 1942 until 1945 Lamb Holm was home to around 500 Italian prisoners of war captured during the North African campaigns of the Second World War and brought to this spot to help construct the Churchill Barriers; however, the men's skills far exceeded the hard labour involved in building causeways and they sought to lift their spirits by performing plays in a makeshift theatre and publishing their own Sunday newspaper, *Il Corriere delia Domenica*. In 1943, attention turned to the construction of a chapel, with two of the camp's long, low-walled, curved-roofed shelters being joined together to create a place for worship for the Catholic prisoners.

Over the entrance of this remarkable building stands a triangular concrete façade built to mimic the traditional Italian style, immaculately whitewashed with deep-red paintwork used to accentuate the shape and, on top of a small porch supported by a circular pillar on either side of the door, highlight a delicately carved face of Christ wearing the crown of thorns. An information sign inside the church explains: 'The face conveys with wonderful skill the expression associated with the paintings of "Ecce Homo" – the famous words of Pontius Pilate – "Behold the Man"'. The scene is completed by a church bell, recovered from a ship sunk in the bay and, at the very top, an eight-pointed cross with a circle at its heart, the current one an identical bronze replacement for the original wrought iron piece which had been destroyed by rust.

One of the prisoners, an artist named Domenico Chiocchetti, oversaw the whole project, even personally designing various features including the altar and tabernacle, as well as reproducing a stunning depiction of the *Madonna of the Olives* from a photograph given to him by his mother. The Mother of God sits, radiant and peaceful, with the baby Jesus on her lap, white cloth wrapped around both of their bodies and her head, as he reaches out with an olive branch. They are framed by angelic children heralding 'REGINA PACIS ORA PRO NOBIS' – Queen of Peace Pray for Us. The angel on the lower right is also holding a sheathed sword – a symbol of peace – while on the opposite side another holds a shield. On the ceiling above, a white dove of peace soars through a golden sky. One prisoner described the chapel as follows:

It was the wish to show to oneself first, and to the world then, that in spite of being trapped in a barbed wire camp, down in spirit, physically and morally deprived of many things, one could still find something inside that could be set free... The statue of St George was built first. It shows the patron saint of soldiers ready to kill the dragon... It is the symbol of a will to 'kill' all misunderstandings among people of different cultures. As the St George was built to express the physical and psychological pain, so was the chapel conceived to meet a spiritual need.

Although it was only used for a short time and never quite completed, as the end of the war in 1945 resulted in the parishioners being returned to their real homes in Italy, the result is a spectacular

Floor mosaic at the Italian Chapel

testament to the human spirit and the power of art, hope and faith, all of which have been brought together to transform a couple of repurposed shelters, some spare concrete and a bit of scrap metal into a place of worship as beautiful and powerful as any cathedral a hundred times its size. When we think of Scotland's history, our mind is naturally drawn to bloody battles and Highland clans, or to the great technological achievements of the people who called this land home – yet here, on a tiny, uninhabited Orcadian island, is something every bit as important: a reminder of the people who have come here, for whatever reason, and by their presence made the country a far better place, as well as the shared humanity which even a great war could not extinguish.

The ferry terminal at St Margaret's Hope was just a short ride from the chapel and I took my time getting there, soaking up as much of the island as I could before departing. I had only been there for two nights, and my exploration had been limited to just Mainland and Wyre, but as I stood on the deck while we set off for Gills Bay, I knew that although I was leaving Orkney it would not be leaving me.

On leaving the ferry at Gills Bay I decided to quickly ride along to John O'Groats for the obligatory photo next to the famous sign pointing out to destinations around the world. It is an amusing novelty but little more, and John O'Groats itself doesn't offer much worth hanging around for. A light rain had also begun to fall and, on the southern horizon, far darker and wetter clouds were threatening, so I left the huddled tourists behind and set off once more. The road south was marked by near-constant smir – a fabulously Scottish word for the sort of bleak, relentless rain that seems to hang in the air rather than fall from the sky – and an increasingly gusty, and cold, wind.

I stopped briefly in Wick for no other reason than to adjust the straps holding my bag to the rear of the bike and found a harbour which, though once the centre of a vast and thriving fishing industry, now seemed almost entirely abandoned. What little fishing still goes on here is focused on crabs and lobsters for luxury restaurants and markets hundreds, even thousands, of miles to the south. It wasn't hard to see what sort of impact this was having. Issues of employment aside, the truth is that when the whole design of your town, and the identity of its community, was built around something which has since disappeared, it makes sense that that the void would be filled, above all, by a profound, inter-generational sense of loss.

The rain continued all the way down the road until I approached Berriedale, with its infamous stretch of steep, contorted tarmac. The weather deteriorated sharply and I was plunged into thick, cold, wet mist. Just like on the Bealach Na Ba a few days earlier, it left me unable to see more than ten or 15 metres in front me, an experience made much more dangerous by the very real risk of another vehicle coming up behind me if I slowed down too much. I had no option but to push on, balancing speed and visibility as best I could, and hope the road would be where I expected as I dipped into each unknown bend. I was relieved to make it to Helmsdale in one piece.

Back in my early 20s I had been on holiday here, renting a huge house on the beach with a group of friends. We spent the week exploring the area during the day, visiting the likes of Brora Beach and Smoo Cave; at night we sat on the balcony or out on the sand, looking over the North Sea, drinking and talking and laughing into the gathering darkness. We had spent very little time in the town itself during that holiday and I had not been back to Helmsdale since, and my memories of the place were, in truth, based more on hazy emotional echoes than genuine recollection.

What I did remember, however, was that something about the town had felt distinctly different from those around it, a sensation which is only brought into focus by an observation of the way in which the streets here are laid out. Helmsdale was a planned town built as part of the Duke of Sutherland's notoriously brutal role in the Highland Clearances, where whole communities were mercilessly, often violently, driven from their land – and it was *their* land – to make way for more profitable sheep farming. It is largely built on a grid system, the ultimate effect of which was to remind me of the housing schemes back home in the Central Belt which had so obviously been designed from the top down instead of growing from the ground up. It feels unnatural and wildly incongruous in this part of Scotland, where small communities expanded naturally, and randomly, over time, and the strangeness of the environment must surely have had an impact upon the people who were forced to call this place home.

Even allowing for the bleakness of the conditions as I arrived, Helmsdale was still a depressed and depressing looking town. Those of a more romantic disposition may legitimately wonder whether the events which birthed this place are still, two centuries on, generating ripples in the world that we can feel if not understand. Although I had come into the town on its northern side most visitors to Helmsdale will enter it from the south, with their first impressions formed by the Bridge Hotel. It is very clearly closed, with an aging façade crumbling and fading as if no attention has been paid to it in many years. To the right is the Green Stag which, despite being in better condition than its neighbour, also seemed devoid of human activity, with La Mirage, which claims to be 'The North's Premier Restaurant', alongside.

What I really wanted to see, however, is found perched on a hill just south of Helmsdale: here, with views over the town below, the sea

NA H-EILTHIRICH

A' CUIMHNEACHADH SLUAGH NA GAIDHEALTACHD AGUS NAN EILEAN A
DH' FHÀG CLADAICHEAN NA TÌRE SEO AN AGHAIDH CHRUADALAN MHÒRA AGUS
A CHAIDH THAR CHUAIN A SHIREADH SAORSA, DÒCHAIS AGUS CEARTAIS. CHAIDH IAD AIR
ADHART, AGUS AN SLIOCHD AN DEIDH SIN, GU BHITH A' RANNSACHADH
MHÒR-THÌREAN AGUS A' CRUTHACHADH DHÙTHCHANNAN AGUS BHAILTEAN
A BHA MÒR AGUS IONGANTACH. TRO AN IOMART AGUS AN DUALCHAS
DH' FHÀG IAD DÌLEAB AIG AN T-SAOGHAL. AIRSON SEO BIDH CUIMHNE ORRA.

CLUINNEAR AN GUTHAN GU BRÀTH ANNS AN FHALAMHACHD A DH' FHÀG IAD
FEADH SHRATHAN AGUS GHLEANNTAN TÌR AN ÀRAICH.

AIR FHOILLSEACHADH LE PRIOMH MHINISTEAR NA H-ALBA, AN T-UAS AILIG SALMOND BPA, 23 IUCHAR 2007

in front and the glen behind, stands a statue called 'The Emigrants.'

The statue depicts a family of four, cleared from their homes and forced, not to Helmsdale, but beyond Scotland and out into the rest of the world. It features a mother clutching her baby, looking back towards the glen to the life that has been taken from them; a father looking out to the sea towards an unknown future in a foreign land; and a boy looking to his parents for comfort as he tries to understand what is happening to his world. This memorial to a lost people includes the following commemoration in both English and Gaelic:

THE EMIGRANTS

Commemorates the people of the highlands and glens of scotland who, in the face of great adversity, sought freedom, hope and justice beyond these shores. They and their descendants went forth and explored continents, built great countries and cities and gave their enterprise and culture to the world. This is their legacy.

Their voices will echo forever thro the empty straths and glens of their homeland.

NA H-EILTHIRICH

A' cuimhneachadh sluagh na gaidhealtachd agus nan eilean a dh'
fhàg cladaichean na tìre seo an aghaidh chruadalan mhòra agus a
chaidh that chuain a shireadh saorsa, dòchais agus certais. Chaidh
iad air adhart, agus an sliochd an deidh sin, gu bhith a' rannsachadh
mhòr-thìrean agus a' cruthachadh dhùthchannan agus bhailtean a
bha mòr agus iongantach. Tro an iomart agus an dualchas dh' fhàg
iad dìlead aig an t-saoghal. Airson sea bidh cuimhne orra.

Cluinnear an guthan gu bràth anns an thalamhachd a dh' fhàg
iad feadh shrathan anus ghleanntan tìr an àraich.

The best compliment that can be paid to the sculptor, Gerald Laing,
is that he has created a fitting tribute to the people who once brought
life to these silenced glens. I'd ridden all the way through swathes
of Scotland affected by the Clearances, through empty straths and
by abandoned coastlines, and for the first time really seen a country
that is beautiful but, in so many places, devoid of human life. We
tell ourselves (and tourists – especially tourists) that this emptiness

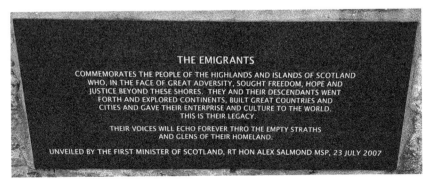

is the beauty, but it's a lie. A prerequisite for any real progress in Scotland is some long-overdue honesty about what the emptiness really represents: the lives, peoples, stories and cultures ripped from the place in which they belonged to make way for wide open grazing land and rich parasites with shotguns.

The statue was inaugurated by then First Minister Alex Salmond on 23 July 2007 at a dreich but well-attended unveiling ceremony, although the most appropriate way to honour the memory of the people being celebrated here, those who had everything taken from them, would have been to immediately head a little further down the coast to tear down the grotesque monument to the Duke of Sutherland which stands on a nearby hill.

From Helmsdale I set off on the final stretch of my eighth day, passing Brora (a beautiful little village in which one of the very best single malt whiskies is made) and Golspie on my way towards Inverness. I had been considering making one more stop, perhaps at Chanonry Point, on the way but as I took to the road the weather began to rapidly deteriorate, with a fine, sticky mist quickly changing into heavy and erratic showers. Things got even worse as I crossed the Dornoch Firth when the rain settled into a consistent downpour; then, as I approached Cromarty, I felt the temperature suddenly drop by several degrees. To make matters worse I encountered an enormous tailback on both sides of the Cromarty Bridge due to road works, leaving me shivering, static and, to be honest, pretty miserable.

When I finally came over the Kessock Bridge into Inverness I, like Muir, found the town to be 'inconveniently crowded with vehicles of all kinds, most of them stationary', a situation made all the worse by the constant deluge of cold, hard rain. Inverness, so small compared to Glasgow or Edinburgh, was nonetheless completely unlike anything else I'd seen for several days. The roads are laid out in the familiar style of rapid, development-driven expansion, all concrete carriageways and congested roundabouts and having spent nearly a week riding through highland and island landscapes I found the scale of it rather disorienting at first. Struggling to get my bearings I stopped somewhere near the centre to ask for directions.

I was told to rejoin the main road and follow it around the town out towards the hospital so I continued on as the rain, somehow, kept on getting heavier. After a couple of unwelcome detours I eventually arrived at the designated meeting point – a large supermarket on the edge of the city – where I hid under a canopy and texted Werner, my host for the evening. He arrived in moments and told me to follow him around the corner; a few minutes later I was out of the rain, sitting in front of a solid-fuel stove, being offered Bavarian meatloaf on a roll with mustard (which I can confirm is delicious) and a glass of shandy.

Werner came to Scotland from Germany in 1985, meaning that he has been here a year longer than me. He initially worked as a labourer in Edinburgh, sharing a room with two others in an overcrowded, rented house. He moved to Inverness five years later and has been here since, now working in a church-run centre supporting vulnerable people experiencing homelessness. It is a role to which he is evidently dedicated and extremely well-suited, though he had doubts about accepting the job when it was offered to him. 'In the end,' he smiled, 'I decided that if I can help one person then it will be worth it.' Though work may have drawn him north, the environment had clearly been a significant factor in keeping him here for nearly 30 years. He told me about growing up in Bavaria and spending glorious summers outside by the lake, though he described those days as if they were from a past life, not this one. Scotland is, very definitely, now home. 'I have absolutely no regrets about moving here,' he smiled. 'Everything is right here.'

When I asked, as I felt I must, about Brexit he reminded me that he did not like swearing in his house, but then went on to surprise me by saying that, in his opinion, the UK should never have joined the EU in the first place. I asked if he worried about having to leave or even simply being made to feel less at home but neither prospect concerned him: he now holds a British passport, addressing the first problem, but was also eager to stress that he had never been made to feel unwelcome in Scotland and saw no reason why that would change now. It cheered me to know that, even amidst all the political turmoil of the past few years, he had never considered going back to Germany but I couldn't help but feel that for those without a UK passport or who have not been here so long this brave new world of British politics might look much more threatening.

I went to bed that night with little idea of what the next day might bring, knowing only that I would be heading east, along a coastline with which I was completely unfamiliar, before turning south at an as yet undecided point and riding to Aberdeen. For the first time since leaving Glasgow I would have no appointments to keep or ferries to catch, and if the weather was good I'd be able to just spend the day riding entirely at my leisure through what was, to me, a largely unknown part of the country.

9
Inverness to Aberdeen

'No one knows what will happen when the oil dries up.'

ON THE WAY OUT of Inverness I passed signs for Culloden, the battlefield on which, in 1746, the Jacobite Rebellion was decisively quashed. The aftermath of this victory for loyalist forces saw a concerted attempt to undermine, and ultimately destroy, highland culture, with land seized, weapons confiscated and even tartan banned. In the years following the battle there were as many as 400 British Army camps in Scotland as the British state sought to ensure that such an uprising would, and could, never happen again. There is little doubt that the policies were broadly successful on those terms or that their effects continue to reverberate to this day; combined with the Clearances, which had begun before Culloden but accelerated in the decades that followed, it is not difficult to understand the current, depressed state of so much of the Highlands.

Despite its historical importance, I did not stop at Culloden, leaving its ghosts behind as I continued east. My first destination for the day was Elgin, which I had never visited and where I had thought I might stop briefly for something to eat and a visit to the ruined cathedral. When I arrived, however, I found a dull, uninviting town, at points not dissimilar from the likes of Cumbernauld – itself quite possibly the most dismal place in Scotland – and not even the cathedral, impressive though it is, could convince me to spend any time here. In the end I stopped long enough to take a few photographs of the tall, rectangular towers and crumbling archways before getting back on the road. Some readers – potentially those from the area – will doubtless be affronted at this description of Elgin, and it may well be the case that somewhere, hidden behind the roads on which I travelled, is another side to the place – but I did not see it.

Indeed, this whole section of my journey had so far been characterised by dull and featureless roads beneath me and an equally dull and featureless sky above. It was one of those days which seems weatherless, where the whole environment appears suspended in lethargic disinterest. I became increasingly eager to escape the grinding monotony of the A96, so when I came upon a sign for the 'Coastal Trail East' it felt like being rescued.

The road took me first to Spey Bay, where that famous river meets the North Sea via a wide, picturesque estuary flecked with tiny islands and the intermittent yellow flash of flowering gorse. Here it meets a huge, bright pebble beach dotted with small conical shelters built of driftwood and gathered debris. As this location is also the home of the Scottish Dolphin Centre, I reasoned that these simple structures had likely been constructed by people hoping to catch a glimpse of the creatures leaping out of the water. I sat myself down on a little pile of stones, with my boots off and my legs outstretched, for around 20 minutes, watching the white waves rise and rush towards the shore, but on this day the cetaceans were either busy elsewhere or not in a performing mood.

The centre itself was too busy to interest me on this occasion and I was about to leave when I noticed something that did grab my attention: three long, low buildings, connected along the parallel sides, with curved, turf roofs – as if a trio of enormous stone Anderson shelters had raised themselves out of the earth rather than being

The Ice House at Spey Bay

placed down into it. The buildings stand on a rise between the car park and the centre, with the vents along the exterior suggesting that the structure continues beneath the surface. These fascinating constructions, according to a small sign warning people not to climb them (which, in fairness, I had been considering) are in fact the old ice houses which would have been used to store the salmon fished from the river until the industry, like so many others, collapsed in the late 1980s and early 1990s.

From Spey Bay I continued along the coastal route, initially following signs for Portgordon before passing through Buckie and then Findochty, where a fine, white-washed church stands on the highest point between the cliffs and the sea, looking back over the harbour and the village it dominates. On the opposite side of the bay a tower – which I was told is the local war memorial – rises out of a similarly commanding position, so that the two seem like sentries keeping watch over the lives below. The homes, which begin by the waterside before stacking up on the hill facing the sea, appear huddled together, as if trying to minimise the gaps and crevices through which the sea winds might attack. Everything before me seemed to have been designed with strictly functional motives, and yet – though my impressions were no doubt coloured by the inevitably novelty of seeing a place for the first time, along with a gradual but very welcome improvement in the weather – this was certainly one of the most beautiful places I had encountered during my journey.

A little further along the coast I reached Portknockie, next to which Bow Fiddle Rock – a stunning natural sea arch formed of a double pyramid of ancient quartzite that rises out of the water and is shaped, as the name suggests, like the tip of a fiddle bow – stands stoically amidst the thundering sea. Then came Portsoy, visibly older than its neighbours and with a harbour which is little-changed since its construction at the end of the 17th century. On the small cliff next to the sea wall, I happened across the gable end of a ruined building, its window space framing a view across the sea to the rocks and cliffs below, a sight which must be all but identical to that enjoyed by the people who lived and worked here more than 300 years ago. This little stretch of coastline, just 20 miles long, possesses a beauty and charm unlike anything I had encountered in the previous week of my travels. Like so many places I had visited, it left me with the urge to return for a longer stay – but, like its equivalents on the country's opposite coast, it nonetheless felt strangely empty, as if something fundamental to life here had slipped away across the generations, with no prospect of it ever coming back.

Continuing eastward, I soon came to the twin towns of Banff and Macduff, which stand on opposite sides of the River Deveron and are connected via a lovely little arched bridge spanning the water. The latter boasts a significant and – despite being sparsely populated

with vessels when I passed – still relatively active harbour supporting shipbuilding, maintenance and engineering jobs. I followed the road along the shoreline and past the Macduff Marine Aquarium, thinking it would eventually take me back up to the A98 above, but instead it lead me to something quite different, which was to become a highlight of my journey.

As the shore road sneaks out of town, it briefly rises over a steep hill before dropping back down to sea level on the other side, affording visitors a tantalising glimpse of a squat white building nestling in the cove below. The approach path passes a sign warning that this is a dangerous site, with slippery surfaces and, at one point, a two metre drop to the sea below. Young children, it insists, must be supervised at all times. But this isn't some ancient, derelict ruin, a relic of times long past – it is Tarlair Pool, an outdoor swimming facility in use from the 1930s until its closure in 1996. It is, without doubt, one of the most remarkable natural amphitheatres I have ever seen in this country or any other, with steep cliffs wrapped around the whole site magnifying the sense of grandeur granted by the views over the sea. I watched a tanker shuffle across the horizon through an awesome, triangular rock formation towering over the water's edge and walked across the dividing wall between the two pools, soaking in as much as I could, before sitting down on the steps of the amazing art-deco pavilion building overlooking it all. It was easy to imagine the scene before me, full of families enjoying a day out in the sunshine, laughter mixing with the roar of the sea, and it seems a terrible shame that it is now unused and, it seemed, largely forgotten, reduced to hosting dog walkers and posing for sombre photographs while it crumbles away. Even if the days of outdoor swimming are gone, there must surely be a better use for such a stunning location – perhaps an outdoor centre or events venue. Fortunately I am not alone in this belief and a local campaign group, Friends of Tarlair, is currently seeking to lease the pavilion building, the first step to securing appropriate funding to bring the whole site back to life again, potentially as a modern adventure and water sports centre. I very much hope that they succeed.

From Tarlair I returned to the A98 and, not far along the road, turned south on the A950, heading for the east coast of the country. I enjoyed the next half hour riding through towns and villages with dependable-sounding names like New Pitsligo, Mintlaw and Longside. The landscape reminded me of parts of Ayrshire as I rode along past a constant patchwork of farmland rolling off in every direction, although both the scale, and the sky, seem a little bigger up here. It's hard to put your finger on, but the whole place feels a little bit richer too.

The road brought me into Peterhead, a town of which I knew little save for the closed prison, a football team playing in the fourth tier of the Scottish game and a historic fishing industry. Over the past 10–15 miles, my right knee had begun to trouble me again so I decided to ride down to the harbour to take a break and stretch my legs, although I was also curious to see if I would find it in the same state of gradual

The abandoned pools and empty buildings at Tarlair

abandonment as most of the others I had passed in the last couple
of days. In reality Peterhead harbour still seemed quite active – so
much so that the water in the harbour was a disconcerting shade of
muddy, rust-like orange – but of course these things are all relative.
Though busier than any other I had encountered it was still clear that
this once-great fishing port is a long way from its peak. The bulk of
Scotland's remaining fishing industry is based here and in nearby
Fraserburgh but its decline has been rapid. Many blame the current
state of Scottish fishing on the UK's membership of the EU which
allowed European fisherman to access the waters around Scotland's
coast, and the industry in general was vocal in its support for a 'Leave'
vote in the 2016 Brexit referendum. The assumption is that Scottish
fisherman will, to borrow a phrase from the campaign, finally be able
to 'take back control' of their waters. But, as BBC Scotland's Business
Editor, Douglas Fraser, has pointed out, the industry experienced a
steeper decline in the 25 years before the UK joined the European
community than in the decades since, and other countries – including
non-EU Iceland and Norway – have also seen reductions in both the
number of boats and the amount of fish caught. Like everything else

connected to this stunning act of national self-harm, the utopian rhetoric seems unlikely to survive contact with cold, hard reality and, as in other sections of society, will likely turn to anger when Brexit does not prove to be the magic bullet or, even worse, requires fishing rights to be exchanged for a more economically critical concession during trade negotiations with the EU. Brexit may well mean Brexit, but it seems fanciful to imagine that it will also mean a renaissance for Peterhead.

On the way out of town, I passed the nearby power station where my attention was grabbed by a sign promising a viewpoint which, I thought, might reveal some glorious hidden vista across the coastline. I decided to investigate and parked in the little car park next to the road and then began to climb the hill. When I got to the top, however, I found that the only thing you get a view of is the power station itself. Although this might be of interest to some (although I cannot for the life of me imagine who) I wasn't terribly fussed about gazing at a collection of grey slabs, cubes and tubes plugged together by the sea. I wondered whether the 'viewpoint' has been designated as part of some skin-deep commitment to protect the environment and animal life around the site, or to maintain the pretence that complexes such as this one do not damage the natural world around them. If so, then it is entirely predicated on the assumption that nobody will ever actually bother to check what is there.

Fortunately my next stop, and the last one before Aberdeen, more than made up for this disappointment. A few miles down the road from Peterhead the signs for the Coastal Trail reappeared, directing me towards a place called Cruden Bay. I hadn't heard of it, but this route didn't let me down at the start of the day so I hoped it would provide a pleasant end to it as well. As I had done so many times on this trip, I followed the road down towards the water, past the curiously named Kilmarnock Arms Hotel (where Bram Stoker, author of Dracula, apparently stayed many times while visiting the area) and finally stopped next to a wooden bridge reaching over a small river towards huge sand dunes. Having spent so much of this trip with water in my boots, it seemed only fair to get some sand between my toes while I had the chance.

Having crossed the bridge and struggled up the dunes – motorbike gear is not designed for such exertions – I was rewarded with a view out over the wide, golden sands. The tide was brushing against this most mutable of borders between land and sea, with the whole scene lit by silken, late-afternoon light. The remarkable beauty of this area is quite distinct from that found out to the west of the country, with a different palette and surrounding landscape affecting both the appearance and the atmosphere of the environment. It is however also the case that this part of the country is nothing like as isolated as the west-coast equivalents, so that the beauty also exists within a different context, framed by wide open farmland and a dual-carriageway instead of high, twisting passes and sparsely populated villages.

From Cruden Bay, I worked my way on down the rest of the coast, over the River Ythan and through Newburgh before rejoining the A90 for the last stretch to Aberdeen. This route took me past the turn off to Donald Trump's infamous golf course, built thanks to backing from the SNP government – and specifically from former First Minister Alex Salmond – despite being rejected by local councillors and opposed by a range of environmental and scientific voices. Trump went on to fiercely, and unsuccessfully oppose the construction of a wind farm off the coast, his relationship with those at the top of

Scottish politics souring in the course of a battle which went all the way to the UK Supreme Course. I did consider a quick stop, even slowing down as I approach the junction for the course, but decided that there was no good reason to spoil what had otherwise been a lovely day on the road.

On reaching Aberdeen I worked my way down to the Esplanade where I parked the bike on the seaward side and stepped off. The weather had started to turn once more and the scene before me was now a bleak one, with a darkening sky meeting the sea on an invisible horizon where a dozen or so ships, all headed east, inched away from an enormous platform resting on the edge of the mist. Aberdeen – the Granite City – is famously grey, but on this occasion the weather seemed determined to magnify this impression as much as possible

Not knowing the city at all I used my phone for directions to where I would be staying that night. The SAT NAV instructed me to follow a route through 'Old Aberdeen', which I thought sounded interesting, but minutes later I was stuck in a traffic jam, inching along roads that were too tight to allow me to squeeze through. By chance, my route took me, slowly, through a fairly deprived area of Aberdeen which, despite having buildings made of granite instead of sandstone and concrete, reminded me of Glasgow, with houses and flats clearly built to very similar designs. The contrast between these places and the street in which I was staying – which is on the edge of a large, affluent block within the city – was as striking as any one might find in the Central Belt. Aberdeen is a rich city, but its wealth has not been shared equally. I finally arrived at my destination – a grand, detached granite house close to the city's western boundary – where I was met by my final host, Darren. Originally from Stewarton, he is an old friend of my wife's uncle with whom he had worked in a number of engineering jobs before moving to the north east. I also met his wife Tracy (whose mother grew up in the exact same part of Glasgow as both of my parents) and her children, Toni and Jack.

Like so many others – directly or indirectly – Darren is employed by the oil industry; his is one of the many land-based jobs which depend on the platforms out to sea, and he was in no doubt that the economy of the whole city, 'one way or another', largely depends on oil. The most immediate effect of this is an extremely high cost of living, something I previously been told of by a friend who works here when he complained about being charged £9.00 for a cooked breakfast (an outrageous amount of money almost anywhere else in the country) and paying 'London prices' for comparatively poor accommodation. These costs had visibly dropped for a few years while the industry had struggled to cope with the plummeting international value of oil – a period in which a large number of people lost their jobs – but, with prospects now beginning to look brighter, prices were starting to creep up once again. While we talked, however, Tracy noted that more lay offs had been announced earlier that very day, news delivered in the sort of matter-of-fact tone that only comes with repetition. We all wondered aloud what will happen when the resource on which Aberdeen's wealth is based finally disappears. 'No one knows what will happen when the oil dries up,' Darren admitted.

All of this makes Aberdeen seem like a boom town always waiting nervously for the bust – and that bust is coming, inexorably and inevitably, to an area whose obvious wealth is derived from a substance which is not just finite, but also poisonous. Even if it were economically viable to extract every last drop of 'black gold' from beneath the North Sea, the results would be environmentally disastrous. Aberdeen, like the rest of Scotland, needs a better future.

10

Aberdeen to Edinburgh

'It's a beautiful day for the end of a journey.'

THE FINAL DAY of my journey began with warm sunshine and fresh blue skies as I set out south from Aberdeen. The end of the road was just 130 miles away with a stop in Arbroath to fit in on the way before a return to the capital. Being unfamiliar with this part of the country, I had asked Tracy if there was anywhere that I should definitely stop on the way and was told that Stonehaven, a historic fishing village about a 30 minute ride away, was a must-see, especially on a day like this. With everything seemingly falling into place, I set off.

The road was a typical, monotonous dual carriageway offering little excitement aside from the occasionally impressive view to my left, where the bright green fields of the farms would tip toe to the edge of the cliffs overlooking the shimmering expanse of the North Sea. Even so, these sorts of roads, especially those where drivers have to cross the opposite carriageway to reach a destination, leave bikers particularly exposed and I experienced two near misses – in both cases caused by drivers not checking their mirrors before changing lane. A well-known rule amongst bikers is that you have to be especially carefully at the end of a journey, as it is the last five minutes, when you can almost see home, when you are mostly likely to drop your guard and end up hurt or worse; for me, this final day was like the last five minutes of a Sunday ride and I was increasingly conscious of the risks that this presented.

Enjoying the sun in Stonehaven

When I did reach Stonehaven, I stopped by the harbour wall and looked out, with the town on my left and the North Sea to my right, and I sat down on the low stone wall, watching as shallow, white-tipped waves rushed landward between the harbour itself and the opposite side of the bay before breaking on the beach amidst the sunshine. Like those I had seen further north, Stonehaven is a town turned, literally and figuratively, towards the sea, although due to its proximity to Aberdeen it seems to have been better able to reinvent itself. Nonetheless, the sense that something is missing is still rather strong.

Riding south from Stonehaven, I stopped for a quick look at Dunnotar Castle, an incredible cliff-top fortress which, though now in ruins, is still surely amongst the most impressive in Scotland. It also boasts a rich history, having been captured by William Wallace (who also burned down a church filled with English soldiers), visited by Mary Queen of Scots and used as a prison for Covenanters from the south and west of the country. Although I did not have time to explore the castle I enjoyed walking down the daffodil-lined path with its ancient silhouette against the blue of the North Sea. The boundary between the sky and the water had blurred together in a pale-blue haze, and I added it to the now vast list of places to revisit in the future. I would have liked to have stayed longer, but I had an appointment to keep in Arbroath so returned to the bike and set off once more, sticking diligently to the coast road rather than wasting my final day on interminable, mind-numbing dual carriageways.

It is impossible not to notice the vibrancy and fertility of the land in this part of Scotland, where even the plants seem to be happy. The greens of the fields and trees seemed to be more radiant than those I had seen elsewhere, although it would obviously be unfair to compare Aberdeenshire and Angus in the sunshine with the soaking wet, snow-covered expanses – as they had been when I passed through them – of the Borders or Ayrshire.

At about lunch-time I arrived in Arbroath, a small town known primarily for two things. The first is fish, specifically a particularly delicious type of smoked haddock known as a Smokie. At the time of writing, this product is even recognised and protected by the EU, although this status is now, of course, at risk. The second claim to fame here is the Declaration of Arbroath, a document dating back to 1320 which sought recognition of Scotland's independence from Pope John XXII. This letter asserts not only the right of Scotland to its own independence and freedom but also – and quite remarkably for the time – the right of the people of Scotland to reject their king – at this point Robert the Bruce – were he to betray them to the English. It is most commonly remembered for these lines:

It is in truth not for glory, nor riches, nor honours that we are fighting, but for freedom – for that alone, which no honest man gives up but with life itself.

For some contemporary supporters of independence, the Declaration is priceless not simply as a historical document but also as the ultimate origin of the movement for self-determination, underpinning the natural justice of the cause. During a recent conversation with an independent broadcaster, I was struck by the conviction with which this argument was made, although I remain far from convinced that harking back 700 years is a particularly sound strategy for those who are seeking to extricate Scotland from the rest of the 21st century United Kingdom. But I hadn't come to the 'Birthplace of Scotland' to ponder the constitutional past and future of the nation – instead, I was on my way to visit Windmill House.

Windmill House, Arbroath

Three stories high and draped in huge windows through which the coastal light floods in, this grand, 19th century building – originally the home of the town clerk – stands proudly on a hill overlooking the seashore below. It is now run as a Christian centre providing affordable conference, residential and holiday facilities for people from across the world, a purpose which has helped to restore the

building to something like its former glory after decades of decline. Even to an avowed atheist like myself, it seems a good life for this fine old place, and I was grateful to Amy, a friend of my wife's family, for welcoming me and showing me around.

Inside its centrepiece is a wide, turning staircase bordered by two show-stopping stained-glass windows, each housing four individually framed images reflecting life across the different seasons. I was told that many years ago, when the building was suffering from serious neglect, much of the valuable materials had been stripped from its interior and that attempts to remove the windows, in order to access the lead in the fittings, had only been blocked at the last minute. Standing looking up at these gorgeous artworks I was very glad of that crucial reprieve.

It is, no doubt, a place filled with stories, but there is one which, though tantalisingly incomplete, stands out. During the Second World War, this building was used to house Polish troops tasked with defending this stretch of coastline and was also the headquarters for the 12th Field Ambulance. There is a memorial stone in the park nearby presented to the people of Arbroath by Polish forces as a 'token of their gratitude', but there is also another, unknown sign of their presence – a fragile ripple in history, long hidden away within the building itself, buried behind layers of wallpaper and years of missing memories.

The simple pencil drawing depicts two wartime planes – a Spitfire, the distortion of its propeller depicting the craft in flight, and a Lancaster Bomber – charging directly towards the viewer through a cloudy sky above what looks like a factory, perhaps the nearby Baltic Works in which troops were billeted. The detail in the airplanes makes them easy to identify, suggesting the sort of familiarity that comes from close contact and impressions deeply ingrained in the consciousness.

Most intriguingly of all, the drawing contains a number etched into the wall beneath the foregrounded Spitfire – 1829802 LA. My initial, hopeful research has failed to establish the meaning of this code; with permission of Windmill House I am therefore including

Pencil drawing found at Windmill House

a photograph of the drawing itself in the hope that its full origins might be uncovered.

Amy is also a keen biker (and a member of the Christian Motorcycle Association, an international, evangelical group of motorcyclists) and offered to join me on the ride down into Dundee, over the Tay Bridge and into Fife, leading the way and therefore allowing me to transfer some of my attention from the road before me to the world around.

We first passed through Dundee, a city in which I would have liked to have spent some time had it been possible. Muir was far from complimentary about it in the 1930s, and the city still faces significant problems, with high levels of poverty and deprivation and some of the lowest life expectancy figures in the country. I was reminded of Glasgow as I passed through, with old stone buildings harking back to a more prosperous past standing alongside the concrete facades of modern shopping centres, office buildings and car parks. The riverside, although being redeveloped, still stands very much in the shadow of declining industry. Dundee is also one of four areas – along with Glasgow, North Lanarkshire and West Dunbartonshire – to vote Yes in the 2014 independence referendum and, like all good cities, has a historical of radical politics.

Today the city is undergoing something of a resurgence, the centrepiece of which is the soon-to-be completed V&A gallery. I was able to catch a glimpse of this new waterfront development as I approached the Tay and it is certainly as striking in real life, even from a distance, as it is in the numerous artists' impressions I had seen. Dundee has recently been named 'Scotland's Coolest City' by the American newspaper, *The Wall Street Journal,* and is also at the heart of the Scottish, and international, video game industry. Kenny Farquharson, one of Scotland's most respected journalists, has described Dundee as a city in the midst of a long overdue change where, crucially, the community's view of itself is beginning to shift:

I have never doubted Dundee's integrity, its decency, its intellect or its creativity. But I have often doubted its ambition. I think I may now have to revisit that opinion. Dundee, finally, has decided to aim for the stars.

We crossed the Tay Bridge and headed into Fife, the mostly flat, fertile peninsula bordered by large river firths to the north and south and the North Sea to the east, with endless rolling farmland and an enormous sky stretched out in all directions. As a child I spent a lot of my summer holidays here, my sister and I staying with my family in Dunfermline while my single mother worked, but I have spent little time in the area during my adult life. Our route took us first to St Andrews, famous for its ancient university and golf course, after which we meandered along the coast road before finally turning towards Glenrothes.

A friend of mine who used to drive deliveries in this part of Scotland always complained about the roads here and I now understood why: overcrowded and badly surfaced, they were by far the worst I'd ridden on throughout the whole trip. Fife shares many of the same features as rural, isolated parts of the country, but actually has the 3rd highest population amongst Scottish council areas, with more residents than North or South Lanarkshire and roughly twice as many as North Ayrshire, and even in the afternoon, during the week and away from the larger towns, this concentration of people is surprisingly obvious.

We had headed to Glenrothes so that I could swap riding companions, with Amy turning back to Arbroath and my father-in-law, Fraser, joining me for the final stretch of my ten-day journey. I have known him for around half my life, having met his daughter when I was 16 years old and been introduced to her family soon after. He is also the reason I learned how to ride a motorbike – my first ever experience of a bike was as his pillion passenger and the experience, though utterly terrifying at first, left me desperate for a motorcycle of my own. Over the years he taught me to be a better rider ('look where you're going, go where you're looking') and how to repair a range of issues, both of which have helped keep me on the road. All of the brilliant experiences I have had on two wheels, including every moment of this journey, are at least in part thanks to him, and it seemed fitting that he would join me as I brought my adventure to a close.

We rode south together through the farmlands of southern Fife towards Rosyth where we met Jamie, a friend of Fraser's and a native of this corner of the country, who had offered to guide us through Edinburgh and back to the parliament building. Once again I was able to shift my attention from street signs and traffic junctions and onto the landmarks of the area, the first of which was the new Queensferry Crossing over the Forth. Like so much else in modern Scotland, the bridge's construction became a political and, inevitably, constitutional battle ground, allegedly highlighting whatever positive or negative aspect of Scottish independence with which myopic obsessives happened to be fixated at any given time. It was precisely the sort of insular, petty bickering that has made Scottish politics so grindingly dull in recent years, made all the more ludicrous by the desperate insistence with which so many people attempted to attach profound political meaning and symbolism to what is, in the end, just an infrastructure project – albeit one opposed by some and described by Patrick Harvie, co-convener of the Scottish Greens, as a 'bung to the road-building lobby'.

Taken on its own terms, however, there is simply no denying that the new bridge is both a wonderful achievement and also a remarkable example of contemporary engineering which, from the northern approach, is every bit as striking and impressive, if not quite as beautiful, as the UNESCO-recognised rail bridge which runs alongside it. Riding across the roadway, the suspension cables produce an intoxicating, shimmering effect between the enormous supporting towers which climb hundreds of feet into the sky. If it is just a bridge then it is a brilliant one – if, as others claims, it is a symbol of what modern Scotland can achieve, then it is a very, very good omen.

We made our way through the mid-afternoon traffic of Edinburgh,

Fraser and I weaving along behind Jamie as he led the way through this unfamiliar labyrinth of streets, past trams and, once again, over cobbled roads. It was only in the final few minutes, as we rode down Leith Walk towards our final destination, that I finally began to recognise the buildings we passed and I felt a weight lift from my aching shoulders as the Scottish Parliament once again appeared before me. Despite the weather, the stresses and the setbacks, I had had the privilege of experiencing the country – my country – in a way that few would be able to, and at a time when Scotland feels on cusp of something new, and difficult, and brilliant.

After ten days, 1,252.3 miles and some of the best experiences of my life, my Scottish Journey had finally come to an end.

Heading Home

ALTHOUGH THE 'OFFICIAL' journey had ended outside the parliament building, I still had a little more riding to do, with my family waiting for me back home. I had expected to be completely exhausted by this stage and dreading the hour or so it would take it to get out of Edinburgh and back across the country to Glasgow – instead I was surprised to find myself energised by the whole experience and, were it not for the fact that I couldn't wait to see my wife and son, felt as though I could simply have turned around and done the whole thing over again.

Once on the motorway it is a simple ride back from Edinburgh, past the towers of Grangemouth and the great shining heads of the Kelpies, on the way across Scotland's Central Belt. By the time I passed Falkirk the adrenaline rush on which I had been depending was beginning to wane and, increasingly conscious of aching muscles and a dull but persistent pain in my temples, I clicked the bike into sixth gear, rested some of my weight on the tank and switched into autopilot.

As the bike swallowed up more miles without complaint I thought back over my journey: those first two days when the whole project almost fell apart; the fun I'd had carving through the Highlands in the sunshine; the boats I'd boarded and the bridges I'd crossed as

I gathered my snapshots of Scotland. I thought, too, about all the places I hadn't seen either as a result of the weather or because ten days is simply not enough time to see more than a fragment of this complicated, conflicted, divided but utterly brilliant little country.

I also thought about people: those I'd met all across the country who had taken time out of their days to talk to me and help me to begin to understand life in their particular corner of Scotland; those missing from the emptied areas of the country whose stories have been lost as a result of political and economic forces entirely beyond their control; and of course those who welcomed me into their homes. But most of all I thought about two people, my wife and son, and although my trip had been every bit as brilliant as I had expected, I couldn't help but smile as I peeled off the motorway to cover the last few miles between me and them.

Reflections

FROM BUSTLING CITIES to tiny island communities, glistening shorelines to towering peaks, suburban sprawl to rural isolation, rapid transit routes to contorted back roads, Scotland more than earns its reputation as a phenomenally beautiful, vibrant and diverse country. It is also one weighed down by inequality, historic failures and contemporary myopia. That all of this is contained within such a small nation makes it all the more remarkable and, all things considered, there can be few countries in the world so well-suited to the type of journey that I was privileged to undertake in the spring of 2018.

Of course I would have liked to have seen more. The reliably unreliable Scottish weather, the great known unknown of any expedition up, down, across or around this land, robbed me of an opportunity to really explore the south of the country, forcing me to race through the Borders, Dumfries & Galloway and Ayrshire. Everywhere I went I felt like I was missing something special, and it was inevitable that I would end up wishing I had been able to stay for longer in each of the places I was able to visit. I could have spent days exploring Wyre alone, and am very much looking forward to returning to places like Waternish, the Aberdeenshire coast and Assynt – hopefully, this time, with my family.

I would also have liked to have spent several days in the bustle of the Central Belt, or meandering through the country's affluent rural heartlands, and was acutely aware of having been unable to include numerous islands – Arran, of course, plus the Hebrides and Shetland – in my journey. The truth is I could have spent ten weeks exploring Scotland and still been left with the same sensation I felt after just ten days.

But even now, looking back on the whole experience, I realise that my reflections remain dominated by the two strongest impressions I felt throughout the journey.

The first is emptiness, which so overwhelmed Muir eight decades ago. The 'disused coal-pits and silent shipyards' are still there, alongside countless abandoned factories and workshops, all casting a long, cold, resolute shadow over parts of the country where deindustrialisation has been one of the few constants over the past three generations. In the north countless silent, songless glens and abandoned communities tell the story of a land that has endured so much, and had such life ripped from it, that now it seems to struggle to draw breath. In the north east, the decline of fishing has left a visible hole in the heart of countless coastal villages and, when the oil disappears, Aberdeen risks a similar, though far more rapid and destructive, reckoning. Scotland has lived with this disease for so long that it too often becomes just another part of the social, economic or geographic landscape, even as it eats the nation alive, and we only ever seem able to motivate ourselves to deal with the symptoms of our sickness, never the root the cause. Even then, our efforts are too often half-hearted and constricted by conservatism.

But the second impression of this land is quite different: anticipation. Despite the inequality, alienation and frustration apparent all over the country there is also a sense of momentum, a feeling that change is coming. Wherever I went I met people bursting with ideas of how to improve their corner of the country and, with it, the nation as a whole. Above all, the Scotland I saw feels like a country where something is about to happen – or, perhaps more accurately, where more and more people realise that something *has* to happen, that Scotland cannot go on like this. Indeed, a recently published survey has shown that Scots are far more optimistic about the future, and much more likely to believe that their country's best days are ahead of it, than their counterparts in England. I saw plenty during my journey to convince me that they are correct. After a generation of devolution and – credit where it's due – a decade of SNP government, and even amidst a battleground of entrenched political division, Scotland, against all the odds, feels ready to build a future.

It will not be easy. When Muir travelled around Scotland the country was caught in the storm of the Great Depression; today we are still threatened by aftershocks from the 2008 financial crash. John Lancaster, writing for the *London Review of Books*, has described the real-terms decline in incomes over this period as being: 'Worse than the decades that followed the Napoleonic Wars, worse than the crises that followed them, worse than the financial crises that inspired Marx, worse than the Depression, worse than both world wars.' The quality of work has also declined with the proliferation of temporary and insecure employment, while the increasing dependence upon voluntary action within communities adds even greater strain. As always, the weakest members of society, those bearing least responsibility for planting the seeds of the crisis into which we have been pulled, bore the brunt of the whirlwind that followed – banks were bailed out, systems shored up, bonuses paid and narratives maintained while people across this country and others saw their lives fall apart. Socialism for the rich and powerful, disaster for the rest of us.

Into this equation must also come Britain's impending exit from the European Union: a final, impotent howl into the void from a collective whose identity has been fatally wounded by the loss of empire and, more simply, power. Brexit represents, in every instance and form, a backwards-looking country scratching and clawing against the tide of history, diminished by its own delusions of grandeur and importance and angrily lashing out at a changing world. Far from reversing the decline of Britain, Brexit has surely accelerated it – and so the people of Scotland, who emphatically rejected an exit from the EU, now find themselves tied to a state in terminal, and overdue, decline.

International concerns aside, our country also has no shortage of internal problems to solve: Scotland's patterns of land ownership, with fewer than 500 families owning half of all private land, are inexcusable and completely unacceptable; widespread problems with housing and homelessness demand policies including rent controls, public support for tenant's unions and a publicly funded programme of house building and renovation right across the nation; Gaelic must be protected, its status as both a link to our past and a living, breathing language respected and supported; people across the country need vital infrastructure, such as transportation, utilities and banking, to be wrestled from the grasp of corporations and a rigged market; and of course the wealthy, who have reaped the greatest benefits from society's protections, still do not make appropriate contributions towards them.

But there's more. During my journey I frequently heard about people who felt that their community had been neglected or even abandoned. I found a 'forgotten corner of Scotland' just a few hours from the steps of the Scottish Parliament and, in the north-west, learned that Edinburgh can sometimes feel as remote as London. These problems are by no means restricted to isolated, far-flung corners of the country – communities in urban Scotland also regularly find themselves on the wrong side of the 'power gap'.

Ideally this obvious social crack would be bridged by local democracy but in Scotland, where sub-parliamentary power structures are regional in design, no such thing really exists. Administrative areas such as the Scottish Borders, Dumfries and Galloway and Aberdeenshire are thousands of square kilometres in size, and the majority have more than 100,000 residents. The Highlands, for example, is bigger than Belgium while being home to a population around two thirds that of the nation of Iceland. Even in the smallest 'local authorities' like Clackmannanshire the council theoretically represents more than 50,000 people.

According to the journalist and land reform campaigner, Lesley Riddoch: 'Across Europe the average council serves 14k people – in Scotland it's roughly 170k. In Germany the average council is 15 square kilometres in size – in Scotland it's 990 square kilometres.'

Scotland is divided between east and west, urban and rural, Central Belt and everywhere else, but the most serious cracks in our hearthstone are ever-widening inequality and the gulf between people making decisions – whether in council offices, corporate boardrooms or national parliaments – and those affected by them.

The problem, as ever, is power. Who wields it? To what end? How is it withheld, hoarded, concentrated and magnified? And, above all, how can it be handed to, or more likely seized by, those who should always have held it: working people in a kaleidoscope of communities across this nation.

Which brings us to the question of independence.

Although this is not a book about Scotland's constitutional future it would nonetheless be ridiculous, and dishonest, to ignore this most fundamental of fault lines in 21st century Scotland, especially when my journey affected my views of Scotland's potential future.

Scotland voted No in 2014 by a margin of 55–45, supposedly settling the matter of independence for a generation. Yet nine months later the SNP rode the surviving wave of the Yes movement to a historic landslide, securing 56 out of 59 Scottish constituencies. A year further on, the SNP lost their Holyrood majority but remained by far the biggest party while crucially, thanks to six MSPs from the Scottish Green Party, pro-independence parties retain a numeral advantage over their unionist opponents. During the snap General Election of 2017 the SNP lost 21 MPs but still secured more Scottish seats than the other parties combined. Support for Scottish independence has not – yet – consistently breached the magical half-way mark but it has not fallen either, while the UK which Scotland voted to remain a part of no longer exists. Quite simply, independence is still very much on the table. In short, independence is still very much on the table.

As my friend, the journalist Jamie Maxwell, rightly argues, independence could make a significant contribution towards tackling our problems, but not if it is pursued for its own sake: 'The only version of independence that would justify all the inevitable disruption and upheaval is one that fundamentally changes Scotland, that takes power away from the people who have always held it – the bankers, and the landowners, and the privately schooled elites – and makes it accessible to those on the margins.' An independence worth having would be based not on ethnicity, or even identity, but rather on the disruption of an untenable status quo.

The Scotland I saw desperately needs that disruption.

Independence would not automatically solve any of the problems of inequality or alienation facing Scotland, nor is it a necessary precondition for resolving at least some of the ills sickening the country, but ultimately I can see no other likely catalyst for fundamental social change in Scotland, no alternative driving force towards a deeply, tangibly better country, than the establishment of an independent nation.

But little glimpses of the country that Scotland could become are already scattered everywhere. In Helmsdale, a community buyout has taken a sizeable chunk of land into the hands of local people, and the entire island of Ulva now belongs to its rightful owners: the people who live there. Facilities like Stramash could change how we view, and value, the vital early years experiences of our people. New media has emerged and, against all odds, thrived, bringing a new challenge to the narrow viewpoints represented in the traditional press. The Time for Inclusive Education (TIE) campaign has transformed the educational landscape and shown that a grassroots campaign group, in a country too often in thrall to slick corporate lobbyists, can effect real change. But these sparks could be easily extinguished. I have been left in no doubt that another Scotland – a better Scotland – is both possible and within reach, but its emergence is by no means inevitable.

Scotland is a complicated and conflicted place, divided by geography and culture and politics and (always) class – a 'confusing conglomeration', to use Muir's phrase. What I realised in the course of my journey is that there are so many versions of this country, so many Scotlands, out there.

Over the course of ten days I saw flashes of some of them: the rural, sparsely populated south of the country which rolls all the way down to the border with England; the physical and social tumult of Glasgow's writhing, pulsing mass; the Highlands, from effervescent western coasts and islands to the great, near-empty expanse in the far north; the mesmerising ebb and flow of Orkney; collections of old fishing villages clinging to stretches of coastline; an economic bubble around Aberdeen; shiny new bridges and broken old homes.

But from those portraits – each its own hastily assembled mosaic of roadside snapshots – a larger picture begins to form. It is obscured, incomplete and certainly imperfect, having been coloured by my existing experiences and impressions of Scotland and, I suppose, those other parts of the world through which I have been lucky enough to travel. In parts it is also a dark and unsettling image, at points dominated by inequality and alienation and in which countless people suffer more than could ever be excused.

Yet above all, that picture of Scotland as I saw it is vibrant and exciting and very much alive, a tartan patchwork of the past, present and future of the country woven together by all those people who have ever called it 'home' and all the others who will. When I think back to my journey it is that image, the one bursting with energy and expectation, that comes to mind and, in those moments, I believe that a better, brighter Scotland, of which I caught so many tentative, tantalising glimpses, might just be on its way.

Sources

Statistics on local authority sizes/populations (pp 32, 46, 175):
http://www.scotlandscensus.gov.uk/documents/censusresults/
release1b/rel1bsb.pdf

Salmon (pp 74–75):
http://scottishsalmon.co.uk/salmon-exports-reach-record-600m/

Lesley Riddoch quote (p 177):
https://www.edinburghnews.scotsman.com/news/politics/lesley-
riddoch-time-to-reform-scotland-s-unloved-councils-1-4286555

Upstart Scotland:
https://www.upstart.scot

Some other books published by **Luath Press**

St Kilda: The Silent Islands
Alex Boyd
ISBN 978-1-912147-18-2
PBK £12.99

Drawn to the Edge: A Lewis and Harris Sketchbook
Anthony J Barber
ISBN: 978-1-912147-63-2 PBK £7.99
ISBN 978-1-912147-64-9 HBK £12.99

Using a 'battered medium format camera' once belonging to Fay Godwin, Alex Boyd captures the archipelago of St Kilda in a new light, from a 21st century perspective. From the crumbling Cold War military base to the wild beauty of the natural landscape, this book is both an ode to the history of the islands and an insight into the modern day lives of those who live and work on St Kilda today.

'*Alex Boyd's images represent a major addition to the tradition of modern landscape photography, of which Fay Godwin – on whose camera these images were taken – was such a crucial 20th-century figure.*' ROBERT MACFARLANE

Since moving to Lewis in 1994, Anthony Barber has used his sketchbooks as source material for his paintings. Working quickly to capture the scene in swiftly changing light, he has created a visual record of his travels around Lewis and Harris.

On pristine summer days or under torrential downpours, here are the standing stones at Callanish, isolated croft houses turning their backs to the sea, fishing boats and peatstacks, moorland, empty beaches and precipitous cliffs. His diary notes bring to the fore the warmth, hospitality and humour of the islanders.

Scotland, the UK and Brexit

Gerry Hassan & Russell Gunson (eds.)
ISBN 978-1-912147-18-2 PBK £12.99

Britain Rebooted: Why Federalism Would Be Good For the Nations and Regions of the UK

David Torrance
ISBN 978-1-910021-71-2 PBK £7.99

What kind of society do the citizens of Scotland and the UK aspire to live in, and what political and social union is the best way to nurture this? That is something that rightly concerns and is the responsibility of all of us.

In this collection of essays from a wide range of leading political specialists, journalists and academics, Hassan and Gunson have assembled a comprehensive guide to Brexit for the UK as a whole, and its constituent parts.

From fisheries and agriculture to higher education and law, the whys and how of Brexit are challenged from all angles. Particular attention is paid to how Brexit will impact Scotland and the viability of a future independent Scotland.

Would federalism work in the UK? Wouldn't England dominate a British federation?
How would powers be distributed between federal and home nation level?

'An impressive and useful contribution to the constitutional debate... For those interested in saving the United Kingdom, federalism makes a great deal of sense.' MURDO FRASER, *Think Scotland*

'Torrance is one of Scotland's best political commentators...' MATT QVORTRUP, *The Scotsman*

Details of these and other books published by Luath Press can be found at:
www.luath.co.uk

Luath Press Limited

committed to publishing well written books worth reading

LUATH PRESS takes its name from Robert Burns, whose little collie Luath (*Gael.*, swift or nimble) tripped up Jean Armour at a wedding and gave him the chance to speak to the woman who was to be his wife and the abiding love of his life. Burns called one of the 'Twa Dogs' Luath after Cuchullin's hunting dog in Ossian's *Fingal*. Luath Press was established in 1981 in the heart of Burns country, and is now based a few steps up the road from Burns' first lodgings on Edinburgh's Royal Mile. Luath offers you distinctive writing with a hint of unexpected pleasures.

Most bookshops in the UK, the US, Canada, Australia, New Zealand and parts of Europe, either carry our books in stock or can order them for you. To order direct from us, please send a £sterling cheque, postal order, international money order or your credit card details (number, address of cardholder and expiry date) to us at the address below. Please add post and packing as follows: UK – £1.00 per delivery address; overseas surface mail – £2.50 per delivery address; overseas airmail – £3.50 for the first book to each delivery address, plus £1.00 for each additional book by airmail to the same address. If your order is a gift, we will happily enclose your card or message at no extra charge.

Luath Press Limited
543/2 Castlehill
The Royal Mile
Edinburgh EH1 2ND
Scotland
Telephone: +44 (0)131 225 4326 (24 hours)
Email: sales@luath. co.uk
Website: www. luath.co.uk

Freud, Sig

Internationaler Zeitschrift für Psychoanalyse XXI 1935 Heft 3

Freud, Sigmund

Internationaler Zeitschrift für Psychoanalyse XXI 1935 Heft 3

Inktank publishing, 2018

www.inktank-publishing.com

ISBN/EAN: 9783750145535

Internationale Zeitschrift für Psychoanalyse

Herausgegeben von Sigm. Freud

| XXI. Band | 1935 | Heft 3 |

Über die Frühstadien der weiblichen Sexualentwicklung[1]

Von

Ernest Jones

London

Dieser Vortrag soll der erste einer Reihe von Austauschvorträgen zwischen Wien und London sein, die Ihr Vizepräsident, Dr. Federn, zu einem speziellen Zweck vorgeschlagen hat. Schon seit einigen Jahren war zu sehen, daß viele Londoner Analytiker über eine Anzahl wichtiger Themen mit ihren Wiener Kollegen nicht derselben Ansicht waren; unter diesen Themen kann ich als Beispiel die Frühstadien der Entwicklung der Sexualität, besonders beim Weibe, die Genese des Über-Ichs und seine Beziehung zum Ödipuskomplex, die Technik der Kinderanalyse und den Begriff des Todestriebs anführen. Ich gebrauche den Ausdruck „viele Analytiker", ohne den Versuch zu machen, sie aufzuzählen, aber es ist klar, daß die Gefahr besteht, lokale Ansichten in einem solchen Grad zu unifizieren, daß man von einer Wiener oder Londoner Schule sprechen könnte, als ob sie verschiedene Tendenzen einer möglicherweise abweichenden Art darstellten. Das ist in keiner Hinsicht wahr, davon bin ich überzeugt. Die Verschiedenheiten sind nur solcher Art, wie sie einem unvollkommenen Kontakt entspringen. In diesem Fall tragen geographische und sprachliche Faktoren zu diesem Zustand bei; die politischen und ökonomischen Störungen der letzten Jahre haben London und Wien einander nicht nähergebracht. Viele englische Analytiker lesen die „Zeitschrift" nicht und noch mehr Wiener Analytiker lesen nicht das „Journal". Auch ist es mir bisher noch nicht gelungen, den Austausch von Übersetzungen so frei zu gestalten, wie ich es wünschen möchte. Zwar sind die deutschen Arbeiten dem Journal viel leichter zugänglich als die englischen Arbeiten der Zeitschrift, aber dieser einseitige

---

1) Nach einem am 24. April 1935 in der Wiener Psychoanalytischen Vereinigung gehaltenen Vortrag; aus dem Englischen übersetzt von Frau Kitty Jones.

Int. Zeitschr. f. Psychoanalyse, XXI/3

13

Weg ist durchaus keine befriedigende Lösung. Tatsache ist, daß in London neue Arbeiten und Ideen entstanden sind, die unserer Meinung nach in Wien noch nicht genügend berücksichtigt worden sind.

Dr. Federn hatte den glücklichen Einfall, dieser Schwierigkeit dadurch abzuhelfen, daß er direkten persönlichen Kontakt und damit persönliche Diskussion herstellte. Auch meiner Ansicht nach ist dieser Weg der meistversprechende. In erster Linie habe ich den Eindruck, daß heutzutage Psychoanalyse viel mehr durch das gesprochene als durch das geschriebene Wort gelernt wird. Die Gewohnheit des Lesens ist sicherlich in den letzten zwanzig Jahren unter den Analytikern zurückgegangen und die Gewohnheit des Schreibens hat daher im gleichen Verhältnis eine mehr narzißtische Richtung angenommen. Zweitens gestattet es diese Methode, gerade jene Redner zu wählen, die sich in hervorstechender Weise mit dem einen oder dem andern Gesichtspunkt oder Untersuchungsweg identifiziert haben.

Daß ich gerade das vorliegende Thema zur Diskussion mit Ihnen gewählt habe, scheint mir natürlich. Schon auf dem Innsbrucker Kongreß vor acht Jahren legte ich eine Darstellung der weiblichen Sexualentwicklung vor, die nicht ganz mit der allgemein akzeptierten übereinstimmte, und auf dem Wiesbadener Kongreß vor drei Jahren erweiterte ich meine Schlußfolgerungen und wandte sie auf die Probleme der männlichen Sexualität an. Einfach gesagt, war mein wesentlichster Punkt der, daß das junge Mädchen mehr Femininität hat, als Analytiker ihr gewöhnlich zugestehen, und daß die männliche Phase, durch welche sie oft geht, in ihrer Motivierung viel komplizierter ist als man gewöhnlich annimmt; mir schien diese Phase sowohl eine Reaktion auf die Angst vor der Femininität als auch etwas Primäres. Viele weibliche Analytiker haben diese Ansicht unterstützt. Karen Horney sagte es zuerst in ihrer energischen Art, daß die Entwicklung des jungen Mädchens zu sehr mit männlichen Augen gesehen worden war; und obwohl einige ihrer späteren Ansichten mir mehr als fragwürdig erscheinen, möchte ich ihr meine Anerkennung für die Anregung aussprechen, die sie für die Aufklärung dieser Probleme gab. Seither konnten die Kinderanalytiker, insbesondere Melanie Klein, diesen Problemen näherkommen und direkte Beobachtungen von unschätzbarem Wert berichten.

Lassen Sie mich nun die Hauptthemen überblicken und die Übereinstimmungen und Verschiedenheiten gesondert erwähnen. Beginnen wir mit den Anfängen. Die Annahme angeborener Bisexualität scheint mir sehr wahrscheinlich, und viele biologischen Tatsachen können zu ihrer Unterstützung angeführt werden. Aber es ist eine sehr schwer zu beweisende Annahme, und darum meine ich, wir sollten sie nicht für absolut selbstverständlich annehmen und sie nicht zu Hilfe rufen, wann immer wir klinischen Schwierigkeiten begegnen.

Wenn wir zu den Anfängen des individuellen Lebens kommen, werden wir darin einer Meinung sein, daß wenigstens im ersten Jahr und wahrscheinlich noch später die Mutter eine viel größere Rolle im Leben des Kindes spielt als der Vater. Von dieser Phase sagt Freud: „Alles auf dem Gebiet dieser ersten Mutterbindung erschien mir so schwer analytisch zu erfassen, so altersgrau, schattenhaft, kaum wieder belebbar, als ob es einer besonders unerbittlichen Verdrängung erlegen wäre." Was wir daher brauchen, ist eine feinere Analyse der ersten Periode der Zuneigung zur Mutter beim Mädchen, und das, meine ich, ist die Frühanalyse im Begriff uns zu liefern. Es ist höchstwahrscheinlich, daß die Meinungsverschiedenheiten in bezug auf die spätere Phase der Entwicklung hauptsächlich und vielleicht vollständig auf die verschiedenen Annahmen hinsichtlich der früheren Phase zurückzuführen sind.

Wir beginnen daher mit dem schwierigsten Punkt, der *crux* all dieser Probleme. Ist diese erste Phase eine Konzentration auf ein einziges Objekt, die Mutter? Und ist sie eine männliche Einstellung, wie die Klitoris-Masturbation anzudeuten scheint? Im großen und ganzen würde dies als die Ansicht Freuds erscheinen. In diesem Fall muß das Mädchen im Laufe ihrer Entwicklung sowohl ihre Sexualeinstellung als auch das Geschlecht ihres Liebesobjekts wechseln und die wohlbekannten Schwierigkeiten, auf die sie in ihrer Entwicklung trifft, können aus der Kompliziertheit dieser Vorgänge erklärt werden.

Im Gegensatz dazu haben wir in London eine ganz andere Ansicht über diese frühe Phase gewonnen, besonders zufolge unserer Erfahrungen in den Frühanalysen Melanie Kleins, aber auch unserer Ergebnisse bei Erwachsenen. Wir halten dafür, daß die Einstellung des Mädchens von Anfang an mehr feminin als maskulin ist, typisch rezeptiv und akquisitiv. Sie beschäftigt sich mehr mit dem Inneren des Körpers als mit seinem Äußeren. Ihre Mutter betrachtet sie nicht wie ein Mann eine Frau betrachtet, als ein Geschöpf, dessen Wünsche, zu empfangen, er mit Vergnügen erfüllt. Sie betrachtet sie eher als ein Wesen, dem es gelungen ist, sich mit all den Dingen anzufüllen, die das Kind so sehr braucht, gutes Material von fester und flüssiger Art. Ihr Ziel ist, dies aus der Mutter herauszubekommen, und die verschiedenen Hindernisse, wie Verzögerung und zahlreiche andere Unvollkommenheiten des Nährens, stimulieren die aggressive Komponente ihrer Wünsche. Die Unzufriedenheit mit der Brustwarze und der Wunsch, an einem mehr adäquaten penisartigen Gegenstand zu saugen, entstehen früh und wiederholen sich in einer späteren Periode in der wohlbekannten Klitorisunzufriedenheit und dem Penisneid. Der erste Wunsch nach einer Art von Penis ist daher durch orale Versagung veranlaßt. In dieser Säuglingsphase sind wir noch mit dem Interesse an einem Teilobjekt beschäftigt, weniger mit der Liebe zum Vater. Dieses Teilobjekt wird noch als dem Körper der Mutter angehörend gefühlt. Der Vater aber kommt als die Quelle in Betracht, von der sie es empfangen hat, und zwar auf oralem Wege, entsprechend der oralen Konzeption des Koitus, die, wie Freud gezeigt hat, die Anfangskonzeption des Kindes ist; soweit das Mädchen auch

23*

die Kehrseite dieser Theorie entwickelt, eine Mammalinguus- sowie eine Fellatio-Theorie des Koitus, betrachtet sie den Vater tatsächlich als einen Rivalen um die Muttermilch. In der zweiten Hälfte des ersten Jahres und regelmäßig bei seiner Vollendung spielt dann die Persönlichkeit des Vaters eine zunehmend wichtige Rolle. Eine echte feminine Liebe zu ihm, verbunden mit dem Wunsch nach Kontakt mit seinem Sexualorgan, beginnt in Konflikt zu treten mit seiner offenbaren Beziehung zu der Mutter. Im zweiten Jahr können wir schon mit Bestimmtheit von einem Ödipuskomplex sprechen. Er unterscheidet sich von der späteren, bekannteren Form dadurch, daß er tiefer verdrängt und unbewußter ist als diese; auch spielt bei ihm die Vorstellung einer „vereinigten Elternimago" eine größere Rolle.

Die sadistische Einstellung des Mädchens zu dem Inhalt des Körpers der Mutter spricht sich in unzähligen Phantasien des Zerschneidens, Beraubens und Verbrennens dieses Körpers aus. Der orale Sadismus wird bald zu urethralem und analem Sadismus ausgedehnt, und es möchte scheinen, daß die Konzeption des zerstörenden Exkrements beim Mädchen sogar mehr ausgesprochen ist als beim Knaben.

Es bestehen zwei bestimmte Gründe dafür, daß die Aufgabe des Mädchens, mit diesem Sadismus fertig zu werden, und die Angst, zu der dies führt, sich viel schwieriger gestalten als beim Knaben. In erster Linie bezieht sich diese Angst auf das Innere des Körpers; das Mädchen hat kein externes Organ, auf das sich die Angst konzentrieren kann, wie dies beim Knaben der Fall ist. Es hat nur die Klitoris, welche als Mittel der Beruhigung unzulänglich ist, wie Karen Horney zuerst betonte, indem sie die Freiheit des Knaben im Sehen, Berühren und Urinieren mit seinem externen Organ hervorhob. In späteren Jahren verschiebt das Mädchen viel von ihrer Angst auf das ganze Äußere des Körpers, die Kleider miteingerechnet, und erhält Beruhigung von dessen Integrität und allgemeiner Zulänglichkeit; aber dies spielt bei dem jungen Kinde eine kleinere Rolle. In zweiter Linie hat der Knabe einen andern persönlichen Blitzableiter für seinen Sadismus und Haß, nämlich seinen Sexualrivalen, den Vater. Das Mädchen hat, im Gegensatz dazu, als ihre Sexualrivalin und als Gegenstand ihres Sadismus die gleiche Person, nämlich die Mutter, von der das Kind sowohl in seinen libidinösen als auch in allen andern Notwendigkeiten des Lebens vollständig abhängig ist. Dies Objekt zu zerstören wäre verhängnisvoll, deshalb ist der Sadismus mit seiner begleitenden Angst viel mehr gestaut und nach innen gekehrt als beim Knaben. Mit einem Wort, das Mädchen hat aus zwei Gründen weniger Gelegenheit, ihren Sadismus nach außen zu richten. Das erklärt die bemerkenswerte Zuneigung zur Mutter und die Abhängigkeit von ihr, auf die Freud in einem vor kurzem veröffentlichten Aufsatz besonders hingewiesen hat. Wir denken, daß diese Betrachtungen auch eine Erklärung dafür geben, was er die Dunkelheit und „unerbittliche Verdrängung" genannt hat, die für diese Entwicklungsphase so charakteristisch sind.

Was ich eben von dieser frühesten Phase, etwa dem ersten Lebensjahr, gesagt habe, scheint in Wien und in London sehr verschieden aufgefaßt zu werden, und ich bin davon überzeugt, daß fast alle Meinungsverschiedenheiten in bezug auf spätere Entwicklungsphasen auf diese fundamentalen Differenzen zurückgehen. Lassen Sie mich versuchen zu zeigen, warum dies so ist.

Glücklicherweise sind wir alle über die Wichtigkeit der oralen Phase einig, und daß die orale Phase das Prototyp der späteren Femininität ist, ist auch ein fast allgemein akzeptierter Grundsatz, obgleich vielleicht weniger als der erstere. Helene Deutsch hat in diesem Zusammenhang auf die saugende Natur der vaginalen Funktion hingewiesen. Die Frage der frühen vaginalen Sensibilität ist zugegebenermaßen noch dunkel, aber mehrere weibliche Analytiker — die letzten sind Dr. Payne und Dr. Brierley — haben, wenn auch nicht restlos überzeugende, so doch höchst wahrscheinliche Beweise ihres Vorkommens, gleichzeitig mit dem Saugen an der Brust, gegeben. Es ist jedoch schwer, zwischen dieser und Vulvasensationen auf der einen Seite und den allgemeinen retentiven Sensationen und Phantasien, die sich auf Anus, Gebärmutter und das Innere des Körpers im allgemeinen beziehen, anderseits zu unterscheiden. Aber man kann kaum länger die Ansicht aufrechterhalten, daß die vaginale Einstellung sich nicht vor der Pubertät entwickle. Die offenbaren Tatsachen der Vaginalanästhesie oder sogar Dyspareunie bei Erwachsenen mit der Andeutung dessen, wovon sie das Negativ sind, scheinen mir die Ansicht zu widerlegen, daß die Vagina ein unempfindliches oder nur ein unentwickeltes Organ sei. Sie beweisen eher die erotische Besetzung der Vagina und die tiefe Angst davor. Die Obskurität des Organs in der Kindheit würde ich drei Ursachen zuschreiben: 1. Phantasien, die sich mit dem Wunsch nach dem Penis eines Mannes und nach einem Kind beschäftigen, sind es, die den stärksten direkten Konflikt mit der Mutterrivalin bewirken; aus einleuchtenden Gründen kann aber das Mädchen ihre Feindseligkeit gegen die Mutter nicht einmal in dem Grad zum Ausdruck bringen, wie es der Knabe dem Vater gegenüber tun kann. 2. Die Vagina ist der Sitz der tiefsten Ängste, deshalb findet eine extensive Verschiebung nach außen statt, sowohl ihrer Erogenität als auch der begleitenden Ängste. Sie wird, wie der Mund, als ein böses und gefährliches Organ empfunden, das daher verborgen werden muß. 3. Sie hat vor der Menstruation keine physiologische Funktion und ist relativ unzugänglich, Tatsachen, die das Mädchen verhindern, die Überzeugung von ihrer Realität zu gewinnen und von ihr für die libidinöse Befriedigung in der Weise Gebrauch zu machen, wie dies mit einem Penis oder sogar mit einer Klitoris möglich ist.

Wir kommen nun zu der Klitoris-Penis-Frage, und hier finden wir die schärfsten Meinungsverschiedenheiten. Das kann man am klarsten zeigen, wenn

man die Verbindung zwischen dieser Frage und der Beziehung zu den Eltern
betrachtet. Wenn Sie mir gestatten, der Kürze wegen die Meinungsverschiedenheiten zu übertreiben, so kann man sagen, daß nach der einen Ansicht das Mädchen ihre Mutter haßt, weil diese sie in ihrem Wunsch, die Klitoris
möge ein Penis sein, enttäuscht hat, während der andern Ansicht nach der
Grund, warum das Mädchen wünscht, daß ihre Klitoris ein Penis sei, der ist,
daß sie gegen ihre Mutter einen Haß fühlt, dem sie nicht Ausdruck verleihen
kann. In ähnlicher Weise liebt — nach der einen Ansicht — das Mädchen den
Vater, weil sie in ihrem Peniswunsch enttäuscht ist, während sie, der andern
Ansicht nach, wegen der Schwierigkeiten, die sich ihrer Vaterliebe in den
Weg stellen, die Klitoris mit einem Penis vertauschen möchte. Sie werden mir
zugeben, daß wir hier sehr entschiedene Meinungsverschiedenheiten vor uns
haben, sogar wenn man die übermäßige Schärfe meiner Formulierung berücksichtigt.

Ich habe an anderer Stelle auf die Verwirrung hingewiesen, die dadurch entsteht, daß das Wort „Peniswunsch" in dieser Verbindung in drei Bedeutungen
gebraucht wird, und ich will versuchen, dies zu vermeiden, indem ich
erkläre, in welchem Sinn ich es hier meine. Momentan sprechen wir von dem
Wunsch, daß die Klitoris ein Penis sei, und ich nehme an, das ist unzwei-
deutig. Wir alle kennen die Unzufriedenheit und das Nachtragen, die mit
diesem Wunsch verknüpft sind, sowie die Rolle, die dies in der Psychologie
des Mädchens spielt. Aber die Tatsache, daß so viele Mädchen Knaben be-
neiden, darf uns für ihre femininen Eigenschaften nicht blind machen, wie,
zum Beispiel, ihre Koketterie und die wichtige Tatsache des Interesses für
Puppen.

Das Problem ist hier die Motivierung dieses Wunsches. Wir stimmen darin
überein, daß ein Teil aus dem einfachen autoerotischen Neid entsteht, den
Karen Horney am gründlichsten beschrieben hat: Neid auf die Freiheit, die
der Knabe im Anschauen, Berühren seines Organs und im Gebrauch desselben
zum Urinieren genießt. Der einen Ansicht nach ist dies jedoch das Haupt-
motiv für den Peniswunsch, während bei andern Autoren dies nur für seinen
kleineren Teil verantwortlich ist. Viel wichtiger sind, meiner Meinung nach,
jene Motive für diesen Wunsch, die man die sekundären nennen kann. Es
sind dies, mit einem Wort, die verschiedenen Versuche des kleinen Mädchens,
mit ihrem gegen die Eltern — besonders gegen die Mutter — gerichteten Sadismus fertig zu werden. Auf die Gefahr hin, mich zu wiederholen, möchte
ich noch einmal erwähnen und hervorheben, was wir als den fundamentalen
Ausdruck dieses Sadismus betrachten, nämlich den Wunsch, sich eine Bahn
in den Körper der Mutter zu brechen und den Penis des Vaters, den das Mädchen darin einverleibt glaubt, zu verschlingen. Was Melanie Klein so glücklich die „vereinigte Elternimago" nennt, entspricht ungefähr dem, was in
Wien die präödipale Phase genannt wird; aber für uns ist sie einfach ein Teil

des Ödipuskomplexes schlechthin. Der für dieses Stadium so charakteristische Sadismus erweckt beim Mädchen die korrespondierende Angst, daß auch ihr eigener Körper ebenso beraubt und vernichtet werden könnte.

Lassen Sie mich nun die Wege aufzählen, auf denen die Phantasie, einen Penis zu besitzen, diesen vehementen Sadismus und die ihn begleitende Angst zu beruhigen sucht. Ich muß damit beginnen, daß der Wert, den diese Penis-idee für das Mädchen hat, wesentlich mit der Fähigkeit verbunden ist, den Urin zu exkretieren und seinen Fluß zu lenken. Helene Deutsch und Karen Horney haben besonders auf diese Verbindung zwischen Penisneid und Urethralsadismus hingewiesen, während Melanie Klein und später Marjorie Brierley sich mit der innigen Beziehung zwischen Oralsadismus und Ure-thralsadismus beschäftigt haben. Nach dem „homöopathischen Prinzip", das ich auf dem Oxforder Kongreß darlegte, geht man gegen diesen verdrängten Urethralsadismus am besten vor, indem man versucht, einen Weg zu finden, auf dem er in der Realität ausgedrückt werden kann, und sich damit die Be-ruhigung zu verschaffen, daß er nicht tödlich wirkt. Das kann der Knabe mit seinen Urinierspielen tun, dank der Beruhigung, die ihm der sichtbar intakte Penis gibt.

Die Vorstellung des Mädchens vom Penis ist natürlich eine ambivalente. Auf der einen Seite ist er gut, freundlich, nahrunggebend, und die Flüssigkeit, die aus ihm kommt, wird der Milch gleichgesetzt. Anderseits ist er böse und zerstörend; er ist eine Waffe, die gegen die Mutter gebraucht werden kann, und zwar in derselben Art, in der, wie das Mädchen glaubt, der Vater die Mutter angreift; sie kann damit bekommen, was sie aus dem Körper der Mutter braucht. Insoweit er gut ist, kann er dazu verwendet werden, der Mutter den Penis zurückzugeben, den — wie das Mädchen glaubt — sie dieser geraubt hat. Das ist besonders dann der Fall, wenn das Mädchen phantasiert, daß der Vater impotent ist; sie will die Mutter befriedigen, da sie den Vater kastriert hat — eine Einstellung, die bei der Homosexualität sehr häufig ist. Er kann ferner gebraucht werden, um den bösen, verinnerlichten Penis zu neutralisieren und gut zu machen, den Penis, den das Mädchen verschluckt und durch ihren Sadismus in ein schädliches und sich selbst zerstörendes Organ in ihrem eigenen Körper verwandelt hat; ein sichtbarer und intakter Penis wäre die beste Beruhigung gegen die unzugänglichen innerlichen Ängste. Schließlich kann er dazu dienen, um den kastrierten Vater zu entschädigen, indem sie sich zuerst mit ihm identifiziert und dann zur Kompensation einen intakten Penis entwickelt.

Hinter dem Wunsch des Mädchens, daß ihre Klitoris ein Penis wäre, liegt daher das komplizierteste Phantasiegewebe. Sein Ziel ist zum Teil libidinös, zum größten Teil aber defensiv; er besteht aus den verschiedenen Versuchen, den Sadismus zu beherrschen und die verzweifelte Angst, die er verursacht hat, zu beruhigen. Freud fragt in bezug auf diese phallische Phase: Warum

10

sollte eine Flucht vor der Femininität stattfinden, außer wenn sie durch primäre natürliche maskuline Strebungen verursacht ist? Ich möchte dies in Übereinstimmung mit Melanie Klein beantworten, die zum Schluß kommt, daß des Mädchens Verdrängung der Femininität mehr von ihrem Haß gegen die Mutter und ihrer Angst vor ihr als von ihrer eigenen maskulinen Einstellung herrührt. Diese Verdrängung geht Hand in Hand mit einer exzessiven Fixierung an die Mutter, einer Fixierung, die die Entwicklung des Mädchens sehr oft ernstlich hindert. Es gibt, unserer Meinung nach, so etwas wie einen primären, natürlichen Peniswunsch beim Mädchen, aber wir finden ihn nicht als ein maskulines Streben in Form von Klitoristendenzen, sondern als einen normalen femininen Wunsch, den Penis eines Mannes sich einzuverleiben — zuerst auf oralem, später auf vaginalem Wege.

Dieser Wunsch scheint uns direkt zu dem Wunsch nach einem Kind zu führen, dem normalen Wunsch, einen Penis zu empfangen und ihn in ein Kind zu verwandeln. Auch das steht im Gegensatz zu Freuds Ansicht, daß der Wunsch des Mädchens nach einem Kind hauptsächlich eine Kompensation für ihre Enttäuschung ist, keinen eigenen Penis zu besitzen. Ich könnte mit Freuds Beschreibung übereinstimmen, wenn sie sich nicht auf das bezöge, was wir den Klitorispenis der phallischen Phase nennen können, sondern auf den ursprünglich oral einverleibten Penis. Ich glaube, es besteht kein Zweifel, daß die Enttäuschung, diesen Penis (und nicht den Klitorispenis) nicht empfangen zu können, zumeist durch die Konzentration auf Kinder kompensiert wird, gewöhnlich schon in der Ersatzform der Puppen. Wir finden dasselbe Phänomen in der exzessiven Mütterlichkeit mancher Frauen, die entweder aus inneren oder aus äußeren Gründen des sexuellen Genusses beraubt sind. Aber in diesem Sinne meint es Freud nicht.

Ich möchte noch ein Wort über die Einstellung des Mädchens zum Vater hinzufügen. Sie überträgt auf ihn das Schuldgefühl und die Angst, die sie gegenüber der Mutter entwickelte, als sie diese in der Phantasie so sadistisch des Penis beraubte. Zuletzt ist es sowohl der Penis des Vaters als auch der der Mutter, den sie verschlungen hat, also ist auch er der geschädigte. Sie fühlt viel mehr Neid und Eifersucht der Mutter als dem Vater gegenüber, und vieles von dem Gefühl, das wir klinisch als gegen den Vater gerichtet bemerken, ist tatsächlich von der Mutter auf ihn verschoben. Aber sobald große Angst in bezug auf den bösen, verinnerlichten Penis besteht, der zufolge der sadistischen Art, in der er empfangen wurde, schädlich ist, kommt das homöopathische Prinzip wieder ins Spiel. Dann muß das Mädchen den Penis des Mannes abbeißen, um eine Beruhigung für die Angst der ursprünglichen Phantasien zu erhalten, ein Wunsch, den wir so oft bei Homosexuellen finden. Ist anderseits die Beziehung zur Mutter vorwiegend gut und zärtlich, dann wird sich das Verhältnis zum Vater auf weniger sadistischen Linien entwickeln und ein gutes werden.

Schließlich kommen wir zum Untergang der phallischen Phase und der Entwicklung einer manifesten Femininität. Auch hier müssen wir verschiedene Meinungen erwarten, denn es ist leicht zu sehen, daß die Ansicht, die man über diese Entwicklungsphase hegt, von jener über die früheren Phasen ernstlich beeinflußt sein muß. Vor allem muß ich sagen, daß, so skeptisch ich über das Bestehen der „phallischen Phase" als eines Entwicklungsstadiums bin, ich noch viel skeptischer, als die Wiener es zu tun scheinen, über die Idee ihres Unterganges denke. — Es scheint mir präziser, den Ausdruck „phallische Position"[2] zu gebrauchen, um die hier in Frage stehenden Phänomene zu beschreiben. Wir haben es hier eher mit einer emotionellen Einstellung[3] zu tun als mit einem Stadium in der libidinösen Entwicklung. Diese Einstellung wird durch gewisse Kräfte oder Bedürfnisse aufrechterhalten; sie verringert sich, wenn diese geschwächt werden, aber dauert fort, solange diese fortdauern — manchmal das ganze Leben. Die „phallische Position" ist nicht selten mit sechs, zehn oder dreißig Jahren ebenso ausgesprochen wie mit zwei oder drei. Was Wiener Analytiker als den Untergang der phallischen Phase bezeichnen, bezieht sich wohl eher auf jene Periode, in der die Femininität des Mädchens sichtbar wird; dagegen sind Londoner Analytiker der Meinung, sie könnten diese schon früher in ihrer mehr verdrängten Form feststellen. Allerdings bleibt die Frage, warum die Femininität oft weniger verdrängt und daher beim Heranwachsen des Mädchens deutlicher sichtbar ist; und diese Frage möchte ich als nächste behandeln.

Sie werden sich an den Unterschied erinnern, den ich in meinem Wiesbadener Vortrag zwischen der protophallischen und der deuterophallischen Phase machte; der Unterschied zwischen ihnen ist durch die bewußte Entdeckung des Geschlechtsunterschiedes gekennzeichnet. Diese Entdeckung hat oft Neid und Nachahmung zur Folge, die die Hauptmerkmale der deuterophallischen Phase sind. Eine sehr wichtige Beobachtung, über die allgemeine Übereinstimmung besteht, ist die, daß der „Untergang" dieser Phase (bzw. das stärkere Sichtbarwerden der Femininität) oft unverkennbar von Feindseligkeit und Groll gegen die Mutter begleitet ist. Freud hat in seiner Erklärung diese beiden Geschehnisse miteinander nicht nur chronologisch, sondern auch dem Zusammenhang nach verbunden. Die Gründe, die er für das Herauskommen des Mädchens aus der phallischen Phase gibt, können in einem Wort zusammengefaßt werden: Enttäuschung. Das Mädchen beginnt einzusehen, daß ihr Wunsch, einen Penis zu besitzen, enttäuscht werden muß, und so verzichtet sie klugerweise zugunsten anderer Lustquellen, die sie trösten sollen. Indem sie dies tut, wechselt sie sowohl ihre eigene sexuelle Einstellung von männlich in weiblich, als auch das Geschlecht ihres Liebesobjekts von

---

2) Vgl. die Begriffe „Libidoposition" und die psychotischen „Positionen" in Melanie Kleins Luzerner Vortrag.
3) Und nicht mit bestimmten Gedankeninhalten.

der Mutter zum Vater. Der Untergang der deuterophallischen Phase kündigt daher den Ödipuskomplex mit seiner Rivalität mit der Mutter an. Das stimmt mit der nicht angezweifelten Beobachtung überein, daß die normale Ödipussituation nach einer Schwächung der phallischen Phase deutlicher sichtbar wird, wie Jeanne Lampl-de Groot dies kurz und bündig ausdrückt: „Das Mädchen muß durch eine invertierte Ödipussituation gehen, bevor sie zu der normalen kommt."

Wir in London dagegen betrachten die deuterophallische Phase im wesentlichen als eine Verteidigung gegen den schon bestehenden Ödipuskomplex. Uns präsentiert sich daher das Problem, warum die defensive phallische Phase zu Ende geht, ganz anders; es ist dem Problem, warum eine infantile Phobie je verschwindet, nicht unähnlich.

Die Antwort, die ich geben würde, ist der Freuds insoweit ähnlich, als beide in der Formulierung „Anpassung an die Realität" gegeben werden könnten. Aber die Art, in der die Realitätserlebnisse sich auswirken, scheint mir nicht dieselbe zu sein, wie sie Freud erscheint. Im Grunde genommen stärkt sie die Ich-Entwicklung auf Kosten der Es-Phantasien. Die Phantasie des Penis als Schutz wird aufgegeben, 1. weil sie als eine Phantasie und daher als ein ungenügender Schutz erkannt wird, 2. weil weniger Angst und daher weniger Notwendigkeit zur Verteidigung vorliegt, und 3. weil andere Schutzmaßnahmen zugänglich geworden sind.

Lassen Sie mich nun diese Gründe der Reihe nach betrachten. Wir wissen, daß der Macht halluzinatorischer Wunscherfüllungen feste Grenzen gesetzt sind, wenigstens bei normalen Menschen — eine Tatsache, die Freud oft am Beispiel des Hungers illustriert hat. Das gilt, ob der Wunsch sich nun auf ein körperliches, z. B. ein libidinöses, Bedürfnis bezieht, oder auf ein Bedürfnis nach Angstschutz. In diesem Fall findet man, daß der phantasierte Schutz nicht gut funktioniert, gerade weil er nicht die Beruhigung äußerer Realität gibt; denn das ist es, was das Mädchen braucht, und was es anfängt, anderswo zu suchen.

Zweitens verringert sich ihre Angst in dem Maße, wie ihr Ich stärker wird. Sie ist besser befähigt, ihre Mutter als eine wirkliche und zumeist zärtliche Persönlichkeit zu sehen, anstatt als eine imaginäre ihrer Phantasie. Sie ist auch nicht mehr so abhängig von der Mutter, wie sie es in den ersten zwei oder drei Jahren ihres Lebens war. Sie kann es sich daher leisten, ihr und andern Personen ihrer Umgebung gegenüber mehr Sadismus zu zeigen, anstatt ihn aufzustapeln und innere Angst zu entwickeln. Das ist die wohlbekannte Phase, in der die Umgebung das heranwachsende Mädchen „schwierig" findet.

Drittens fängt das Mädchen an, zu lernen, sowohl ihre Libido als auch ihre Angst nach außen zu kehren. Sie hat das Stadium der Teilobjektliebe verlassen und interessiert sich mehr für ihren Vater oder Bruder als ein Ganzes. Das ersetzt das frühe, in die Mutter einverleibte Teilobjekt. Ihre Angst ist viel weniger verinnerlicht und nimmt die Gestalt der charakteristischen Angst vor dem Verlassenwerden an, die oft das ganze Leben hindurch anhält.

Das junge Mädchen ist nun viel kühner in seinen Ansprüchen und wagt es zum erstenmal, die ausgesprochene Nebenbuhlerin der Mutter zu sein. Der Groll, den sie gegen diese zeigt, hat nicht nur die Bedeutung, die Freud ihm zuschreibt, des Vorwurfs nämlich, daß ihre Klitoris kein Penis ist, sondern ist auch der Durchbruch der älteren, seit langem aufgehäuften Animosität. Es ist nicht bloß der Vorwurf, daß ihre Mutter ihr nur eine Klitoris gab, es ist der Vorwurf, daß ihre Mutter immer die Brust und den Penis des Vaters in eigener Verwahrung gehalten hat und dem Mädchen nicht erlaubt hat, beide sich selbst nach Herzenslust einzuverleiben. Das Sehen des Penis beim Knaben ist nicht das einzige traumatische Erlebnis, das ihr Leben ändert; es ist nur das letzte Glied in einer langen Kette. Ich glaube auch nicht, daß ein Mädchen, das nie durch dieses Trauma geht, maskulin wird, was aus der Ansicht zu folgen scheint, daß dieses Trauma sie in die Femininität treibt.

Ich kann nun meine Behauptungen in ein paar Sätzen zusammenfassen. Die Haupttatsachen, die wir zu erklären haben, sind der Peniswunsch des jungen Mädchens und ihr Groll gegen die Mutter. Der zentrale Unterschied zwischen den beiden Gesichtspunkten, die ich für die gegenwärtigen Zwecke in übertriebener Weise den Londoner und Wiener nannte, scheint sich mir um die Frage des frühen Ödipuskomplexes zu drehen, der durch orale Unbefriedigtheit eingeleitet wird. Da es dem kleinen Mädchen unmöglich ist, mit der Angst, die jener Zustand hervorruft, fertig zu werden, flüchtet sie zeitweilig mehr oder minder in die „phallische Phase" und nimmt später ihre normale Entwicklung wieder auf. Diese Ansicht scheint mir den uns zugänglichen Tatsachen besser zu entsprechen und ist auch im wesentlichen wahrscheinlicher, als eine, die die Weiblichkeit des Mädchens als das Resultat eines äußeren Erlebnisses (Erblicken des Penis) ansieht. Meiner Ansicht nach entwickelt sich die Weiblichkeit fortschreitend aus dem Antrieb einer triebhaften Konstitution. Kurz gesagt, ich sehe die Frau als ein geborenes Weibchen und nicht — wie die Feministen es tun — als *un homme manqué*, als ein ewig enttäuschtes Geschöpf, das sich mit sekundären Surrogaten zu trösten sucht, die ihrer wahren Natur fremd sind. Die letzte Frage ist also, ob man zur Frau geboren oder gemacht wird.

Allgemeiner gesprochen, würden die Wiener, so glaube ich, uns den Vorwurf machen, daß wir das frühe Phantasieleben auf Kosten der äußeren Realität zu hoch einschätzen. Und wir würden antworten, daß keine Gefahr besteht, daß jemand die äußere Realität vernachlässige; wohl aber, daß man Freuds Lehre von der Wichtigkeit der psychischen noch immer unterschätzen kann.

14

Projektion und Ich=Entwicklung[1]

Von

Ernst Paul Hoffmann

Wien

Es gibt Erkrankungen, bei denen die Libidoposition wohl erforscht ist, die aber nicht genügend geklärt sind, weil die Fixierung des Ichs nicht bestimmt werden konnte. Und doch sind beide voneinander abhängig, denn Änderungen in der Libidoposition gehen Änderungen im Ich parallel.

Zu diesen bisher ungeklärten Erkrankungsformen gehört beispielsweise die Sucht. Glover meint, das libidinöse Moment sei in den Arbeiten über die Sucht genügend betont worden; dennoch ist das Problem nicht gelöst. — Es scheint, daß jede Libidostufe sich als Wunschgehalt der Sucht manifestieren kann; doch muß eine bestimmte Ich-Struktur vorhanden sein, wenn es zur Sucht kommen soll. Deshalb mag das Studium der Süchtigkeit einen Einblick in die Störungen des Ichs versprechen.

Für die Psychoanalyse ist der Begriff der Sucht ein anderer als für die klinische Psychiatrie. Diese versteht unter Süchtigkeit gewöhnlich nur die Rauschgiftsüchtigkeit. Nur nebenbei werden auch Fälle von Süchtigkeit erwähnt, die seltene oder nicht ausgesprochene Rauschgifte betreffen, z. B. Kaffee, Chloralhydrat u. dgl. Die Sprache ist umfassender: Sie operiert mit Worten wie z. B. Eifersucht oder Habsucht. Der Psychoanalytiker kann eine Menge anderer Süchtigkeiten feststellen, die sich als Verschrobenheiten, üble Angewohnheiten u. dgl. darbieten (Glover).

Die Sucht läßt sich nach Federn (1) beschreiben als eine Bedürfnisspannung, die nicht anders zu erledigen ist, als durch sofortige Befriedigung, und zwar durch Einverleibung eines bestimmten Stoffes oder durch Hingabe an eine ganz bestimmte Funktion. Ein Aufschieben der Befriedigung, ein Ertragen, Beherrschen oder Überwinden des Triebes gibt es bei der Sucht nicht. Der davon Betroffene ist nicht oder wähnt sich nicht imstande, die Unlust der Bedürfnisspannung zu ertragen.

Der Wunschgehalt kann verschieden sein. So zeigte ein Patient eine Süchtigkeit, die allen Entwicklungsstufen der Libido entstammte. Er war 35 Jahre alt, Staatsbeamter in sehr hoher und sehr verantwortungsvoller Stellung. Er kam in die Analyse, weil er in kürzeren oder längeren Zeitabständen — einige Stunden bis einige Tage — plötzlich von unwiderstehlichem Sexualverlangen erfaßt zu werden pflegte. Er wurde dann sofort zu jeglicher Arbeit unfähig, mußte alles stehen lassen und sich auf die Suche nach einem Sexualobjekt begeben. War die Dunkelheit bereits eingebrochen, so ging er in einen Park, um unter den Dirnen eine zu wählen; während des Tages ging er jedoch in

---

1) Nach einem am 3. Oktober 1934 in der Wiener Psychoanalytischen Vereinigung gehaltenen Vortrag.

15

ein ganz bestimmtes Pissoir, wo er meist einen Partner traf, mit dem er mutuell onanierte. Im Notfalle onanierte er allein. Sehr bald zeigte es sich, daß er derartige Anfälle auch in bezug auf den oralen Trieb hatte. Er mußte naschen und gab für Süßigkeiten geradezu phantastische Summen aus. Widerstehen konnte der Patient seinem Naschtrieb ebensowenig wie dem Verlangen nach der Onanie. Waren dem Patienten orale und genitale Wünsche bewußt, so erfolgte die Befriedigung seiner analen Wünsche unbewußt, allerdings mit gleicher Sucht. Mit dem Naschen und dem Besuch bei Dirnen verband er den Trieb, Geld auszugeben. Regelmäßig trat die Sucht in dem Augenblicke auf, wenn er unerwartet Geld bekam, z. B. Entschädigungen für gewisse nicht regelmäßige amtliche Funktionen, die ihm erst einige Zeit später entlohnt wurden.

Von Nunberg(1) stammt ein Beispiel, das die Unterschiede zwischen einem gesunden, einem neurotischen und einem psychotischen Menschen demonstriert. Alle drei hätten den gleichen Wunsch, nämlich zu fliegen. Der Gesunde würde im Einklang mit seinen Vermögensverhältnissen, der Jahreszeit und dergleichen, kurz der Realität angepaßt, eine Flugreise unternehmen. Der Neurotiker würde verzweifelte, meist aber erfolglose Anstrengungen machen, um eine Gelegenheit zu fliegen zu bekommen. Und wenn er einmal so weit wäre, würde er wahrscheinlich von heftiger Angst befallen werden. Der Psychotiker würde sich auf den Rücken legen, mit den Armen in der Luft herumfuchteln und überzeugt sein, daß er fliege. Wie würde sich nun ein „Flugsüchtiger" — wenn so etwas gäbe — verhalten? Er würde im Momente des Anfalles alles stehen lassen, raschestens das Flugfeld zu erreichen trachten und ohne Rücksicht auf das Fahrziel jenes Flugzeug besteigen, das als erstes startet.

Bei den genannten vier Typen ist der Wunschgehalt der gleiche. Sie unterscheiden sich voneinander nicht durch das, was sie wünschen, sondern durch die Art, wie sie es wünschen. Nicht der Wunschgehalt und auch nicht die Libidoart ist somit das Entscheidende für das Zustandekommen der Süchtigkeit, sondern der Mechanismus der Krankheit. Es handelt sich nicht darum, welche Art von Libido in der Sucht befriedigt wird, sondern darum, auf welcher Stufe das Ich des Kranken sich befindet.

Hätten wir einen Menschen von der Art des „Flugsüchtigen" vor uns, so würden wir von einem schwachen Ich sprechen, welches nur mit Mühe dem Drängen des Es standhalten kann, einem Ich also, das zeitweilig vom Es überrumpelt wird. Worin liegt nun die Schwäche des Ichs? Ist eine seiner Fronten geschwächt und welche? Die gegen das Es oder die gegen die Außenwelt oder die gegen das Über-Ich? Oder ist nur eine der Funktionen des Ichs „schwach" und welche? Wird etwa nur der Zugang zur Motilität nicht mehr beherrscht? Wie konnte sich das Lustprinzip wieder an die Stelle des Realitätsprinzips setzen?

Wir wollen annehmen, daß die Schwäche des Ichs die Folge einer Entwicklungsstörung ist. Ob diese Störung eine Fixierung oder eine Regression ist, wird seine spezielle Bedeutung haben.

Es wird also der Weg der Ich-Entwicklung zu verfolgen sein, parallel mit der Entwicklung der Objektbeziehungen. Deren intensivste Entwicklung beschreibt Freud (1) folgendermaßen: „Wir sehen auch im Groben einen Gegensatz zwischen der Ich-Libido und der Objektlibido. Je mehr die eine verbraucht, desto mehr verarmt die andere. Als die höchste Entwicklungsphase, zu der es die letztere bringt, erscheint uns der Zustand der Verliebtheit, der sich uns wie ein Aufgeben der eigenen Persönlichkeit gegen die Objektbesetzung darstellt." Das Ich des Süchtigen könnte dem des Verliebten ähnlich sein und die Sucht als eine besondere Art dauernder oder periodischer Verliebtheit erscheinen. Stellt nun diese Höchstphase der Entichung einen Zustand dar, in welchem ein Maximum an Objektlibido gegenüber einem Minimum an Ich-Libido besteht, so zeigt der Beginn der Entwicklung Objektlosigkeit. „Wir dürfen darum nicht vergessen, daß im Intrauterinleben kein Objekt war und daß es damals keine Objekte gab" (Freud [2]). Zu Beginn der Entwicklung gibt es also nur narzißtische Libido, allmählich wird ein Maximum an Objektlibido erreichbar; die Ich-Entwicklung erfolgt am Objekt, so zwar, daß das Ich um so mehr sich festigt, je mehr narzißtische Libido in Objektlibido verwandelt wurde, und je kräftiger diese einer Rückverwandlung in narzißtische Libido standhalten kann; doch gibt es zwischen den beiden Extremen ein Optimum, das nicht mit dem Maximum zusammenfällt. Diese Verwandlung von Ich-Libido in Objektlibido ist keine plötzliche; sie erfolgt in Oszillationen, analog zu den in den „Drei Abhandlungen" erwähnten Oszillationsvorgängen zwischen den einzelnen Entwicklungsstufen der Libido.

Den Beginn der Entwicklung können wir in die pränatale Zeit verlegen. Das ist eine berechtigte Spekulation; Freud (5) sagt: „Intrauterinleben und erste Kindheit sind weit mehr ein Kontinuum, als uns die auffällige Cäsur des Geburtsaktes glauben läßt."

Ein Einfühlen in die pränatale Zeit ist unmöglich; dennoch hat Ferenczi (1) diesen Zustand beschrieben: „Freud erklärt eine Organisation, die dem Lustprinzip frönen, die Realität der Außenwelt vernachlässigen kann, für eine Fiktion, die aber im Säugling, wenn man nur die Mutterpflege hinzunimmt, nahezu realisiert ist. Ich möchte dem hinzufügen, daß es einen Zustand der menschlichen Entwicklung gibt, der das Ideal eines nur der Lust frönenden Wesens nicht nur in der Einbildung und Annäherung, sondern in der Tat und vollkommen verwirklicht. Ich meine die im Mutterleib verbrachte Lebenszeit des Menschen. In diesem Zustande lebt der Mensch wie ein Parasit des Mutterleibes. Eine Außenwelt gibt es für das aufkeimende Lebewesen nur in sehr beschränktem Maße; sein ganzes Bedürfnis nach Schutz, Wärme und Nahrung wird von der Mutter gedeckt. Ja, es hat nicht einmal die Mühe, sich des ihm zugeführten Sauerstoffes und der Nahrungsmittel zu bemächtigen, denn es ist dafür gesorgt, daß diese Stoffe durch geeignete Vorrichtungen geradewegs in seine Blutgefäße gelangen. Im Vergleich hierzu muß z. B. ein Eingeweidewurm viel Arbeit leisten, die ‚Außenwelt verändern‘, wenn er sich erhalten will. Alles Sorgen um den Fortbestand der Leibesfrucht ist aber der Mutter übertragen. Wenn also dem Menschen im Mutterleibe ein wenn auch unbewußtes Seelenleben zukommt, — und es wäre unsinnig zu glauben, daß die Seele erst mit dem Augenblicke der Geburt zu wirken beginnt, — muß er von seiner Existenz den Eindruck bekommen, daß er tatsächlich allmächtig ist. Denn was ist Allmacht? Die Empfindung, daß man alles hat, was man will, und man nichts zu wünschen übrig hat. Die Leibesfrucht könnte aber das von sich behaupten, denn sie hat immer alles, was zur Befriedigung ihrer Triebe notwendig ist, darum hat sie auch nichts zu wünschen; sie ist bedürfnislos.

Der ‚Kindergrößenwahn‘ von der eigenen Allmächtigkeit ist also zumindest kein leerer Wahn; das Kind und der Zwangsneurotiker fordern von der Wirklichkeit nichts Unmögliches, wenn sie davon nicht abzubringen sind, daß ihre Wünsche sich erfüllen müssen; sie fordern nur die Wiederkehr eines Zustandes, der einmal bestanden hat, jener ‚guten alten Zeit‘, in der sie allmächtig waren.“

Aus dem Werke R a n k s „Das Trauma der Geburt“ seien hier folgende Stellen wiedergegeben: „ . . . In zahlreichen Träumen dieses Endstadiums drängte sich immer wieder die endlich unabweisbare Tatsache auf, daß diese Fixierung an die Mutter, welche der analytischen Fixierung zugrunde zu liegen schien, die früheste rein physiologische Beziehung zum mütterlichen Körper beinhaltet.“

„ . . . Daraus ergibt sich, daß die eigentliche Übertragungslibido, die wir bei beiden Geschlechtern analytisch aufzulösen haben, die m ü t t e r l i c h e ist, wie sie in der pränatalen physiologischen Bindung zwischen Mutter und Kind gegeben war.“

„ . . . möchten jedoch schon hier auf die ebenso unzweifelhafte analytische Tatsache verweisen, daß ganz wie jeder Angst die Geburtsangst zugrunde liegt, jede L u s t l e t z t e n E n d e s zur W i e d e r h e r s t e l l u n g der i n t r a u t e - r i n e n U r l u s t tendiert.“

Jedenfalls erfolgt im Intrauterinleben und in der ersten Kindheit die Befriedigung nicht an einem Objekte; soweit man davon sprechen kann, daß die Mutter Befriedigung verschafft, so wird sie doch nicht als Objekt wahrgenommen. Wie tritt nun dieses ins Leben ein? Darüber sagt F r e u d (2): „Seither haben wiederholte Befriedigungssituationen das Objekt der Mutter geschaffen, das nun im Falle des Bedürfnisses eine intensive ‚sehnsüchtig‘ zu nennende Besetzung erfährt.“ „Das Objekt wird zur Befriedigung der autoerotischen Triebe verwendet, denn diese sind uranfänglich“ (F r e u d [1]). Auch können wir nicht von libidinösen Trieben allein sprechen. „Die psychoanalytische Untersuchung, welche uns sonst die Schicksale der libidinösen Triebe ver-

folgen läßt, wenn diese von den Ich-Trieben isoliert sich in Opposition zu
denselben befinden, gestattet uns auf diesem Gebiete Rückschlüsse auf eine
Epoche und eine psychische Situation, in welcher beiderlei Triebe noch ein-
hellig wirksam in untrennbarer Vermengung als narzißtische Interessen auftreten" (Freud[1]).

Das durch wiederholte Befriedigungssituationen geschaffene Objekt hat zwei
wichtige Funktionen. Bei Freud(2) heißt es: „Die Intrauterinexistenz des
Menschen erscheint gegen die der meisten Tiere relativ verkürzt; er wird un-
fertiger als diese in die Welt geschickt. Dadurch wird der Einfluß der realen
Außenwelt verstärkt, die Differenzierung des Ichs vom Es frühzeitig gefördert,
die Gefahren der Außenwelt in ihrer Bedeutung erhöht und der Wert des
Objektes, das allein gegen diese Gefahren schützen und das verlorene Intrauterinleben ersetzen kann, enorm gesteigert." Es wird also das Objekt sozusagen mißbraucht, um in den früheren, lustvollen Zustand, in dem es noch
keine Objekte gab, zurückzukehren.

Die zweite — eng damit verknüpfte — Funktion des Objektes ist, Schutz
vor Gefahr zu bieten. „Die Situation, die er (der Säugling) als ,Gefahr' wertet,
gegen die er versichert sein will, ist also die der Unbefriedigung, des An-
wachsens der Bedürfnisspannung, gegen die er ohnmächtig ist. Ich meine von
diesem Gesichtspunkte aus ordnet sich alles ein: Die Situation der Unbefriedigung, in der Reizgrößen eine unlustvolle Höhe erreichen, ohne Bewältigung
durch psychische Verwendung und Abfuhr zu finden, muß für den Säugling
die Analogie mit dem Geburtserlebnis, die Wiederholung der Gefahrsituation
sein" (Freud[2]).

Erreicht also der Zustand der Unbefriedigung eine gewisse Größe, so wird
infolge ökonomischer Störungen das Geburtserlebnis, die damit verbundene
Gefahr wieder erlebt (vgl. Rank: Das Trauma der Geburt). Allein es tritt
bald eine bedeutsame Änderung ein, die bewirkt, daß auch ohne Störungen in
der Libidoökonomie die Gefahr wieder erlebt wird. „Mit der Erfahrung, daß
ein äußeres, durch Wahrnehmung erfaßbares Objekt der an die Geburt
mahnenden gefährlichen Situation ein Ende machen kann, verschiebt sich nun
der Inhalt der Gefahr von der ökonomischen Situation auf seine Bedingung,
den Objektverlust. Das Vermissen der Mutter wird nun die Gefahr, bei
deren Eintritt der Säugling das Angstsignal gibt, noch ehe die befürchtete
ökonomische Situation eingetreten ist" (Freud[2]). Es ist nicht erklärt, auf
welchem Wege die Verschiebung von der Störung der Libidoökonomie auf das
Vermissen des Objektes zustande kommt. Dies ist nicht ohne weiteres verständlich. Jedenfalls ist in diesem Stadium irgendein Wissen — eine Erfahrung — um die Existenz des Objektes vorhanden. Dieses Wissen um das
Objekt darf nicht mit der Besetzung des Objektes verwechselt werden,
welche erst im Falle der Steigerung des Bedürfnisses eintritt. Die Wahrnehmung
des Nichtvorhandenseins des Objektes bringt Unlustreaktionen gleicher Art

19

hervor, als ob die gefürchtete ökonomische Störung, die Gefahr, tatsächlich Platz gegriffen hätte. Allmählich wird aus der Wahrnehmung eine Vorstellung. Dieses Stadium scheint das früheste zu sein, in dem eine Vorstellung so tiefgreifende Änderungen in der Libidoökonomie zu bewirken imstande ist.

*

Die Wiederkehr überwundener Entwicklungsstufen des Ichs war bei einer Patientin deutlich zu sehen.

Es handelt sich um eine 25jährige Frau, die bereits einmal wegen eines neurotischen Erbrechens eine 17 Monate lange Analyse durchgemacht hatte. Diese war insofern von Erfolg begleitet, als die Patientin symptomfrei wurde und eine befriedigende Beziehung eingehen konnte. Die Patientin war so lange symptomfrei geblieben, als diese Beziehung angedauert hatte. Kaum war diese gelöst, erkrankte die Patientin neuerdings. Zwar kehrten die alten Symptome nicht mehr wieder, doch litt die Patientin nunmehr unter — wie sie es nannte — „Depressionen". Mit diesem Worte bezeichnete sie zwei verschiedene Krankheitsbilder. Es waren Entfremdungs-, bzw. Depersonalisationszustände schwerster Art. Die Welt erschien ihr fremd, farblos, leblos, die Menschen waren nichts anderes als Schattengebilde. Zeitweilig spürte sie sich selbst gar nicht. Es passierte ihr oft, daß sie im Gespräch mit einer Freundin letztere fragte, ob sie (die Patientin) wirklich vorhanden sei. Wenn sie über die Straße ging, hatte sie manchmal das Gefühl, als fehlten ihr die Beine ganz und die Straße würde sich unter ihrem in der Luft schwebenden Oberkörper in entgegengesetzter Richtung bewegen. Sie stieß sich die Fingernägel in das Fleisch der Oberarme, um zu prüfen, ob sie wach sei.

Das zweite, das sie unter „Depressionen" verstand, waren Angstzustände. Eine grenzenlose Angst überkam sie, sie fühlte sich durch ein furchtbares Unglück bedroht, ohne daß sie imstande gewesen wäre, dieses Unglück zu beschreiben. Sie wußte nur, daß es grenzenlos wäre, und daß „alles zusammenstürzen" würde. Nach den Schilderungen der Patientin war es eine Panikstimmung. Die Patientin konnte keinerlei Anlaß für das Auftreten der Panikstimmung angeben, ebensowenig für das — wie sie meinte — unmotivierte Verschwinden dieser Stimmung. Sie wußte auch nicht, daß sie eine Naschsucht hatte, die mit der Panikstimmung in Zusammenhang stand. Sie ging nie aus, ohne einen Vorrat an eßbaren Dingen bei sich zu haben. Ein Apfel, ein Päckchen Bonbons, Haselnüsse u. dgl. — im Notfalle ein Stückchen trockenes Brot — waren in ihrem Handtäschchen stets vorhanden. Das „Süchtige" an dem Naschen wurde erst klar, als die Patientin angab, daß sie, namentlich wenn ihr Chef ihr etwas diktierte, aus Angst, sie könnte in dieser für sie so wichtigen Situation einen Zusammenbruch erleben, irgend etwas Eßbares in den Mund hineinschmuggeln mußte. Sie wußte aus Erfahrung, daß sie, wenn sie etwas — und sei es auch nur ein Bonbon — gegessen hatte, keinen Zusammenbruch mehr erleben werde. Im Gegenteil, sie arbeitete dann viel sicherer. Sie war durch mehrere Jahre bei derselben Firma beschäftigt. Obgleich man mit ihr sehr zufrieden war, gab sie ihre Stellung freiwillig auf, aus Angst, sie könnte einmal einen großen Zusammenbruch erleben und deshalb weggeschickt werden. Bei ihren Bekannten war sie sehr beliebt. Nur ganz wenige Male in ihrem Leben war es zu unangenehmen Auseinandersetzungen gekommen.

In der Analyse zeigte sich, daß sie vorher stets eine Panikstimmung erlebt hatte. Um aus dieser Stimmung herauszukommen, war ihr jedes Mittel recht; in einem solchen Zustande war sie einer Rücksichtnahme auf ihre Mitmenschen nicht fähig und konnte daher den Eindruck eines überaus anmaßenden Menschen erwecken; die Beziehung zu der betreffenden Person fand nach einem solchen Versuch, der Panikstimmung Herr zu werden, meist ihr Ende.

Die Patientin war ein einziges Kind; ihr Vater war ein kleiner Beamter gewesen und starb, als die Patientin im Pubertätsalter war. Mit der Mutter lebte sie seit ihrer Geburt in den gleichen bescheidenen Verhältnissen. Obzwar sie sich mit der Mutter gar nicht verstand, erfüllte sie dennoch äußerlich alle Pflichten einer guten Tochter. Sie war als Kind sehr verzärtelt worden, war immer als die gescheiteste und bravste ihrer Altersgenossinnen gepriesen worden. Beide Eltern bemühten sich sehr, aus ihr ein „Paradekind" zu machen, und sie unterstützte die Eltern darin. Sie gab nie Gelegenheit zu Tadel, war immer still und bescheiden. In jedem Lebensalter konnte sie stundenlang ruhig in einer Sofaecke sitzen und sich beschäftigen, so daß man ihre Anwesenheit in der Wohnung gar nicht wahrnahm. In früher Kindheit war es ein Spiel mit Glaskugeln, das sie so fesseln konnte, später, nachdem sie lesen gelernt hatte, war es die Lektüre eines Buches.

Die Patientin verblieb auch als Erwachsene bei dem gleichen Verhalten. Sie konnte stundenlang im Park sitzen und dem Spiel kleiner Kinder zusehen. Sehr oft pflegte sie, obzwar sie Jüdin ist und vorgibt, Atheistin zu sein, in eine Kirche zu gehen, dort niederzuknien und längere Zeit in Andacht versunken zu bleiben. Verließ sie freiwillig die Kirche, so pflegte sie sich eine Zeit lang sehr beglückt zu fühlen; war sie jedoch — z. B. aus Zeitmangel — gezwungen, ihre Andacht abzukürzen, so fühlte sie sich unglücklich. Die Patientin war stolz darauf, von der Natur mit so reicher Phantasie begabt worden zu sein; auch war sie überzeugt, daß sie etwas Großes werden könnte. Sie sagte: „Ich weiß, daß ich nur eine Kontoristin bin; aber ich könnte ohne weiteres eine berühmte Schriftstellerin oder Schauspielerin sein."

Es zeigte sich, daß die Patientin all das, was sie phantasierte, wirklich zu erleben glaubte. Die Glaskugeln waren für sie Lebewesen, sie war die Heldin der Märchen oder der Romane, sie war das kleine Kind, das im Park betreut wurde, und sie war, so lange sie in der Kirche war, Christus oder Gott. Sie erklärte, wenn sie mit einem von ihr wahrhaft geliebten Manne koitierte, so würde sie die „Urmutter" sein, die die ganze Welt in sich trägt.

Um Phantasien der geschilderten Art zu erleben, brauchte sie in der Außenwelt den dazu passenden Rahmen. Sie begab sich mit Absicht in eine entsprechende Situation. Wollte sie die Wonnen des Kleinkinderdaseins wieder erleben, so suchte sie die Kinderspielplätze im Park auf oder stellte sich im Winter vor die Auslage eines Spielwarenladens. Wenn sie sich allmächtig fühlen wollte, ging sie in die Kirche. Sie brauchte Objekte, um sich mit deren Hilfe in einen Zustand hineinzuphantasieren, der ihr die Befriedigung ihrer narzißtischen Libido ermöglichte.

Ein einziges Mal konnte beobachtet werden, wie diese Patientin das Objekt dazu verwendete, um zu objektlosem Genießen zu gelangen, und da bestätigte sich, daß das Objekt beim Kinde nicht nur dem Schutze vor Gefahr dient, sondern auch das verlorene Intrauterinleben wiederzubeleben vermag.

Die Patientin pflegte während der Behandlung oft von Entfremdung, bzw. Depersonalisation befallen zu werden. Es war für sie sehr peinlich, wenn sie den Analytiker vermißte. Sie wisse zwar genau, pflegte sie zu sagen, daß der Arzt hinter ihr sitze, allein sie fühle ihn nicht. In solchen Situationen pflegte sie den Analytiker anzuflehen, er möge, wenn er schon nicht reden wolle, sich wenigstens eine Zigarette anzünden, damit sie es fühle, daß er da sei. Der Analytiker war ihr also während der Entfremdung sehr wichtig, es war somit die Objektlibido für ihn erhalten. Einmal ereignete es sich, daß der Analytiker der Patientin sagte, sie möge sich darauf einrichten, das nächste Mal vielleicht eine Viertelstunde warten zu müssen. Er wisse nicht, ob er rechtzeitig werde kommen können. Am nächsten Tage nahm sie im Wartezimmer Platz. Während der acht Minuten, die bis zum Eintreffen des Analytikers vergingen, erlebte die Patientin eine Panikstimmung. Eine ungeheure Gefahr bedrohte sie, sie konnte nicht sitzen bleiben, geschweige denn etwas lesen; sie hatte unsägliche Angst, das Telephon könnte läuten, und dann würde man ihr ausrichten, daß die Verspätung so groß werde, daß sie an diesem Tage überhaupt nicht behandelt werden könne. Sie hatte während dieser Minuten nicht etwa die Vorstellung gehabt, dem Analytiker könnte ein Unglück zustoßen. Lediglich für sich befürchtete sie das Ärgste, ohne es jedoch beschreiben zu können. Als der Analytiker kam, war sie hochbeglückt. Sie schilderte die Angst, die sie eben ausgestanden hatte, und wie froh sie sei, daß doch alles sich zum Guten gewendet habe. Plötzlich stockte der Redefluß, und sie verharrte einige Minuten schweigend. Ähnlich wie jemand, der wieder zu sich gekommen ist, begann sie dann wieder: „Herr Doktor, jetzt waren Sie wieder nicht hier, aber das war nicht wie gewöhnlich; es war gar nicht unangenehm, im Gegenteil, vor lauter Glücksgefühl, daß Sie doch gekommen sind, habe ich total vergessen, daß Sie da sind." Eine weitere Analyse dieses Vorganges war unmöglich, die Patientin erklärte immer wieder, sie sei so maßlos glücklich gewesen, daß sie es nicht nötig gehabt habe, auf die Situation zu achten, in der sie sich befinde. Sie habe sich ganz ihrem Glücksgefühl überlassen und infolgedessen „vergessen", wo sie sich befinde.

In dem eben geschilderten Falle hat also das Objekt — der Analytiker — dazu gedient, der Patientin zunächst die Panikstimmung zu nehmen und sie nachher in den lustvollen primärnarzißtischen Zustand der Objektlosigkeit versinken zu lassen. Hatte das Objekt diese beiden Funktionen erfüllt, so wurde ihm die Besetzung entzogen, es konnte „vergessen" werden.

Daß eine solche, subjektiv als vollständig empfundene Stillung der Objektlibido unmittelbar in eine narzißtische Seligkeit überging, war bei der Patientin nur ein einziges Mal zu bemerken. Das sonst für sie charakteristische Verhalten zeigt folgendes Erlebnis:

Sie brauchte nach Schluß der Behandlungsstunde regelmäßig längere Zeit, um sich zum Weggehen herzurichten. Einmal hatte es der Arzt eilig und konnte nicht abwarten, bis die Patientin fertig war; er mußte vor ihr die Wohnung verlassen. Bevor er wegging, übergab er ihr den Schlüssel zur Wohnung mit der Bitte, beim Weggehen die Tür zu versperren und den Schlüssel in den Briefkasten zu werfen. Sie versprrach

24*

es, ohne eine Erregung, merken zu lassen. Tags darauf berichtet sie, daß sie seit der gestrigen Stunde sehr glücklich gewesen sei; während der Stunde hatte sie sich noch sehr elend gefühlt, aber als ihr der Schlüssel übergeben wurde, habe sie ein Glücksgefühl überkommen. Sie sah darin einen Beweis grenzenlosen Vertrauens, denn der Analytiker hatte ihr sein ganzes Hab und Gut anvertraut; sie fühlte sich überhaupt nicht mehr krank — einem Kranken würde der Arzt doch nicht so viel Vertrauen geschenkt haben —, im Gegenteil, seit gestern fühle sie sich so gesund wie noch nie. Die letzten 23 Stunden habe sie überhaupt an nichts anderes denken können, als an dieses sie beglückende Erlebnis.[2]

Ein Vergleich der beiden Erlebnisse der Patientin zeigt folgendes: In dem ersten Erlebnis war die ganze Libido als narzißtische zur Geltung gekommen. Sie hatte dem Objekt die bewußte Besetzung ganz entzogen, den Analytiker, bzw. die Situation, in der sie sich befand, „vergessen". In dem zweiten Falle blieb die Objektbesetzung bewußt, denn das Glück, das sie genoß, war der Ausdruck des vom Objekt Geliebtwordenseins. Deswegen konnte sie zwischen den beiden Behandlungsstunden an nichts anderes denken, als an das Glück, das ihr widerfahren war. Aus vielen anderen Situationen wußten wir, daß die Patientin auf den Verlust eines derartigen Glücksgefühls mit einer von ihr so benannten Depression zu reagieren pflegte, d. h. in eine Panikstimmung oder in einen Entfremdungszustand geraten konnte. Aus dem ängstlichen Vermeiden alles dessen, was ihr eine „Depression" hätte bringen können, aus dem Bestreben, sich das Objekt, bzw. das Geschätztwerden durch das Objekt zu erhalten, sehen wir, wie wichtig ihr dieses ist; es ist demnach eine starke Objektbesetzung vorhanden. Allerdings dient das Objekt hauptsächlich dazu, ihr eine Befriedigung ihrer narzißtischen Libido zu verschaffen. Was die Patientin erlebte, als ihr der Arzt den Wohnungsschlüssel übergab, war — unbeschadet der dem Schlüssel innewohnenden Symbolbedeutung — eine Bereicherung ihrer narzißtischen Libido, was eine Erweiterung ihres frühen, unentwickelten Ichs zur Folge hatte. Sie fühlte sich vollkommen gesund, vertrauenswürdig, sie war ein überglücklicher Mensch, ihr Selbstgefühl war bedeutend gesteigert.

Wir sehen also: Das Objekt diente dazu, eine Erweiterung des Ichs hervorzurufen, indem dieses mehr Libido an sich zog. Vergleichen wir damit den Satz Freuds, wonach die Höchstphase der Verliebtheit mit einer Verarmung an Ich-Libido zugunsten der Objektlibido einhergeht, so ist dagegen diese Ich-Erweiterung als Bereicherung an narzißtischer Libido aufzufassen. Tatsächlich handelt es sich bei dieser Art von Ich-Erweiterung um einen Prozeß, der sich in dem im Zustande der Regression befindlichen Ich abspielt. Das Ich, das sich erweitert hatte, ist nicht identisch mit jener Instanz, die die bekannten

---

2) Die Bedeutung des Schlüssels als Sexualsymbol darf in diesem Falle nicht überschätzt werden. Die Patientin reagierte in ganz der gleichen Art und Intensität auf jede kleine Rücksichtnahme, die ihr der Analytiker beispielsweise bei Festsetzung der Behandlungsstunde beweis.

Funktionen (Realitätsprüfung, Beherrschung der Motilität usw.) zu erfüllen hat, sondern es ist das Gebilde, das der Säugling, bzw. der Kranke als sein Ich bezeichnen würde; ein solches „Ich" ist im Übergange vom Es zum Ich befindlich, also noch im Prozesse der Differenzierung des Ichs aus dem Es. Um Mißverständnissen vorzubeugen, sei vorgeschlagen, dieses noch nicht differenzierte Gebilde das Früh-Ich zu nennen und die Bezeichnung „Ich" für jene vollentwickelte Instanz zu reservieren, die die bekannten Funktionen zu erfüllen hat.

Im Früh-Ich sind auch starke Objektbesetzungen vorhanden, aber das Objekt dient nur zur Befriedigung der narzißtischen Libido. Auf dieser Stufe kann das Objekt nur Änderungen in der Ökonomie der narzißtischen Libido hervorrufen. Und vom Zustande der narzißtischen Libido hängt der Zustand des ganzen Früh-Ichs ab. Denn zu Beginn der Entwicklung fühlt und reagiert das Individuum als Ganzes. „Wenn der Säugling nach der Wahrnehmung der Mutter verlangt, so doch nur darum, weil er bereits aus Erfahrung weiß, daß sie alle seine Bedürfnisse ohne Verzug befriedigt" (Freud [2]). „Die nämliche Steigerung aller Gefühlsregungen zum Extremen und Maßlosen gehört auch der Affektivität des Kindes an und findet sich im Traumleben wieder, wo dank der im Unbewußten herrschenden Isolierung der einzelnen Gefühlsregungen ein leiser Ärger vom Tage sich als Todeswunsch gegen die schuldige Person zum Ausdruck bringt, oder ein Anflug irgendeiner Versuchung zum Anstoß einer im Traum dargestellten verbrecherischen Handlung wird" (Freud [3]). Das Früh-Ich reagiert mit seiner ganzen narzißtischen Libido. Eine durch das Objekt bewirkte Änderung der narzißtischen Libido wird somit als Änderung des ganzen Früh-Ichs empfunden; das Objekt wird auch als zum Früh-Ich gehörig gefühlt. Deshalb ist die Patientin so überglücklich, wenn sie eine Befriedigung erfährt, erlebt aber eine Panikstimmung, wenn ihr eine Gefahr droht, d. h. eine Bedürfnisspannung sie überwältigt.

Daß die Vorstellung des Objektes als zum Früh-Ich gehörig gefühlt wird, hat bedeutsame Folgen: „Kind und Primitiver benehmen sich im Stadium des primären Narzißmus anders als später, nachdem die Ich-Grenze alle Gegenstände der Außenwelt außer dem Individuum gelegen fühlen, nicht nur erkennen läßt. Erstens empfinden Kinder Veränderungen an äußeren Objekten, wie wenn sie ihnen selbst geschehen wären, reagieren deshalb mit Angst und Zorn, mit Lust und Leid, obgleich ihnen nach den Begriffen des Erwachsenen doch ‚gar nichts geschah'. Zweitens aber sind sie andererseits wieder unabhängig von den Geschehnissen der Außenwelt, weil ihre mit vollem Ich-Gefühl erlebten, ständig besetzten Vorstellungen der Außenwelt diese selbst ihnen zu ersetzen vermögen" (Federn [2]).

Auf der eben geschilderten Entwicklungsstufe können Objektbesetzung und Objektlibido miteinander verwechselt werden. Da nämlich einzelne Objekte häufiger, bzw. stärker als andere begehrt werden, kann das Bestehen

von Objektlibido vorgetäuscht werden. In Wirklichkeit ist jedoch nur die
Ich-Libido wirksam, die das Objekt benötigt und begehrt. Im Laufe der
Entwicklung muß schließlich das Objekt die begehrte Befriedigung der Ich-
Libido versagen. Es hört auf, die Ökonomie der narzißtischen Libido zu re-
gulieren, und kann somit nicht länger als zum Ich gehörig gefühlt werden.
Das Objekt wird nunmehr, als in der Außenwelt vorhanden, nicht nur gewußt, sondern auch gefühlt; wenn es jetzt besetzt wird, so ist es mit Objektlibido besetzt (Federn [1]). Den Unterschied möge folgendes Beispiel zeigen:
Wenn das kleine Kind schreit, sobald die Mutter sich entfernt, so tut 'es dies
aus Angst; die Mutter dient zur Aufrechterhaltung der narzißtischen Libidoökonomie, die Entfernung der Mutter würde eine Störung dieser Ökonomie,
somit eine Gefahr für das ganze Früh-Ich bedeuten. Es ist also nicht Objektlibido, die gestört wird. Von Objektlibido können wir erst dann sprechen,
wenn die Entfernung der Mutter ohne Störung der narzißtischen Libidoökonomie, somit ohne Gefahr für das Früh-Ich, also ohne Angst erfolgen
kann.

Die im Früh-Ich herrschende Tendenz nach Befriedigung der gesamten
Libido besteht auch später fort, deshalb wird bei jeder Befriedigung von Objektlibido gleichzeitig auch die Ich-Libido befriedigt. Während jedoch im
Früh-Ich eine Einheit der Libido besteht — die narzißtische Libido reagiert
noch als Ganzes —, erfolgen später die Befriedigungen zwar gleichzeitig und
durch das gleiche Objekt ausgelöst, jedoch nebeneinander.

Daß Entwicklungsstufen verschiedener Höhe nebeneinander bestehen,
darüber äußert sich Freud (4): „Auf seelischem Gebiet hingegen ist die Erhaltung des Primitiven neben dem daraus entstandenen Umgewandelten so
häufig, daß es sich erübrigt, es durch Beispiele zu beweisen."

Ist das Objekt in die Außenwelt entlassen, so ist es aus dem Früh-Ich nicht
spurlos verschwunden, da im Psychischen nichts verlorengeht. Die Erinnerung
an die einst genossene totale Befriedigung der narzißtischen Libido, die das
Objekt brachte, bleibt als dauernde unbewußte Niederschrift bestehen.

Mit fortschreitender Realitätsanpassung wird die Befriedigung der gesamten
Ich-Libido von den Objekten immer mehr versagt werden. Ob diese Versagung leichter oder schwerer hingenommen wird, wird von verschiedenen
Faktoren abhängig sein, beispielsweise etwa von einer konstitutionell bedingten
abnormen Triebstärke. Auch für die einzelnen Triebe, bzw. Funktionen wird
in dieser Hinsicht Verschiedenheit bestehen. Für alle Fälle ist die Freigabe des
Objektes in die Außenwelt für die Gestaltung des Ichs von großer Wichtigkeit,
wie Freud (5) gelehrt hat: „Es war uns gelungen, das schmerzhafte Leiden
der Melancholie durch die Annahme aufzuklären, daß ein verlorenes Objekt
im Ich wieder aufgerichtet, also eine Objektbesetzung durch eine Identifizierung abgelöst wird. Damals erkannten wir aber noch nicht die ganze Bedeutung dieses Vorganges und wußten nicht, wie häufig und typisch er ist.

Wir haben seither verstanden, daß solche Ersetzung einen großen Anteil an der Gestaltung des Ichs hat und wesentlich dazu beiträgt, das herzustellen, was man seinen Charakter heißt." Kurz darauf heißt es: „Soll oder muß ein solches Sexualobjekt aufgegeben werden, so tritt dafür nicht selten die Ich-Veränderung auf, die man als Aufrichtung des Objektes im Ich wie bei der Melancholie beschreiben muß; die näheren Verhältnisse dieser Ersetzung sind uns noch nicht bekannt. Vielleicht erleichtert oder ermöglicht das Ich durch diese Introjektion, die eine Art von Regression zum Mechanismus der oralen Phase ist, das Aufgeben des Objektes. Vielleicht ist diese Identifizierung überhaupt die Bedingung, unter der das Es seine Objekte aufgibt. Jedenfalls ist der Vorgang, zumal in frühen Entwicklungsphasen, ein sehr häufiger und kann die Auffassung ermöglichen, daß der Charakter des Ichs ein Niederschlag der aufgegebenen Objektbesetzungen ist, die Geschichte dieser Objektwahlen enthält." Das reife Ich entsteht also durch Identifizierungen mit dem Objekte, das aufgegeben werden mußte, weil es sich versagte. Dieser Vorgang läßt die Objekte von narzißtischer Besetzung frei werden. Wenn wir die früher vorgeschlagene Scheidung von Früh-Ich und Ich beibehalten, so bedeutet dieser Vorgang: Dadurch, daß eine Identifizierung mit dem aufgegebenen Objekte erfolgte, wurde das Früh-Ich umgewandelt. Es hat das Objekt freigegeben, sich jedoch durch dessen Aufrichtung als Teil des Ichs schadlos gehalten. Dieser Vorgang bedeutet die Umwandlung des Früh-Ichs ins Ich.

Der Identifizierung mit dem aufgegebenen Objekte ist ein langwieriger Prozeß vorangegangen: eine Stufe der Objektlosigkeit, das Auftreten von Objekten durch die Befriedigungssituationen, das Begehren nach dem Objekte zur Befriedigung der narzißtischen Libido. Dieser Entwicklungsgang wird seine Spuren hinterlassen haben. Das Objekt wird also in zweifacher Hinsicht zu beurteilen sein: 1. Seine Rolle vor der Entlassung aus dem Früh-Ich und 2. die Funktion, die darin besteht, daß es das Früh-Ich ins Ich umzuwandeln ermöglicht.

Freud spricht die Vermutung aus, daß die Identifizierung mit dem aufgegebenen Objekte überhaupt die Bedingung sei, unter der das Es seine Objekte aufgibt. Allein Freud bezeichnet die Identifizierung als einen Vorgang, der sich auch viel früher abspielt, lange bevor ein Aufgeben des Objektes in Frage kommt. Er nennt die Identifizierung die früheste Gefühlsbeziehung zu einem Objekt: „Das aus diesen drei Quellen Gelernte können wir dahin zusammenfassen, daß die Identifizierung die ursprünglichste Form der Gefühlsbindung an ein Objekt ist." „Wir haben gehört, daß die Identifizierung die früheste und ursprünglichste Form der Gefühlsbindung ist" (Freud[3]). „Wie immer sich aber die spätere Resistenz des Charakters gegen die Einflüsse aufgegebener Objektbesetzungen gestalten mag, die Wirkungen der ersten, im frühesten Alter erfolgten Identifizierungen werden allgemeine und nachhaltige sein. Dies führt uns zur Entstehung des Ich-Ideals zurück, denn hinter ihm verbirgt sich die erste und bedeutsamste Identifizierung des Individuums, die mit dem Vater der persönlichen Vorzeit. Diese scheint zunächst nicht Erfolg oder Ausgang einer Objektbesetzung zu sein, sie ist eine direkte und unmittelbare und frühzeitiger als jede Objektbesetzung. Aber die Objektwahlen, die der ersten Sexualperiode angehören und Vater und Mutter betreffen, scheinen beim normalen Ablauf den Ausgang in solche Identifizierung zu nehmen und somit die primäre Identifizierung zu verstärken" (Freud [5]).

Wir sehen also zwei Arten von Identifizierung: eine spätere, die zustande kommt, weil das Objekt aufgegeben werden mußte, und eine frühere, die eine direkte und unmittelbare war, frühzeitiger als jede Objektbesetzung und deren Wirkungen von Freud allgemein und nachhaltig genannt werden. So können zwei Niederschriften des Objektes zustande kommen. Die eine stammt aus der Zeit vor der Entlassung des Objektes aus dem Früh-Ich und dankt ihre Entstehung der primären, also vor der Objektbesetzung erfolgenden Identifizierung; die andere ist die Folge der Freigabe des Objektes aus dem Früh-Ich und der Wiederaufrichtung desselben als Teil des Ichs.

Die Wirkungen der primären Identifizierung sind andere als die der späteren; auch unterscheiden sie sich in ihren Mechanismen. „Es kann leicht sein, daß der seelische Apparat vor der scharfen Sonderung von Ich und Es, vor der Ausbildung eines Über-Ichs, andere Methoden der Abwehr übt, als nach Erreichung dieser Organisationsstufen" (Freud [2]).

Die primäre Identifizierung erfolgt vor der Objektbesetzung, auf einer Stufe, wo es nur narzißtische Libido gibt. Alles, was im Individuum vorgeht, kann in diesem Stadium nur die Ökonomie der narzißtischen Libido betreffen. Diese reagiert jedoch stets als ein Ganzes. Der Zustand der Befriedigtheit ist ein totaler, ebenso der Zustand der Bedürfnisspannung. Das Verhalten der früher erwähnten Patientin, als sie auf den Analytiker warten mußte, kann als Beispiel dafür dienen. Jede Änderung der Libidoökonomie wird als Änderung der Gesamtorganisation empfunden, als Änderung jenes Gebildes, das wir vom Standpunkte des Erwachsenen als Es, bzw. als Früh-Ich bezeichnen, welches aber für den Säugling sein Ich darstellt.

Solcher Änderungen wird es im Beginne der Entwicklung nur wenige geben. Je primitiver die Organisation, desto weniger differenziert ist das Gefühlsleben. So zeigte auch die erwähnte, primärnarzißtisch gebliebene Patientin eine sehr primitive Art, ihre Gefühle auszudrücken. Wenn sie z. B. sagen wollte, daß ihr der Ausflug auf den Kahlenberg oder an die Donau viel Lustgewinn gebracht habe, so drückte sie das durch die Worte aus: „Gestern war der Kahlenberg gut, war die Donau gut." Hatte sie keinen Lustgewinn, so waren Kahlenberg und Donau „schlecht" gewesen.

Auch eingetretene Differenzierungen der Organisation ändern noch lange nichts daran, daß die Befriedigung der gesamten Libido als Ziel fortbesteht.

Von jedem Partialtrieb aus wird m a x i m a l e Befriedigung der gesamten narzißtischen Libido begehrt. Darin gleichen alle Quellen einander, daß aus
ihnen die gleiche Lust — die maximale Befriedigung der gesamten narzißtischen Libido — fließt. Die Patientin pflegte, wenn die Übertragung ein po-
sitives Vorzeichen hatte, zu erklären, daß sie genau so glücklich wäre, wenn
der Analytiker sie zur Geliebten nähme, wie wenn er mit ihr ein Buch zusammen läse oder einen gemeinsamen Spaziergang unternähme. Tatsächlich
erlebt sie manchmal orgasmusähnliche Sensationen, wenn ihr ein von ihr ge-
schätzter Mann Feuer für die Zigarette reicht. — Manche Erscheinungen, die
als „Verschiebung von unten nach oben" geschildert werden, mögen dadurch
ermöglicht worden sein, daß von jeder der beiden erogenen Zonen aus seinerzeit die maximale Befriedigung erfolgt war. Auch mag das Stürmische mancher
Übertragung darin seinen Grund haben, daß der aus der Kindheit übertragene
Wunsch die Befriedigung der gesamten narzißtischen Libido erstrebt hatte.

Wie sollen wir uns nun das Zustandekommen der primären Identifizierung
erklären? Welcher Grund kann auf einer Entwicklungsstufe, auf der es nur
narzißtische Libido gibt, das Früh-Ich dazu antreiben, sich zu verändern, und
zwar als G a n z e s zu ändern? Die spätere Identifizierung, die durch Versagung bedingt ist, ist eine Entschädigung für den Verlust des Objektes und
hält dieses fest; eine Voraussetzung für das Festhalten des Objektes ist dessen
Besetzung. Diese Besetzung fehlt noch, wie F r e u d ausführt, bei der primären
Identifizierung. Über die Möglichkeit, daß eine Identifizierung vor der Objektwahl — nicht zu verwechseln mit Objektbesetzung — zustande kommt,
äußert sich F r e u d (3): „Die erstere" (sc. Identifizierung) „ist darum bereits
vor jeder sexuellen Objektwahl möglich. Es ist weit schwieriger, diese Verschiedenheit metapsychologisch anschaulich darzustellen. Man erkennt nur, die
Identifizierung strebt darnach, das eigene Ich ähnlich zu gestalten, wie das
andere, zum Vorbild genommene."

Die primäre Identifizierung ist stets eine totale, da auf dieser frühen Stufe
das Individuum stets als Ganzes reagieren muß. Das Objekt w a h r n e h m e n
bedeutet — wahrscheinlich durch eine Art bedingten Reflexes (P a w l o w-I s c h-
l o n d s k y) — für das Kind Befreiung von Gefahr, d. h. von übergroßer Bedürfnisspannung, und, nachdem dies geschehen ist, Zurückversetzung in
den maximal lustvollen Zustand des Intrauterinlebens. Das Objekt sich v o r-
s t e l l e n, bedeutet das gleiche, denn zu dieser Zeit haben die Vorstellungen
noch Wirklichkeitswert. N u n b e r g (1) spricht den Satz aus: „Das psychische
innere Erlebnis besitzt sogar, da es unmittelbar gegeben ist, mehr Evidenz,
als das äußere." Halten wir uns vor Augen, daß auf dieser Entwicklungsstufe
das Lustprinzip noch uneingeschränkt herrscht, und daß die ganze narzißtische
Libido aktiviert wird. Es werden somit folgende Gleichungen bestehen: Sich
die M u t t e r vorstellen, bedeutet: sich eine L u s t vorstellen. (Die Mutter ist
noch ausschließlich die „Gute" auf Grund des Lustprinzips.) Sich e i n e Lust

vorstellen, bedeutet: sich totale, bzw. maximale Lust vorstellen. (Total, weil die ganze Libido befriedigt wird.) Totale Lust sich vorstellen, bedeutet: totale Lust fühlen. (Wegen der Evidenz des psychischen Erlebens und des Fehlens jeder Realitätsprüfung.) Totale Lust fühlen, bedeutet: die gesamte narzißtische Libido befriedigt haben, bedeutet somit: als Ganzes sich als lustvolles Subjekt fühlen.

Stellen wir in den eben angeführten Gleichungen die erste und die letzte Größe einander gegenüber, so ergibt sich wie mit mathematischer Notwendigkeit: Das Objekt sich vorstellen, bedeutet: sein Ich — das Früh-Ich — als lustvolles Subjekt fühlen. Könnte der Säugling reden, so müßte er sagen: „Wenn ich mir die Mutter vorstelle, so bin ich sofort ein anderer Mensch, und zwar ein maximal ‚guter‘."

Dieser Vorgang ist bekannt. Freud hat ihn beschrieben, als er lehrte, daß sich der „Inhalt der Gefahr von der ökonomischen Situation auf seine Bedingung, den Objektverlust" verschiebt und schon das Vermissen der Mutter zur Gefahr wird. Nur haben die Vorgänge der Trennung und der Identifizierung entgegengesetzte Vorzeichen.

Daß sich diese Identifizierung nicht nur auf libidobedingte Gemeinsamkeiten bezieht, zeigt z. B. eine Stelle aus dem Roman „Die Gezeichneten" von Aage Madelung. Ein Sohn steht nach jahrzehntelanger Abwesenheit an dem Sterbelager seiner Mutter. Der Dichter schreibt: „Er hatte plötzlich ein Empfinden, als wäre er es selber, der da starb, als stürbe er zugleich mit der Mutter und alle anderen Menschen mit ihr ... Ja, das ist es, dachte er. Eines Menschen Tod ist aller Menschen Tod, denn sie müssen alle sterben. Eines einzigen Menschen Tod ist der Menschheit und der Welt Tod ..."

Die primäre Identifizierung hat das gleiche Resultat wie jede Identifizierung: Zwischen Subjekt und Objekt besteht Gleichheit; diese Gleichheit kam dadurch zustande, daß sich das Subjekt dem Objekt angeglichen hat.

Das lustvolle Sich-selbst-Fühlen des Subjektes ist das Resultat der Angleichung an das lustspendende Objekt; Lustquelle ist das Objekt, Lustempfänger ist das Subjekt.

*

Nun bestätigt die Klinik die von Federn gegebene Erklärung der Entfremdungs-, bzw. Depersonalisationszustände: Den Kranken erscheint die Außenwelt, also das Objekt, traumhaft, wie tot. Sie beklagen sich darüber, benehmen sich jedoch so, als würde ihnen das Objekt lebendig erscheinen. Aus der Wichtignahme des Objektes ist zu sehen, daß Objektlibido vorhanden ist. Was nicht vorhanden ist, ist die Besetzung des dem Objekte zugewendeten Teiles des Ichs mit narzißtischer Libido. Vor der Entlassung des Objektes aus dem Früh-Ich gehörte das Objekt zum Früh-Ich. Es wurde mit nur narzißtischer Libido besetzt. Die Realitätsanpassung erzwang die Freigabe des Objektes, d. h. die Abgrenzung von Ich und Objekt. Soll nun ein psychischer Akt voll, d. h. nicht entfremdet erlebt werden, so müssen gleichzeitig Ich-Libido und Objektlibido befriedigt werden, es müssen die mit narzißtischer Libido besetzte Ich-Grenze und das Objekt aneinander herankommen. Wo der Ich-Grenze die narzißtische Besetzung fehlt, kommt es zur Entfremdung. Beim normalen, nicht entfremdeten Ablauf kommt es mitunter zu einer vorübergehenden Erweiterung der Ich-Grenze. Für ganz kurze Zeit stellt sich der Zustand her, wie er vor der Freigabe des Objektes in die Außenwelt, vor der Abgrenzung von Ich und Objekt bestanden hat (Federn [2, 3, 4, 5]).

. Wenn die Entfremdeten in der Analyse erkannt haben, worauf es ankommt, so kann man oft sehen, daß gerade jene Teile, bzw. Funktionen des Ichs, an denen über Entfremdung geklagt wird, zu anderen Zeiten mit narzißtischer Libido überstark besetzt sind. Als Beispiel diene die erwähnte Patientin. Zeitweilig spürte sie sich gar nicht gehen, sondern glaubte, die Erde bewege sich unter ihr. Mitunter jedoch hatte sie ein starkes wohliges Körpergefühl in ihren Beinen. Sie war geradezu ekstatisch, wenn sie nackt vor dem Spiegel stand und ihre Beine bewunderte; sie war überglücklich, daß sie gerade solche Beine habe. Auch beim Schwimmen hatte sie ein überstarkes Körpergefühl in ihren Beinen. Spielte sie mit vollem Körpergefühl auf einer Wiese, so bezeichnete sie die Wiese als „gut". Ging sie mit Entfremdungsgefühlen in den Beinen, so war die Wiese „schlecht". Auch für viele andere entfremdete Funktionen der Patientin ließ sich das gleiche nachweisen.

Ob dem Entfremdeten das Objekt lebendig oder wie tot erscheint, hängt von dem Zustande seiner narzißtischen Libido ab. Ist jener Teil des Ichs, mit dem er das Objekt erfassen soll, mit narzißtischer Libido gar nicht oder nur mangelhaft besetzt, so erfolgt Entfremdung; bei überstarker Besetzung erfolgt Ekstase (Federn [6]).

Bei den Entfremdeten handelt es sich um einzelne Teile des Ichs, deren Besetzung mit narzißtischer Libido gestört ist. Auf jener frühen Entwicklungsstufe, auf der das Ich — das Früh-Ich — noch nicht in Teilen, sondern als Ganzes reagiert, wird also das Objekt dadurch maximal lustvoll gefühlt, daß das Früh-Ich sich selbst als maximal lustvolles Subjekt empfindet. Was für einen einzelnen Teil gilt, muß vor der Differenzierung für das ganze Früh-Ich gelten. Wir kommen also zu dem Schlusse: Wenn das Früh-Ich sich als lustvolles Subjekt fühlt, so wird ihm auch das Objekt als lustspendend erscheinen; oder: eine Bedingung für das Fühlen des Objektes ist, daß das Früh-Ich sich als Subjekt fühlt.

Einen Anlaß dazu, daß das Früh-Ich sich als lustvolles Subjekt fühlt, sahen wir in der primären Identifizierung. Was geschieht nun, wenn die Empfindung des „Sich-als-lustvolles-Subjekt-Fühlens" durch irgendeine andere Ursache hervorgerufen wird als durch primäre Identifizierung mit dem Objekte? Durch hormonale Änderungen oder beim Erwachsenen etwa durch Einverleibung eines Rauschgiftes? Lustvolles Subjekt und lustvolles Objekt sind ja, wenn einmal eine gewisse Entwicklungsstufe erreicht ist, fest miteinander verbunden. Wenn also dieses Rauschgift nicht in einen Zustand der völligen Objektlosigkeit versetzt, vielmehr das Objekt erhalten bleibt, so wird die Empfindung „ich bin ein lustvolles Subjekt" sich auch auf das Objekt auswirken müssen. Da zwischen beiden Gleichheit besteht, so wird, wodurch immer die Empfindung „ich bin ein lustvolles Subjekt" verursacht sein mag, diese Empfindung begleitet sein von der Vorstellung, bzw. Empfindung „das Objekt ist lustspendend". Es müßte also der dem Säugling in den Mund gelegte Satz sich auch umkehren lassen: „Wenn ich — aus was für Gründen immer — ein ‚guter' Mensch bin, dann ist auch die Mutter ‚gut'."

Wiederum kommt es zur Gleichheit zwischen Objekt und Subjekt. Während bei der primären Identifizierung das Subjekt sich dem Objekte angeglichen hatte, findet hier eine „Umkehrung der Identifizierung", eine Angleichung des Objektes an das Subjekt statt. Als Lustspender könnte man das Subjekt bezeichnen, als Lustempfänger das Objekt.

Beispiele: Ein Patient litt, als er die Analyse begann, an schweren Minderwertigkeitsgefühlen. Seine Mutter haßte er, soweit er sich erinnern konnte. Als er den Höhepunkt seiner Ödipussituation erinnerte, rief er geradezu ekstatisch aus: „Nie in meinem ganzen Leben habe ich mich so wertvoll gefühlt wie in jenem Augenblicke, und nie mehr wieder ist mir ein Mensch so liebenswert erschienen wie damals meine Mutter!"

Ein anderer Patient leidet u. a. daran, daß er kein Körpergefühl für seinen Penis hat. In solchen Stunden ist er nicht imstande sich vorzustellen, daß der Analytiker ein Genitale hat. In dem gleichen Maße, wie sein Körpergefühl für seinen Penis zurückkehrt, kann er sich auch das Genitale des Analytikers vorstellen. Wenn der Patient in seiner beruflichen Tätigkeit eine Anerkennung gefunden hat, so fühlt er seinen Penis und stellt sich auch den Analytiker mit einem großen Penis vor; hatte der Patient im Beruf Mißerfolg, so verliert der Analytiker sein Genitale.

Tausk meint: „Wir können also sagen, bei einer krankhaft veränderten Libido findet das Ich eine verrückte Welt zu bewältigen, und darum benimmt es sich verrückt."

Goethe sagt:

> Willst du dich deines Werts erfreu'n,
> So mußt der Welt du Wert verleih'n.

Daß bei gehobenem Selbstgefühl die Welt liebenswert erscheint, ist allgemein bekannt. — Verkehrungen ins Gegenteil, Verwechslungen von Ursache und Wirkung, Umkehrungen überhaupt sind uns aus der Traumdeutung schon lange bekannt.

Bei der Identifizierung auf der Objektstufe nimmt das Ich eine Qualität des Objektes an; letzteres bleibt jedoch in der Außenwelt und ist durch das Ich nicht beeinflußbar, d. h. das Ich fühlt, daß das Objekt seine ihm eigene Qualität beibehält. Bei der primären Identifizierung, bzw. deren Umkehrung wird eine Gleichheit zumindest des Affektes, bzw. Triebes bei Objekt und Subjekt als vorhanden gefühlt.

*

Wir hörten früher, daß das Objekt durch wiederholte Befriedigungssituationen geschaffen wurde. Wir können jetzt sagen: Ist das Objekt einmal vorhanden, so wird, so oft es vorgestellt wird, das Früh-Ich geändert.

Aus zwei Gründen ist die primäre Identifizierung nachhaltig. Erstens: Sie erfolgt mit der ganzen narzißtischen Libido und verändert das ganze Individuum. Zweitens: Sie erfolgt nach dem Lustprinzip und hat zur Folge, daß das Individuum sich als lustvolles Subjekt erlebt. Anders jene Identifizierung, welche uns nach der Aufklärung der Melancholie die Bildung des Ichs aus dem Früh-Ich hat verstehen lassen. Diese Identifizierungen kommen zustande, wenn ein Sexualobjekt aufgegeben werden muß. Weil dies ein schmerzhafter Verzicht auf das begehrte Objekt ist, ist der Vorgang sehr unlustvoll. Deswegen können die Wirkungen dieser — das Ich bildenden — Identifizierungen nicht so stabil sein. Der Verzicht wird nämlich — nach Nunberg sogar in allen Fällen — nur mit einer *reservatio mentalis* geleistet. „Die Tendenz, das Ich mit dem Es immer wieder von neuem zu vereinigen, ihre Einheit zu wahren, geht niemals gänzlich verloren, wenn sie auch im Einzelfalle gestört sein mag. In dieser selbstgenügsamen Einheit erfolgt am Ich die Befriedigung des Narzißmus des Es. Ein Bestreben, die Differenzierung zwischen Ich und Es rückgängig zu machen, die auseinandergehenden psychischen Kräfte wieder miteinander zu vereinigen und zu verschmelzen, ist unverkennbar" (Nunberg [2]). Es besteht das Bestreben, das Ich in das Früh-Ich rückzuverwandeln, oder anders ausgedrückt: die das Ich bildende Identifizierung zugunsten der primären Identifizierung aufzugeben.

Die das Ich bildende Identifizierung erfolgt, im Gegensatz zur primären, nicht mehr mit der ganzen Libido. Letzteres war möglich, solange nur eine einheitliche narzißtische Libido bestand. Die das Ich bildende Identifizierung bedeutet infolge Entlassung des Objektes aus dem Früh-Ich eine Zerstörung der bis jetzt vorhandenen narzißtischen Einheit. Wo jedoch auch die das Ich formende Identifizierung mit der gesamten Libido erfolgt, kommt es zur Melancholie. So mag es zu verstehen sein, daß der Melancholiker neben dem Kleinheitswahn stets auch den Größenwahn zeigt, beispielsweise der „größte Verbrecher aller Zeiten" zu sein.

Die primäre Identifizierung erfolgt vor der Objektbesetzung, die das Ich bildende hingegen hat eine Besetzung des Objektes zur Voraussetzung. Wir dürfen jedoch nicht annehmen, daß mit der Objektbesetzung die primäre Identifizierung aufgehört hat. Da im Psychischen nichts verlorengeht, so muß im Stadium der Objektbesetzung auch das der primären Identifizierung erhalten bleiben. Das Objekt wird also begehrt, nicht nur zwecks Beseitigung der Bedürfnisspannung, sondern auch wegen der Lust, die in der primären Identifizierung enthalten ist.

Nach Freud sind in der primitiven oralen Phase Objektbesetzung und Identifizierung „wohl nicht voneinander zu unterscheiden". Später finden Oszillationen zwischen beiden statt. Eine Regression von der Objektbesetzung zur Identifizierung zeigte die Patientin folgendermaßen: Ihre Sehnsucht, in die Kirche zu gehen und dort in Andacht zu versinken, hatte sie seit ihrer Kindheit. Als vorschulpflichtiges Kind hatte sie vom Christkind gehört, das alles Gute zu verteilen habe und überhaupt allmächtig sei. Sie begann zu wünschen, daß das Christkind auch sie besuchen möge. Die Patientin sagte wörtlich: „So sehr habe ich mich nach dem Christkind gesehnt, daß ich den ganzen Tag daran gedacht habe; ich wünschte, daß es ständig bei mir ist, und zwar ganz nahe, noch näher, so nahe, daß schließlich jeder Zwischenraum zwischen uns verschwunden ist, und wir eins geworden sind. Dann bin ich im Besitze aller Geschenke, die es zu vergeben hat, und bin selbst das allmächtige Christkind."

*

Nach Entlassung des Objektes aus dem Früh-Ich in die Außenwelt und nach Besetzung des Objektes mit Objektlibido stellt sich zwischen dieser und der Ich-Libido das bekannte Korrelationsverhältnis nach dem Muster zweier kommunizierender Gefäße her: Je mehr die eine für sich verbraucht, desto mehr verarmt die andere. Anders ist die Situation auf der Stufe der Besetzung des Objektes mit narzißtischer Libido, die der das Ich bildenden Identifizierung vorausgeht. Nach der Gleichung „sich das lustspendende Objekt vorstellen, bedeutet: sein Ich — das Früh-Ich — lustvoll fühlen" ergibt sich für diese Stufe: Je stärker die Besetzung des Objektes, desto stärker das Selbstgefühl, desto lustvoller das Früh-Ich. So kommt es, daß Ferenczi(2) jede Objektliebe als eine Ausweitung des Ichs auffaßt. Die Verarmung des Ichs an Libido zugunsten des Objektes, die Freud beschreibt, betrifft das Ich nach Vollzug der das Ich bildenden Identifizierung, während die Ausweitung des Ichs nach Ferenczi für das Früh-Ich Geltung hat. Für das Früh-Ich hat das Objekt die Funktion, das Selbstgefühl zu steigern; für das Ich hingegen ist das Objekt Träger einer „auffälligen Sexualüberschätzung, welche wohl dem ursprünglichen Narzißmus des Kindes entstammt und somit einer Übertragung desselben auf das Sexualobjekt entspricht" (Freud [1]). Um den Betrag der Sexualüberschätzung verarmt das Ich an Libido.

Wie verhält sich nun das Ich, bzw. Früh-Ich bei der Süchtigkeit? Fenichel nennt die Süchtigkeit einen Reizschutz nach innen, der sekundär lustvoll geworden ist. Aber wovor soll geschützt werden, und worin besteht das Lustvolle dieses Schutzes bei der Süchtigkeit? Geschützt wird offenbar vor der alten Gefahr, die in der erhöhten Bedürfnisspannung besteht; sie zu beseitigen, war die erste Aufgabe der Objekte. Geschützt wird also immer auch vor dem Objektverlust. Es ist die Frage, wie das reife Ich sich bei einem solchen Objektverlust verhält, und wie das Früh-Ich. Das reife Ich wird auf den eingetretenen Objektverlust mit der normalen Trauer reagieren, einen drohenden Objektverlust aber realitätsangepaßt hintanzuhalten trachten. Anders das Früh-Ich: Droht diesem ein Objektverlust, so betrifft er ja nicht das mit Objektlibido besetzte, also in der Außenwelt gefühlte Objekt, sondern das zum Früh-Ich gehörige. Wegen der primärnarzißtischen Besetzung der Vorstellung — das Vorgestellte wird sofort g e f ü h l t — bedeutet auch der drohende Objektverlust soviel wie der tatsächlich eingetretene. Wenn das Objekt als nicht vorhanden gefühlt wird, so fehlt dem Früh-Ich die Möglichkeit erstens: Schutz zu haben vor der Angst, d. i. jener großartigen Störung in der Ökonomie der narzißtischen Libido, welche das Geburtserlebnis einmal tatsächlich gebracht hatte; zweitens: die volle Befriedigung der narzißtischen Libido zu erlangen, d. h. sich selbst lustvoll zu fühlen. Deshalb ist für das Früh-Ich der drohende Objektverlust gleichzeitig ein drohender Ich-Verlust, bei welchem die gesamte Libido in Aktion tritt. Deshalb bleibt keine Instanz übrig, die ein Ertragen der Spannung, ein Beherrschen des Triebes ermöglichen könnte.

Lustvoll wird der Schutz sekundär dadurch, daß die Introjektion des schützenden Objektes eine Ausweitung des Früh-Ichs zur Folge hat. F e n i c h e l sagt wörtlich: „Aber der vermittelte Genuß hat, wie R a d o wahrscheinlich gemacht hat, auch hier am ehesten Ähnlichkeit mit der Befriedigung des gesättigten Säuglings, die er den ‚alimentären Orgasmus‘ nennt. Wahrscheinlich gemacht wird das vor allem durch den Umstand, daß das hervorstechendste Moment des Rauscherlebnisses die überwältigende Erhöhung des Selbstgefühls ist." Durch die Bezeichnung „alimentär" hat R a d o ausgedrückt, daß die Erhöhung des Selbstgefühles — anders ausgedrückt: die Ausweitung des Früh-Ichs — durch Befriedigung des oralen Triebes bewirkt wird. Wenn es aber richtig ist, daß die totale narzißtische Befriedigung auch von anderen Quellen her erreichbar ist, so würde dem oralen Trieb für das Zustandekommen der Süchtigkeit nicht die Bedeutung der einzigen Ursache zukommen. Die orale Libido hätte dann nur insofern Bedeutung, als deren Fixierung die Weiterentwicklung des Ichs, bzw. Früh-Ichs gestört und so zu einer geringeren Resistenzfähigkeit geführt hätte.

*

„In den tiefsten Schichten der Psyche wie beim Beginne der psychischen Entwicklung herrscht noch das rohe Unlustprinzip, der Drang nach unmittelbarer motorischer Befriedigung der Libido; das ist die Schichte (oder das Stadium) des Autoerotismus nach F r e u d. Diese Region in der Schichtung der Psyche eines Erwachsenen ist als direkte Reproduktion meist nicht mehr

34

zu erreichen; sie muß aus ihren Symptomen erschlossen werden. Was reprodu-
zierbar ist, gehört zumeist schon der Schichte (dem Stadium) der Objektliebe
(Freud) an..." (Ferenczi [3]). Den Grund für die Schwierigkeit, in so frühe
Stadien vorzudringen, hat uns Freud (2) erklärt, indem er sagte, daß der seelische Apparat vor der scharfen Sonderung von Ich und Es andere Methoden
der Abwehr übt. Wir dürfen annehmen, daß auch die Besetzungen in anderer
Art gemacht werden. Die öfters erwähnte Patientin ließ einen neuen Einblick
in die Art und Weise dieser Mechanismen gewähren.

Schon die Übertragungssituation bot ein etwas ungewöhnliches Bild, und zwar
so, daß die Patientin vom Beginne an paranoid in bezug auf den Analytiker eingestellt war. Die ersten Worte, mit denen sie diese ihre zweite Analyse begann,
drückten ihre Überzeugung aus, daß der Analytiker mit ihr ein Liebesverhältnis anfangen werde. In der ersten Analyse sei es nur deswegen nicht zu
einem Liebesverhältnis gekommen, weil ihr erster Analytiker eine Frau war.
Wenn sie auch wisse, daß dem Analytiker seine Vorschriften es verbieten, mit
ihr werde er dennoch eine Ausnahme machen. Daß der Analytiker sie liebe,
sei doch schon durch die Tatsache bewiesen, daß er sie analysiere. Es sei doch
unmöglich — äußeren Zwang ausgenommen —, sich mit einem Menschen ab-
zugeben, den man nicht liebt. Der Analytiker dürfe seine Liebe nur nicht zur
Kenntnis bringen, da dies den Gang der Analyse stören würde. Aber er werde
nicht lange widerstehen können.

Diese positiven Beziehungsideen verkehrten sich bald ins Gegenteil. Die
Patientin konnte unvermittelt, ohne Zusammenhang mit dem, was sie gerade
sagte, den Wunsch äußern, die Analyse abzubrechen, da der Analytiker sie
weghaben wolle. Das Wegblasen eines Aschenrestes hatte sie für einen Seufzer
gehalten, und geseufzt konnte der Analytiker doch nur deswegen haben, weil
er mit ihr unzufrieden war. Die Patientin paßte ungemein scharf auf das
Verhalten des Analytikers auf und deutete beispielsweise jede Veränderung
seiner Körperhaltung als ein Zeichen seiner Ungeduld, seines Wunsches, sie weg-
zuschicken; um sich diese Erniedrigung zu ersparen, wollte sie selbst die
Analyse abbrechen.

Die Patientin hatte starke Wünsche nach irgendeiner Gemeinsamkeit mit
dem Analytiker. Sie bot sich zu verschiedenen Diensten an, phantasierte von
gemeinsamen Spaziergängen; sie wünschte zu wissen, was für Bücher der
Analytiker lese; sie wollte die gleichen Bücher lesen, um auf diese Art eine
geistige Gemeinschaft herzustellen. Sie fühlte alles mit, was sich an dem für
sie erkennbaren Leben des Analytikers änderte. Sie war aufgeregt, als er
übersiedelte, und war hochbeglückt, als sie zum erstenmal das neu ein-
gerichtete Warte-, bzw. Ordinationszimmer betrat.

Von den vielen Erscheinungen, die die Patientin bot, waren es zwei, die
lange Zeit jedem Verständnisse trotzten: 1. Es zog sie immer zu einer be-

stimmten Stelle der Stadt hin, wo sie mit Begeisterung bestimmte Brunnen-figuren betrachtete; 2. eine ähnliche starke Sensation (Ekstase?) drohte sie zu überkommen, wenn sie in der Analyse von der geometrischen Figur eines Kreises zu sprechen begann.

Ein beinahe unmerkliches Agieren in der Außenwelt ermöglichte ein Ver-ständnis für diese Erscheinungen und ihre Analyse. Die Patientin schwimmt sehr gerne, und zwar seit vielen Jahren immer in einem nahe ihrer Wohnung gelegenen Schwimmbad. Eines Tages begann sie eine Schwimmhalle zu be-suchen, die ziemlich weit entfernt von ihrer eigenen, wohl aber in nächster Nähe der Wohnung des Analytikers gelegen war. Sie brachte eine Menge Rationalisierungen, denn es war ihr unbewußt, daß sie dies getan hatte in der Hoffnung, mit dem Analytiker dort zusammenzutreffen. Die Vorstellung, mit dem Analytiker gemeinsam in demselben Bassin zu schwimmen, war für sie sehr lustvoll. Alte Exhibitions-, bzw. Voyeurwünsche machten sich geltend. Die Phantasie änderte sich bald dahin, daß beide — Patientin und Analytiker — in einem gemeinsamen Moorbad liegen. Hier erinnerte die Patientin früh-kindliche Begebenheiten. Es war für sie eine besondere Lust, daß der Vater sie ins Bett nahm. Sie erinnert sich deutlich der Wärme und der Ausdünstung — zu jener Zeit war es für sie Wohlgeruch —, die an dem Bette hafteten und es wohlig warm machten. Dazu sei erwähnt, daß der Vater sich bis zu seinem Tode keinerlei Zwang in seinen analen Betätigungen auferlegt hatte. Er pflegte ungeniert in Gegenwart der Patientin und deren Mutter Winde zu lassen und auf den Kübel zu gehen. Das gleiche tat auch die Patientin bis lange nach der Pubertät. Eine sehr frühe Erinnerung, verlegt in das Lebens-alter von $1^1/_2$ Jahren, war ihr schon früher aufgetaucht: Sie hatte in das Bett des Vaters defäziert, die Mutter hatte sie angeschrien, der gute Vater jedoch hatte sie gereinigt und vor der bösen Mutter in Schutz genommen. Die Analyse eines Traumes, der um diese Zeit vorfiel, konnte einen noch tieferen Sinn der analen Phantasie der Patientin ergeben. Der Traum lautet: *Sie sitzt auf einem Klosett und defäziert. Durch den herabfallenden Kot wird ein Rad, das sich in der Klosettmuschel befindet, und das sie mit ihrem Körper berührt, in Rotation versetzt.* Bei der Besprechung dieses Traumes geriet die Patientin in einen Er-regungszustand. Schon früher hatten die vom Kreis ausgehenden Assoziations-ketten in eine bestimmte Richtung gewiesen, z. B. Kreis — Mond — fran-zösisch *la lune* — vulgäre Bezeichnung für das Gesäß. Oder: Kreis — zwei Halbkreise, wie die Gesetzestafeln Mosis — Horizontalschnitt durch die Nates usw. Die Analyse des Traumes ergab eine Phantasie, die die Patientin unter starkem Affekt und nur äußerst widerwillig preisgab. Sie lautet: Sie und der Vater defäzieren gleichzeitig gegenseitig jeder in den After des anderen. Sie erinnert sich der Lust, welche ihr die Vorstellung der sich gegen-einander bewegenden Kotstangen machte. Dabei sind sie und der Vater eins, ein einziger Körper. In dieser Phantasie besteht für die Patientin eine Einheit zwischen ihr und dem geliebten Objekt, das höchste Glücksgefühl, das die Patientin kennt.

Auch der Kreis gewann hier eine neue Bedeutung. Er war nicht nur wegen seiner Form ein Symbol für die Körperrundungen, sondern hatte als Begriff, ähnlich wie für den Patienten, über den Weizsäcker berichtete, viel tiefere Bedeutung. Der Kreis stelle etwas in sich Geschlossenes dar. Wenn man sich von einem bestimmten Punkte aus bewege, so komme man zu dem gleichen Punkt zurück, wobei es gar keinen Unterschied mache, ob man sich rechts herum oder links herum, oben herum oder unten herum bewegt habe. Gerade die Vorstellung, daß man so gar nicht darauf zu achten brauche, ob man sich nach der einen oder nach der entgegengesetzten Seite bewege, daß man sich sogar gleichzeitig nach beiden einander entgegengesetzten Richtungen bewegen könne und unter allen Umständen wieder den ersehnten Ausgangspunkt erreiche, bringe sie so in Erregung.

Wenn die Assoziationsreihe nicht zu den Nates führte, so bestand sie aus einer einzigen Vorstellung: „Es dreht sich alles um mich herum." Aus Angst, es könnte sie ein Schwindel befallen, lehnte sie das weitere Assoziieren ab. Nachdem starke Widerstände beseitigt worden waren, ergab sich Gelegenheit, eine weitere Bedeutung des Kreises zu finden. Wenn die Patientin sich einen Koitus vorstellte, so gebrauchte sie stereotyp die gleichen Worte „wir liegen übereinander". Diese „Fehlleistung" war das Resultat folgender Phantasie: Der Koitus beginnt in normaler Lage, doch bald legt sie sich über den Mann, dann wieder der Mann über sie usw. Diese Drehungen werden immer rascher und rascher, so daß schließlich ein einziger Körper vorhanden ist, der in rasender Rotation begriffen ist. Sie erinnerte das Schulexperiment, bei welchem eine Scheibe mit verschieden gefärbten Teilen bei rascher Rotation eine einzige Farbe annimmt. Bei dem so phantasierten Koitus machte es für die Patientin gar nichts aus, ob der Mann sein Glied in ihrer Scheide hatte oder nicht. Das Lustvolle war das Einssein mit dem anderen. Von dieser Phantasie führte auch ein Weg zum Verständnis des Interesses an den Brunnenfiguren. Diese überrasche Rotation nannte die Patientin das „Chaos", nach welchem sie sich sehnte. Die Brunnenfiguren stellten für sie wegen der verschlungenen und verrenkten Gliedmaßen auch eine Art Chaos dar. Nach diesem Chaos hatte sie sich als ganz kleines Kind gesehnt, als sie einen Koitus der Eltern beobachtete. Sie wünschte mit als dritte im Bunde zu sein. Sie sagte wörtlich: „Ich muß verrückt gewesen sein: Ich wünschte sowohl der Vater zu sein als auch die Mutter, als auch das Kind. Irgendwie hätten wir alle drei uns zu einer einzigen Masse vermischen sollen."

In noch einem Zusammenhange kehrte der Kreis wieder. Die Patientin träumte: „Ich liege im Bette nur mit einem Nachthemd bekleidet. Mein Vater neigt sich über mich und küßt meine linke Brust. Gleichzeitig führt er sein Glied in meine Scheide ein. Das ist der lustvollste Verkehr." Dieser Traum enthielt in genitalem

Gewande einen oralen Wunsch. Sie läßt den Vater trinken, und gleichzeitig läßt der Vater sie mit ihrem unteren Mund an seiner Brust, d. h. Penis, saugen. Die Milch durchläuft also einen Kreis. In diesem Traum durchlebte die Patientin wieder einmal das „Kinderwagerlgefühl". So nannte sie nämlich das Glücksgefühl, das sie genoß, wenn sie in ihrem Kinderwagen lag und die Mutter sich über sie neigte.

Was die Patientin wünscht, ist: eins zu sein mit dem Objekt. Die erogenen Zonen sind für sie vor allem ein Mittel, diese Einheit zu erreichen. Bei dieser Einheit gibt es keine Trennung nach Ich und Objekt; sie nimmt die Form des Objektes an, das Objekt die Form ihres Ichs. Sie träumte einmal: *„Ich bin in einem Spital und soll operiert werden. Der Arzt nähert sich mir mit einem langen Messer und operiert an meinem Genitale. Jetzt werde ich befähigt sein, ein Kind zu gebären."* Die Analyse ergab: Sie trägt ständig ein Kind, d. h. einen Penis in sich. Der Vater sollte ihr durch seinen Penis den in ihrem Leib verborgenen herausheben. Wenn der Vater mit seinem Penis etwas tut, so nur zu dem Zwecke, um mit ihrem Penis zusammen zu sein. Wenn der Analytiker seine geistigen Fähigkeiten bei ihr verwendet, so tut er dies doch nur, um die verborgenen Fähigkeiten zu wecken, die in der Patientin schlummern.

Bei der Besprechung dieses Traumes phantasierte die Patientin eine Liebesszene mit dem Analytiker. Plötzlich sprang sie auf. Nachdem sie sich beruhigt hatte, gab sie an, ihr Körper sei plötzlich ganz unnatürlich groß geworden, sie sei ganz hart und steif geworden. Diese Sensation habe sie bei der Vorstellung überkommen, daß sie das Glied des Analytikers in die Hand nehme und dieses groß und steif würde.

Diese Sensation der Patientin zeigt, daß sie die Vorstellungen primärnarzißtisch besetzt. Wenn sie an das Glied denkt, so ist sie selbst ein Glied. Was dem Objekt geschieht, geschieht auch ihrem Ich.

Auch die Vorliebe für das Schwimmen entsprang — abgesehen von Voyeurund Exhibitionswünschen — der Sehnsucht nach Einheit. Sie phantasiert, „mit dem unendlichen Ozean vermischt zu sein"; ihr Wunsch, daß ihre eigenen „Körpergrenzen" aufhören mögen, wird ihr im Wasser zum Teil befriedigt. Sie fügte hinzu: „Es ist so unendlich traurig, hier steht ein Mensch allein, dort steht ein Mensch allein, jeder einsam für sich. Warum sind sie so abgegrenzt voneinander?"

Nachdem die Patientin erkannt hatte, daß ihre erotischen Triebe ein Mittel waren, um mit dem Objekt zu verschmelzen, erinnerte sie eine Phantasie, die sie vom 4. bis zum 6. Lebensjahr beherrscht hat. Soweit sie sich erinnern kann, hat sie stets bedauert, das einzige Kind ihrer Eltern zu sein. Sie wäre glücklich, wenn sie eine Schwester hätte. Vom 4. bis 6. Lebensjahr nun phantasierte sie, daß sie eine Zwillingsschwester habe, mit der sie als siamesisches Zwillingspaar verwachsen lebe. Diese Phantasie befriedigte ihren Wunsch, mit einem geliebten Objekt verwachsen zu sein, und dieses Objekt wurde des-

25*

wegen so geliebt, weil es gleichzeitig ihr Ich war. Als eine ihrer Bekannten einem Zwillingspaar das Leben schenkte, konnte die Patientin durch Wochen von nichts anderem sprechen.

Auch bei anderen Patienten war ein ähnliches Verlangen nach der Einheit des Ichs mit dem Objekt und dem gleichzeitigen zentrifugalen und zentripetalen Strömen der Libido zwischen beiden zu beobachten. Ein 35jähriger, akademisch gebildeter Mann brachte folgende Erinnerung: Er ist ein Kind von noch nicht zwei Jahren. Er soll defäzieren, kann aber nicht, und die Mutter legt ihre Handfläche auf seinen nackten Bauch. Er empfindet ein Glücksgefühl dabei und defäziert. Er war voll Liebe und Dankbarkeit der Mutter gegenüber und wünschte auch ihr das gleiche Glücksgefühl zu bereiten. Der Patient äußerte seinen Zweifel darüber, ob er der Mutter aus Dankbarkeit seine Hand auf den Bauch legen wollte, oder ob er der Mutter zuerst diesen Liebesdienst erweisen wollte, damit sie sich ihm gegenüber in der gleichen Art revanchiere. Plötzlich schwieg der Patient einige Augenblicke. Er berichtete, daß er während des Schweigens ein intensives Glücksgefühl genossen habe; er hatte sich vorgestellt, wie er und die Mutter gleichzeitig ihre Handflächen auf dem Bauch des Gegenübers liegen haben. Das Beglückende lag für ihn eben darin, daß er „unbeschwert von jeder Logik und jedem Kausalitätsbedürfnis" fühlen konnte, er und die Mutter erwiesen einander gleichzeitig den gleichen Liebesdienst. Wenn er anfange nachzudenken, ob einer von den beiden und welcher angefangen, bzw. reagiert habe, so werde das Ganze ein Geschäft und habe mit Liebe nichts mehr zu tun. Das Glücksgefühl verschwand in dem Augenblicke, als die logische Funktion des Ichs eintrat, d. h. die Besetzung vom Früh-Ich auf das Ich verschoben wurde.

Ein Patient wurde einmal bei der Lektüre einer kleinen Arbeit über Palindrome von Glücksgefühl überkommen. Er fand dort etwas über das sogenannte Satansquadrat. Dieses Quadrat besteht aus fünf Wörtern, jedes zu fünf Buchstaben. Aneinandergereiht lauten diese Wörter:

SATOR — AREPO — TENET — OPERA — ROTAS.

Er wollte sich überzeugen, ob diese fünf Wörter vor- und rückwärts gelesen wirklich gleichlauten. In dem Momente, als er in Eile gleichzeitig vor- und rückwärts lesen wollte, empfand er ein wohliges Gefühl. Die Empfindung, daß etwas gleichzeitig nach zwei entgegengesetzten Richtungen geht, hatte ihm das wohlige Gefühl verschafft.

Ein vierter Patient, ein 28jähriger Handwerker mit starker Begeisterungsfähigkeit, schilderte einmal, wie gut es ihm ergangen sein mag, als er noch an der Mutterbrust trinken durfte. In seiner übertreibenden Art beschrieb er, wie glücklich er gewesen, als die Mutter noch so gut zu ihm war, und wie sehr er die Mutter damals geliebt hatte. Er rief dann aus: „Zu jener Zeit hat zwischen meiner Mutter und mir die heilige Zweieinigkeit bestanden!" Er begründete dann dieses neue Wort „Zweieinigkeit" in Analogie zu dem kirchlichen Begriff der Dreieinigkeit. Er und die Mutter hätten zusammen ein einziges Wesen gebildet. Wäre dieses Wesen entzweigeschnitten worden, so hätten beide Teile — einzeln — keine Existenz mehr gehabt. Denn er fühlte, daß die Mutter, wenn sie ihn nicht säugte, einfach nicht existierte, und damit die Welt überhaupt zu existieren aufgehört hatte. Gab ihm die Mutter zu trinken, so floß ein Strom von Liebe von der Mutter zu ihm — in Form der Milch —, aber auch von ihm zur Mutter — er meinte in Form des Harnes. Der Patient glaubte, wenn er heute fähig wäre, das gleiche zu empfinden, wie er es als Säugling empfunden haben mußte, so wäre er imstande, sich die Unsterblichkeit zu erringen. Denn eine solche „Zweieinigkeit" sei nicht etwa die Addition der Fähigkeiten zweier Menschen, sondern sie hole das Letzte heraus, was ein Mensch in sich trage, und befähige ihn geradezu, die ganze Welt zu ändern, z. B. auf dem Wege der Politik oder Literatur.

Diese Stufe der Entwicklung des Ichs, die der Patient als „Zweieinigkeit" bezeichnete, und für welche die erwähnten Patienten Beispiele bieten, läßt sich folgendermaßen beschreiben: Es besteht keine Trennung zwischen dem Objekt und dem Früh-Ich. Es hat einerseits eine primäre, demnach totale Identifizierung mit dem Objekt stattgefunden, anderseits eine Umkehrung dieser Identifizierung, d. h. eine Angleichung des Objektes an das Früh-Ich. Was an Trieben oder Affekten gespürt wird, wird in ganz der gleichen Weise als auch beim Objekt vorhanden empfunden. Der Strom der Liebe — um mit den Worten des Patienten zu reden — geht gleichartig vom Früh-Ich zum Objekt und vom Objekt zum Früh-Ich. Die Bezeichnung „gleichartig" will hier und im folgenden besagen: Es wird völlige Identität der beiden Libidoströme in bezug auf Qualität, Intensität und zeitlichen Ablauf gefühlt. Es wird doch die gleiche narzißtische Libido von dem dem Früh-Ich gleichenden, sich somit wie ein Spiegel verhaltenden Objekt reflektiert.

In höherer Schichte dient die Einheit mit dem Objekt der sexuellen Verdrängung, der Erleichterung des sexuellen Dimorphismus.

Die Verschmelzung von Ich und Objekt, das Einswerden mit dem All, die *unio mystica* ist als Ziel aller Mystiker bekannt. Die Ubiquität dieser Erscheinung hat auch Helene Deutsch hervorgehoben, indem sie schrieb: „Jeder ästhetische Genuß, mag er bei der Betrachtung einer Landschaft oder eines Kunstgegenstandes entstehen, bei der Lektüre einer Dichtung oder beim Hören von Musik, immer kennzeichnet er sich dadurch, daß zwischen dem Ich und dem von der Außenwelt zuströmenden Eindruck auf dem Wege der Einfühlung eine Ich-Welt-Identität entsteht. Das Beglückende ist eben in diesem Identitätsgefühl zu suchen."

Auch Jekels und Bergler sehen das Wesentliche der Liebe in der Re-Introjektion des Objektes ins Ich. Sie schreiben: „Steckt doch hinter dem geliebten Objekt eigentlich das eigene, im manischen

Rausch des Geliebtwerdens schwelgende Ich, das das Objekt für würdig befunden hat, das Allerwertvollste auf Erden, sein Ich-Ideal, in der Wirklichkeit zu vertreten."

Bei dem Zustande der Einheit zwischen Objekt und Ich muß genau unterschieden werden, wieweit es sich um die Wiedervereinigung mit dem bereits in die Außenwelt entlassen gewesenen, mit Objektlibido besetzten Objekte handelt (Re-Introjektion) und wieweit um die daneben bestehende „Zweieinigkeit", d. h. jene Entwicklungsstufe, auf der das Objekt noch nicht mit anderer als narzißtischer Libido besetzt ist. Anders ausgedrückt: wieweit die Einheit zwischen Objekt und Ich besteht und daneben zwischen Objekt und Früh-Ich.

Diese Unterscheidung ist deswegen so bedeutsam, weil die „Zweieinigkeit" uns ein Verständnis der Projektion ermöglicht.

Freud (6) äußert sich über die Projektion folgendermaßen: „..., daß sie nicht nur bei Paranoia, sondern auch unter anderen Verhältnissen im Seelenleben vorkommt, ja, daß ihr ein regelmäßiger Anteil in unserer Einstellung zur Außenwelt zugewiesen ist. Wenn wir die Ursachen gewisser Sinnesempfindungen nicht wie die anderer in uns selbst suchen, sondern sie nach außen verlegen, so verdient auch dieser normale Vorgang den Namen einer Projektion." Ferner: „Eine innere Wahrnehmung wird unterdrückt, und zum Ersatz für sie kommt ihr Inhalt, nachdem er eine gewisse Entstellung erfahren hat, als Wahrnehmung von außen zum Bewußtsein."

Wie ist nun die Beziehung zwischen Projektion und „Zweieinigkeit"? In dem Zustande der Zweieinigkeit geht der „Strom der Liebe" gleichartig vom Subjekt zum Objekt und umgekehrt. Es ist dies nur narzißtische Libido. Subjekt und Objekt fühlen das gleiche. Ist der Zustand der „Zweieinigkeit" noch ungestört, so müßte das Individuum sagen: „Ich und mein Gegenüber, wir haben die ganz gleichen Gefühle, die ganz gleichen Gedanken." Auf dieser Stufe besteht noch kein Grund, den Empfindungen, die sowohl „innen" als auch „außen" vorhanden sind, das Wohnrecht im „Innen" zu entziehen.

Ein Beispiel einfachster Art für diesen Vorgang: Jemand bekommt unerwartet Besuch, über den er sehr erfreut ist. Als Motiv für den Besuch setzt er bei dem Gast etwas voraus, was ihm selbst (dem Besuchten) Freude bereiten würde. Er fühlt, daß ihm der Gast etwas „Gutes" erweist, bzw. erweisen wird und wünscht, dem Gaste auch etwas „Gutes" zu tun; nicht etwa, das „Gute" auf Grund einer verstandesgemäßen Überlegung zu vergelten, sondern aus einer rein gefühlsmäßigen liebevollen Einstellung. So gleichen alle dem Patienten, der sein Glücksgefühl nur dann genoß, wenn er sich „unbeschwert von jeder Logik und jedem Kausalitätsbedürfnis" vorstellte, daß er und die Mutter gegenseitig die Handflächen auf dem Bauch des Gegenübers liegen haben; sobald er nachzudenken begann, wer provoziert, und wer sich revanchiert hatte, hörte die Liebe auf, und das Ganze wurde ein Geschäft.

Unser Gastgeber wird etwa seinem Besucher etwas anbieten, was er selbst für „gut" hält, und wovon er fühlt, daß es auch der Gast für „gut" halten wird. Das wäre ein einfachster Fall von „Zweieinigkeit", wo der „Strom der Liebe" noch ungestört gleichartig zentrifugal und zentripetal sich bewegt.

Man wird fragen, ob derlei Regressionen zu so frühen Entwicklungsstufen wirklich so ubiquitär sind, ob sie wirklich so häufig im alltäglichen Leben vorhanden sind. Diese Frage ist zu bejahen. Erinnern wir uns: Wenn ein psychischer Akt nicht entfremdet erlebt werden soll, so muß die mit narzißtischer Libido besetzte Ich-Grenze an die mit Objektlibido besetzte Vorstellung des Objektes herankommen. Vorübergehend kann eine Erweiterung der Ich-Grenze eintreten. Für kurze Zeit kann es zu einem Überschwemmen des Objektes mit narzißtischer Libido kommen, kann jener Zustand wiederhergestellt werden, wie er einstmals, nämlich vor der Freigabe des Objektes in die Außenwelt, bestanden hatte (Federn [2]). Solange dieser vorübergehende Zustand andauert, solange besteht „Zweieinigkeit". Werden Früh-Ich und Objekt voneinander abgegrenzt, hat die Ich-Grenze sich wieder zurückgezogen, befindet sich das Objekt wieder ganz in der Außenwelt, so hat auch die „Zweieinigkeit" aufgehört.

Wenn in unserem Beispiele der unerwartete Besuch Befürchtungen betreffs des Besuchszweckes beim Besuchten hervorruft, so wird dieser leicht seinem Gast ein Motiv zuschieben, das diesem zwar fernliegt, aber im Bewußtsein des Besuchten aufgestiegen ist. Es ist dies ein Fall, von dem wir sagen können, daß die Ursache einer Empfindung nach außen verlegt wurde. Auch in diesem Falle besteht „Zweieinigkeit" zwischen Besucher und Besuchtem; doch ist diese nicht mehr ungestört, es ist vielmehr zur Projektion gekommen.

Normale und paranoische Projektion haben beide den gleichen Mechanismus: Das Subjekt fühlt, daß das Objekt ihm etwas zusendet; es hält dies für eine spontane Äußerung des letzteren. Wir wissen, daß das Objekt nichts anderes tut, als ganz das gleiche zurückzusenden, was es vom Subjekt erhalten hat. Dies kann nur sein, wenn zwischen Subjekt und Objekt jene Gleichheit besteht, wie sie vor der Entlassung des Objektes in die Außenwelt durch die primäre Identifizierung, bzw. deren Umkehrung herbeigeführt wird; wenn also das Objekt noch nicht eine ihm eigene Qualität hat, sondern — bildlich ausgedrückt — das Spiegelbild des Subjektes ist. In diesem Stadium geht ein Strom narzißtischer Libido vom Objekt zum Subjekt (ergibt die primäre Identifizierung) und gleichartig vom Subjekt zum Objekt (ergibt die Umkehrung der primären Identifizierung) — es ist das Stadium der „Zweieinigkeit". Die Projektion entsteht auf dem Boden der „Zweieinigkeit": Wenn nämlich der Inhalt des vom Subjekt zum Objekt gehenden Libidostromes unbewußt, bzw. entstellt worden ist, dann fühlt das Subjekt, daß es etwas erhält, ohne zu wissen, daß es selbst es aussendet.

Bei ungestörter „Zweieinigkeit" wird der Psychotiker das Bild des positiven Beziehungswahnes bieten; der entsprechende Fall des Normalen würde durch das vorhin erwähnte Beispiel des freudig überraschenden Besuches dargestellt sein. In beiden Fällen besteht kein Grund, das Aussenden der Libido, bzw. das Empfangen derselben zu inhibieren. Anders wenn die „Zweieinigkeit" durch Unbewußtwerden, bzw. Entstellung des vom Subjekt ausgesendeten Libidostromes gestört wird. Dann erhalten wir das Bild der paranoischen (beim Psychotiker), bzw. normalen Projektion.

Die normale Projektion, der ja „ein regelmäßiger Anteil an unserer Einstellung zur Außenwelt zugewiesen ist", ist leicht korrigierbar, genau so leicht oder so schwer, wie der Boden, auf dem die Projektion entstehen kann, die „Zweieinigkeit", korrigierbar ist. Mit anderen Worten: genau so leicht, wie die beschriebene vorübergehende Erweiterung der Ich-Grenze rückgängig gemacht werden kann, d. h. wie das Ich, bzw. Früh-Ich das Objekt wieder in die Außenwelt entlassen, sich von ihm abgrenzen kann.

Wir verstehen jetzt auch, weshalb die Projektion bei Kindern so häufig und so auffallend ist. Wir hörten doch, daß bei ihnen die Vorstellungen der Objekte noch dem Ich zugehören. Das Früh-Ich hat die Objekte noch nicht in die Außenwelt entlassen, es sendet einen Strom narzißtischer Libido zu den Objekten und empfängt den gleichen Strom zurück: Der Zustand der „Zweieinigkeit", auf deren Boden die Projektion entstehen kann, ist viel häufiger zu sehen als beim Erwachsenen.

Wie ist es nun in der Paranoia? Wir wissen, daß hier die Projektion nicht korrigierbar ist. Der Paranoiker hat ja seine Libido zur Gänze in narzißtische umgewandelt und damit das Objekt verloren. Den Restitutionsversuch, der uns das Bild seines Wahnes darbietet, kann er nur mit narzißtischer Libido unternehmen. Je mehr Libido er also an das Objekt aussendet, desto mehr gleicht er es seinem Ich an. Was sein Ich vom Objekt zu empfangen wähnt, ist nichts anderes, als seine eigene narzißtische Libido. Da das Objekt seinem Ich gleicht, funktioniert es wie ein Spiegel: Es wirft die Libido zurück, die das Ich aussendet. Der Paranoiker befindet sich also in dem Zustande der (gestörten) „Zweieinigkeit", doch ist dieser Zustand nicht korrigierbar. Das ist eben das Psychotische, daß die Ich-Regression eine definitive ist, daß den Wahnvorstellungen Wirklichkeitscharakter verliehen wird. Für den Paranoiker ist die „Zweieinigkeit" zum Dauerzustand geworden. Da er das Objekt mit Objektlibido nicht besetzen kann, würde er es bei einer Freigabe in die Außenwelt ganz verlieren, also den Restitutionsversuch, der sich uns als Wahn darbietet, rückgängig machen.

Bei normaler Entwicklung wird das Stadium der „Zweieinigkeit" verschwinden und der Anerkennung des Objektes als eines in der Außenwelt vorhandenen, eine andere Qualität als das Früh-Ich habenden Etwas weichen. Nun wissen wir, daß Störungen in der Ökonomie der narzißtischen Libido auch durch Schreckerlebnisse verursacht werden können. Nehmen wir nun an, ein solches Trauma treffe das Individuum gerade in dem Zustand der „Zweieinigkeit" und zerstöre diesen. Es wird das „zweieinige" Wesen gespalten werden in 1. das Früh-Ich und 2. das Objekt, welches vom Früh-Ich so empfunden wird, als wäre es das Früh-Ich selbst. Wir hörten ja, daß eine Umkehrung der primären Identifizierung möglich ist in dem Sinne: Nicht nur mein Ich hat sich dem Objekte angeglichen, sondern ich habe auch das Objekt meinem Ich angeglichen. Die gewaltsam zerrissene „Zweieinigkeit" wird also empfunden werden, als wäre der eine Teil des Früh-Ichs verblieben, und es hätte sich der andere Teil, der durch das Objekt als den Träger der Eigenschaften des Früh-Ichs sozusagen dargestellt wurde, in die Außenwelt entfernt. So mag es zu verstehen sein, daß in der Schizophrenie das eigene Spiegelbild in der Außenwelt gesehen wird. Es sei hier an all die Sagen und Märchen erinnert, in denen geschildert wird, wie jemand dem Teufel sein Spiegelbild oder seinen Schatten verkauft.

Was die Ökonomie betrifft, könnten wir sagen: Je stärker die maximal erstrebte Befriedigung der narzißtischen Libido empfunden wird, desto mehr wird Gleichheit zwischen dem Früh-Ich und dem introjizierten Objekte bestehen. Als Beispiel diene die Phantasie der Patientin, mit einer Zwillingsschwester verwachsen zu sein. Diese Phantasie läßt die Körpergrenzen aufhören und verwandelt das Objekt in das Spiegelbild des eigenen Ichs. Sie unterscheidet sich von der schizophrenen Wahnbildung nur dadurch, daß die Patientin phantasiert, mit ihrem Spiegelbild verbunden zu sein, während der Schizophrene sein Ebenbild in der Außenwelt wirklich sieht.

Von der Patientin wissen wir, daß ihre Sehnsucht dem Zustand der Einheit mit dem Objekte gilt, der mit der beschriebenen „Zweieinigkeit" identisch ist, und den sie dadurch herbeizuführen phantasiert, daß ihre Körpergrenzen und die des Objektes ineinander aufgehen. Die Patientin schildert, daß es ihr ganz gleichgültig sei, auf welchem Wege sie ihr Ziel — die Verschmelzung mit dem Objekte — erreiche. Sie tut so, als vernachlässige sie die Libidopositionen vollständig. Aus den Widerständen bei der Besprechung einzelner Libidostufen ließ sich erkennen, daß starke Affekte verdrängt waren. Festgestellt wurde: Die „Zweieinigkeit" auf genitalem Wege wird durch die normale Annäherung mit dem Objekte — Gesicht gegen Gesicht — erstrebt, ebenso die orale. Auf analem Wege wird die Verschmelzung mit dem Objekte dadurch hergestellt, daß beide sich mit dem Rücken gegeneinander annähern.

Auf dieser frühen Entwicklungsstufe sind die libidinösen Triebe von den Ich-Trieben nicht zu unterscheiden, beide dienen narzißtischen Interessen (Freud[1]). Im Laufe der Entwicklung kommt es zur Verdrängung, und es ist nicht gleichgültig für die Art der Erkrankung, welche Triebe verdrängt wurden. Wir sehen in der Psychose: Sind die erotischen Triebe der Verdrängung anheimgefallen, so haben wir das Bild des Verfolgungswahnes vor uns, bei Verdrängung des Todestriebes hingegen das Bild der Erotomanie.

Auch wird es seine Bedeutung haben, ob das Früh-Ich das Verbot der Triebbefriedigung nur für sich allein akzeptierte oder auch für das introjizierte Objekt. Die erwähnte Patientin z. B. sehnt sich ständig nach der „Zweieinigkeit", sie tut jedoch nichts, um diese herbeizuführen, sondern sie wartet darauf, daß das Objekt dies tue. Sie lebt in einer ekstatischen Hingabe, da sie das Bestehen eines Verbotes der Triebbefriedigung wohl für ihr Ich, jedoch nicht für das introjizierte Objekt angenommen hat.

Vielleicht ließe sich ganz allgemein folgende Formel aufstellen: Mancher Kranke ersehnt die „Zweieinigkeit". Es fragt sich nun, ob er darauf wartet, daß das Objekt diesen Zustand herbeiführt (durch Befriedigung des libidinösen Triebes). Auf dieser Stufe befindet sich die geschilderte Patientin. Hierher könnten auch alle jene Individuen gehören, die eine besondere Bereitschaft zeigen, sich vom Affekte, den sie beim Objekt bemerken, induzieren zu lassen. Anders, wenn das Ich die „Zweieinigkeit" herzustellen bestrebt ist. Hierher dürften jene gehören, die das Objekt mit ihrem eigenen Affekt zu induzieren wünschen, beispielsweise jene Rauschgiftsüchtigen, welche ihre Sucht zu verbreiten trachten.

In der Psychose ist die „Zweieinigkeit" gegeben. Es ist die Frage, auf welche Weise das in Regression befindliche Ich diesen Zustand akzeptiert oder abwehrt. Es können folgende Möglichkeiten bestehen: 1. Ich und Objekt unternehmen beide die Befriedigung; das ergibt den positiven Beziehungswahn, bzw. jene scheinbar überglückliche Liebesbeziehung, die der Psychose häufig vorangeht. 2. Es wird phantasiert, daß das Objekt die gegenseitige Befriedigung unternimmt, das Ich hingegen wehrt ab; dies ergibt die Verfolgungsideen. 3. Das in Regression befindliche Ich bewerkstelligt die Befriedigung, das Objekt ist „neutral"; das ergibt den Welterlösungswahn.

Alle jene Fälle, in denen das Ich, bzw. das Früh-Ich das Verbot für sich wohl akzeptiert, aber für das Objekt das Nichtbestehen des Verbotes angenommen hat, werden in dem Zustande der „Zweieinigkeit" den Mechanismus der Projektion zeigen. Denn nur der vom Subjekt gegen das Objekt gerichtete „Strom der Liebe" mußte unbewußt werden, nicht aber auch der vom Objekt gegen das Subjekt gerichtete.

Daß derlei Beziehungen, die sich von einem Teile des Ichs zu einem anderen abspielen, möglich sind, hat Freud (3) durch folgenden Satz ausgedrückt: „Denken wir daran, daß das Ich nun in die Beziehung eines Objektes zu dem aus ihm entwickelten Ich-Ideal tritt, und daß möglicherweise alle Wechselwirkungen, die wir zwischen äußerem Objekt und Gesamt-Ich in der Neurosenlehre kennengelernt haben, auf diesem neuen Schauplatze innerhalb des Ichs zur Wiederholung kommen." — Wir wollen nicht vergessen: Hinter dem

Ich-Ideal verbirgt sich die erste und bedeutsamste Identifizierung des Individuums, die primäre.

Literaturverzeichnis.

Deutsch, Helene: Über Zufriedenheit, Glück und Ekstase. Int. Ztschr. f. Psa., Bd. XIII,
1927.

Federn: 1. Zunahme der Süchtigkeit. Almanach der Psychoanalyse 1935. 2. Das Ich als
Subjekt und Objekt im Narzißmus. Int. Ztschr. f. Psa., Bd. XV, 1929. 3. Variationen des
Ich-Gefühls, Int. Ztschr. f. Psa., Bd. XII, 1926. 4. Narzißmus im Ich-Gefüge, Int. Ztschr. f.
Psa., Bd. XIII, 1927. 5. Die Ich-Besetzung bei den Fehlleistungen. Imago, Bd. XIX, 1933.
6. Das Erwachen des Ichs im Traume. I. Die Orthiogenese. Int. Ztschr. f. Psa., Bd. XX, 1934.

Fenichel: Perversionen, Psychosen, Charakterstörungen. Int. Psa. Verlag, 1931.

Ferenczi: 1. Entwicklungsstufen des Wirklichkeitssinnes. Int. Ztschr. f. Psa., Bd. I, 1913.
2. Zur Begriffsbestimmung der Introjektion. Zentralblatt f. Psa., Jg. 1912. 3. Introjektion
und Übertragung. Jahrbuch f. psa. und psychopathol. Forschungen, Jg. 1909.

Freud: 1. Zur Einführung des Narzißmus. Ges. Schr., Bd. VI. 2. Hemmung, Symptom
und Angst. Ges. Schr., Bd. XI. 3. Massenpsychologie und Ich-Analyse. Ges. Schr., Bd. VI.
4. Das Unbehagen in der Kultur. Ges. Schr., Bd. XII. 5. Das Ich und das Es. Ges. Schr.,
Bd. VI. 6. Psychoanalytische Bemerkungen über einen autobiographisch-beschriebenen Fall
von Paranoia. Ges. Schr., Bd. VIII.

Glover: Zur Ätiologie der Sucht. Int. Ztschr. f. Psa., Bd. XIX, 1933.

Jekels und Bergler: Übertragung und Liebe. Imago, Bd. XX, 1934.

Nunberg: 1. Allgemeine Neurosenlehre. Verlag Hans Huber, Bern-Berlin. 2. Die syn-
thetische Funktion des Ichs. Int. Ztschr. f. Psa., Bd. XVI, 1930.

Rank: Das Trauma der Geburt. Int. Psa. Verlag, 1924.

Tausk: Über die Entstehung des „Beeinflussungs-Apparates" in der Schizophrenie. Int.
Ztschr. f. Psa., Bd. V, 1919.

Weizsäcker: Körpergeschehen und Neurose. Int. Ztschr. f. Psa., Bd. XIX, 1933.

46

Harntriebäußerungen, insbesondere Enuresis, Urophilie und Uropolemie [1]

Von

Hans Christoffel

Basel

Der Umfang des Stoffes, der uns heute abend beschäftigen soll, kann durch zwei Punkte annähernd angegeben werden. Sie stammen aus dem Lebenswerke desjenigen, der heute seinen 79. Geburtstag begeht, und zu dessen Ehrung Sie diese Sitzung veranstaltet haben: Sigm. Freuds. Die Formulierung der zwei Punkte liegt zeitlich ein Vierteljahrhundert auseinander und kann mit den Jahreszahlen 1905 und 1930 fixiert werden; inhaltlich erstreckt sich der gemeinte Weg von der Entwicklung des einzelnen in der Kinderstube bis zur Problematik der menschlichen Kulturgemeinschaft. Sie erraten, was ich meine. Die beiden Grenzpunkte sind: 1. Die Enuresis der kindlichen Frühblüte, wie sie ihre prägnante Formulierung in den „Drei Abhandlungen..." gefunden hat; 2. das, was in einer Fußnote des „Unbehagens in der Kultur" unter dem Stichwort „Zähmung des Feuers" angedeutet und etwas später unter dem Titel „Zur Gewinnung des Feuers" in einem Imagoaufsatz 1932 ausgeführt ist.

In diesen Rahmen möchte ich dasjenige spannen, was ich, der freundlichen Aufforderung Ihres Herrn Vorsitzenden folgend, Ihnen aus meiner 1934 in der Zeitschrift für Kinderpsychiatrie erschienenen Arbeit „Zur Biologie der Enuresis" vorzutragen das Vergnügen habe. Manches dort Geschriebene muß im Rahmen eines Vortrags unterdrückt werden, anderes, hoffe ich, tritt damit deutlicher hervor. Es sind in erster Linie klinische Ausführungen, die ich Ihnen zu bieten habe. Als Arzt und ethnologischer Laie habe ich nur wenig zum zweiterwähnten Punkte zu sagen. Die Enuresis als somatische Dysergie bei körperlicher Integrität bildet die Basis meiner Betrachtungen. Von ihr aus soll uns das Walten der beiden Triebarten, wie wir es in den Funktionen und Funktionsstörungen des Harnapparates ersehen können, soll uns die Urophilie und Uropolemie, mit welchen Ausdrücken ich Eros und Thanatos in den Harntriebäußerungen unterscheide, bis in die Nähe des zweiten Punktes führen. Bloß bis in die Nähe. Zu mehr reicht es nicht. Wohingegen eine Überschreitung des ersten Punktes, der Enuresis um das 3. bis 4. Lebensjahr, sehr wohl möglich ist, und die Harntriebäußerungen über die Frühblüte bis zum Beginn des extrauterinen Lebens zurückverfolgt werden können. — Wenn von Enuresis die Rede ist, so liegt gewöhnlich — nicht immer — eine Abkürzung vor; gemeint ist nämlich Enuresis nocturna. Berührt wird mit diesem *nocturna* ein Problem des Schlafens, d. h. nach

---

1) Gastvortrag, gehalten in Berlin in der Sitzung der Deutschen Psychoanalytischen Gesellschaft am 6. Mai 1935.

Freudscher Formulierung der annähernden „Herstellung des fötalen Ruhezustandes" (s. der Vorl. z. Einf. i. d. Psa.; Ges. Schr., Bd. VII). Damit ergibt sich, abgesehen von einem kurzen Blick auf den Fötalzustand selbst, die Aufgabe, das Verhältnis der Harnentleerung zum Schlaf — im weiteren zum Bewußtseinszustand — zu untersuchen. Liegt diese Prüfung noch durchaus in analytischer Linie, so mag die scharfe Abgrenzung der Enuresis als frühkindliches Normalverhalten und später psychogene Miktionsstörung von den Verhaltungsweisen bei körperlicher Erkrankung vielleicht überflüssig erscheinen. Ich bin aber der Meinung, daß es für den Analytiker ebenso wesentlich ist, über den Unterschied von Enuresis und Inkontinenz im klaren zu sein wie über denjenigen zwischen Stottern und Stammeln! Die so skizzierte Klinik der Harntriebäußerungen kann endlich eine nicht unwesentliche Bereicherung dadurch erfahren, daß man die einfache Alltagsbeobachtung des menschlichen und tierischen Zusammenlebens mitsprechen läßt.

Wenn der Schlaf ein Zustand von Bewußtseinsverminderung ist, so ist diese um so stärker, je tiefer der Schlaf ist. Es führt somit die öfter Behauptung eines „Tiefschlafs" der Enuretiker zur Frage: Wie verhält sich die Blasenfunktion bei Bewußtlosigkeit? Die Antwort lautet: Charakteristisch für Zustände von Bewußtlosigkeit ist die Ischurie, die Harnverhaltung. Nun erhebt sich sofort ein Einwand: Wie ist es denn bei Epilepsie? Ist es nicht ein Widerspruch, wenn tiefe Bewußtlosigkeit infolge von epileptischen Zuständen Harnverhaltung bewirkt, und andernteils gerade die Epilepsie zu Enuresis Anlaß geben soll? Es kommt Ihnen doch wohl gleich die als Punkt eins erwähnte Freud-Stelle in den Sinn, wo es von den Triebäußerungen der Frühblüte heißt: „Die Symptomatik dieser Sexualäußerungen ist armselig; für den noch unentwickelten Geschlechtsapparat gibt meist der Harnapparat, gleichsam als sein Vormund, Zeichen. Die meisten sogenannten Blasenleiden dieser Zeit sind sexuelle Störungen; die Enuresis nocturna entspricht, wo sie nicht einen epileptischen Anfall darstellt, einer Pollution." Beachten Sie bitte das Wort Anfall! Die Einzelheiten eines solchen epileptischen Anfalls zu kennen ist wichtig. Ich erwähne hier nur, daß es im vollausgebildeten, im sogenannten großen epileptischen Anfall, im klonischen Stadium zur Urinausstoßung kommt; also nicht in der initialen Bewußtlosigkeit, nicht während der tonischen Phase und wiederum nicht im oft stundenlangen Koma nach den Kloni, den Zuckungen. Die Harnentleerung bei epileptischen Attacken ist kein der Bewußtlosigkeit, sondern den Zuckkrämpfen koordiniertes Symptom. Dazu darf als weitere wichtige Einzelheit vermerkt werden, daß ein Parallelismus zwischen Pupillen- und Blasenverschlußspiel in der Weise offenbar besteht, daß Pupillenweitung und Öffnung des Blasensphinkters sich entsprechen, im epileptischen Anfall eine Gleichschaltung der beiden Verschlüsse zu beobachten ist, wie wir ihr bei Betrachtung von Schlaf und Erwachen wiederum begegnen werden. — Also

48

nochmals: die eben erwähnte epileptische Harnausstoßung ist ein Anfallssymptom, während für epileptische wie für anderweitige Zustände von Bewußtlosigkeit Blasenverschluß statthat. Auch stößt weder der Fötus Urin aus, obwohl er solchen bildet, noch entleert sich die Blase im Tod. Vom „fötalen Ruhezustand" bis zum definitiven Erlöschen des Bewußtseins gilt es also für alle normalen und krankhaften Zustände von mehr oder weniger starkem Bewußtseinsverlust die Tatsache festzuhalten, daß dabei Harnblasenverschluß statthat. Dagegen kann eine durch Ischurie geschädigte Harnblase sekundär inkontinent werden.

Das für Bewußtseinsverminderungen Gesagte trifft im großen und ganzen ebenfalls für die organischen Leitungsstörungen zu, z. B. bei Verletzungen, Mißbildungen und degenerativ-entzündlichen Krankheiten des Rückenmarks. Die Klinik lehrt eindeutig, daß so bewirkte Zustände von Ischurie und Inkontinenz niemals isoliert vorkommen, sondern nur mit anderweitigen körperlichen Krankheitsäußerungen zusammen. Diese Erfahrung besagt, daß der so oft aus einer Enuresis gezogene Rückschluß auf organische Störung im Zentralnervensystem ein Fehlschluß ist und jeglicher materiellen Grundlage entbehrt. Desgleichen muß gewarnt werden, aus röntgenologisch nachweisbaren hintern Spaltbildungen der Lenden- und Kreuzwirbel, d. h. aus der Spina bifida occulta lumbosacralis posterior auf eine Mißbildung des untersten Rückenmarkabschnitts mit dem sogenannten sakralen Blasenzentrum zu schließen. Allerdings ist eine solche Schädigung möglich und verrät sich durch charakteristische Symptome von Ischurie-Inkontinenz, kombiniert mit allerhand Störungen, besonders an den Beinen. Es besteht aber keinerlei Berechtigung, einen eventuellen bloßen Knochenspalt mit einer Enuresis in ursächlichen Zusammenhang zu bringen. Völliger Verschluß der unteren Lendenwirbel und des Kreuzbeins ist übrigens während der ersten fünf Lebensjahre die Ausnahme und nicht die Regel und wird fernerhin noch zu Anfang der Zwanzigerjahre nur bei der Hälfte der Gesunden angetroffen!

Es ist keineswegs exakt, aber für kurze Verdeutlichung anschaulicher, den Unterschied zwischen Inkontinenz und Enuresis so zu erläutern, daß wir es bei inkontinenter Harnblase mit einem lecken Flüssigkeitsbehälter zu tun haben, während bei Enuresis zwar das Gefäß dicht ist, jedoch sein Inhalt zu leicht unter Pressung gerät. Während im ersten Falle es eher zu einem Abtröpfeln kommt, erzwingt sich im zweiten die Flüssigkeit ihren Austritt strahlweise. Ich kann beifügen, daß die Pressung durch Zusammenziehung der Muskelwand der Harnblase stattfindet. Es ist diese Wandspannung und nicht die Blasenfüllung als solche, welche als Harnreiz empfunden wird. Man kann auch sagen: Harndrang ist die psychische Repräsentanz dessen, was körperhafterweise als Blasenwandspannung sich ausdrückt. Schenken wir uns viele, an sich wichtige Einzelheiten, und tun wir nunmehr einen Blick auf die Ana tomie, so zeigt ein Vergleich zwischen den beiden Geschlechtern, daß der Blasenverschluß beim männlichen Geschlecht ein bedeutend mehr ausgebauter und voluminöserer ist als beim weiblichen, während die Blasenwand keine Geschlechtsdifferenz aufweist. Man müßte also, rein anatomisch genommen, die Kontinenz weiblicherseits geringer vermuten als auf der männlichen Seite. Wahrscheinlich hat diese anatomische Folgerung ihre physiologische Richtigkeit: Entleerung kleinster Harnmengen beim weiblichen Geschlecht bei plötzlichen Bewegungen, beim raschen Bergabgehen, beim Lachen usw. sind ein öfteres Vorkommnis. Wollte man also, wie das bei der Enuresis so oft mißbräuchlich geschieht, von einer „schwachen Blase" reden, so wäre diese das Privileg der Weiblichkeit. Fragen wir aber die Autoren über die Verteilung der Enuresis auf die Geschlechter, so kommen auf eine weibliche Enuresis deren zwei männliche, besteht jedenfalls ein Überwiegen der männlichen Enuretiker. So fehlt es an jeglichem Hinweis, daß die Enuresis mit irgendwelcher lokalen Minderwertigkeit etwas zu tun hat. Die Behauptungen von A. Adler über „Organminderwertigkeit" stehen auch hier in der Luft.

Mit der Prädilektion der Enuresis für das männliche Geschlecht stoßen wir vermutlich auf ein Problem der Konstitution, wie es in ähnlicher Weise für das Stottern besteht. Nur daß bei diesem der Prozentsatz der Erkrankenden noch viel mehr zu ungunsten des männlichen Geschlechts verschoben ist und 7 bis 8 stotternde Knaben auf bloß 2 bis 3 Mädchen, später sogar 9 stotternde Männer auf bloß eine einzige Frau kommen (H. Gutzmann [1]). — Es ist sehr wenig Genaues, was über Konstitution bekannt ist. Zwillingsuntersuchungen von H. W. Siemens ergeben, daß eineiige Zwillinge punkto Enuresis sich viel ähnlicher verhalten als zweieiige, auch wenn für diese die Umweltbedingungen gleichgestaltet sind; ferner sollen seine Befunde zeigen, daß die Enuresis in hohem Maße von nicht erblichen Faktoren abhängig ist. Nach Stirnimann verhält sich das Neugeborene während der ersten 4 bis 5 Lebenstage auf Selbstbenässung indifferent; aber die Empfindung des Nassen, die ihm doch vom Fruchtwasser nicht unbekannt sein sollte, löse vom 5. bis 6. Tage an „Unruhe und sichtliche Unlust" bei der Mehrzahl der Kinder aus. „Einzelne ältere Säuglinge empfinden das Liegen im Nassen lustbetont. Man kann sie lange erfolglos über den Topf halten; bettet man sie ein, so erfolgt bald eine Urinentleerung, die eine behagliche Stimmung auslöst." Dies sei besonders dann der Fall, wenn dem Kind durch Trockenbett das Naßliegen ohne sein eigenes Zutun immer vorenthalten worden sei. Halten wir also vorläufig fest, daß eine Näßlust nicht von Anfang des extrauterinen Daseins an deutlich da ist, sondern eher bei „älteren Säuglingen" sich zeigt. Das Problem wird uns in anderm Zusammenhange nochmals beschäftigen. — Wenn es auch vorläufig der exakten Erblichkeitsforschung nicht gelungen ist, Wesentliches über die Harntriebhaftigkeit als Erbeigentümlichkeit beizubringen, so besteht doch der bestimmte Eindruck, daß wir es mit einer solchen zu tun haben. So ist mir z. B. eine Familie bekannt, wo der Vater seinerzeit Enuretiker war und so, wie ich ihn geschildert bekam, als Erwachsener die unverkennbaren Züge dessen, was wir einen urethralen Typ heißen, aufwies; von seinen sieben Kindern waren fünf männlichen Geschlechts, zwei weiblichen; sämtliche fünf Jungen, nicht aber die zwei Töchter, haben bis in und einer sogar bis über die Pubertät genäßt. Eindrücklich ist mir auch eine andere Familie, die ich in drei Generationen ziemlich genau kenne, und von deren Mitgliedern ich mehrere in analytischer Arbeit hatte. Es überwiegen in ihr die Knabengeburten sehr stark, die Prägenitalität spielt bei allen, besonders im Sinne der Analität, eine große Rolle; in zweiter Linie sind die urethralen und in dritter die oralen Qualitäten auffällig. Ein 11- bis 12jähriger Junge aus dieser Familie beginnt nach onanistischer Reizung durch den zwei Jahre älteren Bruder an imperativem Harndrang untertags und Bettnässen zu leiden. Er zeigt ein Symptom, das ich die Harnverhaltung enuretischen Typs heiße; wenn ihn nämlich der anfallsweise Harndrang veranlaßt hat, den Abort aufzusuchen, ist der Drang plötzlich verschwunden; nun provoziert ihn der Junge wieder, indem er sein Glied reibt. Samenentleerungen hat er keine; sondern, wie es in den „Drei Abhandlungen" heißt, seine Harnentleerungen stehen an Stelle von Pollutionen. Wie groß die konstitutionellen Unterschiede sein können, erhellt aus dem Vergleich dieses 11- bis 12jährigen mit einem 8jährigen Jungen aus der Beobachtung von Moll, der bereits volle geschlechtliche Erregung mit Samenerguß hatte. Ein anderer 8jähriger aus meiner Praxis, der in Schule und Musikunterricht Vorzügliches leistete, in Trennung von einem Kindermädchen, das er sehr geliebt, seit einem Jahr in exzessive Onanie verfallen war, hat nie genäßt, sondern als Abschluß des onanistischen Akts ein die Wäsche sehr beschmutzendes Sekret entleert, das von den Eltern als Samenerguß taxiert wurde, und dessen mikroskopische Untersuchung zu veranlassen ich leider versäumt habe. — Daß aus den meisten Enuretikerstatistiken kaum etwas über eine Sonderkonstitution ersehen werden kann, liegt an der unkritischen Anfertigung dieser Arbeiten; hingegen kann man aus ihnen entnehmen, daß unter Sonderbedingungen, d. h. in Anstalten und Waisenhäusern, der Prozentsatz der Nässer ein besonders hoher ist. Wie sehr es eben diese Sonderbedingungen und nicht die Sonderkonstitution ist, zeigte mir eine eigene Beobachtung an einer Anstalt für schwererziehbare Kinder, deren Leiter sich gelegentlich mit mir beraten. Mit höchst einfachen und fast selbstverständlichen pädagogischen Mitteln, vielfach damit, daß man die Sonderbehandlung der Jungen eben nicht mehr praktiziert hat, ist eine Reduktion der vorher 40prozentigen Enuresis auf $4^0/_0$, zeitweise sogar auf $0^0/_0$ erfolgt. — Die Prädilektion des männlichen Geschlechts für Harntriebsäußerungen geht andeutungsweise auch aus Brauch und Sprache hervor. Es ist mir z. B. nicht bekannt, daß der Vorgang des Pissens auf Brunnen anders als durch Knabenfiguren zum Ausdruck kommt; deren bekannteste steht in Brüssel als Manneken-pis. Die Plastik stammt aus dem 17. Jahrhundert von einem künstlerischen Zeitgenossen von Rubens. In unsern modernen Städten fällt auf, daß Pissoirs entschieden häufiger sind als Bedürfnisstellen für das weibliche Geschlecht. Sowohl das griechische Wort „νεφρός" wie das deutsche „Niere" bedeuten sowohl Niere als Hoden. Wenn uns also die Entwicklungsgeschichte über einen Urogenitalapparat belehrt, so ist in der Sprachgeschichte die urethrale Funktion besonders mit der männlichen Genitalität verlötet. Eine vor 8 Jahren in der Münch. med. Wschr. erschienene Anekdote erzählt aus Niederbayern, daß ein Bauer den Arzt, der seine nierenkranke Frau behandeln sollte, auf die Eröffnung der Art des Leidens grob fortwies mit den Worten: „Daß meine Frau nierenleidend ist, das ist ganz unmöglich; denn die Nieren habe ich und nicht die Frau!" Harnspiele aus unseren Gegenden sind mir, wenn auch nicht ausschließlich, so doch weitaus vorwiegend von Knaben bekannt. — Und lassen wir endlich noch Beobachtungen an unseren Haustieren mitsprechen, so zeigt sich auch hier ein Vorwiegen, wenn nicht sogar die Pachtung der Harnexkretionslust bei den Männchen. Das bekannteste Beispiel bieten die Hunderüden ab dem Alter von $^3/_4$ Jahren; aber auch die Hauskater weisen ähnliche Züge auf. Und bei den Pferden, die mit Harn im Gegensatz zum Kot außerordentlich zurückhaltend sind, vielfach nur „stallend" urinieren, ist es eher noch ein Wallach — über Hengste fehlen mir Beobachtungen und Auskünfte — der als Seltenheit gehend oder trabend uriniert.

Im Zusammenhange mit der Konstitution wäre endlich noch die Frage des Typus zu erörtern. Hier helfen uns bewährte psa. Grundsätze; ich meine, die Arbeitsweise, Triebäußerungen sowohl in ihrer Ursprünglichkeit als auch in der Form zu untersuchen, die sich geradlinig oder reaktiv aus jener gestaltet hat. Gewohnt sind wir ferner, die um den Miktionsakt gruppierten Harntriebäußerungen als phallisch zu betrachten. Ich glaube nun, unbeschadet der theoretisch gewohnten zeitlichen Reihenfolge der prägenitalen Trieborganisationen, deren späteste, wenigstens in ausgeprägter Form, die phallische ist, diese Qualität des Phallischen schon den allerfrühesten exkretorischen Harntriebäußerungen zuschreiben, mithin schon hier die — vorübergehend vielleicht wieder zurücktretenden — ersten Ansätze dessen sehen zu dürfen, was dann besonders deutlich erst um das 3. bis 4. Lebensjahr wieder hervortritt. In dieser Annahme mag uns das körperliche Faktum unterstützen, daß Neugeborene normalerweise „makrogenital" sind, d. h. daß ihre Genitalien im Vergleich zu später verhältnismäßig größer sind; ein Zustand, der von Flusser (2) betont und mit der eigentlichen Überschwemmung des Neugeborenenorganismus durch mütterliche Sexualhormone in ursächlichen Zusammenhang gebracht wird. Immerhin ist weiblicherseits das anatomische Substrat der unmittelbar postnatalen Phallizität nicht nur ein Miniaturorgan, sondern ein Rudiment, das außer der Harnröhre deren sowie der Eichel

Schwellkörper völlig entbehrt. Es fehlt also den Harntriebäußerungen beim weiblichen Geschlecht weitgehend an einem Exekutivorgan. Umgekehrt erfährt dieses beim urinierenden männlichen Säugling von Lebensanfang an und hier sogar am allerdeutlichsten, mit dem Miktionsakt eine Vergrößerung, indem es in Erektion gerät, durch eine Erektion schon die Miktion sich ankündigt, ein Zustand, der sich bloß allmählich im Laufe der Jahre verliert und als morgendliche Wassersteife sich über Jahrzehnte erhalten kann. — Auch unter Würdigung dieser Fakten leuchtet es ein, daß die um den Miktionsakt gruppierte Harntriebhaftigkeit mehr auf Seiten des männlichen Geschlechts sich findet und von weiblicher Seite, wie psa. Erfahrung lehrt, Männlichkeitswünschen Ausdruck zu geben pflegt. Daß zu Lebensbeginn Ich- und Es-Funktionen mehr oder weniger zusammenfallen, bedarf kaum der Erwähnung. Was die beim Knaben den Miktionsakt begleitende Erektion anbetrifft, so ist bemerkenswert deren allmähliche Ablösung vom Uriniervorgang mit Zuordnung zum eigentlichen Genitalakt in den Pubertätsjahren. Marcuse hat gelegentlich über einen Patienten berichtet, der zum erstenmal onanierte, als er an den Genitalien Sensationen bekam, die er als Urindrang auffaßte und erst allmählich als Genitaldrang zu differenzieren lernte. Und Flesch teilte dann später aus eigener Jugenderinnerung mit, daß diese Analogie in den Gesprächen der Mitschüler eine Rolle gespielt habe: es hieß bei der Onanie, wenn es zur Ejakulation kam, es werde einem so „pisserig" zumute. — Im Gegensatz zum Hunger, der das Kind unruhig macht, wird der Säugling bei Harndrang ruhig; ja, er kann absorbiert wirken. Sein Gesichtchen rötet sich, und mit oder nach der Entleerung kann sein Körperchen wie von einem wohligen Schauder befallen sein. Man wird bei diesem Schüttelzittern auch daran denken dürfen, daß das, was wir später Orgasmus heißen, sein körperliches Substrat in Muskelkontraktionen hat. (Nach L. R. Müller ist es nämlich nicht die Ausscheidung der Geschlechtsprodukte, sondern sind es Kontraktionen glattmuskeliger Elemente der Geschlechtsorgane, welche das Wesen des Orgasmus ausmachen.) — Wie gesagt, erfolgt eine Harnentleerung niemals im Tiefschlaf, sondern im Teil- oder Ganzerwachen. Russische Autoren haben 2- bis 3jährige Kinder im Schlummer beobachtet und bloß zusammen mit rascherer Atmung, Pulsbeschleunigung, allerhand Körperbewegungen und Lächeln, Urinentleerung festgestellt. Charakteristisch sind auch für den Säugling Schlafkontinenz und gehäufte Harnentleerungen mit dem Erwachen. — Man kann sich nun auch fragen, warum gerade ältere Säuglinge eine deutlichere Harntriebhaftigkeit zeigen. Erinnern wir uns daran, daß die Säuglingsmasturbation erst etwa mit ¹/₂ Jahr eintritt, so liegt es nahe, die Harnäußerung, bzw. die Enuresis als Antwort auf die Genitalpressungen bei Mädchen und das Zupfen der Knaben zu vermuten. — Um nochmals auf den Lebensanfang zurückzugreifen, so ist noch dessen zu gedenken, was Abraham „den primi-

tivsten Liebesbeweis" geheißen hat, „weit ursprünglicher als Kuß und Um-
armung", nämlich die Benässung einer geliebten Person durch einen z. B. im
Familienkreis herumgereichten Säugling. — Es klaffen riesige Beobachtungs-
lücken zwischen diesen Säuglingsbeobachtungen und demjenigen, was wir als
urethralen Typ gemeinhin bezeichnen. Für die Frühblüte mag ihn die schon
erwähnte Brüsseler Brunnenfigur von Duquesnoy aus dem Jahre 1648 ver-
bildlichen als schöner, stolzer, lächelnd den Wasserstrahl aus dem mit der
linken Hand gehaltenen Glied spritzender Knabe. Wie übrigens solche Trieb-
entäußerung bewertet wird, deuten Verkleidungsgebräuche an: Manneken-pis
hat eine große Garderobe der verschiedensten Uniformen und stolzen Ge-
wänder und wird mit diesen ihm wechselnd angezogenen, immer wieder bis
in die letzten Jahre durch neue bereicherten Kostümen als Held gefeiert.
Andernteils begegnen wir noch im Pfaundlerschen Handbuch der Kinderheilkunde der Strafverkleidung enuretischer Knaben in Mädchen als einer,
wenn auch abgelehnten „Behandlungsmethode" der Enuresis. — Für den
Habitus der kindlichen Enuretiker ist nach dem eben genannten Handbuch der
— heißen wir ihn zur schnellen Verständigung Manneken-pis —, also der
phallische Typ in der Minderzahl; er hat nach jener Beschreibung „etwas un-
verschämt Herausforderndes" in seinem Wesen, während das eigentliche
Enuretikergesicht Scheu und Verschämtheit ausdrücke. Meiner Beobachtung
nach gilt diese Duplizität der Enuretikertypen für Bub und Mädchen.
Daß aber das eigentliche Enuretikergesicht, eben das scheu-verschämte, nicht
der eigentliche, der Urtyp der Harntriebhaftigkeit ist, sondern deren Verleugnung Ausdruck gibt, geht schon einigermaßen aus den Säuglingsbeobachtungen hervor. Auch Abraham hat die ehemaligen Enuretiker, welche
er als Männer wegen ihrer Ejaculatio praecox zu analysieren hatte, in zwei
Gruppen geteilt, solche, „deren gesamtes Wesen schlaff, energielos, passiv —
kurz unmännlich erscheint", und solche „von erethischem, überlebhaftem,
beständig hastendem Wesen". Auch er faßt die ersterwähnte Kategorie der
Schlaffen als reaktiv auf und fügt bei, daß freilich die beiden Gruppen nicht
scharf gegeneinander abzugrenzen sind. Seiner Skizzierung entnehme ich
weiter: „Die Neigung zur Ausfälligkeit in Worten, zum Jähzorn, zu gewalt-
tätigen Handlungen ist... außerordentlich groß, soweit sie nicht gelähmt
wird durch einen anderen... Charakterzug: die Feigheit. Übertriebene Zorn-
mütigkeit und Lähmung der normalen männlichen Angriffslust finden sich
hier in naher Nachbarschaft beieinander... Nebeneinander von übergroßem
Ehrgeiz und schweren Arbeitswiderständen." Die Polarität der beiden Typen
findet sich auch in Fenichels spezieller Neurosenlehre angedeutet. Im
ganzen ist es aber der aktive Typ, der Mensch mit dem brennenden Ehrgeiz,
der die psa. Anschauungen vom Enuretiker illustriert. — Muß nun
schon nach eben mitgeteilten Erfahrungen für den Großteil der Enuretiker die Verleugnung der Phallizität, also der Sekundärtyp als cha-

rakteristisch angesehen werden, so führen uns nun die Forschungen von
Abraham noch weiter in dieser Richtung. Ich vermute, daß dasjenige, was er als die spezifischen Lustsensationen seiner Patienten beschrieben hat, deren Entleerung dem Stoffe nach eine Ejakulation, hingegen nach dem Modus der Ausstoßung eine Miktion ist, dem reaktiven
Urethraltyp entspricht und sich aufs engste berührt mit dem, was neu-
lich E. Kemper die „rezeptive Urethralerotik beim Manne" geheißen hat (Int.
Ztschr. f. Psa., Bd. XX, 1934). Abraham nämlich gibt für seine Urethralerotiker mangelhafte Erregbarkeit der Eicheloberfläche, hingegen die Lust-
empfindungen in der hintern Harnröhre unter dem Damm lokalisiert an. Die
„rezeptiven Urethralerotiker" als extremste Vertreter des reaktiven oder Se-
kundärtyps der Urethralen haben ihre Harnröhre empfindungsgemäß zur
Vagina umgestaltet. Neu war mir aber, bei Kemper zu ersehen, daß Frauen
häufiger als Männer unter diesen Rezeptiven sich finden.[2] Ich selber kenne
aus der analytischen Arbeit bloß männliche Patienten dieser Art. Stricknadel
und Fiebermesser dienen ihnen z. B. als Reizkörper, die sie in die Urethra
einführen; einer hat sich dabei eine Striktur zugezogen. Ein anderer pflegte
Samenentleerung durch reibende Einführung eines Pinselstiels zu bewirken
und seinen Verweiblichungswünschen außerdem durch Tragen eines eng ge-
schnürten Korsetts Ausdruck zu geben. In der Hauptsache sind es die Chirur-
gen, welche mit diesen scheu-femininen Typen zu tun haben; dann nämlich,
wenn ein Fremdkörper abbricht oder in die Blase gleitet. Die Anamnese über
diese Vorfälle bleibe „meist stumm", ironisiert dies de Quervain in seiner
„chirurgischen Diagnostik". — So viel oder so wenig über die beiden urethralen Typen.

Es wäre nun weiterhin verlockend, die Harntriebäußerungen unter dem
Gesichtspunkt der beiden Triebarten zu betrachten. Doch muß ich mich
darauf beschränken, das und jenes herauszugreifen. Soviel ist schon für rasche
Übersicht deutlich, daß von demjenigen, was Abraham den primitivsten
Liebesbeweis genannt hat, bis zum „Genuß der männlichen Potenz im homosexuellen Wettkampf", nach Freudschem Ausdruck, eine Linie zu verfolgen
ist, auf der sich mehr und mehr die der Harnerotik beigemengte Aggression
manifestiert. Ich bediene mich zur Kennzeichnung der beiden Strebungen
der Ausdrücke Urophilie und Uropolemie. Ohne nun die Enuresis, wie
ich es in meiner biologischen Arbeit getan, genauer über die verschiedenen
Lebensphasen vom Beginn der Säuglingszeit über Ödipussituation, Latenz und
Pubertät ausführlicher zu verfolgen, sei kurz gesagt, daß Marie Bonapartes
Terminus „aggressiver Autoerotismus" manche Fälle von Enuresis in

---

2) Das ist nach Kempers ergänzender mündlicher Mitteilung eine chirurgische, keine
psychologische Erfahrung! Aus anatomischen Gründen gleitet beim weiblichen Geschlecht
der in die Harnröhre geschobene Fremdkörper eher bis in die Blase und bedarf daselbst
chirurgischer Intervention.

trefflicher Knappheit charakterisiert, wobei wir zugleich an die Reaktivform des Urethraltyps denken mögen. Hätten wir hier die Uropolemie gegen den betreffenden Enuretiker zugleich mit der libidinösen Komponente selber gewendet, also ein Stück Masochismus, so erweist sich der sogenannte „Tiefschlaf" der Enuretiker gleichwie das Sträuben des Säuglings, sich abheben zu lassen, als eine Abwehr der Erzieherperson gegenüber. Natürlich ist es berechtigt, diese „Harnverhaltung enuretischen Typs", wie ich sie genannt habe, der Einwirkung analer Strebungen zuzuschreiben. Solche Betrachtung läge vor allem in der Richtung derjenigen Auffassungen, wie sie Ferenczi in seiner „Genitaltheorie" vertritt. Noch näher aber liegen Bezüge auf die Oralität. Ich brauche nur an den Terminus „Harnstottern" zu erinnern. Bei Erwachsenen begegnet man ja viel häufiger als der Enuresis in vollausgeprägter Form des Einnässens einer bloßen Pollakurie. Dies in einer Unzahl von psychoneurotischen Zusammenhängen. Diese Pollakurie kann nachts zu mehrmaligem Aufstehen zwingen und untertags die größten Einschränkungen und Vorsichtsmaßnahmen erfordern. Zola z. B. war während seiner schriftstellerischen Arbeit der Mannesjahre ein solcher Sklave seines Nachttopfs; und wenn er ihn 20mal im Tage benützen mußte, war es wenig. Die Kombination dieses imperativen Harndrangs mit ebenso plötzlicher unfreiwilliger Harnverhaltung enuretischen Typs, d. h. in Gegenwart anderer, dies beides zusammen wird als Harnstottern bezeichnet, wobei die Beschreibung hier nicht auf weitere Einzelheiten und Zusammenhänge eingehen kann. Um nochmals auf die ursprüngliche Harnverhaltung enuretischen Typs zurückzukommen, so muß gesagt werden, daß das schlafende Kind sich der weckenwollenden Erzieherperson gegenüber verhält wie jener Frontsoldat, der mächtigen Kanonendonner verschläft. Und wie der gleiche Soldat auf das leise Ticken des Telephonapparats, auf dessen Bedienung er eingestellt ist, trotzdem erwacht, so hat man sich beim Enuretiker den Harnreiz als „spezifischen Weckreiz" vorzustellen. Im übrigen dürfen wir uns zur Zerstörung der Legende vom Nässen im Tiefschlaf — die Blase wird wie der Telephonapparat in erwachendem oder wachem Zustand bedient! — an Freuds Traumdeutung wenden. Und sollte diese Anleihe für ein bioanalytisches Problem bei der Psychoanalyse beanstandet werden, so darf auf Pötzls schöne Arbeit verwiesen werden, in der er dartut, wie die Auffassung des Schlafes, die Freud rein von der psychischen Seite her gewonnen hat, im wesentlichen übereinstimmt mit den modernen physiologischen Schlaftheorien. Mir selber hat die direkte Säuglingsbeobachtung die wesentlichen Aufschlüsse darüber verschafft, daß das Kind im Tiefschlaf nicht näßt, wobei mir weiter aufgefallen ist, daß gleichzeitig mit dem Springen der schlafverengten Pupillen der Harnstrahl einsetzt. Betrachten wir den Sachverhalt von Freuds Traumdeutung her, so ergeben sich kurz folgende Ableitungen: Der Traum ist der Hüter des Schlafs, indem er u. a. störende Leibreize verarbeitet. So kann ein

Harnreiz zum Harnreiztraum führen. Dort nun, wo wir es mit einer Enuresis als mehr oder weniger stereotyper Verhaltensweise zu tun haben, scheint der Traum keineswegs regelmäßig eine Rolle zu spielen; wenn schon, dann vorbereitend, vielleicht kurze Zeit aufschiebend, worauf dann, im eigentlichen Sinne infolge des Traumes, die Handlung des Nässens sich anschließt; mir ist das nur von sporadischer Enuresis bekannt und dann oft so, daß mit beginnendem Nässen der Schläfer erwacht. Wenn man das Denken als Probehandeln bezeichnet, so ist es wohl nicht zu gewaltsam, das Halluzinieren des Traums einigermaßen dieser Kategorie des Probehandelns zugehörig zu erachten und in Gegensatz zu eigentlicher Handlung zu stellen. Als solche Schlafhandlung fasse ich die Enuresis nocturna auf. Statt der mittelbaren Abfuhr, der Verarbeitung des Harnreizes in einem Traum, glaube ich also eine unmittelbare Abfuhr in Form des Nässens behaupten zu dürfen; d. h. eine Verhaltensweise, wie sie überhaupt das Kindes- und Jugendalter im Vergleich zu reiferen Jahren auszeichnet. So rückte also die Enuresis nocturna klinisch in die Nähe der Zustände von Schlafwandel und Schlaftics, die einem partiellen Wachsein offensichtlich entsprechen, wobei man, wie das Trömner tut, von einem „rein motorischen Erwachen" sprechen mag, jedenfalls aber wie bei Tics und Schlafwandel die morgendliche Amnesie für dieses Wachsein, bzw. die Handlung des Nässens als typisch anzusehen hat.

Die Empfindung des körperwarmen Nassen, wie sie durch Enuresis zustande kommt, muß dem Neugeborenen von seiner intrauterinen Fruchtwasserexistenz vertraut sein. Logischerweise ist Enuresis im Resultat annähernde Wiederherstellung eines vorgeburtlichen Zustandes.[3] Wie früher erwähnt, sind die Reaktionen der Säuglinge auf die Selbstbenässung verschieden: vom heimisch-vertrauten, behaglichen — wofür Schweizer Mundart den Ausdruck „heimelig" hat — bis zum unheimlichen dürfen wir eine ganze Gefühlsskala annehmen und dementsprechend die Quantität der Regression verschieden. Tatsache ist jedenfalls, daß, je mehr das Kind durch Liebe und Betreuung in seinem extrauterinen Dasein heimisch wird, es um so weniger die Wiederherstellung des intrauterinen Milieus enuretisch praktiziert. Kleine, die zu Hause nicht mehr nässen, tun das an fremdem Ort, z. B. auf einer Reise oder bei Wechsel der Pflegepersonen. Weiterhin nässen Kinder, die überhaupt eines eigentlichen Heims entbehren, nässen z. B. Anstaltskinder mehr als andere, so daß der Prozentsatz der Enuretiker als Qualitätsmesser für Waisenhäuser und ähnliche Institutionen zum Teil verwendet werden kann. Aus einer Anstalt für schwachsinnige Kinder ist mir als nach Bericht des Hausvaters erfolgreiche Behandlung von Enuretikern das abendliche heiße Bad bekannt. Es wird jeweils während ungefähr drei Wochen gegeben; dann müsse die Behandlung

---

3) Etymologisch ist in diesem Zusammenhang interessant, daß das lateinische Verb *urinor* = untertauchen, *urinator* = der Taucher heißt!

abgebrochen werden, weil sie zu starke Müdigkeit und Schwäche untertags bewirke. Im allgemeinen ist es aber das lauwarme bis warme Bad von 37 bis 37,5 Grad Celsius, das — wenigstens vom Kleinkinde — wohlig empfunden wird. „Vielleicht wird so auch unser Verständnis für die therapeutische Wirkung warmer Bäder vorbereitet", meint Freud bei Darlegung erogener Hautreizungen in den „Drei Abhandlungen". Daß Bad und Selbstbenässung sich auch beim Erwachsenen verhältnismäßig oft kombinieren, zeigt die Errechnung von 60 ccm Urin pro Besucher von Hallenschwimmbädern! Ich kenne einen unzufriedenen Mann mit starker ubw. Mutterbindung. Er neigt zum ungeselligen Trunke; und eine ähnlich wohlige Empfindung, wie er sie sich damit verschafft, eine Art Nirwanastimmung, überkommt ihn auch im sommerlichen Bade sowie auf einer Meerfahrt. Feucht und Warm kennzeichnen für ihn die Heimat; und dementsprechend hat sich dieser Mitteleuropäer während seines mittleren Mannesalters jahrelang in den Tropen aufgehalten und im späteren dorthin zurückgesehnt.

Wir sind von der Reaktivierung des intrauterinen Zustandes durch Enuresis ausgegangen und können von hier eine Linie triebhaften Verhaltens vorwärts verfolgen, die irgendwie und als eine unter andern auf das von Freud herausgestellte, anfangs erwähnte kulturpsychologische Problem zielt.

Der Hamburger Physiologe J. v. Uexküll hat an vielen Beispielen dargelegt, wie die objektive Umgebung in sehr subjektiver Weise vom Individuum zur Umwelt gestaltet wird, die Art der leiblichen und psychischen Organisation die gleiche Umgebung eine sehr verschiedene Umwelt sein läßt. In Uexkülls Schilderungen von „Heim und Heimat" findet sich folgende Darstellung: „Eine besondere Beachtung verdient die Art und Weise, wie die Hunde ihre Heimat ihren Artgenossen gegenüber kenntlich machen. (Eine Abbildung stellt die Karte des Zoologischen Gartens in Hamburg dar mit den Wegen, auf denen die Stellen angegeben sind, wo auf Spaziergängen zwei täglich ausgeführte Rüden urinierten.) — Es waren immer die auch für das menschliche Auge besonders kenntlichen Orte, die sie mit ihren Duftmarken belegten. Wenn beide Hunde zugleich ausgeführt wurden, trat regelmäßig ein Wetturinieren ein. — Ein temperamentvoller Hund zeigt immer die Neigung, sobald ihm ein fremder Hund begegnet, sogleich den nächsten in die Augen fallenden Gegenstand mit seiner Visitenkarte zu versehen. Auch wird er, wenn er in die durch Duftmarken eines andern Hundes kenntlich gemachte Heimat... dieses... eindringt, diese fremden Marken nacheinander aufsuchen und sorgfältig überpinseln. Ein temperamentloser Hund hingegen wird in der Heimat des fremden Hundes scheu an dessen Duftmarken vorübergehen und seine Anwesenheit durch kein Duftzeichen verraten. — Das Markieren der Heimat ist... auch bei den großen Bären Nordamerikas üblich. Der Bär reibt, in seiner ganzen Höhe aufrecht stehend, mit Rücken und Schnauze die Rinde einer einzeln stehenden, weithin sichtbaren Kiefer ab. Dies wirkt als Signal

für andere Bären, die Kiefer in weitem Bogen zu umgehen und das ganze Gebiet zu meiden, wo ein Bär von solchen Ausmaßen seine Heimat verteidigt."
— Die Hundeschilderung läßt sich zusammenfassen in die Worte: Urinieren
als Markieren der Heimat im mann-männlichen Wettkampf.
Uropolemie als Wetturinieren der Knaben fällt einem weiter in diesem Zusammenhange ein, wobei nach eigener 4 Jahrzehnte zurückgreifender Erinnerung aus dem 6. bis 7. Altersjahr die Enantiodromie, das Ineinanderübergehen
der Polaritäten Wasser und Feuer im Scherz eine Rolle spielte, ein Junge, der
ohne sein Wissen die Hose nicht ganz geschlossen trug, darauf aufmerksam
gemacht wurde mit dem Zuruf: „Hör, du hast Kerzen feil!" Róheim erzählt
von erwachsenen Zentralaustraliern, daß einer, aufgefordert das große Glied
des andern zu loben, bei Weigerung entweder vom ersten geschlagen werden
darf oder von dessen Urin trinken muß. — Damit hätten wir uns von dem,
was Abraham die primitivste Liebesbezeugung nennt, schon ziemlich weit
entfernt. Die Uropolemie wäre recht deutlich geworden. Wenn Sie sich aber
erinnern, wie nach Pipals Schilderungen Halterbuben um Wiener-Neustadt
spielen, so sehen wir doch noch deutlich die erotische Komponente auch
dabei: Gemeinschaftlich und auf Kommando eines Anführers löscht die
Bubenhorde das Weidefeuer mit dem natürlichen Löschwerkzeug; gemeinschaftlich wird das Anpissen desjenigen, der neu zur Horde stößt, geübt. Ich
schildere Ihnen einen solchen primitiven Initiationsritus, wie ihn einer meiner
Analysanden in Südbaden als ca. 11jähriger vor 25 Jahren mitgemacht hat.
Der Neuankömmling wird zum „Tüpflezählen" aufgefordert. Zu diesem
Zwecke stellen sich alle Buben, Rücken außen, zum Kreis. Ein großes bunt-
gedrucktes Taschentuch wird zwischen ihnen ausgespannt und von jedem mit
der Hand gehalten. Der Neuling muß nun die farbigen Tupfen auf dem
Tuche zählen. Während er sich bemüht, dieser Aufforderung nachzukommen,
haben die andern, verdeckt durch das Tuch, ihre Hosen geöffnet und über-
raschen nun den Neuen mit einer Harntaufe. Zeigt hier die Horde ihre über-
legene Macht und Schlauheit, so läßt mit gleichen Mitteln Rabelais seinen
Riesenjüngling Gargantua die Masse besiegen. „Wie Gargantua den Parisern
sein Willkomm bezahlt" wird im 13. Kapitel des Buches folgendermaßen geschildert: „Vom gaffenden Volk vor der Tür von Notre Dame umringt, setzt
er sich und spricht laut zu seinem Begleiter: ‚Ich glaub, die Schlingel meinen,
daß ich ihnen hie mein Pflastergeld und meinen Willkomm zahlen soll. Ist
billig; sie sollen ihren Wein han, aber par ris, per risum, spottweis.' — Da lupft'
er lächelnd seinen schönen Hosenlatz, zog sein Ablaufrohr an die Luft herfür
und bebrunzelte sie so haarscharf, daß ihrer 260418 elend ersoffen, ohn die
Weiber und kleinen Kinder." — Der Rettung von Besitz gibt, wie mir eine
kurze Einzelbeobachtung zeigte, der Harnstrom auch von Seiten der Frau
Ausdruck: Die 39jährige Gattin eines Zimmereibesitzers wird durch Brand-
stiftung aus dem Schlafe geschreckt. Ab dieser Zeit stellen sich bei ihr —

sicherlich mehrfach determiniert — nächtliche Angstzustände mit eigentlicher Harnflut alle paar Wochen ein. — Interessant sind in diesem Zusammenhang auch die verschiedenen Versionen über das Urbild des Manneken-pis. Nach einer dieser Legenden gilt die Brunnenfigur dem ehrenden Andenken eines kleinen Jungen, der im 13. Jahrhundert eine Lunte gelöscht, mit der die Feinde die Stadt in Brand stecken wollten. Nach anderer Version erinnere das Standbild an den zweijährigen Gottfried den III., Herzog von Brabant, gegen dessen und seiner Mutter Herrschaft sich zwei mächtige Vasallen empört. Der dem Kind getreue Heerführer verlangt für die Schlacht mit den Rebellen die aufmunternde Gegenwart des Kleinen, und so wird dessen Wiege an einem hohen Eichenast auf dem Schlachtfelde aufgehängt, über ihr die Standarte von Brabant. Der Kampf dauert drei Tage. Viermal werden die Getreuen vom Feinde zurückgetrieben; aber niemals weiter als bis zur Eiche. Um die Mitte des dritten Tages hilft neuer Zuzug zum Sieg über die Rebellen. Während des ganzen Schlachtgetümmels aber hat der kleine Fürst von Zeit zu Zeit, allen sichtbar, in seiner Wiege sich erhoben, stolz und ohne Scham Richtung Feind gepißt, *„satisfait fièrement à ce léger besoin que l'enfance accomplit sans rougir."* (Das Nichterröten könnte uns dabei nach früher erwähnten Kinderbeobachtungen besonders legendär vorkommen!) Und jedesmal, wenn der Kleine urinierte, wurde dieser Akt von seinen Truppen mit Freudebrüllen begrüßt. — A b e r n i c h t n u r u n p e r s ö n l i c h e m B e s i t z u n d d e s s e n E r o b e r u n g u n d B e h a u p t u n g k a n n d e r M i k t i o n s a k t A u s - d r u c k g e b e n , s o n d e r n e r s p i e l t a u c h e i n e R o l l e b e i m K a m p f u m s W e i b c h e n , wobei es nach einer Beobachtung aus der Tierpsychologie folgendermaßen zugehen kann: Ein einjähriger Riesenjüngling unter Katzen, ein prächtiger weißer Kater, zieht im Vorfrühling 1935 zum erstenmal auf Paarung aus. Aber, weit entfernt davon, die Rolle des Gargantua in Paris zu spielen, kommt er jeweils so übel begossen heim, daß man ihn von dem stinkenden Urin, mit dem ihn die älteren Kater bespritzt, baden muß. Diese Phase dauert wenige Tage. Es folgt eine zweite, für die der Beobachter den Ausdruck brauchte, nunmehr habe der Kater ausgesehen wie ein Student nach der Mensur, blutig verletzt an Ohren und Schnauze. Dritte und letzte Phase innerhalb einiger Wochen: Sämtliche andern Kater sind vom Bauhof, wo sich alles abspielt, verschwunden und der weiße Kater bleibt im Besitz des ganzen Harems. — Ein letztes Beispiel endlich mag uns in dichterischer Darstellung die Rolle der Uropolemie im tötlichen Kampf eines 14- bis 15jährigen Jungen mit dem erwachsenen Rivalen zeigen. Es stammt aus dem mir mit der Jahreszahl 1928 vorliegenden Roman von Manfred H a u s m a n n: „Lampioon küßt Mädchen und kleine Birken. Abenteuer eines Wanderers" (Schünemann, Bremen): Dem Handelslehrling und spätern Vagabunden Lampioon hat der dreiste, protzige Buchhalter Tilken ein Mädchen, das der Junge mit scheuer Sinnlichkeit und viel Schwärmerei verehrt, geraubt. Es ist zum Kampf zwischen Lampioon und Tilken gekommen; jener ist trotz Rasen und Beißen unterlegen und von Tilken vor der Geliebten auf den nackten Hintern geschlagen worden. Lampioon trollt sich verzweifelt, will den Tod suchen, bis ihm rasch der Entschluß reift, den andern zu ermorden. Es ist Nacht, und Tilken muß mit dem Motorrad des Wegs kommen. Lampioon spannt ihm einen Stacheldraht, Tilken saust richtig darein, überschlägt sich, zuckt ein paarmal und liegt dann, aus dem Munde blutend, tot am Boden. „Da schoß ein Wirbel von Triumph, Krankheit und Entsetzen durch mich hindurch, daß mir das Wasser in die Hose lief", läßt der Dichter Lampioon erzählen, „da rannte ich weg und merkte, daß ich in einemfort hähähä machte und die Zähne bleckte". —

Obwohl wir uns mit dieser Schilderung weit von der nüchternen Klinik entfernt haben, besteht doch kein Anlaß anzunehmen, daß wir damit den Boden seelischer Tatsachen unter den Füßen verloren hätten. Hingegen hat sich unter der Niederschrift dieser Ausführungen meine ursprüngliche Absicht der bloßen Kürzung, Kompression und Umstellung, wie sie einem Referate dienlich sein möchte, insofern nicht ganz verwirklichen lassen, als sich allerhand Frisches unversehens eingeschlichen hat. Wieviel von Tatsachensammlung noch aussteht, zeigt eine vorläufige Sichtung. Wieviel von Anregungen aus Freuds Traumdeutung für die Erforschung motorischer Schlafphänomene noch unausgeschöpft ist, konnte ich bloß notdürftig zeigen. Auch hat in meinem Vortrag die Angst in ihren Zusammenhängen mit der Harntriebhaftigkeit keinen Platz gefunden. Was diese Angst betrifft, so sähe ich unter dem Gesichtswinkel der drei Abhängigkeiten des Ichs ihre Sichtung gegeben auf einer Strecke, die mit Freuds Angstneurosenmonographie von 1895 etwa ihren Anfang nähme, wobei der Weg, auf dem die Urophilie und Uropolemie zu verfolgen wäre, so bezeichnet werden könnte: von der Aktualangst bis zum Unbehagen in der Kultur.

Literatur

Sofern hier bloß die Autorennamen angeführt sind, genauer in H. Christoffel: Zur Biologie der Enuresis. Zeitschr. f. Kinderpsychiatrie, 1934, H. 1—4; Verlag Benno Schwabe & Cie., Basel.

1. H. Gutzmann: Sprachheilkunde. II. Aufl. Fischer, Berlin, 1912.
2. E. Flusser: Zuwachsen des Vestibulums kleiner Mädchen. Münch. med. Wschr., 1935, Nr. 5, S. 172.

Der Kern des Ödipuskomplexes[1]

Von

C. D. Daly

Kalkutta

VII. Klinische Beweise für die zentrale Bedeutung des
Menstruationskomplexes in der Ätiologie der Neurosen

Beispiel A
Ein Traum

I. Bruchstück. *Der Träumer macht sich auf die Suche nach einer ihm bekannten
älteren Prostituierten, und zwar in der Absicht, mit ihr sexuell zu verkehren. Er kannte
sie als nett und sauber, wenn auch ihre Vagina trocken und sie selbst alt und reizlos
war. Als sie sich jedoch entblößte, merkte er, daß ihre Geschlechtsteile abscheulich und
ekelerregend waren; der Anblick war unbeschreiblich abstoßend.*

II. Bruchstück. *Er veranlaßte dann einen Mann mit einem roten Hut, ihm
eine Frau ausfindig zu machen. Der Mann führte ihn an einen Ort, an dem sich eine
Anzahl junger Mädchen befand, alle sauber und anziehend; sie standen in der Obhut
einer alten Frau. Er wählte eine; sie saß oben auf einem Regal. Er hätte gern ihre
Klitoris geküßt, fürchtete aber, sich eine Krankheit zu holen. Er griff ihr mit der Hand
zwischen die Beine und war entzückt, als er merkte, daß sie feucht und erregt war.
Ihm galt das als ein Zeichen der Liebe und der Sicherheit. Dann merkte er, daß sie
ein wenig unwohl war und aus der Vagina blutete. Jede weitere Erinnerung schwand
sofort.*

III. Bruchstück. *Er ging mit einer anziehenden schwarzgekleideten Frau spa-
zieren. Sie hielt die Landschaft, die sich zu den schönen Bergen hinzog, für sehr hübsch.
Er war nicht ihrer Ansicht — er hatte die Gegend schon früher gesehen und fand sie
in keiner Weise schön. Die großen länglichen Flecken roten Lehms, die zu sehen waren,
dünkten ihn sehr häßlich. Sie jedoch machte ihn auf einen schönen Fleck blauer Blumen
in der Mitte des Tals aufmerksam. Er sah die Blumen an und wurde sofort bewußtlos.
Als er zu sich kam, hing er mit einem Arm am Rand eines Felsens. Sie lag auf einem
Pfad über ihm. Er bat sie, sich nicht zu bewegen, denn wenn sie es täte, würde er sicher
abstürzen und getötet werden. Gelänge es ihm aber, sich auf den Pfad auf dem Felsen hin-
aufzuarbeiten, dann würde alles gut sein, und er würde Verkehr mit ihr haben.*

Fassen wir alle Punkte der Analyse, die für unsern Gegenstand von Bedeutung sind, kurz zusammen: Das erste Bruchstück bezieht sich auf die Groß-
mutter des Träumers. Er berichtet, daß der zufällige Anblick ihrer Vagina
seinen ersten Ohnmachtsanfall verursacht habe. Die spätere Analyse ergab
jedoch, daß der Anblick nicht zufällig gewesen war; er war an sie heran-
gekrochen, um ihr zwischen die Beine zu sehen. Er erinnerte sich, daß der An-

---

1) Fortsetzung der in Int. Ztschr. f. Psa., Bd. XXI, Heft 2, erschienenen Arbeit; aus dem
Englischen übersetzt von Helene Reiff.

blick abstoßend und von einem scharfen Geruch begleitet gewesen sei. Tiefere Analyse zeigte, daß dieser Geruch und dieser Anblick einst, in der frühen Zeit der Freiheit in seinen Beziehungen zur Mutter, für ihn von großem Reiz gewesen waren. Es ist zu beachten, daß im zweiten Bruchstück alle Erinnerung schwand, nachdem er im Traum die blutende Vagina gesehen hatte; ferner, daß er diese Feststellung mit dem Gedanken verknüpfte, er könnte sich eine Krankheit holen. In der weiteren Analyse zeigte es sich, daß er die gefürchtete Kastration durch die Mutter auf die Schwester verschoben hatte.

Das dritte Bruchstück enthält das Wissen um die Menstruation seiner Mutter sowie auch das Verstehen seines eigenen Anfalls. Sowohl die Schwester als auch die Mutter sind in dem Traum enthalten. Der Fleck auf den Hügeln gegen die Berge hin ist die Vagina, die ihn häßlich, seine Schwester jedoch schön dünkte.[2] Die Berge, auf denen Quellen entspringen, sind die Brüste der Mutter. Der Blumenfleck in der Mitte des Tals bedeutet symbolisch die menstruierende Vagina.

Die einzige Spur des Vaters in diesem Traum ist der Mann mit dem roten Hut (= Penis), der ihm als Führer (= Kuppler) diente und ihn nach dem Ort brachte, in dem die Frauen wohnten. In der Analyse dieser Einzelheit kamen verschiedene Tendenzen zutage. Eine ging dahin, den Vater herabzuwürdigen, teils wegen seiner sexuellen Beziehungen zur Mutter, teils auch weil er in Wirklichkeit der in diese Richtung gehenden Neugier des Sohnes Schranken gesetzt hatte; deshalb war ihm die Rolle eines Kupplers, eines verachteten Menschen also, zugewiesen worden. Gleichzeitig erreichte der Träumer damit aber auch die Befriedigung eines unbewußten Wunsches, nämlich Vater und Mutter würden seiner Neugier und seinen inzestuösen Neigungen zur Schwester keine Hindernisse in den Weg legen, ihm vielmehr helfen, daß er ans Ziel gelange, anstatt ihn zu hemmen und zu bestrafen, was sie in Wirklichkeit getan hatten. Bis zu einem gewissen Ausmaß mißlingt jedoch diese List des Unbewußten, denn selbst im Traum wird er beim Anblick des Blutes ohnmächtig, wodurch er dem Tod entgeht.

Mit der Furcht vor dem Vater und der Bewunderung für ihn verband sich auch eine homosexuelle Strebung: deshalb kann er in dem Traum erst, als der Vater ihn führt, zu dem Mädchen (= Schwester) gelangen. Vom Vater also fürchtete er den Tod.

Auf diesen Traum folgten eine Zeitlang Träume *von einer Frau mit einem Penis, bei der er eine Ejakulation hatte,* später *von einer Frau mit einem oder mehreren Penissen.* Auch träumte er, *daß er in eine Felsenspalte stürze oder magnetisch in einen Abgrund gezogen werde;* dann wieder, *daß er in irgendwelche Schlingen gerate und sich nicht befreien könne,* oder *daß sich seine Angel beim Fischen*

---

2) Die Schwester pflegte ihm ihre Vagina zu zeigen und zu sagen, daß sie viel schöner sei als sein Penis; dabei freute es sie offenkundig, daß er sich vor der Vagina fürchtete. Hinter dieser Handlung steckte offensichtlich ihr Penisneid.

in einem Felsen festhake, und er sie nicht losbekommen könne. Die Analyse dieser Träume bewies unbewußte Furcht davor, von einer Frau sexuell so sehr angezogen zu werden, daß er gezwungen sein würde, Beziehungen zu ihr anzuknüpfen; er fürchtete, daß diese sexuelle Beziehung irgendwie zu seinem Tod führen werde. Nachdem die tiefere Schicht des oben angeführten Menstruationstraums erreicht worden war, entwickelte der Patient starken Haß gegen jede Frau, die seinem Empfinden nach sein Recht auf freies Interesse an ihrer oder anderer Menschen Sexualität irgendwie einschränkte oder sich auf irgendeine Weise dem Gedanken der freien Liebe widersetzte. Darauf folgte eine Phase heftiger Sehnsucht nach Vaterliebe und schließlich von Identifizierung mit Jesus Christus, was für ihn mit der Übernahme der passiven Rolle gleichbedeutend war.

Sein Ohnmachtsanfall war demnach ein Versuch seines Ichs, der Todesstrafe zu entgehen, der verfallen ist, wer den Inzestverboten der Eltern trotzt.

Auch ein zweiter Traum, der von Defloration während der Menstruation handelt, ist sehr aufschlußreich. Der Träumer berichtet:

Ich sah einen steilen Felsen hinab und erblickte einige wunderschöne Obstbäume in voller Blüte. Sie interessierten mich so sehr, daß ich das Gleichgewicht verlor und auf sie hinabfiel, wobei ich einen blühenden Zweig abbrach. Ich hob den Blütenzweig auf, denn ich dachte, da er doch abgebrochen war, könnte ich ihn wohl meiner Frau nach Hause bringen; da erschien ein Polizist auf dem Schauplatz und verhaftete mich wegen Blumendiebstahls. Ich erklärte dem Polizisten, daß es sich um einen Unfall handle, und daß mich daher keine Schuld treffe; ich hätte nicht die Absicht gehabt, den Zweig vom Baum zu brechen, die Blüten seien jedoch so unwiderstehlich schön und hätten mich so sehr entzückt, daß ich gar nicht gewußt hätte, was ich tat; so hätte ich das Gleichgewicht verloren und sei von dem Felsen herabgestürzt. Ich könne doch nicht wegen eines Geschehnisses zur Verantwortung gezogen werden, über das ich keine Gewalt gehabt hatte.

Die Analyse dieses Traumes enthüllte den unbewußten Impuls, weibliche Genitalien zu betrachten, und den verdrängten Wunsch, mit Mädchen, deren Menses eben begonnen hatten, sexuell zu verkehren. Der Gedanke, junge Mädchen im Pubertätsalter zu deflorieren, war überaus verlockend für den Träumer, obgleich er in früheren Jahren ein solches Beginnen für eine große Sünde gehalten hatte, eine Sünde, die Gott nie verzeihen würde.

Die weitere Analyse ergab, daß der Mann seinen Eltern heftig grollte, weil sie ihn dafür bestraft hatten, daß er sexuellen Neigungen oder von außen kommenden Reizen nachgab (so z. B. wenn seine ältere Schwester ihn zu sexuellem Tun verführte oder seine Mutter seine Genitalien liebkost hatte); diese Reize waren so stark gewesen, daß er ihnen nicht hatte widerstehen können; die Schuld lag aber an den Reizen, nicht an ihm. Das war zumindest seine Meinung. Daß die Genitalien seiner Mutter so schön waren und so gut rochen, war ebenfalls nicht seine Schuld, er konnte nichts dafür, daß sie so heftiges Verlangen in ihm erweckten.

Der Traum enthielt auch eine aggressiv-sadistische Tendenz. Der Gedanke, daß er den Zweig zufällig abgebrochen habe, war eine Art Rache, eine Kastration seiner Mutter zur Strafe dafür, daß sie ihn mit Kastration bedroht hatte; er ahmte damit den Vater nach, von dem er meinte, daß er die Mutter kastriert habe. Der Zweig war jedoch ein mehrfach determiniertes Symbol: Er war auch der Ölzweig, mit dem er seiner Mutter Frieden anbot. Obgleich er sich der Mutter gegenüber schuldig fühlte, weil er in der Phantasie die Schwester defloriert, ferner weil er seine Liebe zur Mutter zum Teil auf die Schwester übertragen hatte, war es klar, daß er sich auch vor dem Vater (= Polizist = Über-Ich) fürchtete, d. h. auch diesem gegenüber ein Gefühl der Schuld empfand.

Er glaubte nicht wirklich daran, daß der Sturz auf die Bäume durchaus nur Zufall gewesen war. Aber es dünkte ihn tatsächlich absurd, daß er für Taten bestraft werden sollte, die zu vermeiden er nicht stark genug gewesen war, — die Verlockung war zu groß gewesen. Seine Schwester habe ihn verlockt. Auch habe er um den Geschlechtsverkehr der Eltern gewußt, ebenso um den der Vögel und anderer Tiere.

Der Traum enthält eine Reihe von Phantasien, die auf realen Faktoren fußen. Der männliche und der weibliche Sexualtropismus sind in jenem frühen Alter von tiefer Wirkung auf das Kind; denn das frühe Kindesalter entspricht jener frühen Stufe in der Kindheit des Menschengeschlechts, auf der, ehe noch der traumatische Einfluß des Inzestgesetzes und der Sexualtabus den Geschlechtstrieb hemmten, Hör-, Tast-, Seh-, Schmeck- und Riechreize die Geschlechter so mächtig zueinander zogen.[3] Daß der Träumer seine Angriffslust immer wieder als Folge von Verlockungen hinstellte, zeigte, wie stark seine Männlichkeit in der Kindheit gewesen war; von übergroßer Wißbegier in bezug auf Sexuelles erfüllt, war er entschlossen gewesen, alle Rätsel des Geschlechtlichen zu lösen und es seinem Vater gleichzutun.

Der Traum erfuhr aber noch eine weitere Deutung, und zwar auf Grundlage der Darstellung durch das Gegenteil: Das einstmals Schöne war häßlich geworden, ein Ergebnis der Strafandrohungen von seiten des Vaters (= Polizist) wie auch der Furcht vor Kastration durch die Mutter. Er fiel, kastriert aber

3) Die Einfälle zu den Obstbaumblüten brachten die tiefe Verdrängung bezüglich des Geruchs der Vagina ans Licht. Anfänglich sagte der Patient, Obstbaumblüten hätten keinen Geruch; dann erinnerte er sich des angenehmen Empfindens, das der Duft von Rosen und der Parfüms, die seine Mutter zu verwenden pflegte, in ihm ausgelöst hatten; schließlich fiel ihm das lebhafte Interesse ein, das er an dem Sexualgeruch seiner Eltern genommen hatte, besonders an dem der Mutter. Dieses verknüpfte er auf dem Weg der Tatsachen, daß aus Obstbaumblüten Früchte werden, und Blüten einen besonderen Geruch haben, mit seinem Interesse an der Fortpflanzung. — Der englische Schriftsteller Galsworthy hat darauf hingewiesen, daß der Grund, warum viele Menschen gern Blumenausstellungen besuchen, oft ausschließlich in der Sinnenfreude liegt, die der Duft der Blumen gewährt.

wurde die Mutter oder die Schwester — er verschob Haß und Furcht auf die
Quelle der Versuchung, fühlte sich darob dann schuldig und wollte die Frauen
(= Gattin = Mutter) versöhnen, jene Frauen, von denen die Kastration gefürchtet wird, weil ihre blutende Vagina die Furcht bestätigt, welche die
eigentliche Quelle des aus dem Inzestverbrechen entspringenden Schuldgefühls
ist (Schuldgefühl = Furcht vor Strafe). Deshalb erschien der Vater (= Polizist = Über-Ich) auf dem Schauplatz und verhaftete ihn.

Daß der Sohn das Bedürfnis hatte, die Mutter wieder zu versöhnen, weil
er Geschlechtsverkehr mit einer reifen jungen Frau (= Obstbaum in Blüte =
= menstruierende Frau; siehe Freuds Bericht über ähnliche Symbole in der
„Traumdeutung") gehabt hatte, brachte die unbewußte Quelle des Schuldgefühls ans Licht, welches ihn in seiner Ehe nicht recht glücklich werden ließ.

Die Verleugnung der Mutter infolge des Menstruationstraumas ist bei vielen
Menschen eine Quelle des Schuldgefühls. Edgar Allan Poe beleuchtet diese
Tatsache auf eine besonders umfassende Art in verschiedenen seiner Er-
zählungen.

Unser Verständnis für den Ursprung des Schuldgefühls und die Art und
Weise, in welcher Angst aus der Wunschverdrängung entsteht (Freud macht
wiederholt auf die Dunkelheit dieser Vorgänge aufmerksam), wird durch die
Erkenntnis des Menstruationskomplexes gefördert.

Auf die traumatische Verdrängung der Libido und die Flucht des Ichs aus
der Wirklichkeit folgte die Verwandlung der positiven Eroberungswünsche
der Inzestphase in Angst. Das Angstgefühl entsteht in großem Ausmaß dadurch, daß das Ich die Wiederkehr jener instinktiven libidinösen Reaktionen
fürchtet, über die es im kindlichen Alter so wenig Gewalt hatte. Diese Reaktionen brachten das Kind mit den Eltern und der übrigen Umgebung in
Konflikt, es wurde mit Strafe bedroht oder wirklich bestraft; beim reifen
Menschen rufen sie gegen das Ich den introjizierten Sadismus des Über-Ichs
wach.

Beispiel B
Ein Traum

I. Bruchstück. *Ich sah eine Schar schwarzer Menschen, die, auf Schnee oder
Gras schreitend, einen steilen Berg hinanstiegen zu einem Heiligtum auf dem Gipfel.
Ich dachte, wie fromm und ehrlich oder wie angsterfüllt diese Pilger sein müßten, da
sie sich so schwer mühten. Dann überquerte ich den Fluß, um an den Fuß des Berges
zu gelangen, nach der Stelle, an der der Pilgerzug begann; dort war auch ein Heiligtum in einer Höhle, in der sich ein Priester befand. Viele Frauen waren da; die meisten
von ihnen litten an Schwindsucht und spuckten unaufhörlich Blut in kleine Schalen.
Ich hatte das Gefühl, daß es hier gefährlich sei, da man sich diese entsetzliche Krankheit holen könne; um nicht mit den Frauen in Berührung zu kommen, trat ich auf eine
erhöhte Steinplatte. Von hier führte eine eiserne Leiter nach dem Heiligtum auf dem
Bergesgipfel hinauf. Der Priester war oben — irgendwie schien er aber auch unten*

zu sein, bei den blutenden Frauen, die ihm gehörten. Ich begann, die Leiter Sprosse um Sprosse hinaufzusteigen, merkte aber, daß ich nicht bis hinauf gelangen würde, und begann zu fürchten, ich könnte fallen und so sterben. Als ich ein Stück hinaufgelangt war, fürchtete ich mich auch hinabzusehen, denn das würde mich von der Gewißheit meines Todes überzeugt haben, und ich wäre erst recht gefallen.

II. Bruchstück. Ich kam dann an einen Ort, an dem ich schon früher als Tuberkuloser behandelt worden war; ich sollte meine Kur zu Ende führen. Die Patienten gingen auf einem offenen Platz im Kreise umher wie Pferde oder Maultiere, die man zureitet; sie sahen entsetzlich krank aus, man merkte ihnen an, daß sie bald sterben würden. Es waren nur Männer und Knaben. Ich hoffte, daß der Arzt sich meiner erinnern und sich freuen würde, mich zu sehen, denn ich war ja anders als seine sterbenskranken Patienten. Ich hatte nur noch eine kurze Zeit der Behandlung nötig, dann würde ich geheilt sein — was ich brauchte, war Liebe, dann würde ich von selbst gesund werden. — Ich erwachte dadurch, daß ich meine Mutter (oder Schwester oder Frau) um Hilfe rufen hörte. Allmählich wurde mir klar, daß niemand gerufen hatte, daß dies nur ein Traumbild gewesen war.

Analyse des Traumes

Ich gebe hier die Analyse zum Teil in direkter Rede, möglichst mit den eigenen Worten des Patienten, wieder:

„Als meine Frau schreit, daß sie in Gefahr sei, und mich zu Hilfe ruft, springe ich nicht gleich auf, um ihr zu Hilfe zu eilen, — obwohl ich im Traum das Gefühl hatte, sie werde von einem Dieb getötet: Da ist es, glaube ich, klar, daß ich meine Furcht davor, von meinem Vater (dem Dieb, der, wie ich dachte, meine Genitalien stehlen wollte) getötet zu werden, auf sie verschiebe und wünsche, er möge sie und nicht mich töten. Eine gerechte Strafe dafür, daß sie mir gedroht hatte, mich zu kastrieren, wenn ich masturbierte, denn ich hatte nur masturbiert, weil ich nicht die Möglichkeit hatte, sie zu lieben. Aber wenn ich auch den Haß meiner Frau fürchte, so hat sie doch nie geradeheraus gedroht, sie werde mich kastrieren; ich verschiebe also offenbar meine haßerfüllte Furcht vor meiner Mutter auf sie.

Ich muß mir in der Kindheit eingebildet haben, daß mein Vater die Mutter töte oder kastriere, wenn er auf ihr liege, und hinter dieser Vorstellung stand, das ist klar, ein Wunsch. (Der Vater bestätigte, daß der Patient als Kind in einem Bettchen im Schlafzimmer der Eltern geschlafen habe.) Wenn mein Vater in das Schlafzimmer kam, dachte ich immer, daß er meiner Mutter nun dasselbe tun werde, was die Stiere den Kühen tun. (Der Patient hatte seine ersten vier Lebensjahre auf einem Landgut verbracht.) In dem Traum ruft zwar meine Frau (= Mutter) nach mir, aber man muß das zum Teil umkehren, damit es verständlich wird: Ich pflegte angsterfüllt meine Mutter zu rufen, wenn der Vater Geschlechtsverkehr mit ihr hatte, aber sie antwortete mir nicht. Dafür strafe ich sie im Traum, indem ich sie ihrem Schicksal und dem Dieb überlasse.

Da ich auf meinen Vater eifersüchtig war und ihm den Tod wünschte, überkam mich die Furcht, er könnte mich ebensosehr hassen wie ich ihn und mich töten.

Ich haßte ihn, weil er mit meiner Mutter schlief, während ich in ein kleines Bettchen neben ihrem Bett verbannt worden war, — da mußte ich liegen, während er die Mutter liebkoste und alles Mögliche mit ihr anstellte und mich dadurch in Erregung versetzte, so daß ich masturbierte. Dafür strafte mich meine Mutter dann, wenn sie es entdeckte, und drohte mir mit Kastration. Das ließ mich wünschen, ich hätte eine Waffe gleich der meines Vaters, mit der ich sie strafen könnte. Es ist also klar, daß ich mich nun mit meinem Vater identifizierte und wünschte, ich hätte einen Penis, mit dem ich meine Mutter angreifen könnte. Ich masturbierte, wenn ich mich vor meinem Vater fürchtete, und sehnte mich dabei, an der Brust meiner Mutter zu saugen, — aus dieser Phantasie scheine ich ein Gefühl des Schutzes vor dem Angriff meines Vaters gewonnen zu haben.

Obgleich die Kastrationsdrohung meiner Mutter den sadistischen Wunsch in mir erweckte, ich könnte sie so behandeln wie mein Vater sie, und wie alle männlichen Tiere die weiblichen behandeln, glaubte ich doch nicht wirklich an ihre Kastrationsdrohung, bis ich eines Tages entdeckte, daß sie zwischen den Beinen blutete. Das bestätigte mir die Möglichkeit der Kastration, und die Furcht, daß man mich kastrieren und ich wie meine Mutter und meine Schwester werden könnte, machte mir die beiden und alle Frauen abscheulich und verhaßt.[4] Ich wünschte sie zu lieben, konnte es aber nicht aus Furcht vor ihrer blutenden Vagina. Liebe war mir jedoch eine Notwendigkeit, ich fühlte, daß ich ohne sie nicht leben konnte; daher begann ich zu wünschen, ich würde wie meine Mutter bluten und so die Liebe meines Vaters gewinnen, denn ich hatte bemerkt, daß er sie trotz seiner sadistischen Angriffe auf sie oft liebkoste und küßte und überhaupt liebevoll gegen sie war. So hatte sie mich liebkost, als sie noch ganz mir gehört hatte. Ich wünschte, daß entweder meine Mutter einen Penis anstatt einer blutenden Vagina hätte, so daß sie mich hätte lieben können, wie mein Vater sie liebte; oder daß ich selbst eine blutende Vagina hätte, damit mein Vater mich hätte lieben können, wie er sie liebte, bevor sie ein Kind bekam.

Als sie schwanger wurde, haßte und verabscheute ich sie sogar noch mehr als zu der Zeit, da ich ihr Bluten entdeckt hätte; sadistische Wünsche gegen sie und ihren dicken Bauch regten sich in mir, wie so viele meiner Träume gezeigt haben. Woher ich wußte, daß ich ein Rivalen enthielt, kann ich nicht sagen, daß ich es aber wußte, haben meine Träume klar bewiesen.[5] Ich fühlte, daß sie auf das Kind urinieren würde, wenn es geboren war, und ihm erlauben würde, auf sie zu urinieren und an ihren Brüsten zu saugen, — dafür haßte ich sowohl sie als auch das Kind."

Mit der Geburt des kleinen Bruders und Rivalen erreichte sein Haß einen Höhepunkt. Er verschob dann den Haß gegen die Eltern auf das Kind und war so allmählich imstande, seinen negativen Ödipuskomplex zu verdrängen. Dies vollzog sich, indem er für seine grausamen Impulse Betätigung fand: Er übertrug sie auf Geschöpfe, die kleiner und schwächer waren als er selbst, auf

---

4) Tiefer dringende Analyse ergab eine hinter diesem Haß und Abscheu stehende Tatsache, nämlich daß er in der Vorstellung, ein Mädchen zu deflorieren und zu verwunden, die tiefste sadistische Befriedigung empfand. Er lebte jedoch auf der Stufe der Reaktionsbildung, legte übertriebene Zärtlichkeit für Frauen an den Tag nebst dem Zwang, ihre Liebe zu gewinnen und sie dann im Stich zu lassen.

5) In einem früheren Zeitpunkt der Analyse waren folgende Phantasien ans Licht gekommen: Er hatte den Leib der schwangeren Mutter mit einem Messer aufgeschlitzt und den Feind, der da seinem Empfinden nach war (= der Penis des Vaters und das werdende Kind, das ihn seiner Rechte berauben würde), getötet. (Er war bei der Geburt des kleinen Bruders vier Jahre alt.) Vielleicht ist das Wissen um die Schwangerschaft der Mutter ererbt; jedenfalls zeigt sich der Haß gegen die schwangere Mutter sogar schon bei zweijährigen Kindern. Möglicherweise läßt der dicke Leib der schwangeren Mutter im Kind die Furcht, von den Eltern gefressen zu werden, neu aufleben.

Int. Zeitschr. f. Psychoanalyse, XXI/3   27

Insekten, Frösche, Kröten usw. Indem er solche Tiere quälte und tötete, vermochte er seinem Haß und seinen sadistischen Wünschen gegen den kleinen Bruder und gegen den Phallus des Vaters Ausdruck zu geben. Sein Ingrimm richtete sich anfänglich gegen Wesen, die krochen und in Teichen lebten, später gegen Ratten und Mäuse, die aus Löchern hervorkommen und wieder darin verschwinden. Seinen Höhepunkt erreichte dieses sadistische Haßgefühl, wenn er die Tiere tötete und Blut floß: Er hatte dann eine von freudigem Lustgefühl begleitete Erektion. Er spielte Begräbnis mit den toten Tieren, setzte ihnen Leichensteine und empfand Kummer und Reue darüber, daß er sie getötet hatte; dann stellte er sich vor, daß es sich um den Leichnam seines Vaters handle, und daß er nun mit der verwitweten Mutter lieb sein werde.

Später bereitete es ihm großes Vergnügen, Vögel mit einer Schleuder zu töten, insbesondere Rotkehlchen und Zaunkönige, weil diese als heilige Vögel gelten. Die Analyse ergab, daß er, indem er sie tötete, die Mutter tötete und daß die rote Kehle (Verschiebung von unten nach oben) besondere Anziehungskraft besaß. Durch die Analyse seines sadistischen Verhaltens gegen das Rotkehlchen und der „Heiligkeit" dieses Vogels kamen wir endlich zu einer unmittelbaren Analyse des Traumes, denn wir entdeckten, daß die rote Kehle die blutende Vagina der Mutter symbolisierte, welche anzubeten die schwarzen (= schuldigen) Pilger (= sein zweites Selbst) den Berg emporkeuchten, und das sowohl aus Liebe als auch aus Furcht; sie sollten oben Gott anbeten — er war der Meinung, daß das Weib in ihm Gott anbetete, der Mann in ihm jedoch das Weib anzubeten scheine, vor dem er sich aber, das war ihm klar, auch fürchtete; irgendwie, fand er, enthalte diese Furcht vor der Mutter auch die Furcht vor dem Vater.

Die schwarzen Menschen, die mühselig über Rasen hinweg den Berg hinaufkeuchen, um anzubeten, sind jene Schuldigen, für die der Koitus ebensosehr Qual ist wie Freude, weil sie den Vater fürchten, der im Heiligtum (= blutende Vagina) wohnt. Das Gras auf dem Berg ist das Haar des Mons veneris, der Schnee symbolisiert die Leidenschaft (Darstellung durch das Gegenteil). Der Vater, der als in der Vagina wohnend gefürchtet wird, ist der introjizierte Vater, den der Sohn unbewußt fürchtet; dieser Vater zwingt den Sohn, seine Schuld einzugestehen und um die Liebe der Eltern zu bitten, die ein Schutz ist gegen ihren Zorn. Die Darstellung durch das Gegenteil spielte in allen Träumen dieses Patienten eine Rolle.

„Die Blut spuckenden, schwindsüchtigen Frauen vor dem Heiligtum in dem Flußtal, wo sie mit dem Priester lebten (vielleicht in der Hoffnung, geheilt zu werden), mußten um jeden Preis gemieden werden, denn sie waren gefährlich; jede Berührung mit ihnen mußte den Tod bringen, den Tod durch die Hand des Priesters (= Vater), dessen Schatten in der Höhle (= Vagina) zu sehen war.[6] Eine dieser Frauen glich

---

6) Auch Hindu-Künstler lassen, wenn sie in der Durga-Mythe den Tod des bösen Asura (= Sohn) durch die Hand der Mutter darstellen, Gott den Vater als schattenhafte Gestalt zwischen Wolken erscheinen.

einer alten Hexe, ganz schwarz, mit blutigem Mund; ich hätte mich ihr gern zärtlich
genähert, wenn ich das gekonnt hätte, denn so entsetzlich und hassenswert ihr Bild
ist, scheine ich sie doch auch innig zu lieben. Ich konnte mich ihr aber nicht nähern,
denn sie war zu abscheulich, als sie von Zeit zu Zeit Blut in einen Topf spuckte, den
sie zwischen den Beinen hielt — das Gefäß floß fast schon über von schleimigem
Blut, sie aber betrachtete es wohlgefällig. Ich fürchtete mich entsetzlich vor einer
Berührung mit ihr und ihrem Blut; deshalb wandte ich mich von ihr ab und versuchte, die Leiter zum Himmel emporzuklettern, — Stufen hinaufzusteigen, bedeutet
aber Koitus, wie ich aus anderen Träumen schon weiß: also bedeutet dies, daß ich
mich ihr zuwandte (d. h. das Bluten war sowohl anziehend wie auch abstoßend). Ich
begann emporzusteigen, blieb aber auf halbem Weg stecken, die Furcht, daß ich
hinunterfallen und sterben könnte, lähmte mich. Je höher ich stieg, desto gewisser
schien es zu werden, daß ich hinabfallen und sterben würde. Ich fürchtete mich vor
der Furcht und war gelähmt von Furcht. Offenbar ist der Mann, der oben auf dem
Gipfel wohnt, mein Vater, und er wird mich um meines Inzestverbrechens willen
erschlagen. Die Leiter, die ich emporsteige, bedeutet symbolisch seinen Koitus mit
meiner Mutter, und ich darf nicht hinaufsteigen so wie er, denn das würde unbedingt
mein Tod sein.

Der Berg symbolisiert auch einen riesigen Phallus und der Fluß die Vagina meiner
Mutter. Ich darf die beiden anbeten, aber, es ihnen sexuell gleichzutun, ist mein Tod.
Der blutende Mund der schwarzen Frau symbolisiert die blutende Vagina meiner
Mutter. Ich verschiebe meinen Haß gegen meinen Vater und meine Furcht vor ihm
sowie auch meine eigene Schuld auf sie; die Schuld zeigt sich darin, daß sie schwarz
ist; ihre blutende Vagina erinnert mich an meine Todesfurcht. Ich verschiebe das
Bluten nach oben in ihren Mund, weil ich den Mund meines Vaters fürchte; ich
fürchte, daß er mich fressen wird, so wie ich einst, von sadistischer Lust erfaßt, die
Brüste meiner Mutter fressen wollte, später seinen verhaßten Penis, der in die Mutter
eindringt und sie bluten macht. Dieser Anblick erweckte lustvolle Leidenschaft in
mir, bis das Bluten sich mit der Kastration und dem Tod verknüpfte, und so das
Lustgefühl sich in Furcht und Haß verwandelte. Ich gehe dann an einen Ort, an
dem ich von meiner Krankheit geheilt werden soll." (Krankheit = Schuld = Angst
zu verbluten = Kastration = Furcht, gefressen zu werden = Furcht, verzehrt zu
werden = Auszehrung.) „Daß diese Krankheit, die Strafe für ein Vergehen ist, die
Lunge (= Brust) befällt, hat nichts Überraschendes, denn ich hatte einmal versucht,
meine Mutter in die Brust zu beißen." (Der Geschmack der Mutterbrust erweckt die
aggressive Komponente des Ernährungsinstinktes, jeder Widerstand der Mutter
steigert sowohl sie wie auch den Wunsch, die Mutter zu besitzen, sie sich einzuverleiben.) „Später, als sie mir meines Masturbierens wegen mit Kastration gedroht
hatte, wünschte ich, ihr die Brüste abzuschneiden.

Ich ging an den Ort, an dem sich die Lungenkranken befanden, und gesellte mich
zu ihnen, denn auch ich war schuldig. Sie gingen auf grasbedecktem Boden im Kreis
umher wie Pferde, die zugeritten werden. Dies Imkreisumhergehen gehörte zu den
Freiluftübungen, die der Arzt (Vater) mit ihnen durchführte. Eine erbärmliche
Schar war es, alle todkrank zur Strafe dafür, daß sie masturbiert und sich des Inzests
schuldig gemacht hatten. Der Penis war ihnen abgeschnitten worden, sie mußten
verbluten, und es hatte nicht den Anschein, als ob der Arzt (= mein Vater) sie wirklich zu retten gedachte; denn er liebte sie nicht wirklich, mindestens hoffte ich das,
obgleich sie mir leid taten, — ich wünschte aber, daß er nur mich allein lieben solle.
Doch stellten sie in Wirklichkeit alle mich dar, der ich wenig Hoffnung auf Rettung
habe, weil ich haßte und meinem Vater den Tod wünschte und nun fürchte, daß er

27*

Gleiches mit Gleichem vergelten, mich sterben lassen und sich an meinen Leiden weiden würde. Ich brauche eine Versicherung seiner Liebe, weil ich so sehr fürchte, durch seine Hand sterben zu müssen."

Ein Bruchstück der Analyse kam erst später ans Licht: die Deutung des Umstands, daß der Träumer auf eine Steinplatte tritt, um nicht mit dem Blut der Mutter in Berührung zu kommen. Der Stein bedeutet etwas Hartes im Gegensatz zu dem weichen Körper der Mutter, etwas, das nicht riecht und deshalb sicher ist, — denn der Geruch der menstruierenden Mutter erfüllte jetzt seine Seele mit Furcht, obgleich er ahnte, daß dieser Geruch einstmals, während der Entwicklungsphase vor dem Ödipuskomplex, etwas Anziehendes für ihn gehabt hatte. Ebenso waren damals auch seine analen Gerüche sowie die anderer Menschen und die der Tiere anziehend für ihn gewesen.

Was uns an dem Traum vorwiegend interessiert, ist, daß er sehr klar beleuchtet, **wie unter dem Einfluß der Menstruation der Mutter die Inzestwünsche des Kindes sowohl erweckt als auch gehemmt werden und die libidinösen Kräfte auf dem Wege der Regression ein anal-sadistisches Ziel erhalten.** Außerdem zeigt er, daß eine der wesentlichen Ursachen für die Verdrängung der tropistischen Reaktionen auf Geruchsreize im Menstruationstrauma liegt und nicht nur, wie Freud vermutet, in der Annahme der aufrechten Haltung.

Die weitere Analyse dieses Traumes brachte eine Erinnerung an die Mutter ans Licht: Die Mutter sitzt auf dem Nachttopf (das Gefäß zwischen ihren Beinen), und es läuft Blut in den Topf. Es ließ sich nachweisen, daß dieser Vorfall stattgefunden haben mußte, als der Patient noch nicht dreieinviertel Jahre alt war, denn als er in diesem Alter stand, wurde seine Mutter wieder schwanger. Das Bluten aus dem Mund ist eine Verschiebung nach oben, das Spucken eine Projektion seines Hasses gegen die Mutter auf diese selbst. An diesem Punkt der Analyse fiel ihm der Priester in der Höhle wieder ein: Er meinte, daß der Mann zwar gewiß ein Priester, trotzdem aber von böser Wesensart sei, das Bluten der Frauen nicht heile, sondern vielmehr schuld daran sei und sich in böser Lust an ihren „scheinbaren" Schmerzen weide. Als ich ihn fragte, warum er das Wort „scheinbar" gebraucht habe, sagte er, daß er an ihre Leiden nicht wirklich glaube, es komme ihm vielmehr so vor, als ob die Frauen ihre Krankheit ganz gleichgültig hinnähmen. Dazu fiel ihm wieder etwas ein: Als er noch ein ganz kleines Kind gewesen war, pflegte seine Mutter ihre blutigen Monatsbinden in seiner Anwesenheit zu wechseln, ohne zu merken, wie schrecklich, abscheulich und ekelhaft ihm ihr Bluten geworden war. Irgendwie, sagte er, scheine sowohl die heilige als auch die unheimliche Atmosphäre, die Frauen umgibt, mit ihren Vaginalblutungen zusammenzuhängen.

Beispiel C
Ein Traum

„Ich traf zwei Mädchen an Bord eines Schiffes und verlobte mich mit dem einen. Jemand sagte mir, daß das schöne Mädchen krank sei oder die Auszehrung habe. Da wurde ich sehr ängstlich und überlegte unruhig, wie ich es dem süßen, lieblichen Geschöpf beibringen sollte, daß ich sie nicht mehr liebte und nun, da ich um ihre Krankheit wußte, nicht mehr daran dächte, sie zu heiraten. Die Vorstellung, sie zu küssen, war mir nun durchaus abstoßend geworden. Ich ging den Hügel hinunter zu dem kleinen Haus ihrer Freundin, wo ich sie treffen sollte. Als ich dort angelangt war, legte ich mich mit der Freundin ins Bett. Wir waren beide nackt, und ich hätte gern Geschlechtsverkehr mit ihr gehabt, fürchtete aber, sie würde denken, ich sei ihrer Freundin, meiner Verlobten, untreu. Ihr warmer nackter Körper, den ich an meinem fühlte, war aber eine zu große Versuchung, er verlockte mich wider meinen Willen, und ich hatte, an sie geschmiegt, eine Ejakulation. Ich bat sie um Verzeihung und brachte zu meiner Entschuldigung vor, daß ich eben eine fieberhafte Enteritis überstanden hätte und infolgedessen schwach sei. Sie zeigte sich sehr liebevoll und sagte, daß sie mich ganz und gar verstehe. Dann kam irgendwie ein böser Mann in das Haus, und ich war bemüht, mich davonzustehlen, denn ich wollte nicht, daß er denke, ich hätte Geschlechtsverkehr mit diesem Mädchen gehabt."

Die Analyse des Traumes

ergab, daß die gefürchtete Krankheit eine Verschiebung seiner Furcht vor der Menstrualblutung nach oben war. Als der Patient entdeckt hatte, daß seine Mutter zwischen den Beinen blutete, hatte er sich vor ihr zu fürchten begonnen; er hatte sie nicht mehr geliebt und war von dem Gefühl erfüllt gewesen, daß sie gefährlich sei und um jeden Preis gemieden werden müsse. Er erinnerte sich nun mehrerer Erlebnisse aus verschiedenen Zeiten mit Frauen oder Mädchen, zu denen er in Liebesbeziehungen gestanden hatte. Als er die Geliebte nach einer Zeit des Getrenntseins unter günstigen Umständen traf, menstruierte sie, so daß ein Verkehr unmöglich war; zwei der in Frage stehenden Frauen sagten ihm, daß sie bei dieser Gelegenheit ihre Menses zu früh und gerade am Tag seiner Ankunft bekommen hatten. (Der Leser erinnere sich an die Feststellung Groddecks, daß die Frau in solchen Fällen unbewußt die Menstruation hervorruft, um die Leidenschaft des Mannes zu vergrößern; meine eigenen Beobachtungen haben diese Feststellung vielfach bestätigt.)

In zwei Fällen, in denen es sich um verheiratete Frauen handelte, war mein Patient nach jenem Erlebnis der zu früh eingetretenen Menstruation von Furcht befallen worden, daß der Gatte der Geliebten der Sache auf die Spur kommen könnte; in einem dritten Fall, in welchem es sich um ein unverheiratetes Mädchen handelte, hatte er sich vor ihrem Vater zu fürchten begonnen, obgleich er vor jenem Erlebnis an solche Furcht nicht gedacht hatte. In einem vierten Fall hatte es sich um eine sehr schöne Prostituierte gehandelt:

72

Er hatte Verkehr mit ihr gehabt, während sie menstruierte, und litt danach unter heftiger Furcht, daß er sich mit Syphilis angesteckt haben könnte; dabei fühlte er sich sowohl seiner Mutter als auch seinem Vater gegenüber sehr schuldbewußt. Er fürchtete sich vor dem Menstruationszustand der Frau, überdies auch vor der „Auszehrung"; denn Berührung mit einer solchen Frau, sagte er, bedeute, daß der Mann auch krank werde und sterbe; außerdem werde er von der Gesellschaft verabscheut und verachtet, weil er sich von einer Frau habe anstecken lassen. Hier fiel ihm ein, daß er zu verschiedenen Zeiten unter hypochondrischer Angst vor allerlei Krankheiten gelitten hatte, vor Auszehrung, Syphilis, Leberabszeß, Blattern usw.; und immer war er zur Zeit solcher Angst entweder in ein besonders schönes Mädchen verliebt gewesen, das er aus einer Hemmung heraus nicht heiraten konnte, obgleich er das zu tun wünschte, oder er hatte in erzwungener Enthaltsamkeit gelebt. Ich konnte diese Angaben in zwei Fällen nachprüfen. Er hatte tatsächlich die Liebe zweier besonders anziehender und geistig hochstehender Mädchen gewonnen. Keine der beiden scheint ihm gegrollt zu haben, weil er sie verließ, denn sie erkannten offenbar mit weiblicher Intuition, daß er gegen etwas Unbewußtes ankämpfte, das sich seiner Beherrschung entzog: In beiden Fällen konnte er wieder lieben, sobald von Heirat nicht mehr die Rede war, und mit dem einen der beiden Mädchen hatte er sehr genußreiche sexuelle Beziehungen. Die Ehe hatte für ihn also die Bedeutung des Inzests. Ich habe in mehreren Fällen feststellen können, daß dies die Grundlage von Ehekonflikten bildete. Die Analyse der erwähnten Hypochondrie brachte verschiedenes Interessantes ans Licht. Hinter der Furcht vor Krankheit lag der negative Ödipuswunsch des Patienten, krank zu werden, aber, wie er betonte, nicht der Wunsch zu sterben. Vielmehr lag darin unmittelbare, echte Todesfurcht, die den positiven Ödipuswunsch nach Verkehr mit Frauen zu gewissen Zeiten verdeckte, nämlich dann, wenn sie für ihn verboten, jedoch anziehend waren. Anziehend waren sie, wie er sagte, teils durch gewisse Merkmale in ihrem Blick und in ihrem Teint, besonders aber durch den süß verlockenden Geruch ihres Atems. Er erkannte, daß die Todesfurcht um so größer wurde, in je stärkerem Maße er unter dem Zwang stand zu heiraten; besonders fürchtete er, daß der Vater irgendeines Mädchens ihn zwingen werde, es zu heiraten. Er sagte, der Vater würde das aus Rache tun, denn er würde finden, das Mädchen sei durch die Liebesbeziehung entehrt. Er würde also gezwungen werden zu heiraten, somit an eine Frau gefesselt sein und alle Freiheit verloren haben. Dies erwies sich als eine Wiederkehr verdrängter Gedanken über die Beziehungen des Vaters zur Mutter in der Urszene.

Als ich ihn fragte, warum er der Anziehung durch den Atem der Frau solche Bedeutung beimesse, erwiderte er: „O, man nennt sie blutige Hündinnen, und das sind sie auch, wenn sie bluten. Ich finde sie aber hinreißend, wenn sie gleich den Hündinnen läufig sind." Als ich ihn nach Einfällen zu dem Umstand fragte, daß er die Mädchen im Traum an Bord eines Schiffes getroffen habe, sagte er, er habe sie in einem tropischen Landstrich getroffen; dann meinte er, daß „an Bord eines Schiffes" einen warmen Ort bedeute und den Körper seiner Mutter symbolisiere.

Es wurde schließlich klar, daß die beiden Frauen seine Mutter und seine Schwester darstellten — diejenige, mit der er sich verlobte, war seine Mutter, gehörte also seinem Vater, und zwar besonders im Zusammenhang mit dem augenfälligen Kennzeichen ihrer Periode; die andere, die seine Schwester war, schien in gewissem Ausmaß auch dem Vater zu gehören, doch konnte er sich ihr leichter nähern, weil sie nicht krank war (= nicht menstruierte). Mit ihr durfte er aber gewisser Gesetze wegen keinen Geschlechtsverkehr haben, außerdem wäre er dadurch seiner Mutter untreu geworden, an die ihn eine Liebeserklärung band, die er aber im Unbewußten haßte und verabscheute, weil sie krank war. An sie war er doppelt gebunden: unbewußt durch den verdrängten Haß und die Schuld der grausamen Wünsche einer frühen Phase, bewußt durch eine später entwickelte, auch zärtliche Liebe von mehr geistiger Art.

In dem Traum war nicht nur die Mutter, sondern auch er selbst krank gewesen. Und auf die Freundin (= Schwester) übertrug er in dem Traum zur Zeit seines Menstruationstraumas seine Liebe. Als er sich aber von seiner fieberhaften Enteritis (= Menstruationstrauma) erholt hatte, bedurfte er aufs neue der Liebe der Mutter und entschuldigte sich bei ihr im Traum, etwa in diesem Sinn: „Deine körperlichen Reize waren so groß, und ich war so schwach, daß meinem Gewissen zum Trotz die Begierde überstark in mir wurde und ich eine unwillkürliche Ejakulation hatte, obgleich ich bewußt dagegen ankämpfte."

Darauf antwortete die alles begreifende Traum-Mutter mitfühlend, daß sie ihn ganz und gar verstehe. Das bezog sich auf ihr Verständnis und ihr Mitgefühl anläßlich seines Bettnässens in der Kinderzeit, welches eine inzestuöse Grundlage gehabt hatte. Er fühlte, daß diese Freundin ihn für untreu gegen seine Braut halten würde, wenn er tatsächlich in sie eindränge; dennoch bewies die Tatsache, daß sie sich nackt mit ihm ins Bett gelegt hatte, wie wertvoll ihr seine Liebe war, solange keine bestimmte sexuelle Annäherung stattfand. Das zeigte, daß wir es mit der vergangenen Situation seiner Mutter gegenüber zu tun hatten, zurückverlegt auf den Perseus-Andromeda- oder sekundären Ödipuskomplex,[7] und daß daher die beiden Freundinnen nichts anderes sind als zweierlei Aspekte seiner Mutter, die er auch in jeder anderen Frau sieht. Hier erkannte er klar, daß er an seine Mutter gefesselt war, und zwar auf eine besonders heilige Art, wie man durch heilige Schwüre gebunden ist; infolgedessen war es ihm unmöglich, den Geschlechtsverkehr mit irgendeiner anderen Frau völlig zu genießen: Immer fürchtete er die Vorwürfe seiner Mutter.

7) Vgl. Daly, Int. Journ. of Psa., XI.

Die Freundin seiner Verlobten war nicht krank, sie hatte einen rosigen Teint und war begehrenswert. Er fühlte den Wunsch in sich, sie zu lieben, wurde aber durch ihren kranken Widerpart — den er als die Mutter erkennt — daran gehindert. An diesem Punkt des Traumes erschien der Vater als ein böser Mann auf dem Schauplatz. Hier ergab die Analyse, daß er gewünscht hatte, wirklich in das Mädchen einzudringen, daran aber durch Furcht vor dem Vater und ein Schuldgefühl gegen diesen gehindert worden war. Der böse Mann war der Vater, von dem er dachte, daß er die Mutter bluten gemacht habe. Das zeigt, daß auf der tiefsten Stufe die Furcht vor dem Vater den Sohn hemmt, daß diese Furcht aber auf die Mutter verschoben wird, und zwar infolge des Schrecks, den sowohl der Anblick wie auch der Geruch der mütterlichen Vagina während der Menstruation in der Seele des kleinen Jungen hervorrufen. Dieser Schreck bewirkt die Verdrängung seines tiefsten Hasses, des Hasses gegen den Vater, und seiner Leidenschaft für die Mutter.

Während der Analyse gähnte der Patient unaufhörlich und sagte immer wieder, er sei so müde, daß er gar nicht wieder würde aufstehen können. Dahinter stand deutlich die verdrängte Leidenschaft für seine Mutter.

Ich will seine Assoziationen möglichst wörtlich anführen:

„Ihr liebes, rosiges kleines Hinterteil war mir zugekehrt, es war süß, sie so warm an mir zu fühlen, ich spürte, daß ich sie von ganzem Herzen liebte und sie begehrte. Ich durfte sie aber nicht haben, weil ich ihrer kranken Freundin, die ich nun verabscheute und haßte, verpflichtet war. Sie, das weiß ich jetzt, stellte die Mutter dar, die ich einst so leidenschaftlich liebte, — alle Frauen stellen mir die Mutter dar. Ich habe eine Ejakulation an ihrem lieben, rosigen Hinterteil, weil ich die Vagina vorne fürchte; aber ich dringe selbst im Traume nicht in ihren After ein, weil der Schmutz und der Geruch des Kots mich an meine schmutzige Tat (= Schuld) erinnern würden, auch sehne ich mich ja tief in meiner Seele danach, in ihre geliebte Vagina einzudringen, doch hindert mich daran meine Furcht vor der Blutung, hinter welcher die Furcht vor meinem Vater steht.

Ich erkenne jetzt so klar, daß alle Strafen, die sie mir auferlegte, zweifach begründet waren: durch ihre Eifersucht auf meine Schwester (ihre Tochter) und durch ihre Furcht vor meinem Vater.

Ich schämte mich im Traum, nachdem ich eine Ejakulation an ihrem Körper gehabt hatte — der wahre Grund dafür war aber, daß es so schnell gekommen war, bevor ich noch Zeit gehabt hatte, in sie einzudringen. Dieses Gefühl der Scham, das sehe ich jetzt klar, kommt daher, daß ich halb bewußt seine Ursache erkenne und fühle, wie sie mich ob meiner Feigheit verachten wird. Ich war nicht imstande, ihr volle Befriedigung zu geben, — daran ist die Furcht vor meinen Eltern schuld, besonders die vor meinem Vater, der jetzt, obgleich ich mein leidenschaftliches Verlangen nur halb gestillt habe, auf dem Schauplatz des Traumes erscheint, so daß ich mich wie ein geschlagener Hund oder wie ein Dieb davonstehle. Ich hasse und verabscheue ihn um meiner eigenen Feigheit willen und verschiebe meine eigene Schlechtigkeit auf ihn. Aber ich habe schon entdeckt, daß ich meinen Vater für schlecht halte, weil er meine Mutter bluten machte; also sehe ich ein, daß unter allen meinen auf Bluten bezüglichen Verdrängungen zutiefst ein Wunsch verborgen liegt, Frauen zu deflorieren und sie bluten zu machen — denn dieses Bluten ist das Symbol meiner Männlichkeit, d. h. der Tapferkeit und der Eroberung.“

Phylogenetisch mag dem der Wunsch entsprechen, alle Rivalen zu besiegen und das reife junge Weib zu zwingen, sich zu ergeben. Die analytische Überwindung des Menstruationskomplexes könnte nun bewirken, daß unsere Art in einer zukünftigen Entwicklungsphase ihre Todesfurcht (die durch die Kastrationsfurcht verstärkt wurde) in hinreichendem Maße überwindet und so vielleicht imstande sein wird, sich des Lebens ungestörter zu freuen.

Die weitere Analyse brachte zutage, daß seine Hypochondrie sowie gelegentliche tatsächliche Erkrankungen den Sinn einer Abwehr gegen die Ehe hatten, die für ihn Inzest bedeutete; denn mit der Eheschließung hätte seine Frau die Bedeutung einer Mutter-Imago in vollem Ausmaß gewonnen.

Auf ähnliche Art bedeutete auch die Beziehung zu Prostituierten Inzest, denn diese Frauen waren kranke Imagines der Mutter. Daher ersehnte er Strafe durch Infektion: Strafe hätte sein Gewissen erleichtert, das schuldbeladen war, weil er seinen inzestuösen Wünschen nachgegeben hatte.

An Lungenschwindsucht (oder an Hämorrhoiden) zu erkranken, stellte den tiefsten Wunsch seiner negativen Ödipusphase dar, denn er glaubte tatsächlich, daß er durch Blutungen unwiderstehlich anziehend für Männer werden würde, daß Ärzte, die Ersatzpersonen des Vaters für ihn waren, ihn innig bemitleiden und lieben würden. Wenn ein Arzt, den er aufsuchte, ihm sagte, er sei nicht krank, überkam ihn tiefste Niedergeschlagenheit; wollte ein Arzt ihn aber operieren oder ihm eine Injektion geben, so wurde er heiter und unterzog sich dem Eingriff mit offensichtlicher Befriedigung. Die Ähnlichkeit zwischen diesem Fall und dem Patienten in Freuds „Geschichte einer infantilen Neurose" ist auffallend.

Beispiel D

Der Träumer erwachte aus einem Traum und sprach mit lauter Stimme die folgenden Worte:

„Der tiefere, kürzere Weg muß von Blut gesäubert werden, bevor man den Geschlechtsakt genießen kann."

Er war wütend, als er erwachte. Seiner Erinnerung schwebte das Bild zweier Röhren vor, die kürzere war voll Blut. Diese stellte den Vaginalgang einer Frau dar, die längere ihren Analgang.

Analyse

Die Liebe des Patienten zu seiner Frau war plötzlich in Haß umgeschlagen, nachdem er eines Tages ihre blutige Monatsbinde und Blutflecken auf dem Bettlaken gesehen hatte. Er wurde infolge dieses Erlebnisses passiv, hatte keine Erektionen mehr, und sein Penis schrumpfte zusammen.

Früher war er sehr potent gewesen, hatte häufige und kräftige Erektionen gehabt und den Geschlechtsakt mit Freundinnen vollzogen, selbst wenn diese menstruierten.

Der Grund für jene außerordentlich starke Reaktion wurde klar: Sie war erstens nach einem Ereignis eingetreten, das symbolisch eine Kastration bedeutete, nämlich nach einem Verlust von Besitz und Geld. Zweitens trat sie ein, während er zu Besuch in einer Stadt weilte, in welcher eine sehr gefürchtete Ersatzperson des Vaters lebte. (Ich möchte hier den Leser noch einmal daran erinnern, daß im Folklore und in der Mythologie die Frau Gott gehört, wenn sie menstruiert.) Als ein Ergebnis dieses Traumas wiederholte er, was anläßlich seines infantilen Traumas geschehen war: Damals hatte er seine Männlichkeit von sich gewiesen und war passiv homosexuell geworden; er hatte um die Liebe des Vaters geworben, die Mutter als Nebenbuhlerin empfunden und ein Kind vom Vater ersehnt.

Als Nächstes kamen Assoziationen zu der Mandelentzündung, an der er häufig litt. Er neigte ganz besonders zu dieser Krankheit, wenn er Verkehr mit einer Prostituierten gehabt hatte. Jedesmal bekam er Schmerzen in der rechten Mandel nebst beträchtlicher Eiterbildung. In der Analyse identifizierte er seine rechte Mandel mit seinem Vater und seinem schuldbeladenen Gewissen, die linke dagegen, die sauber war, mit seiner reinen Mutter. Der Vater hätte ihm ein Führer zum Guten sein sollen, in Wirklichkeit aber war er ein ausschweifender Mensch gewesen; als der Sohn das entdeckte, hatte er das Gefühl, vom Vater verraten worden zu sein, — deshalb war es gerecht, wenn er nach jedem Fehltritt sich selbst und somit indirekt den Vater bestrafte. Denn indem der Vater die ideale Meinung, die er, der Sohn, von ihm gehabt hatte, zerstörte, hatte er ihn sozusagen des Ruders beraubt, mit dessen Hilfe er durchs Leben hätte steuern können. So verschob er die Krankheit der Mutter (symbolisch für Prostitution und Verbrechen) auf den Vater (= rechte Mandel).

In der Kindheit hatte er jedoch offenbar den Vater als Ideal und wunderbaren Menschen betrachtet; die Mutter hingegen hatte ihm als niedrig, schmutzig und krank gegolten und das infolge ihres Geschlechtsverkehrs mit dem Vater und ihrer Blutungen.

Im späteren Leben hatte sich sein Vater als feiger Taugenichts erwiesen, die Mutter hingegen als eine tapfere und gute Frau. Sein Verhalten gegen die Frauen zeigte einen oberflächlichen Idealismus, der einen tief ins Unbewußte gesunkenen Haß und Abscheu verdeckte; der Mann mit seinem prächtigen Phallus war das Ideal, die Frau, die immer wieder krankhaft blutete, war verächtlich und konnte schlecht behandelt und mißbraucht werden. Seine Mutter war heilig (aber auch gefährlich = schmutzig = unrein).

„Warum", fragte ich ihn, „waren Sie so wütend, als Sie erwachten?" „Ich wollte", erwiderte er, „den Geschlechtsakt vollziehen und konnte es nicht, weil ich mich vor der Berührung mit ihrem Blut fürchtete. Der Gedanke, daß sie blutete, machte mich wütend und aggressiv, gleichzeitig erfüllte er mich aber auch mit Angst vor dem Verlust der Fähigkeit zu lieben. Ich sehe jetzt ein, daß ich meinen Vater gehaßt und mich wegen der Monatsblutungen meiner Mutter vor ihm gefürchtet haben muß. Ich erinnere mich, wie warm und lieb meine Mutter zu Zeiten war. Eines Tages hatte ich, an sie geschmiegt, bei ihr im Bett gelegen — als sie aufstand, konnte ich von hinten zwischen ihre Beine sehen und entdeckte, daß sie eine große blutende Wunde hatte, eine fürchterliche, von langen Haaren umgebene Wunde. Ich empfand Zorn gegen sie und fürchtete mich entsetzlich, denn ich bildete mir ein, daß sie irgendwie auch mich auf ähnliche Art bluten machen könnte." Hier fiel ihm ein, daß er in einem andern Traum Haß gegen eine Frau empfunden hatte, die zweifellos seine Mutter war; diese würde, so fürchtete er, einen Hund (= Vater) auf ihn hetzen, der ihn beißen und verstümmeln würde.

Die Analyse dieses Traumes zeigte seine Kastrationsfurcht und ergab, daß er infolge dieser Furcht seinen früheren Haß gegen den Vater und dessen Penis auf die Mutter verschob. Er kam zu der Erkenntnis, daß das Bluten seiner Mutter ein völliges „Erschlaffen" seines Verlangens bewirkt hatte. Einfälle zu dem Wort „Erschlaffen" zeigten, daß er den Begriff nicht nur mit dem Verlust der Erektionskraft in Zusammenhang brachte, sondern auch mit jener Angst vor dem Verlust der Fähigkeit zu lieben, vor dem Verlust seines Ichs also (das ist der Zustand, den Jones so treffend als Aphanasis bezeichnet hat).

Als er sich schließlich die rechte Mandel hatte entfernen lassen, bekam er am ganzen Körper einen rötlichen Ausschlag; sofort vermutete er, er habe sich mit Syphilis angesteckt. Er stürzte zu einem Spezialisten, der ihm versicherte, daß das nicht der Fall sei, um ihn zu beruhigen, aber trotzdem eine Blutprobe machte. Die klinische Widerlegung dieser Furcht reaktivierte seine unbewußte Angst — er träumte, daß er Syphilis habe. Dahinter lag der Wunsch, schwanger zu werden, als Kompensation für die gefürchtete Kastration; denn indem er sich mit der Mutter identifizierte, gewann er in der Phantasie die Fähigkeit, sich etwas sogar noch Größeres wachsen zu lassen als einen Penis, nämlich ein Kind.

In dem nun der Analyse unterzogenen Traumbruchstück trat zutage, daß Furcht, Schuldgefühl, Haß und Zorn des Patienten mit den Blutungen der Mutter und den Todeswünschen gegen beide Eltern zusammenhingen. Seine Einfälle zu Blut ergaben folgendes: Obwohl er in dem Traum ganz besonders helles, scharlachrotes Blut in dem Vaginalgang zu sehen vermeint hatte und gerade durch den Anblick dieses scharlachroten Blutes von Wut übermannt wurde, war ihm doch dunkles Blut und insbesondere der Geruch des Menstrualblutes im späteren Stadium der Periode anstößig, denn beides war mit der Vorstellung des Todes verknüpft. Von der Vorstellung des Todes kam er auf die der Geburt und auf den ekelerregenden Geruch der Blutung beim Gebären. Er brachte diesen merkwürdig süßlichen Geruch mit der Todesfurcht in Zusammenhang und mit der Verdrängung seines Wunsches, vom Vater geschwängert zu werden (die sogenannte negative Ödipusphase). Weiters verknüpfte er diesen Geruch mit der Geburt seines kleinen Bruders, die später stattgefunden hatte als das Erlebnis des Menstruationstraumas.

Die Entfernung seiner Mandel symbolisierte zweierlei: einerseits Kastration und Strafe für seine Inzestgedanken, anderseits Aufhebung seiner Weiblichkeit, d. h. Entfernung der krankhaften Wunde. Die rechte Mandel stellte also das schuldbeladene, kranke, unreine Weib (= der sündige, kastrierte Mann) dar, die linke dagegen die Idealgestalt der Mutter (seine reine Mutter, die kein Menstruationsanzeichen aufzuweisen hat). Die schlechte und gute Bedeutung von links und rechts war umgekehrt worden. Die Notwendigkeit, daß der kleinere Gang von Blut gesäubert werde, brachte er schließlich mit seinen homosexuellen Neigungen in Zusammenhang. Er sagte wütend: „Wie kann man den Geschlechtsakt mit einer Frau vollziehen, deren Gang voll Blut ist — ihr After ist sicherer und sauberer, aber der eines Jungen ist noch sauberer und sogar auch noch weniger gefährlich."

Als ich darauf hinwies, daß gegen die Berührung mit den Faeces Einwände erhoben werden könnten, erwiderte er, sie sei ganz gewiß der mit Blut vorzuziehen, Blut könne ihn über und über bespritzen. Faeces seien, selbst was den Geruch betrifft, ganz angenehm; sich mit Blut zu besudeln, sei hingegen unsagbar schrecklich. Man stürbe gewiß daran; schon bei dem Gedanken daran überkomme ihn ein Gefühl der Schwäche.

In der folgenden Nacht wurde er im Schlaf immer wieder ohnmächtig und erwachte immer wieder aus dem Ohnmachtsanfall. Schließlich fürchtete er sich davor, wieder einzuschlafen. Damit wiederholte er offensichtlich das Trauma der Kindheit, und die Erlebnisse jener Nacht überzeugten ihn davon, daß es der Anblick der blutenden Vagina seiner Mutter gewesen war, was seine männliche Angriffslust gehemmt hatte.

Wenn in der Analyse ein Abreagieren des Hasses gegen den Vater und dessen Penis, der Furcht vor ihm und des Schuldbewußtseins in bezug auf ihn erreicht werden soll, ein Abreagieren der der positiven Phase des Ödipuskomplexes angehörenden Gefühle also, dann ist eine vollständige Entwicklung der Mutterübertragung wesentlich, so daß jene Haltung der Mutter und ihrer Vagina gegenüber durchgearbeitet wird, in welcher die Wiedererweckung der anziehenden und der abstoßenden Charakteristika, d. h. der Menstruationskomplex inbegriffen ist, der für das Kind die tiefste Bestätigung der Kastrations- und Todesfurcht bedeutet.

Wenn die Neurose ihren Ursprung in der positiven Phase des Ödipuskomplexes hat, kann dies das Abreagieren der Affekte bewirken und dazu führen, daß der Patient fortan eine positive Haltung dem Leben gegenüber einnimmt; wo noch frühere Fixierungen den Ödipuskonflikten zugrunde liegen, erschließt die Auflösung des Menstruationskomplexes einen Weg für die Analyse der oralen und analen Symptome in ihrer ursprünglichen, nicht lediglich in ihrer späteren, regressiv entstellten Form.

Wenn jedoch der Menstruationskomplex des Analytikers nicht gelöst ist und er daher in gewissem Ausmaß noch unter dem Einfluß des Kastrationskomplexes auf dessen tiefster Stufe steht, wird sich ein Stillstand ergeben, sobald die Arbeit an jene Phase des Inzestkomplexes herangekommen ist. Der Patient und der Analytiker werden sich in einem verhängnisvollen Kreis um den toten Punkt drehen — dabei mag der Patient zwar durch Neuerziehung von seiten des Analytikers gefördert werden, doch wird das mögliche Ausmaß an Tiefenanalyse unter diesen Umständen verringert sein.

Beispiel E

Zwei meiner Patienten begannen ihre Analyse am ersten Tag der Behandlung damit, daß sie einen Menstruationstraum erzählten. Ich will so kurz wie möglich die Bedeutung dieser beiden Fälle für meine Theorie darlegen.

Beide Patienten waren infolge des Menstruationstraumas an ihre Mutter fixiert.

Der Traum des Patienten X: *Ich begab mich in ein W.C., sah aus dem Fenster und erblickte den Mond, der aber nicht silbrig glänzte, wie man erwarten würde, sondern blutrot war.*[8]

Die Analyse ergab, daß der Patient einst nicht aus dem Fenster, sondern in die Klosettschale gesehen hatte; das runde Loch am Grunde war voll Blut gewesen. Er war hinter seiner älteren (sechzehnjährigen) Schwester hergegangen, die das Klosett soeben benützt hatte; es war ihm aufgefallen, daß sie sich geheimnisvoll benahm. Der Vorfall muß sich ereignet haben, als er 2½ bis 3½ Jahre alt war. Im weiteren Verlauf der Analyse stellte es sich jedoch heraus, daß er sogar noch früher schon andere auf die Menstruation bezügliche Erlebnisse gehabt hatte.

Als er ungefähr drei Jahre alt gewesen war, hatte seine Mutter ihre blutige Binde in den Nachttopf getan. Er war in das Zimmer gekommen, hatte das Ding entdeckt und in die Hand genommen. Erregt roch er daran, als die Mutter in das Zimmer zurückkehrte, ihm die Binde aus der Hand nahm, ihn schlug und zur Tür hinausschob.

Er wurde nach diesem Vorfall aus dem Schlafzimmer der Eltern entfernt und begann, wie es scheint, unmittelbar danach, ständig vor dem Einschlafen zu masturbieren. Die Mutter pflegte in sein Zimmer zu kommen, und wenn sie ihn bei seinem Tun ertappte, drohte sie ihm ganz eindeutig mit Kastration. Seiner Meinung nach war es eine kurze Zeit später, als er, immer noch neugierig mit dem Gedanken an die Blutung seiner Mutter beschäftigt, sich in das Klosett begab, um den Angelegenheiten seiner Schwester nachzuspüren.

8) Mehrere Patienten erzählten ganz ähnliche Träume. Der Mond ist ein Symbol des weiblichen Prinzips.

Die weitere Analyse ergab jedoch, daß das eigentliche Trauma durch ein
Kindermädchen hervorgerufen worden war, das die Beine geöffnet und das
Kind seine blutende Vagina hatte sehen lassen. Welche Absicht das Mädchen
verfolgte, als es das tat, bleibt unbekannt, doch ist es möglich, daß es dem
Beispiel mancher Bauernfrauen Mitteleuropas folgte, die, wie man weiß, in
solchem Beginnen ein wirksames Mittel kennen, dem autoerotischen Tun des
Sohnes zu steuern und ihn zu disziplinieren. Nach meinen Erfahrungen in
ähnlichen Fällen ist es aber ebenso möglich, daß die Handlungsweise des Mädchens seinem unbewußten Wunsch zu exhibieren, entsprang, der zur Zeit der
Menstruation stärker ist als sonst.

Das Wesentliche an diesem Fall jedoch ist, daß in dem Hause insgesamt
sechs Frauen im Alter von 16 bis 40 Jahren lebten und daher sechsmal im
Monat eine Scheidenblutung vorkam. Trotzdem ist mir sogar von Psycho-
analytikern feierlich erklärt worden, eine zufällige Entdeckung der Blutung
eines weiblichen Wesens sei in einigen vereinzelten Fällen zwar möglich,
komme aber so selten vor, daß von einer allgemeinen Reaktion darauf nicht
die Rede sein könne, — die Tatsache, daß Mütter menstruieren, werde übersehen. In jenem Haus fanden 72 Menstruationen im Jahr statt. Überdies war
es ein Landhaus, in dem es zahlreiche Hunde gab.

Es stellte sich im Verlauf der Analyse heraus, daß der Patient sehr früh
großes Interesse an läufigen Hündinnen gehabt und auch das Wittern und
die Erregung der männlichen Hunde beobachtet hatte. Um dieselbe Zeit war
er Zeuge der Urszene geworden und hatte sein Wissen um die Sexualität der
Tiere auf die Eltern verschoben. Infolge dieses Interesses war die Neugier in
bezug auf Mutter und Schwester in ihm erwacht; er kam in Konflikt mit
beiden Eltern, begann übermäßig zu masturbieren und erlebte das Menstruationstrauma, das seine Kastrationsangst verstärkte. Erst nachdem der
Menstruationskomplex in der Analyse wiedererweckt worden war, gelangten
wir zu dem noch tieferen Gefühl der Furcht und des Hasses gegen den Vater,
das dahinter steht; dieses muß aufgelöst werden, bevor eine positive Phase in
der Beziehung zur Frau erreicht und ein zufriedenstellendes therapeutisches
Resultat erzielt werden kann.

Die Urszene erweckt den stärksten Haß gegen den Vater, wobei die
Machtlosigkeit des Zuschauers (Laforgue) eine so wichtige Rolle spielt.
Der stärkste Haß gegen die Mutter jedoch wird durch die Verhinderung der
Masturbationsneigungen erweckt.

Die Reizbarkeit, die viele Männer gegen ihre Frauen an den Tag legen,
wenn diese ihnen vorhalten, sie verschwendeten Geld, hat ihren Ursprung oft
in jenen verdrängten Masturbationsneigungen. Denn die Masturbation auf der
Inzeststufe ist immer auch ein Versuch, sich von Angst zu befreien — von
Angst, die einer durch das Menstruations- oder Kastrationstrauma bewirkten
Verdrängung entstammt. Es reizt den gehemmten Mann, wenn er — gar von

seiner Frau — an seine verschwenderischen Neigungen erinnert wird; er fühlt sich schuldig wegen seines verdrängten Hasses gerade gegen die Eigenschaften des Weibes, die einst seine stärksten Leidenschaften erweckt hatten, und er fühlt sich schuldig, weil er Geld (= Samen) vergeudet, das der Befruchtung des Weibes (= Mutter) dienen sollte.

Traum des Patienten Y: ,,*Ich stand in der Ecke eines Zimmers an einer Tür, die in ein kleineres Zimmer führte, und beobachtete fasziniert zwei Leute, die an einem Tisch saßen und miteinander aßen. Auf dem Tisch lag ein fleckenlos reines Tischtuch von lebhaft weißer Farbe. Plötzlich kam aus dem Schränkchen in dem Tisch unterhalb des weißen Tuches eine Schlange hervor, deren Kopf eine sonderbare Form aufwies. Eine Zeitlang zog sich die Schlange immer wieder in das Schränkchen zurück, um gleich darauf wieder hervorzuschnellen. Schließlich kam sie in das Zimmer heraus und verschlang sich zu einem Dreieck besonderer Art. Während ich das Dreieck betrachtete, wurde es plötzlich wieder zur Schlange und diese schnellte mit geöffnetem Rachen bösartig auf mein Bein los. Ich sprang beiseite, um ihr auszuweichen, und erwachte in schrecklicher Angst — mein Herz schlug heftig.*''*

In der ersten Zeit der Analyse dieses Traumes erzählte der Patient verschiedene, sein Geschlechtsleben betreffende Vorfälle, die deutlich Exhibitionswünsche, begleitet von Furcht vor der Vagina verrieten. Er hob hervor, daß er als Knabe und als junger Mann viel masturbiert habe. Ferner, daß er sowohl im Wachen wie im Schlaf Pollutionen habe.

Seine Sexualität war stark verdrängt, was er der Religion zuschrieb und auch so rationalisierte.

Während der Analyse des wiedergegebenen Traumes fielen ihm andere Träume ein, die stärkste Furcht davor verrieten, vom Vater angegriffen und getötet zu werden.

Sehr klar kamen verdrängte vatermörderische Wünsche zutage, die auf Feinde des Landes verschoben worden waren; Einfälle dazu führten auf die Urszene zurück. Der Patient erinnerte sich, daß er in einem kleinen Ankleidezimmer neben dem Schlafzimmer der Eltern geschlafen habe, wo er hören konnte, was im elterlichen Schlafraum vorging. Weitere Erinnerungen kamen: Wenn es in der Nacht viel Bewegung im Zimmer der Eltern gegeben und das Bett darin gekracht hatte, pflegte die Mutter am Morgen zu ihm zu sagen: ,,Vater wälzte sich die Nacht unruhig im Bett, er träumte von Schlangen.''

Er kam selbst auf den Gedanken, daß die Schlange in seinem Traum den Penis des Vaters symbolisiere, denn er hatte allerlei über Symbolismus gelesen; doch war seiner Meinung nach das Besondere an seinem Traum die Art und Weise, in der die Schlange aus dem Schränkchen in dem Tisch hervorgekommen war.

Assoziationen zeigten, daß die Leute, die an dem Tisch gegessen hatten, sein Vater und seine Mutter waren; bald wurde auch klar, daß, miteinander zu essen, symbolisch Geschlechtsverkehr bedeutete.

Zu dem Tisch kam der Einfall: ein Bett, auf dem seine Mutter lag.

Zu dem weißen Tischtuch fiel ihm ein weißes Bettuch ein und die Flecken darauf, die von seinen Masturbationssünden, bevor er geheiratet hatte, und von dem Verkehr mit seiner Frau, seit er verheiratet war, Zeugnis ablegten. Als ein Ergebnis der bereits analysierten Assoziationen verknüpfte er dann sowohl Masturbation als auch Geschlechtsverkehr mit seinen verdrängten Inzestphantasien; er habe, sagte er, in bezug auf beide ein Schuldgefühl, besonders aber in bezug auf die Masturbation.

So heftig waren seine sexuellen Konflikte früher gewesen, daß er sich während des Krieges wiederholt exponiert hatte in der Hoffnung, er werde erschossen werden und so seinen Konflikten ein Ende setzen. Der Wunsch, seinem Leben ein Ende zu machen, führte zu einer Kriegsverwundung. Als er heiratete, wußte er nichts vom Geschlechtsleben, doch hat eine geduldige Gattin ihm sehr geholfen. Alle seine sexuellen Beziehungen erweckten ein Schuldgefühl in ihm; dieses war seiner Überzeugung nach eine Folge seines Masturbierens in der Jugend.

Als ich ihn fragte, was es seiner Meinung nach bedeute, daß der Traum die fleckenlose Reinheit des Tischtuches und dessen weiße Farbe hervorhebe, antwortete er erregt: „Das weiß ich nicht. Ein weißes Tuch — ein schmutziges Tuch — ein gefährliches Tuch. ‚Wirf es von dir, wie du das Tuch einer menstruierenden Frau von dir werfen würdest.'" Er erinnerte sich nicht, wo er diesen Satz gelesen hatte, meinte aber, er müsse gleich vielen anderen ähnlichen Anspielungen aus der Bibel sein. Wie z. B. auch das Wort: „Ihre Unreinheit ist in ihren Röcken." Der Traum stellte also den Geschlechtsverkehr zwischen seinen Eltern dar und zeigte zunächst, wie der Vater seinen Phallus in die Mutter — d. h. in das Schränkchen zwischen den Tischbeinen — stieß und wieder herauszog. „Ein abscheuliches, ein schmutziges Beginnen."

Er erinnerte sich nun, daß er an die Tür seines kleinen Zimmers gekommen war und die Eltern auf ihrem Bett in dem andern Zimmer liegen gesehen hatte. Plötzlich hatte der Vater seinen roten, geschwollenen Penis aus der Mutter herausgezogen und den kleinen Jungen böse angestarrt. Dieser hatte sich sowohl vor dem Vater als auch vor dem Penis entsetzlich gefürchtet. Kurze Zeit später bemerkte er, daß der Nachttopf im Schlafzimmer seiner Mutter oft Blut enthielt, und er vermutete, dies komme daher, daß der Penis des Vaters, indem er in sie eindrang, ihr eine Wunde beigebracht habe.

Als er von dem Schränkchen sprach, fiel ihm ein, wie seine etliche Jahre ältere Schwester ihm ihre Vagina gezeigt, seinen Penis betrachtet und dann gesagt hatte: „Wir sollten das nicht tun."

Unter Angstreaktion in bezug auf seinen Vater zitierte er noch einmal, erregt und von Abscheu geschüttelt, den Satz vom Tuch einer menstruierenden Frau. Damit brachte er die Versuchung ans Licht, die verdrängt hinter dem individuellen Menstruationstabu liegt — die Versuchung, sich mit der

Mutter zu begatten, und gleichzeitig auch die Furcht, von dem Penis des Vaters getötet zu werden, falls er dieser Versuchung nachgeben sollte. Dies erklärt, warum in der Mythologie und im Folklore die Frau zur Zeit der Menstruation Gott gehört, und warum es heißt, Gott sei in ihrem Menstruationsblut gegenwärtig. In der Ontogenese besteht auf der Höhe der Inzestphase, jedoch vor dem Menstruationstrauma, die größte Versuchung zur Zeit der Monatsblutung der Mutter.

Die Prämenstruationsphase ist die Zeit des positiven Tropismus, in der Kinder ebenso auf Gerüche reagieren wie die übrige Tierwelt. Während der Inzestphase sind sie sozusagen natürlich, aber nicht zivilisiert. Sie fürchten, gefressen zu werden, aber sie glauben noch nicht an die Möglichkeit der Kastration.

Die Fixierung des Patienten an die Mutter zeigte sich darin, daß er eine kränkliche Frau geheiratet hatte, obgleich er von gesunden und dabei anziehenden Mädchen geliebt worden war.

Die Analyse der Verwandlung der Schlange (= Penis) in ein Dreieck (= Vagina) ergab, daß sich darin die Verschiebung der Furcht vor dem Penis des Vaters auf die Mutter symbolisierte; diese Verschiebung ist ein Ergebnis der Tatsache, daß ihre Menstruation die Kastrationsfurcht bestätigt. Die Vagina ließ jedoch die Furcht vor des Vaters Penis (Schlange) aufs neue erwachen, so daß er anstatt der faszinierenden Vagina, die seine infantile Leidenschaft erweckt hatte, nur den väterlichen Penis und dessen drohende Angriffe auf sich sah. Hinter seiner Verehrung für Frauen liegt tief verdrängter Sadismus. Er ist sehr unterwürfig gegen Ersatzpersonen des Vaters und hat zahlreiche analerotische Züge.

Es wird vielleicht eines Tages zugegeben werden, daß der Sadismus des Über-Ichs seinen Ursprung in den Konflikten des Menstruationskomplexes hat, welcher der Kern des Inzestkomplexes ist. Das Wesentliche an einem Komplex ist, daß er sowohl anziehende als auch abstoßende Elemente enthält, d. h. einen gehemmten Wunsch. In der Phylogenese müssen der Wunsch, eine Frau zu schwängern, und die sozialen Verbote, die die Erfüllung dieses Wunsches verhinderten, den größten Konflikt gebildet haben. In der Ontogenese liegen die Dinge nicht viel anders, nur daß die Verdrängung jenes Wunsches jetzt in einer frühinfantilen Phase der seelischen Entwicklung stattfindet.

Der erste der beiden erwähnten Patienten hatte eine Frau von kräftig harter Wesensart geheiratet, vergleichbar der indischen Göttin Kali; der zweite hingegen eine kränkliche von sanftem, gütigem Wesen, die, wie er sagte, „einen geschwollenen und verhärteten Darm" hatte, — d. h. sie war krank wie seine Mutter und hatte eine Vagina gleich dieser, verbarg aber einen Penis in sich.

Beide Patienten waren in ihrem Geschlechtsleben gehemmt und hatten sich anfänglich gefürchtet, die Vagina ihrer Frau mit der Hand zu berühren (d. h.

sie hatten sich vor der darin enthaltenen Schlange = Penis gefürchtet, was
sich in den Träumen beider Fälle deutlich zeigt).

VIII

Schluß. Über die Bedeutung organischer und psychischer
Faktoren für die Hemmung des Sexualtriebes

Freud hat mir die Ehre erwiesen, in den Anmerkungen zu seinem Werk
„Das Unbehagen an der Kultur" meine Forschungsarbeiten zu erwähnen. Da
jedoch seine Ansichten nicht völlig mit den meinen übereinstimmen, scheint
es wünschenswert, daß ich meine Theorien noch einmal vorbringe.

Freud bespricht die von mir[9] nachdrücklich hervorgehobene Tatsache, daß
die Periodizität der Sexualvorgänge zwar bestehen geblieben, die seelische
Wirkung auf die Geschlechtserregung jedoch beinahe ins Gegenteil verkehrt
worden ist, und er bringt diesen Wandel vor allem mit der abnehmenden Bedeutung der Riechreize in Zusammenhang, die sich seiner Hypothese nach ergab, als der Mensch sich vom Boden aufrichtete, d. h. einen aufrechten Gang
annahm. Seiner Meinung nach ging die Funktion der Riechreize, die früher
die Geschlechtserregung beim Manne hervorgebracht hatte, auf die Sehreize
über, die dauernd, und nicht gleich den Riechreizen nur intermittierend, am
Werke sein können.

Freud stellt ferner fest, daß das Menstruationstabu seinen Ursprung in
dieser „organischen Verdrängung" hatte, die als eine Schranke gegen eine
Phase der Entwicklung wirkte, über die der Mensch hinausgekommen war.

Während diese letztere Annahme einleuchtet, können wir der Theorie, jene
organische Verdrängung sei dadurch entstanden, daß der Mensch eine auf-
rechte Gangart annahm, nicht so leicht zustimmen. Ebensowenig klar ist
mir, wie das Menstruationstabu in irgend einem unmittelbaren Zusammenhang
damit stehen könnte. Ich stelle dieser Ansicht meine Theorie entgegen, welche
besagt, daß eine physiologische Veränderung in der Frau vor sich ging infolge
der Maßnahmen zur Unterdrückung des Inzests und der dadurch bewirkten
Unterbindung des Geschlechtstriebs in einem Zeitpunkt, in dem in der Tierwelt unwiderstehliche Anziehung besteht (d. h. zur Zeit der Brunst) und
Schwängerung stattfindet.

Dadurch, daß der Mensch sich vom Erdboden aufrichtete, seien die Geschlechtsteile exponiert worden, sagt Freud; es sei notwendig geworden, sie
zu schützen, und daraus sei ein Gefühl der Scham entstanden. Mir scheint das
Gefühl der Scham, das mit jener Exponiertheit im Falle des Mannes in Zusammenhang steht, ein unmittelbares Ergebnis der Sexualverdrängung zu sein,
die aller Wahrscheinlichkeit nach einer beträchtlich späteren Zeit angehört
als die Annahme einer aufrechten Haltung. Jenes Gefühl der Scham dürfte

---

9) Imago XIII, 1927.

also weit eher eine Folge der Triebhemmung als eine der Erhebung vom Erdboden sein — diese letzte Anpassung kann sich auch nur ganz allmählich vollzogen haben. Es ist zwar richtig, daß das männliche Genitale bei einer aufrechten Haltung stärker exponiert ist; im Fall der Frau verhält es sich aber
anders: das weibliche Genitale war stärker exponiert vor Erreichung des aufrechten Ganges.

Alle solchen Überlegungen rücken jedoch in die zweite Reihe, wenn wir
ihnen das machtvolle Phänomen entgegenhalten, das die Unterdrückung der
Paarung zur Zeit der weiblichen Brunst darstellt.

In der Phylogenese erweckte die Brunst der Frau die aggressiven Instinkte
des Mannes und war daher das stärkste treibende Moment der Auflehnung
gegen die Herrschaft des Urvaters. In der Periode, die der Auflösung der
Horde folgte, wurde aber der Zustand der Rivalität unter den Männern tatsächlich zu einer Bedrohung des Fortbestands unserer Art. Dies
führte zur Schaffung des Inzestgesetzes und des Tabus der
Paarung zur Zeit der weiblichen Brunst. Die ältere Furcht, gefressen
zu werden, die in der Phase der Horde genügt hatte, die Inzestneigungen des
Sohnes zu hemmen — der Vater-Tochter-Inzest war in dieser Phase noch
normal —, erfuhr in der späteren Phase eine Verstärkung durch die Bedrohung mit Kastration zur Zeit der Pubertät; und diese Bedrohung wurde
der wichtigste Hemmungsfaktor im Dienste der Sexualunterdrückung, d. h.
der Unterdrückung der Paarung zur Zeit der weiblichen Brunst.

Das junge Weib wurde mit dem Tode bedroht, wenn es jene sichtbaren Anzeichen der Sexualanziehung zu verbergen unterließ, denen der Mann zu
widerstehen nicht imstande war. Daß der Fortpflanzungsprozeß bei der Frau
nicht zur natürlichen Zeit seinen Fortgang nehmen konnte, führte den Zustand reichlichen Blutens herbei, den wir als Menstruation bezeichnen; und
dieses Bluten spielte dann eine wesentliche Rolle bei der Unterdrückung der
Inzestneigungen in der menschlichen Gesellschaft infolge seines Zusammen-
hangs mit der Furcht, gefressen zu werden, und mit der Kastrationsfurcht.
Die Monatsblutung der Frau wurde allmählich eine Bestätigung für die Möglichkeit der Kastration und des Todes; und die mit dieser Blutung verknüpfte
Furcht verdrängte die angenehme Assoziation der anziehenden Gerüche. Daher
genießt in unserer zivilisierten Gesellschaft der normale Mann starke sexuelle
Gerüche nur, wenn er sich in sexueller Erregung befindet oder unter dem Einfluß eines künstlichen Anregungsmittels, etwa des Alkohols, steht. In pathologischen Fällen jedoch spielt der Geruchsinn eine bedeutende Rolle. Wir
müssen uns über die volle Tragweite dieser Tatsache erst klar werden und
werden finden, daß sie oft den Schlüssel für die Fixierung des Patienten an
den Tropismus der positiven Phase des Ödipuskomplexes bildet.

Freud meint, daß die Umkehrung in der Bewertung der Exkremente durch
die frühe Erziehung der Kinder herbeigeführt werde und nur möglich sei, weil

28*

das positive Interesse an den Exkrementen infolge ihres starken Geruchs dazu
bestimmt sei, das Schicksal zu teilen, das infolge der „organischen Verdrängung"
die Riechreize ereilte. Mir scheint es besonders bedeutungsvoll, daß unter den
Bedingungen unseres zivilisierten Lebens die Erziehungsmaßnahmen in der
Kinderstube — abgesehen von ihrer Notwendigkeit im Dienste der sozialen
Hygiene — der späteren Hemmung der inzestuösen Sexualneigungen den
Weg bereiten.

Ich möchte den Leser hier darauf hinweisen, daß der orthodoxe Hindu sich
nach jeder Handlung, von der angenommen werden kann, daß sie eine Ver-
unreinigung verursache, den Mund spülen muß. Es ist Vorschrift, sich nach
dem Urinieren den Mund viermal zu spülen, nach dem Stuhlgang[10] achtmal,
nach jeder Nahrungsaufnahme zwölfmal, nach Geschlechtsverkehr[11] sechzehnmal. Wenn auch die Zahl bei verschiedenen Rassen verschieden ist, gibt uns
ein solches Ritual doch wertvolle Aufschlüsse für die Abschätzung der
Wichtigkeit der Hemmung in jeder Phase, in der oralen, der analen
und der genitalen. Wir können durch die Betrachtung dieser Reinigungsmaß-
regeln zu dem Schluß kommen, daß die oralen und die phallischen Faktoren
von größerer, die analen und urethralen dagegen von geringerer Wichtigkeit
sind; doch stimmen wir der Ansicht zu, daß die angenehmen Attribute der
analen Phase infolge ihres starken Geruchs das Schicksal der sexuellen Riechreize teilen mußten. Aus der Vorschrift, sich den Mund nach dem Geschlechtsverkehr sechzehnmal und nicht nur zwölfmal, wie nach der Nahrungsaufnahme, zu spülen, schließen wir, daß die Befriedigung des Geschlechtstriebs
eine noch stärkere Reaktion weckt als die des älteren oral-kannibalischen
Verlangens.

Ich habe in der Analyse oft gefunden, daß bei Personen, deren Inzestneigungen nicht erfolgreich verdrängt worden waren, wenig oder gar keine ausgesprochene Abneigung gegen den Geruch des Kotes bestand; diese wirkten bei
manchen dieser Patienten sogar angenehm. Sexualgerüche wirkten bei solchen
Menschen stets sehr angenehm. Deshalb kann die Wertumkehrung in bezug
auf die Analerotik historisch als ein sekundäres Ergebnis der Hemmung des
Geschlechtstriebs angesehen werden, welche gleichzeitig mit der Bildung der
nicht inzestuösen Gesellschaft stattfand.

In der auf dieser Grundlage gebildeten Gesellschaft ist das Streben nach
Reinlichkeit ein Ergebnis, das nachträglich durch Erwägungen der Hygiene
gerechtfertigt wurde: Trotzdem kam es nach Freud[12] zum Ausdruck, bevor
noch die Hygiene Würdigung fand, und hat seinen Ursprung in dem Ver-

---

10) Durch diesen wird man rein, da man Unreine aus dem Körper ausgeschieden hat.
11) Weisheit, Tatkraft, Stärke, Gesichtssinn und Lebenskraft schwinden, so sagt der alte
Gesetzgeber der Hindus, wenn ein Mann mit einer menstruierenden Frau Verkehr hat. Die
christliche Kirche schrieb vierzig oder fünfzig Tage der Buße für den Geschlechtsverkehr
während der Menstruation vor (Havelock Ellis).
12) Das Unbehagen in der Kultur, Ges. Schr., Bd. XII, S. 66 f. (Anm.).

langen, Ausscheidungen loszuwerden, die der Sinneswahrnehmung unangenehm geworden sind.

Es ist interessant, daß Freud die Bedeutungsverminderung der Geruchsreize mit der Abschließung der Frauen zur Zeit ihrer Monatsblutung in Zusammenhang bringt. Ich möchte aber noch besonders darauf hinweisen, daß die Abschließung der Frau zu dieser Zeit ein endgültiges Resultat der Unterdrückung des Inzests war und der frühesten Phase der menschlichen Kultur angehört, ferner daß eine der Aufgaben dieser Abschließung zweifellos die Unterdrückung des anziehenden Geschlechtsgeruches war. Durkheim[13] hat schon vor langer Zeit bezüglich des Inzestverbotes bei den Wilden bemerkt: „Die Geschlechtsorgane müssen beizeiten verhüllt werden, damit die gefährlichen Ausdünstungen, die von ihnen ausgehen, die Umgebung nicht erreichen können."

Wenn tatsächlich die Geruchsreize durch Gesichtseindrücke Ersatz fanden, dann können wir nur zu dem Schluß kommen, daß diese Änderung keinen Erfolg hatte; denn psychische Reaktionen auf das weibliche Genitale haben den Mann veranlaßt, die anziehende Vorstellung, die ursprünglich im Genitale zentriert war, davon weg auf die Brüste, das Gesicht und die Gestalt zu verschieben. Es war insbesondere der Anblick der blutenden Vagina etwas Schreckliches für den Mann geworden. Wir schreiben das Menstruationstabu genetisch der Notwendigkeit zu, die Frau für die Zeit, in welcher sie sich in jenem Zustand befand, der im Manne unbezwingliche kannibalische Gier und Aggressivität erweckte, aus dessen Umkreis zu entfernen, und wir erkennen dann, auf welchem Wege die reichliche Blutung, die infolge dieser Vereitelung der Schwangerschaft im naturgegebenen Zeitpunkt der Befruchtung entstand, so große Bedeutung als traumatischer Faktor der Neurosen erlangte, ferner auch, wie diese Blutung die sadistische Komponente der menschlichen Natur besonders verstärkte. Die Voraussetzung dieser Annahme füllt eine Lücke in der psychoanalytischen Lehre und bestätigt in erwünschter Weise etliche der wertvollsten Theorien Freuds. Alles, was das männliche Individuum veranlaßte, seine Sexualwünsche zur Zeit der stärksten weiblichen Anziehung zu zügeln, und eine so tiefgreifende physiologische Veränderung in der Frau wie das reichliche Bluten der menschlichen Menstruation hervorbrachte, ist sicherlich von großer Bedeutung. Einzig und allein die zur Verhinderung des Inzests ergriffenen Maßregeln tragen Schuld an der schweren Hemmung des gesamten Sexualtriebs.

Warum tötet ein Wilder eine menstruierende Frau, die ihn verunreinigt hat, indem sie ihn mit ihren Kleidern in Berührung kommen ließ, — warum tötet er sie und stirbt dann selbst vor Furcht? Es gibt über die Antwort keinen Zweifel.

Es ist möglich, mit Hilfe der psychoanalytischen Methode die traumatische

13) L'année sociolog., 1896.

Wirkung zu illustrieren, die das blutende Genitale der Mutter in der Ontogenese hat, und aufzuzeigen, welchen Einfluß es bei der Verdrängung der angenehmen Reaktionen auf Geruchreize ausübt.[14] Wir können ferner nachweisen, daß das blutende Genitale der Mutter eine überaus große Rolle bei
der Verdrängung der inzestuösen Sexualität der Menschheit gespielt hat; und
in einigen pathologischen Fällen können wir eine Reaktion von solcher Heftig-
keit demonstrieren, daß der Geruch der Genitalien die Potenz zu hemmen imstande ist, während in anderen die Potenz nur bei starkem Geruch möglich
wird.

Róheim[15] bestätigt in seinen Beobachtungen über die Subinzisionsriten
bei zeitgenössischen wilden Völkerstämmen Australiens meine Theorie in
weitgehendem Maße, daß der Mann sich die „furchterregenden" Attribute
der Frau — d. h. der Menstruation — angeeignet hat, um die Kastrationsangst
der jüngeren Generation zu verstärken. Mir will scheinen, daß sich der Mann
den „schrecklichen" Anblick der Frau auch zum Zwecke der Verstärkung
seiner dahinschwindenden Autorität angeeignet hat — daß seine Autorität
abgenommen hatte, war eine Folge der Unterdrückung des Kannibalismus
(des früheren Mittels zur Aufrechterhaltung der Zucht innerhalb der Horde).
Róheim schildert auch, wie der junge Eingeborene in der Zeit, die auf die
Subinzisionsriten folgt und der Heirat vorangeht, sich in homosexueller Er-
gebenheit seinem Schwiegervater passiv unterwerfen muß; erst dann darf er
die Tochter heiraten und selbst eine Familie beherrschen. Dieser unmittelbare
Beweis aus dem Leben zeitgenössischer Primitiver bildet eine wertolle Stütze
meiner auf klinischen Befunden ruhenden Theorie. Die Subinzisionsriten
sichern die Unterwerfung des Sohnes unter die Gepflogenheiten des Stammes
und die endgültige Unterdrückung seiner Inzestneigungen.

Zu beachten ist auch folgende Tatsache: Vor dem Verbot der Paarung zur
Zeit der weiblichen Brunst brauchte das Menschenweibchen (gleich den Weibchen der meisten Tiere) keine anderen Reize als die von seinem Genitale ausgehenden Riech- und Schaureize, um vom Männchen geschwängert zu werden.
Die Aufgaben der Geruchsreize sind zum Teil auf die Gesichtsreize über-
gegangen — besonders in den Anfangsstadien der sexuellen Erregung. Trotzdem kann eine sexuelle Beziehung nicht dauernd aufrechterhalten werden,
wenn die Geruchreaktionen, die sich bei naher Berührung ergeben, keine angenehmen sind.

Die ursprünglich positiv gewesenen Sexualreize wirken jetzt zu Beginn des

14) Brill berichtet über zwei Fälle von Zwangsneurose, bei denen ein hervortretendes
Symptom übler Geruch des Atems war. Dieses Symptom ließ sich unmittelbar auf einstige
Lust an dem Geruch zurückführen, der von der Mutter ausging. Bei dem einen Patienten
hing die geschlechtliche Potenz völlig von dem Geruchsinn ab — hatte eine Frau einen Geruch, der den Patienten an seine Mutter erinnerte, so wurde er völlig impotent (Psa. Quarterly, Vol. I, 1932).
15) Imago XVIII, 1932.

Kontaktes negativ. Dennoch bleiben sie in vielen Fällen auch bei normalen Menschen lustvoll, wenn die hemmenden Schranken überwunden worden sind und ein tieferes sexuelles Verlangen sich regt.

Es ist vielleicht richtiger zu sagen, daß die Sinne sich von den früheren Quellen sexueller Reize abgewendet haben, damit nicht der Widerwille neu auflebt, der eine Folge tief sitzender Ängste ist. Das angeschwollene, stark-gefärbte weibliche Genitale, die männliche Erektion und die sexuellen Ge-rüche beider Geschlechter sind heute für den normalen zivilisierten Menschen nicht mehr von Anfang an anziehend, d. h., es muß eine indirekte Anreizung stattgefunden und einen gewissen Grad von Erregung hervorgerufen haben, bevor diese primären Reize anziehend wirken. Schöne Kleider, die Gestalt, Bewegungen, diskret zur Geltung kommende Parfüms geben heute dem Sexual-trieb die erste Anregung. Später jedoch können unmittelbare Sexualreize eine Rolle spielen. Niemals aber ist für den normalen Mann die Blutung der Frau anziehend — der Grund hiefür ist in dem Einfluß des Menstruations-tabus (und des verdrängten Menstruationstraumas) zu suchen. Das Men-struationstabu wird, wenn es auch vielleicht erblich erworben ist, in der Onto-genese verstärkt und äußert bis auf den heutigen Tag seine Wirkung.

Im Fall von Tieren, bei denen das Weibchen eine Brunstzeit durchmacht oder — wie bei manchen Affenarten — eine primäre Menstrualperiode hat, die dem Prä-Ostreus anderer Tiere entspricht, belecken und beriechen die Männchen unaufhörlich das geschwollene weibliche Genitale — diese Vor-stellung ist höchst abstoßend für den normalen Mann, solange er sich nicht in Erregung befindet, obgleich manche Männer sie zwischen den Perioden als eine normale Form der Vorlust in die Tat umsetzen.

Der Anblick der Menstrualblutung der Frau jedoch kann eine tiefe Hem-mung auf das Geschlechtsleben ausüben, kann Liebe in Haß verwandeln und manchmal — wie in einem Fall Ferenczis — sogar Impotenz beim Manne hervorrufen.

Es ist mir hoffentlich durch das in dieser Schrift zusammengetragene Material und durch die unmittelbaren Beweise aus dem Unbewußten, welche in den Traumbeispielen enthalten sind, gelungen, meine Ansicht zu begrün-den, daß der Menstruationskomplex der Kern des männlichen Ödipuskomplexes ist, und auch bis zu einem gewissen Maße nachzuweisen, daß die lustvollen Geruchreize infolge des Menstruationstraumas ver-drängt worden sind.

Die Furcht vor dem Gefressenwerden, die ich gleich der Kastrationsfurcht mit dem Menstruationskomplex in Beziehung setze, kann als eine instinktive Furcht bezeichnet werden. Sie ist allen Lebewesen eigen. Wir nehmen an, daß sie durch den Kampf ums Dasein in der Eiszeit verstärkt wurde, ferner, daß sich der Urvater in der vormenschlichen „Horde" ihrer bediente, um

Zucht zu erzwingen und den Inzest (Sohn-Tochter- und Sohn-Mutter-Inzest) zu verhindern.

Als die Phase der Urhorde zu Ende ging und die primitive menschliche Familie an Stelle der Horde trat, wurde die Furcht vor dem Gefressenwerden durch die in den Pubertätsriten der Wilden enthaltene Kastrationsdrohung verstärkt. Der Zweck dieser Riten war, die Inzestneigung zwischen allen nahen Verwandten zu hemmen. Das Menstruationstabu war jedoch von noch tieferer Wirkung: Es hinderte die erwachsenen Männer, ihre Töchter zur Zeit der Pubertät zu befruchten. Denn nur durch das Verbot jedweden Geschlechtsverkehrs zur Zeit der weiblichen Brunst wurde das Inzestgesetz der Menschheit möglich. — Menschenblut zu vergießen wurde in jeder Form (von zeremoniellen Bräuchen abgesehen) innerhalb des Stamms tabu.

Auch in der Ontogenese geht die Furcht vor dem Gefressenwerden der Kastrationsfurcht voran. Es scheint, daß sie durch die Kastrationsdrohung in der phallischen Phase verstärkt wird und dann bei der Verdrängung die frühesten Kastrationsängste mit sich zieht. Dann geschieht es, daß beide Arten von Furcht infolge des Menstruationstraumas auf die Mutter und ihre Vagina verschoben werden. In dieser Verschiebung der Furcht vom Mund des Vaters auf die Vagina der Mutter liegt die Genese der Vorstellung von der Vagina dentata. Hinter dieser Angst verbirgt sich die Anziehung, die ursprünglich von der Vagina ausgegangen ist.

Wenn einmal die unheilvollen Wirkungen des Menstruationstabus überwunden sein werden, dann wird, so möchte ich glauben, die bisherige Entwicklungsphase allmählich zu Ende gehen und eine wahrhaft „menschliche" beginnen, eine Phase, in der sich die Ambivalenz zwischen Eltern und Kindern und zwischen den Geschlechtern um vieles verringern wird. Vielleicht ist es die Hauptaufgabe der Psychoanalyse, die ontogenetische und die phylogenetische Vergangenheit zu entschleiern, durch deren Nachwirkungen das Menschengeschlecht immer noch geknechtet wird.

Die Traumsymbolik der analytischen Situation[1]

Von

Maxim. Steiner

Wien

Die Gesichtspunkte, die Freud bei dem Studium des Traumes fand, erschienen zuerst nicht nur den Fernerstehenden absurd, sondern auch den Fachgenossen fremdartig. Sie sind inzwischen allgemein akzeptiert worden und haben uns nicht nur das Verständnis der wunderbaren Struktur der Neurosen und Psychosen erschlossen, sondern auch ganz neue Aspekte für alle Gebiete des Wissens und der Kunstbetrachtung eröffnet, ja man kann sagen, unsere Auffassung vom gesamten Weltbild grundlegend verändert. So wurde die Traumdeutung zwar zum täglichen Arbeitsfeld und vielleicht zum sichersten Besitz der Psychoanalyse, sie gilt aber heute zu sehr als abgeschlossenes Thema. Seit dem Erscheinen des Standardwerkes tauchte, von den sehr bedeutsamen Arbeiten Federns abgesehen, kaum mehr ein wirklich neuer Gesichtspunkt auf. Das ist um so mehr verwunderlich, als im übrigen Lehrgebäude der Psychoanalyse kein ähnlicher Konservatismus herrscht, sondern im Gegenteil immerfort gebaut, renoviert, mitunter auch demoliert wird. Für uns alle hat sich demnach die Theorie der Traumlehre als so tragfest erwiesen, daß sie keiner neuerlichen Untersuchung oder gar Abänderung bedarf. Auch die vorliegende Arbeit hat nicht die Theorie des Traums zum Gegenstande, sondern nur die Rolle, die der Traum in der analytischen Praxis spielt. Im Laufe der vielen Jahre bin ich im Zuge meiner therapeutischen Analysen vielleicht mehr als mancher andere mit dem Traumproblem in Berührung gekommen. Denn ich bin infolge der Eigenart meines Analysandenmaterials genötigt, kurze[2] Analysen durchzuführen, die zum größten Teil nur einige Monate, mitunter sogar nur einige Wochen dauern. Dadurch wurde mein Traummaterial, oder besser gesagt meine Traumkasuistik besonders groß und ich konnte daher gewisse typische Traumstrukturen öfter beobachten als viele meiner Kollegen.

Nach wie vor bildet der Traum den besten Zugang zum Unbewußten und gilt auch in den Augen der Analysanden als der unanfechtbarste. Er ist eine seelische Leistung, zu der sie sich bekennen müssen, so unsinnig und ichfremd sie sich ihnen darstellen mag. Denn der Patient kann ihn ebensowenig verleugnen wie der darstellende oder bildende Künstler seine Schöpfung. Und wie diese nach unserer analytischen Auffassung und nach Goethes Worten ihm ermöglicht, das, was ihn bedrängt, zu sagen, ist auch der Traum ein Kunstwerk, das den Patienten allnächtlich in die Lage versetzt, sich mit seinen

---

1) Vortrag, gehalten in der Wiener Psychoanalytischen Vereinigung am 26. November 1934.
2) Ich habe in meinem Oxforder Kongreßvortrag die Gründe angeführt, die mich veranlaßt haben, in diesen speziellen Fällen von der klassischen Technik abzugehen.

Konflikten, allerdings meist erfolglos, auseinanderzusetzen. Daher fehlt dem
Traum diese soeben erwähnte reinigende und befreiende Wirkung. Das scheint
unter anderem das Kunstwerk von den Träumen, Symptomen und Wahn-
gebilden zu unterscheiden, und es scheint mir die Hauptaufgabe unserer
Therapie zu sein, diesen Unterschied zu beseitigen und durch unser Eingreifen
das künstlerische Schaffen in der ganzen Lebensführung unserer Patienten frei-
zumachen. Hat nicht, wie schon so oft, auch hier der tägliche Sprachgebrauch
in seiner Hellsichtigkeit diesen Zusammenhang erfaßt, indem er einen Menschen, der seinen Weg mit Sicherheit und Festigkeit geht, als Lebenskünstler
bezeichnet?

Wir pflegen bei Beginn der Analyse den Patienten auf die Bedeutung des
Träumens aufmerksam zu machen und ihm zu sagen, daß wir für die Dauer
der Behandlung nebst den anderen seelischen Äußerungen, in denen seine
gesamte Persönlichkeit zum Ausdruck kommt, ganz besonders auch seine
Träume für uns reklamieren. Heutzutage kommen ja die meisten unserer
Patienten mit einer Kenntnis dieses Sachverhaltes zu uns und viele von ihnen
äußern mit einer gewissen Beklommenheit Zweifel an ihrer Eignung für die
Analyse, da sie nicht oder nur sehr selten träumen oder aber beim Erwachen
sich des Trauminhaltes kaum je erinnern. Wir beruhigen solche Patienten
wahrheitsgemäß mit dem Hinweis, daß wir eine ganze Reihe von Analysen
erfolgreich zu Ende geführt haben, bei denen keine oder sehr spärliche Träume
geliefert wurden. Aus alter Erfahrung aber könnten wir den Patienten sagen,
daß auch bei vielen Menschen, die vorher nie geträumt haben oder sich
ihrer Träume nie erinnern konnten, kaum ein Tag vergehen wird, an dem
sie uns nicht einen oder mehrere Träume vorlegen werden. Dieses Phänomen,
das trotz seiner Regelmäßigkeit auch uns stets von neuem frappiert, findet
wohl seine Erklärung durch die Eigenart der analytischen Situation, und wir
werden darauf mit um so größerer Sicherheit rechnen können, je besser es
uns gelingt, dem Analysanden die Bedeutung dieser Situation zu unterstreichen.
Wenn ein Mensch eine Beziehung eingeht, die sich von allen bisherigen so
grundlegend unterscheidet, tritt eine Revolutionierung des seelischen Gesamt-
haushaltes ein, die sich am eindrucksvollsten gerade an jenen Leistungen äußern
wird, welche vom bewußten Ich am schwächsten kontrolliert werden. So
wird die analytische Situation zum Ariadnefaden, mit dessen Hilfe wir uns in
den labyrinthisch verschlungenen Pfaden der Analyse durch ihren ganzen Verlauf zuverlässig orientieren werden.

Obgleich für unsere Vereinigungen diese Erkenntnis ein Gemeinplatz zu
sein scheint, kann ich mich als aufmerksamer Zuhörer der in den Vereins-
sitzungen und im therapeutischen Seminar gehaltenen Vorträge nicht des
Eindrucks erwehren, daß die analytische Situation in der Technik der Traumdeutung lange noch nicht die ihr gebührende Beachtung gefunden hat.

Wenn wir einen Traum deuten sollen, stehen wir vor der Aufgabe, eine

Gleichung mit mehreren Unbekannten aufzulösen, und ebenso wie bei einer solchen ergeben sich unendlich viele Lösungsmöglichkeiten. In gewissen Fällen setzen wir bei solchen Gleichungen bestimmte einschränkende Bedingungen, wodurch die Anzahl der möglichen Lösungen erheblich reduziert wird, so z. B. wenn wir nur Lösungen in ganzen Zahlen suchen. In ähnlicher Weise können wir die unendlich vielen Deutungsmöglichkeiten des Traums auf ein erträgliches Maß herabsetzen. Eine einschränkende Bedingung, deren wir uns zu diesem Zwecke bedienen, ist die Einführung der analytischen Situation. Diese ist, wie wir wissen, eine Resultierende aus Übertragung und Widerstand. Die erstere ist unser Bundesgenosse; sie ist die eine Hand, der wir wahrscheinlich das uns überbrachte Traumgeschenk verdanken, aber der Widerstand ist die andere Hand, die es uns wieder zu entreißen oder unbrauchbar zu machen trachtet. Er ist es daher, mit dem wir uns bei der Traumdeutungsarbeit in erster Reihe auseinanderzusetzen haben.

Der mitgebrachte Widerstand wird u. a. aus narzißtischen Quellen gespeist. Diese narzißtische Position (Reich nannte sie die narzißtische Schranke) wird durch den ganzen Verlauf der Analyse zähe verteidigt und kann so fest ausgebaut werden, daß an ihr alle Führungskünste des Analytikers zuschanden werden. Der Kampf, der sich während der Analyse abspielt, hat weit eher den Charakter eines aufreibenden Stellungskrieges als eines offenen Kampfes und sein wechselvoller Verlauf wird sehr wesentlich durch den Ambivalenzkonflikt determiniert. Betrachten wir den Traum als funktionales Phänomen, so tritt diese Ambivalenz ganz besonders eindrucksvoll in Erscheinung. Es ist, als würde der Analysand dem Analytiker nur zögernd einen Finger entgegenstrecken, damit dieser ihm helfe. Der Traum ist also gewissermaßen der slang des Unbewußten, mit dessen Hilfe es zum Unbewußten des Analytikers spricht. Andererseits ist aber auch der Traum ein Akt der Selbsthilfe des Analysanden, durch die er nächtlicherweile wie in der voranalytischen Zeit seine Konflikte selbständig und ohne Hilfe des Analytikers zu erledigen sucht. Im Traum kommt die narzißtische Position zum Ausdruck, während in der analytischen Stunde in der Zusammenarbeit zu zweit die Objektbeziehung ihre Darstellung findet. Der Traum ist also auch von diesem Gesichtspunkt betrachtet eine Kompromißbildung (ich gebrauche absichtlich diesen schlechten Witz). Das zeigt sich auch darin, daß der Träumer sich selbst (und während der Analyse auch den Analytiker, der sein *alter ego* ist,) in allen möglichen Symbolen und Gestalten darstellt, um sich selbst (und auch dem Analytiker) eine Objektbeziehung vorzutäuschen, zu der er in Wirklichkeit nicht fähig ist.

Die Tendenz, die narzißtische Position gegen jeden Angriff von seiten des Analytikers zähe zu verteidigen, ist namentlich in der ersten Phase der Analyse so deutlich, daß sie kaum zu übersehen ist. Sie äußert sich in unendlich vielen symbolischen Darstellungen, in denen der Unmut des Analysanden über die

Störung seiner „privacy" zum Ausdruck kommt, und in Träumen, in denen der Analytiker herabgesetzt, beschimpft und in allerhand geringgeschätzten Personen meist niedriger oder dienender Stellung, als gefährlicher oder verdächtiger Mensch dargestellt wird, das Haus des Analytikers als Spelunke, verrufenes Haus, Spielhölle, Leichenhalle, Friedhof, Operationssaal oder als irgendwie gefährliche, unheimliche Gegend. Diese Symbolik ist so durchsichtig, daß wir dem Analysanden, wenn wir ihn in die Geheimnisse der Traumdeutung einführen, geradezu die „Bauernregel" an die Hand geben können, daß in allen Personen im Traum, die irgendwie unsympathisch sind, der Analytiker seine symbolische Darstellung findet.

Für die Träume dieser Phase sind bestimmte Typen von Widerständen charakteristisch, die in den folgenden Traumbeispielen vielfach verschränkt und variiert wiederzufinden sind. In einer künftigen ausführlichen Arbeit sollen diese Traumbeispiele im Zusammenhang mit den Krankengeschichten das eben Gesagte eindrucksvoll illustrieren, während ich hier nur Bruchstücke von Träumen bringen oder sie auch nur skizzieren werde.

Das Motiv der Stornierung findet seine symbolische Darstellung in allen Träumen, in denen irgend eine Bewegung (Spaziergang, Reise usw.) unternommen und sogleich wieder durch Rückkehr zum Ausgangspunkt aufgehoben, irgend eine Handlung ausgeführt und wieder rückgängig gemacht, irgend eine Äußerung getan und wieder zurückgenommen wird. Diese Stornierungstendenz, welche das ganze Leben des Neurotikers erschwert und im extremsten Fall sogar zur Vernichtung des Lebens führen kann, bringt in der analytischen Situation den unbewußten Wunsch des Patienten zum Ausdruck, die Analyse rückgängig zu machen. Ein Beispiel eines solchen Stornierungstraumes wäre der folgende:

Der Patient fährt mit seiner Freundin von der Inneren Stadt nach Hietzing, um dort mit ihr in ein Hotel zu gehen, doch kehrt er unverrichteter Dinge in die Stadt zurück, wo er ein Hotel aufsucht. Dort gefällt ihm das Zimmer nicht und er geht mit der Freundin ins Kino. Aber auch dort ist seines Bleibens nicht und er kehrt wieder ins Hotel zurück.

Das Motiv der Störung der „privacy" (durch den Analytiker) mag durch folgenden Traum eines jungen Rechtsanwaltes illustriert werden:

Ein Klient erscheint in seiner Kanzlei und macht sich, während der Träumer ins Vorzimmer geht, um den betreffenden Akt zu holen, an seinem Schreibtisch zu schaffen und steckt, wie er durch die Türe deutlich sieht, ein auf dem Tisch liegendes Schriftstück ein.

Ein anderer Traum sieht so aus:

Patient sitzt auf dem Klosett und verrichtet seine Notdurft. Plötzlich erscheint sein Stubenmädchen, das die Tür trotz seines Protestes geöffnet hat.

Dieses Motiv findet seine symbolische Darstellung auch in Träumen, in denen der Träumer in einem Bette liegt, das in einem Stiegenhaus steht, oder in einem Durchgangszimmer, oder sonst in einem Raum, wo man voraussichtlich nicht ungestört bleiben wird; ferner in Träumen, wo man in sonstigen Situationen, etwa beim Geschlechtsverkehr, gestört wird; endlich in Träumen, in denen man durch indiskretes Benehmen irgend einer Person in Verlegenheit gebracht wird (zugleich als Darstellung des Zweifels an der Diskretion des Analytikers).

Motiv der topischen Darstellung: Hierher gehören die Träume, in denen der Analytiker als irgend eine Person dargestellt wird, die hinter dem Träumer sitzt oder steht, dann die Träume, in denen der Analysand sich selbst in einer auf einem Bett oder Sofa liegenden Person darstellt, überhaupt solche Träume, in denen Sitzen, Liegen, Aufstehen oder sonstige durch den manifesten Trauminhalt nicht hinreichend motivierte Lageveränderungen eine Rolle spielen. So träumt besonders die große Anzahl von Patienten, welche sich, namentlich anfangs, nur sehr ungern dem Zwang zum Liegen unterwerfen.

Das oft verwendete Motiv der Nacktheit, mangelhaften Bekleidung usw. stellt in vielen Situationen eine unbewußte Auflehnung gegen die Befolgung der „Grundregel" dar, die ja vom Analysanden verlangt, daß er sich vollkommen entblöße. Noch deutlicher verrät sich die Tendenz des Analysanden, dem Analytiker etwas zu verheimlichen, in Träumen, in denen von An-, Um- und Verkleiden oder gar von Verstecken und Verschließen die Rede ist, wie z. B. im folgenden:

Ich bin mit meiner Tante in einem Zimmer. Ich merke, daß sie sich umzukleiden beabsichtigt und will daher hinausgehen. Ehe ich das Zimmer verlasse, versperre ich einen Schrank, da sie aus ihm, wie ich weiß, nichts benötigt.

Das Motiv des Wunders dient dem Widerstand gegen die langsame, mühselige und peinliche Kur und dem unbewußten Wunsch, lieber durch eine wunderbare oder magische Prozedur geheilt zu werden.

Ein Patient träumt, daß er ein entstellendes Mal auf der Wange hat; er sieht in einen Spiegel mit dem Erfolg, daß das häßliche Mal verschwindet.

Ähnlich ist der Widerstand der „kalten Methode". Damit bezeichne ich alle jene aus der Beschäftigung mit der analytischen Theorie geschöpften Versuche, in bewußter aber auch unbewußter Darstellung dem Analytiker zu helfen, ihm „einzusagen", ihn etwa auf die ätiologische Bedeutung des Mutterinzestes für die vorliegende Neurose aufmerksam zu machen, wie z. B. im folgenden Traum:

Patient liegt mit seiner Tante in einem Bett, um mit ihr zu verkehren. Seine Schwester, die zusieht, geht ins anstoßende Zimmer, um die dort befindliche Mutter herbeizurufen.

Der Widerstand des Fach- und Besserwissens wird sehr häufig bewußter- und unbewußterweise vom Analysanden verwendet, um so sich und sein Geheimnis dem Analytiker „unauffällig" zu entziehen. Nicht nur Fachgelehrte, sondern auch Handwerker, Kaufleute u. a. schaffen sich auf diese

Weise einen „*jardin secret*", den der Analytiker nicht betreten soll. In diesem
Sinne spielen z. B. auch Damen ihre Überlegenheit in Mode- und Toilette-
fragen gegen den männlichen Analytiker aus.

Auch die Zahlensymbolik soll nie der Aufmerksamkeit des Analytikers
entgehen, denn sonst übersieht er Anspielungen, die sich auf die Anzahl der
bereits vergangenen oder noch bevorstehenden Sitzungen, mitunter auch auf
das Honorar beziehen. Das Unbewußte wendet in diesem Falle dieselbe
Technik an wie z. B. ein ungeduldiger Schüler, der unausgesetzt die Tage bis
zum Eintritt der Ferien zählt. Eine besondere Bedeutung vom Gesichtspunkt
der analytischen Situation kommt den Zahlen 1 und 2 zu. 1 ist die symbolische
Darstellung der narzißtischen Position, 2 die Darstellung der Objektbeziehung.
Wenn man auf diese Symbolik achtet, so werden besonders solche Träume,
in denen 1 und 2 abwechselnd und oft in auffälligen Beziehungen vorkommen,
besonders aufschlußreich dadurch, daß sie ein Licht auf die ambivalente Einstellung des Analysanden zum Analytiker und auf die Akzeptierung oder Ablehnung der Analyse werfen. So gibt es Träume, in denen der Analysand mit
jemandem eine Reise antritt und sich plötzlich allein findet. Die Zahl 2 für
sich allein wird sehr oft, namentlich wenn sie in einem Traum gehäuft auf-
tritt, zur symbolischen Darstellung von Ambivalenz und Zweifel verwendet.

Der Widerstand des Zahltags findet seine symbolische Darstellung in
Träumen, in denen der Analysand gewöhnlich unter starken Affektäußerungen
von Bettlern, Kellnern, Kokotten usw. ausgenützt oder übervorteilt wird. Da
diese Träume auch bei zahlungswilligen Patienten fast regelmäßig bei jedem
Zahlungstermin auftreten, sind sie besonders geeignet, dem Analysanden die
Autonomie des Unbewußten vor Augen zu führen.

Der Widerstand der Umkehrung dient der Tendenz, die Beziehung
zwischen Analytiker und Analysanden gewissermaßen auf den Kopf zu stellen.
Sie wird in Träumen so dargestellt, daß der Schüler den Lehrer, das Kind die
Gouvernante terrorisiert, der Patient den Arzt operiert, der Schaffner dem
Fahrgast den Fahrpreis entrichtet usw.

Schließlich sei noch eines der allerhäufigsten Widerstandsmotive, nämlich
das der Degradation des Analytikers und seiner Leistung angereiht:

*Ein Patient, der mit seiner Frau im Gasthaus sitzt, wird von einem hinter ihm an
einem anderen Tisch sitzenden Menschen von ordinärem Aussehen aufgefordert, in
den Vorraum zu kommen. Dort legitimiert sich der Mann als Detektiv und teilt ihm
mit, daß seine Gattin ihn betrüge, sich als Prostituierte herumtreibe und namentlich
am letzten Donnerstag (Datum des Traums) in ganz gemeiner Weise mit einem Mann
auf einem Klosett verkehrt habe.*

Dieser Traum bringt übrigens nicht nur die Degradation des Analytikers
(Mensch von ordinärem Aussehen), das Motiv der Störung der „*privacy*"
(Detektiv), die topische Darstellung (der Mann, der hinter dem Träumer sitzt),
die Umkehrung (in Wirklichkeit ist er es, der die Gattin, die von der Analyse

nichts weiß, mit dem Analytiker betrügt), sondern auch die Herabsetzung der Analyse selbst, indem er sie symbolisch als Akt der Prostitution und Verkehr auf einem Klosett darstellt.

Dies sind einige der wichtigsten Situationswiderstände, die ganz typisch in der ersten Phase der Analyse beobachtet werden können. Wenn sie auch im obigen einzeln besprochen wurden, dürfen wir nicht erwarten, sie immer so schön isoliert vorzufinden. Die Träume werden vielmehr, ähnlich wie es der zuletzt ausgeführte gezeigt hat, fast stets Kombinationen verschiedener typischer Motive aufweisen.

Ich möchte bemerken, daß ich den Begriff der analytischen Situation vom ersten Augenblick an zum „Orgelpunkt" der Analyse mache. Sie ist gewissermaßen das Koordinatensystem, auf das alles in der Stunde Vorgebrachte bezogen wird, mag es Traum, Assoziation oder Bericht über das aktuelle Erlebnis sein. Diese Annahme wird zur gemeinsamen, sehr fruchtbaren Arbeitshypothese. Schon nach kurzer Zeit lebt sich der Analysand in diese Ideologie hinein, und er lernt auf diese Weise drei der tiefsten Wahrheiten der Analyse erfassen, nämlich die Existenz und die Autonomie des Unbewußten und die symbolische Bedeutung alles Geschehens. Er erfaßt die Überwertigkeit der psychischen Realität im Verhältnis zur aktuellen Realität. Für die Dauer der Analyse wird die Stunde zum eigentlichen Erleben und alles andere wird unwichtig, mitunter fast traumhaft. Diese Zumutung, diese Suggestion, wird nach anfänglichem Sträuben stets akzeptiert und hat eine vielfach günstige Wirkung. Sie begünstigt das Auftreten der Übertragungsneurose, macht dadurch längst vergangene Konflikte aktuell, bringt das Verdrängte in die Gegenwart und nähert es dem Bewußtsein. Sie macht die Stunde zu einem konzentrierten Erlebnis und erleichtert dadurch dem Analysanden die Befolgung der Vorschrift, untertags der Analyse keine Gedanken zu widmen, da er es ohne Mitwirkung seines lebhaft agierenden Gegenspielers gar nicht vermag. Eine gewisse Aktivität des Analytikers ist, wie ich schon seinerzeit in Oxford gesagt habe, der Technik ähnlich, die Anna Freud für ihre Kinderanalysen empfohlen hat. Sie erweist sich als ebenso erfolgreich bei der Analyse der großen Kinder, die wir Erwachsene nennen und denen wir auch, wenigstens im Anfang, imponieren müssen. Sie sind mindestens so bösartig, mißtrauisch und feindselig wie die Kinder, nur noch gefährlicher, weil sie all diese Feindseligkeit unter der Maske einer gleisnerischen Freundlichkeit verbergen. Dadurch, daß wir ihnen Tag für Tag und Stück für Stück diese Maske vom Gesicht reißen, gelingt es uns, ihre wilde Gegnerschaft zu zähmen und die Übertragung zustande zu bringen. In diesem Kampfe müssen wir jedes Mittel des Verständnisses verwenden, denn sonst wird der Analysand jede Blöße, die er zu sehen meint, zum Anlaß nehmen, um seine Absicht, der Analyse auszuweichen oder gar zu entfliehen, zur Durchführung zu bringen.

Die Technik, mit der wir alles psychische Geschehen der Analysanden in eine Einheit zusammendrängen, ist in Wirklichkeit gar nicht der Gewaltakt, als der sie im ersten Augenblick imponiert. Unser Verfahren ahmt eigentlich nur die Technik unserer Patienten nach oder parodiert sie sogar, indem ja auch deren neurotisches Verhalten häufig eine unentwirrbare Verknüpfung von Traum und Wirklichkeit darstellt. Indem wir uns mit unserer Technik dieser Verhaltungsweise anpassen, tun wir nichts anderes als die Mutter, die sich dem slang ihres Babys anpaßt und erfahrungsgemäß für diese Entgegenkommen reichlich entschädigt wird, indem sich das Kind eines Tages als Revanche herbeiläßt, die Sprache der Mutter zu sprechen. Das wunderbare Phänomen der Erlernung der Muttersprache wiederholt sich beim Zustandekommen der Übertragung in der Analyse. Ihren symbolischen Ausdruck findet diese Phase in den Mischfiguren, in denen die Identifizierung mit dem Analytiker dargestellt wird, und in den Träumen, in denen der Analytiker persönlich erscheint.

Ich brauche hier wohl nicht eigens zu erwähnen, daß außer der Situationsdeutung auch alle Inhaltsdeutungen zur Sprache kommen, unter ihnen besonders auch die Sexualdeutungen. Die Situationsdeutung ist aber stets in erster Linie das Barometer, das uns über das jeweils herrschende Analysenwetter orientiert, und alle anderen Deutungen werden uns mühelos in den Schoß fallen, ja sie werden uns, wenn wir nur ein bißchen Geduld haben, vom Patienten selbst gebracht werden. Ich mache sogar eine Regel daraus, selbst naheliegende Sexualdeutungen vorerst zu unterdrücken. Diese Technik erweist sich als vorteilhaft, da das auf diese Weise gewissermaßen angestaute Material früher oder später geradezu explosiv durchbricht und dadurch für den Patienten zum eindrucksvollen Erlebnis wird; das Material deutet sich fast von selbst.

In dem Maß, als die Übertragung zustande kommt, ändert die analytische Situation ihren Charakter. Nicht als ob sie an Bedeutung verlöre, aber sie ist eine fast unumstrittene analytische Institution geworden, die Plattform, auf der sich Analytiker und Analysand zu gemeinsamer Arbeit gefunden haben und die auch zwischen ihnen eine Beziehung herstellt, die kaum in irgend einer anderen ihr Analogon findet. Ein juristischer Spaßvogel hat einmal festgestellt, was für eine Unsumme von juristischen Verträgen nötig wäre, um den Rechts- und Pflichtenkreis einer Ehe zu erfassen, und daß selbst diese Menge von Verträgen noch nicht den ganzen Gehalt des „Ehekomplexes" restlos ausschöpfen würde. In eine noch viel größere Schwierigkeit würde der geraten, der die Beziehung zwischen Analytiker und Analysanden im Stadium der Übertragung in ähnlicher Weise erfassen wollte. Sie hat etwas von der Art der Beziehung zwischen Beichtvater und Beichtkind, zwischen Lehrer und Schüler, zwischen Chef und Angestelltem, zwischen Eltern und Kindern, zwischen Geschwistern untereinander, zwischen gleich- und verschiedengeschlechtlichen Freunden, zwischen Verliebten und zwischen Eheleuten; aber wir empfinden, indem wir das aussprechen, daß alle diese Darstellungen nur unzulängliche Versuche sind, um der Eigenart dieses Verhältnisses gerecht zu werden, das eigentlich alle die soeben genannten Beziehungen in sich begreift und noch viele andere dazu, aber mit einem Quantum von Affektivität und Ambivalenz, das in den banalen Beziehungen in diesem Ausmaß nicht zu finden ist. Und so wird auch in der Traumsymbolik die Analyse in den angeführten Bildern dargestellt, und die begleitenden Affekte und Ambivalenzkonflikte machen die uns in dieser Zeit gelieferten Inhalte zum analytischen Erlebnis, welches auch in dieser Phase durch die stete Betonung der analytischen Situation an dramatischer Lebendigkeit gewinnt. Wir können uns überzeugen, daß auch jetzt die Situationswiderstände nicht erloschen, sondern nur abgeschwächt sind. Den strikten Beweis hiefür liefert uns das Verhalten der Patienten im Endstadium der Analyse, wo fast immer ein neues Aufflackern des bisher nur unter der Asche glimmenden Widerstandes wahrzunehmen ist, des typischen „Widerstandes der letzten Zeit". Doch bevor ich mich mit diesem Phänomen befasse, will ich kurz skizzieren, was inzwischen vor sich gegangen ist.

Der Patient hat nach den eindrucksvollen Erlebnissen der Kur die relative Bedeutungslosigkeit der aktuellen im Vergleich zur Überwertigkeit der psychischen Realität erfaßt. Sein Ich hat die kriminellen Tendenzen des Es durchschaut und das strafende Über-Ich als Popanz erkannt. Er ist freier, heiterer, selbstbewußter geworden. Die von so mannigfachen Hypotheken entlastete Libido äußert sich bei Männern in der Besserung der Potenz, im Auftreten von kräftigen Morgenerektionen, bei Frauen in der Aussöhnung mit ihrer weiblichen Rolle, was häufig genug in der Besserung ihrer aktuellen Liebesfähigkeit zum Ausdruck kommt, besonders eindrucksvoll bei solchen, die bisher noch nie richtig empfunden hatten. Auch die Träume haben ihren Charakter geändert; ursprünglich angstvoll, sind sie jetzt mehr reflektierend und kritisierend geworden. Es treten Träume auf, die Emanzipationsbestrebungen, Entwertungstendenzen, schließlich auch die Parodierung und Verulkung des Analytikers und der Analyse selbst bringen. Einige Traumbeispiele mögen dies zeigen:

Der Träumer, der in einem Auto fährt, nimmt dem links neben ihm sitzenden Chauffeur den Volant aus der Hand und übernimmt selbst die Führung des Wagens. (Emanzipationstendenz.)

Die Entwertung des Aktuellen kommt dadurch zum Ausdruck, daß anscheinend gefährliche Situationen in den Träumen angstlos erledigt werden. So wird etwa die Mitteilung der unmittelbar bevorstehenden Hinrichtung ohne Angst entgegengenommen; oder es kommen wilde Tiere auf den Träumer zu, die sich in der Nähe als harmlos erweisen, oder es bricht Feuer aus, ohne Schaden zu stiften. In diesen Träumen zeigt der Analysand sich selbst und den anderen die Tatsache, daß er dem Analytiker „über den Kopf gewachsen ist". Noch deutlicher wird das, wenn ein sich feminin identifizierender Patient, bei dem Ideen seiner hormonalen Minderwertigkeit eine große Rolle gespielt haben, nun träumt, *daß ihm ein Hoden samt dem Penis, der auffallend klein ist, abgefallen sei. Es ist ein lehmartiges Gebilde, das er einer im Zimmer zugleich mit ihrer kleinen Tochter befindlichen Frau überreicht, die es mit Behagen verspeisen, wobei er ein Gefühl unendlicher Überlegenheit hat.*

Das ist wohl eine besonders schöne Darstellung der analytischen Erledigung eines früher angstbetonten Komplexes.

Am augenfälligsten ist dieses Entwertungsmotiv in Träumen, in denen Personen oder Dinge, die einst groß oder bedeutend waren, nunmehr klein erscheinen, z. B. in folgendem:

Der Träumer befindet sich auf dem Friedhof beim Grabdenkmal des verstorbenen Prof. Schwind. Aber das ganze Denkmal ist eigentlich nur ein kleiner, würfelförmiger, durchsichtiger Kasten und der darin stehende Prof. Schwind füllt selbst diese Kiste nur zur Hälfte aus.

Diese Symbolik ist deutlich genug. Der Analytiker ist erledigt (tot und klein). Für den, der die Beziehung zwischen Traum und Witz kennt, ist es ziemlich wahrscheinlich, daß hier auch der Analyse selbst (kleiner Schwind = Schwindel) der Garaus gemacht wird.

Wenn sich nun der Analytiker unter diesen Umständen zur Beendigung der Analyse entschließt und dieses Vorhaben dem Analysanden zur Kenntnis bringt oder auch nur andeutet, dann erwacht plötzlich der oben erwähnte „Widerstand der letzten Zeit". Der Sinn dieses Widerstandes ist, entweder dem Analytiker zu zeigen, daß man genau so krank und elend ist wie zuvor, oder aber daß man ihm den Erfolg nicht verdanken will. Der erfahrene Analytiker merkt aber an gewissen Anzeichen, daß dieser Widerstand, so ähnlich er auch in seiner manifesten Äußerung dem gleichen Phänomen der Anfangszeit sein mag, sich dennoch von ihm unterscheidet. Der Affekt ist unecht, gespielt, man könnte sagen, arrangiert. Der Fachmann wird ihn durchschauen, und das Verständnis dieser letzten Phase der Analyse erschließt sich ihm durch Träume, in denen das „Motiv des Rückzugsgefechts" symbolisch dargestellt wird.

Ein Patient mit einer psychischen Sexualstörung, der im Laufe der Behandlung zu einer sehr zufriedenstellenden Potenz gelangt ist, bringt vor der Beendigung der Analyse folgenden Traum:

Ich soll in ein Haus gehen, wohin mich mein Vater gerufen hat, damit ich vorsinge. Als ich dort eintrete, sagt mein Vater, es sei nicht mehr nötig. Ich bin sehr gekränkt und sage es auch, aber ich werde anscheinend nicht ernst genommen.

Ein anderer Patient mit einer Potenzstörung, in dessen Neurose die feminine Identifizierung eine große Rolle gespielt hat, aber nunmehr einer betont männlichen Einstellung gewichen ist, träumt unmittelbar nach der „Kündigung", daß er ein Mädchen aus einem Zimmer hinausgeschickt hat, sie aber heimlich bei einer Seitentüre wieder hereinläßt.

Ein Patient, der nebst anderen Symptomen namentlich an gehäuften Pollutionen gelitten hat, die während der Kur vergangen sind, träumt unmittelbar nachdem ich den Termin ausgesprochen habe, daß er eine Pollution bekommen hat und sich über den Analytiker, der es mit Bestürzung wahrnimmt, wundert.

Ich bin mir natürlich vollkommen darüber im klaren und will es nochmals betonen, wie unendlich schwierig es ist, meine Formulierungen durch einzelne aus dem Zusammenhang gerissene Traumfragmente hinreichend zu stützen. Die von mir in Aussicht gestellte ausführliche Publikation wird dieser Aufgabe hoffentlich besser gerecht werden. Für den Augenblick aber würde ich sehr glücklich sein, wenn es mir durch diese Arbeit gelungen wäre, die Kollegen zu veranlassen, die Richtigkeit der von mir gebrachten Traumsymbolik der analytischen Situation an ihrem eigenen großen Traummaterial nachzuprüfen.

Beiträge zu einer Psychopathologie des Traumes II

Von

Eduard Hitschmann

Wien

Die Widerstände der Psychologen und Psychiater gegen die Beschäftigung mit dem Thema der Träume sind so verbreitet, daß wir Psychoanalytiker die einzigen Fachleute auf diesem Gebiete, das viel praktische Erfahrung erfordert, sind.

Der Traum ist für uns Gegenstand täglicher Beobachtung. Der Schüler der Psychoanalyse lernt in seiner Lehranalyse seine Träume deuten. Macht er dann, nach Schulung in Kursen und gründlicher Lektüre von Freuds „Traumdeutung", selbst seine ersten Analysen unter der Kontrolle eines erfahrenen Analytikers, so berichtet er diesem regelmäßig über die Träume seines Analysanden in der abgelaufenen Woche. So berichtet etwa der Schüler in der internen Medizin über den Verlauf des Organ- oder Harnbefundes bei dem ihm anvertrauten Patienten. Ich beschreibe dies hier, um zu zeigen, wie selbstverständlich die objektiven Traumbeobachtungen und -deutungen Gegenstand ärztlicher Erfahrung geworden sind.

Wird erst eine Psychopathologie der Träume all das Gesetzmäßige, Unbezweifelbare, Erwiesene über dieses Stiefkind der Medizin und Psychologie darstellen, so wird ein Ausweichen und Verleugnen nicht mehr gut möglich sein.

Die Erkenntnis wird sich Bahn brechen, daß „wer sich die Entstehung der Traumbilder nicht zu erklären weiß, sich auch um das Verständnis der Phobien, Zwangs- und Wahnideen, eventuell um deren therapeutische Beeinflussung, vergeblich bemühen wird" (Freud).

Mit Kretschmer die Überzeugung vertretend, daß es den Grundsätzen einer soliden wissenschaftlichen und ärztlichen Urteilsbildung widerspricht, ein so umfangreiches Stück Erfahrungsmaterial wie die Träume zu vernachlässigen, kommen wir hier nochmals auf die Anregung zu einer Psychopathologie der Träume zu sprechen, die vor allem das Gesetzmäßige dieser seelischen Erscheinung festzulegen hat, aber auch zur Vervollständigung unserer Befunde beitragen wird.

Wenn ich mit meinem ersten Aufsatz über dieses Thema[1] durch die Betonung des Wertes auch der manifesten Traumbilder und der durchschaubaren Träume neues Interesse unter den Psychiatern und Psychologen geweckt habe, kann ich nun erst recht der Tiefendeutung, deren jeder längere, ausführlichere Traum für die Psychoanalyse bedarf, mit allem Respekt gedenken. Das reiche Material, das in einem solchen Traum verdichtet ist, seine volle Ein-

---

[1] Int. Ztschr. f. Psa., Bd. XX, 1934, Heft 4.

103

ordnung in das Seelenleben des Träumers, der latente unbewußte Wunschgehalt, die Wertung von Widerstand und Übertragung im Traum, seine Bedeutung für den Verlauf der Psychoanalyse kann natürlich nur durch regel-
rechte Deutung hervorgeholt werden. Ein leuchtendes Beispiel einer extensiv
und intensiv erschöpfenden Bearbeitung eines Traumes finden wir in Freuds
Arbeit „Aus der Geschichte einer infantilen Neurose".[2] Es heißt dort: „Ich
will bemerken, daß diese Deutung eine Aufgabe war, deren Lösung sich durch
mehrere Jahre hinzog ... Nachdem uns die Synthese dieses Traumes gelungen
ist, will ich versuchen, die Beziehungen des manifesten Trauminhaltes zu den
latenten Traumgedanken übersichtlich darzustellen."

* * *

Das Kapitel „Phänomenologie der Träume" wird ein umfangreiches
werden müssen und fast aller Vorarbeit erst bedürfen. Abgesehen von den
Differenzen der Zahl, des Umfanges, der zugehörigen Deutungsbereitschaft,
wie sie davon abhängig ist, ob und mit welchem Vorzeichen die Träume
während einer Analyse „in den Stromkreis der Übertragung eingeschaltet
sind" (Sachs), — stellen wir solche Differenzen auch sonst in den Eigenheiten
verschiedener Träumer fest, so daß all diese verschiedenen Typen beschrieben
werden müssen, der Ursprung dieser Arten des Träumens, des Festhaltens oder
des Berichtens erst gesucht werden muß. Zwei Gattungen von Träumen
hat der Dichter Gottfried Keller in seinem Traumbuch (15. September 1847)
differenziert:

„Auch dem Schulz werde ich beim Frühstück keine Träume mehr erzählen,"
heißt es dort, „weil er den Verdacht aussprach, daß ich dieselben vorweg er-
sinne und erfinde. Er kennt nur die einfachsten Träume als: heute träumte ich
von einem Sarg, oder von Rauten, oder: ich fing Fische, oder: ich sah einem
die Nägel abschneiden usf. Weil er keine Phantasie hat, welche auch im
Schlafe schafft und wirtschaftet, so hält er einen wohlorganisierten Traum, der
einen ordentlichen Verlauf und schöne künstlerische Anschauungen hat, für
unmöglich ..."

Über die „Qualitätenskala der Träume von der Verworrenheit bis zur Klarheit" (Freud) und vieles andere finden wir Aufklärung in der „Traumdeutung". Allenthalben finden sich hier Bruchflächen, welche Kontaktstellen
mit der Psychologie entsprechen. Manche stehen schon in Erörterung, z. B.
der scheinbar beschleunigte Ablauf des seelischen Geschehens, wie ihn die
Traumarbeit zeigt. Seltsamerweise hat die Universitätspsychologie sonst fast
all diese Fragen unbeantwortet gelassen; hier eröffnet sich ihr noch ein großes
Arbeitsfeld.

Was die Psychologen so lange hat zögern lassen, die Freudsche Traumdeutung anzuerkennen, waren die bekannten Widerstände gegen die Psycho-

2) Ges. Schr., Bd. VIII.

analyse, besonders die Einwände gegen ein unbewußtes Seelisches; dann gegen das Sinnvolle der Träume und gegen die Wissenschaftlichkeit der Symbolik, zumal der sexuellen. Durch tendenziöse Kritik der Psychoanalyse wurden zahlreiche Jahrgänge von Studierenden der Psychologie dem Thema der Traumdeutung entfremdet.

So erklärt es sich, daß die Träume, eine solche Fundgrube psychologischer Erkenntnisse, von der Psychologie vernachlässigt erscheinen. Eine Arbeit wie die von Karl S i e b e r t über „Fehlleistung und Traum"[3] zeigt noch die ganze Überheblichkeit und Oberflächlichkeit des Besserwissers. Aber in einer Arbeit desselben Autors, zwei Jahre später, „Die Gestaltbildung im Traum. Eine experimentelle Untersuchung"[4] finden wir schon mehr Respekt und Einsicht.

Hier wäre aber des wichtigen Beitrages des Psychiaters O. P ö t z l „Experimentell erregte Traumbilder in ihren Beziehungen zum indirekten Sehen" zu gedenken.[5] Die Versuchsergebnisse können als experimentelle Illustrationen der F r e u d schen Traumanalyse betrachtet werden und sind geeignet, diese auch den Experimentalpsychologen näherzubringen. Sie bestätigen wichtige Tatsachen der Psychoanalyse.

Der Leidener Psychiater J e l g e r s m a hat schon im Jahre 1914[6] in seinem Vortrag „Unbewußtes Geistesleben" sich voll Bewunderung für die Anerkennung der Traumdeutung eingesetzt, ohne daß viele andere Psychiater davon beeinflußt worden wären. S c h i l d e r behandelt in seiner „Medizinischen Psychologie" (1924) das Traumproblem ausführlich im psychoanalytischen Sinn.

Das ausgezeichnete kleine Werk von L. B i n s w a n g e r, „Wandlungen in der Auffassung und Deutung des Traumes von den Griechen bis zur Gegenwart"[7] steht ganz auf dem Boden der Psychoanalyse. Die überraschende Übereinstimmung antiker Traumdeutung mit der der Psychoanalyse hat H. W. G r u h l e in einem Vortrag in der Versammlung der südwestdeutschen Neurologen und Psychiater nachgewiesen (1928). P ö t z l verdanken wir weiters mehrere bedeutsame Arbeiten zum Traumproblem: „Schlafzentrum und Traum" (Med. Klinik, Jg. 22, 1926); „Über richtende Momente im Traum" (W. med. Wochenschr., Jg. 77, 1927); „Analyse eines Traumes mit Zoopsie" (Psych. neur. Wochenschr., 29, 1927).

A. v. M u r a l t hat bereits im Jahre 1922 die Erwartung ausgesprochen, daß die Traumdeutung zu einer generalisierenden, w i s s e n s c h a f t l i c h e n M e t h o d e nach Art anderer naturwissenschaftlicher Methoden in der Medizin auszubauen sei.[8] L a i g n e l - L a v a s t i n e sprach 1926 die Hoffnung aus, daß

---

3) B r a u m ü l l e r, Wien, 1932.
4) A. f. Psychologie.
5) Ztschr. f. d. ges. Neurol. u. Psych., 73, 1917.
6) Beihefte zur Int. Ztschr. f. Psa., 1914, Nr. 1.
7) Berlin, 1928, J. Springer. Dem gleichen Autor verdanken wir auch die ebenfalls von hoher Bildung zeugende Arbeit „Traum und Existenz" (Neue Schweiz. Rdsch., 1930).
8) „Zur Frage der Traumdeutung", Schw. A. f. Neur. u. Psych., Bd. 11.

im Laufe der Zeit die Untersuchung der Träume eine feinere Klassifizierung der Charaktere ermöglichen werde.[9]

Havelock-Ellis veröffentlichte in „The Psychoanalytic Review"[10] eine Arbeit „Die Traumsynthese: Studie einer Reihe von 100 Träumen", in der er 100 Träume einer Frau ohne psychologische Auswertung bringt, nur um ein Bild ihrer Traumtypik und der in ihr sich auswirkenden Phänomene und Funktionen zu geben.

Selbst ein Skeptiker wie J. Meinertz[11] gibt zu, die Traumdeutung trage „zur seelischen Morphologie der einzelnen menschlichen Seele, einschließlich ihrer Verwurzlungen" bei und gebe „einen Zipfel in die Hand, an dem wir uns in die Tiefe tasten können". Psychoanalytische Theorie und Traumforschung stehen im Verhältnis gegenseitiger Befruchtung; so betrachten z. B. Jekels und Bergler in ihrem Vortrag „Triebdualismus im Traum" (XIII. Int. Psa. Kongreß, 1934) auch das Traumphänomen unter dem Aspekt des Ringens von Eros und Todestrieb und finden dann im Traum Manifestationen des Todestriebes. Oder: Die bekannte symbolische Gleichung Zahn = Penis „muß" nach Jones aus einer gewissen sadistischen prägenitalen Phase „stammen", ist also ein Beweis für sie („Die phallische Phase", Int. Ztschr. f. Psa., Bd. XIX, 1933). Jones' grundlegende Arbeit „Der Alptraum" (Schr. z. angew. Seelenkunde, 1912) gibt Beweise für die Theorie der hysterischen Angst. — Hier mögen auch Federns Ausführungen über „Das Ich-Gefühl im Traum" (Int. Ztschr. f. Psa., Bd. XVIII, 1932) Erwähnung finden.

* * *

Die feinsinnige Ausführung eines Psychiaters, Griesinger, „die mit aller Klarheit die Wunscherfüllung als einen dem Traume und der Psychose gemeinsamen Charakter des Vorstellens enthüllt", hat seinerzeit neben seinen eigenen Untersuchungen Freud gelehrt, daß hier der Schlüssel zu einer psychologischen Theorie des Traumes und der Psychose zu finden ist.

Über die Beziehungen zwischen Traum und Geisteskrankheiten hat Freud sich dann in der Traumdeutung ausführlich geäußert und Autoren angeführt, die zu dem Thema berichtet haben. Die Ansicht, daß ein Traum eine Geisteskrankheit verursachen könne, stellt Freud dahin richtig, daß in diesen Fällen besser ausgesagt wird, die geistige Störung habe ihre erste Äußerung am Traumleben gezeigt, sei im Traume zuerst durchgebrochen. Auch wird z. B. von Féré von einem Traume berichtet, „der eine hysterische Lähmung zur Folge hatte".

Ich selbst habe einmal eine hysterische Patientin zu behandeln gehabt, die Wochen vor dem Eintritt der Lähmung von ihr geträumt hatte: dieselbe war

---

9) „Der semiologische Wert der Träume", Journ. méd. franc., Bd. 15.
10) Bd. 12, 1925.
11) Z. f. d. g. Neur. u. Psych. 1935, Bd. 153, H. 1.

auf Selbstbestrafungstendenzen zurückzuführen, die, bevor sie an einem Buß-
tag nach dem Besuch des Gotteshauses die Lähmung hatten in Erscheinung
treten lassen, im Traum bereits sich gemeldet hatten. Träume, deren leidender
Inhalt durch solche Tendenzen charakterisiert sind, haben wir schon hervorgehoben. Daß die Analyse die Paraparese als Kastration deuten ließ, wird
nicht wundernehmen. Es ist nicht ausgeschlossen, daß eine rechtzeitige Kennt-
nisnahme ähnlicher Träume durch den Arzt zur Verhütung des Ausbruches
des Symptoms verwendet werden kann.

Aber über die Träume der Geisteskranken muß erst ausführlich
gearbeitet werden, und zwar unter Zugrundelegung der psychoanalytischen
Traumdeutung. Eine Deutung mit Hilfe der Einfälle des Kranken wird nicht
immer möglich sein. Hollós verdanken wir eine Studie über „Die Arbeit
des Traumes und der Geisteskrankheiten", ihre Analogie (in „Psa. Studien",
Budapest, 1933). Ebendort berichtet Almasy über Psychoanalyse von amentia-
artigen Krankheitsbildern.

Es sei hier eine Arbeit über das Traumleben chronischer Alkoholiker herangezogen, um zu zeigen, wieviel hier noch zu leisten ist, und wieviel Anregung
zu wissenschaftlicher Weiterarbeit von den Traumbeobachtungen ausgehen
kann. Das Traumleben chronischer Alkoholiker, sobald sie
abstinent werden, wird von J. G. Jislin sehr charakteristisch geschildert.[12] Gedrückte Stimmung, Angst, paranoische Einstellung gehen schon
voraus. Dann beginnt der Schlaf sich zu verschlechtern, und der Patient wacht
aus schweren Träumen auf. „Er fällt irgendwohin, bricht durch irgendetwas
durch; ihn überfallen Banditen, zerlumpte Kerle von schrecklichem Aussehen,
mit ungewöhnlich verzerrten Gesichtern; er sieht in großer Anzahl verschiedene Tiere: Wölfe, Bären, Löwen, öfters aber Hunde, Katzen, Mäuse,
Pferde. Die Hunde und Pferde beißen ihn, er will sich von ihnen befreien,
dabei schlägt er im Bett mit den Händen um sich, nicht selten beschädigt er
sie und erwacht dann. Er hört Gebell, Geschrei, Gesang, Musik, wacht in
Schweiß gebadet auf, aber die Figuren der Menschen und sich bewegenden
Tiere stehen gleichsam einige Zeit noch vor seinen Augen."

Ein erster solcher Traum lautete: „Zu ihm kam eine Militärperson, ein Oberst
mit blankem Säbel und schrie: ‚Wirst du, Hundesohn, noch lange hier saufen?
Wenn du es tust, haue ich dir gleich den Kopf ab,‘ wobei er den Säbel gegen ihn
hob." — Der psychoanalytische Traumdeuter wird hier auffallende Ähnlichkeit
mit den Träumen von Homosexuellen feststellen. Der Zusammenhang zwischen der Intoxikation mit Alkohol und der Homosexualität könnte von
hier aus angegangen werden. Der Autor nimmt jedoch auf letztere gar nicht
Bezug.

Die Psychoanalyse hat schon seit langer Zeit auf die homosexuelle Kom-

---

12) „Zur Klinik der Abstinenzerscheinungen beim Alcoholismus chronicus", Ztschr. f. d.
ges. Neurol. u. Psych., 136, 1931.

ponente bei Trinkern hingewiesen. Abrahams Arbeit aus dem Jahre 1908[13] entnehme ich nur folgenden Satz: „Durch jede Kneipe geht ein Zug von Homosexualität. Die gleichgeschlechtliche Komponente, die wir unter den Einflüssen der Erziehung verdrängen und sublimieren gelernt haben, kommt unter der Wirkung des Alkohols unverkennbar wieder zum Vorschein."

A. Kielholz machte einen „Analyseversuch bei Delirium tremens",[14] den er mit folgender Zusammenfassung schließt: „Die Einfälle eines Alkoholdeliranten zu seinen wahnhaften Erlebnissen weisen auf eine Verstärkung der homosexuellen Triebkomponente, des Narzißmus und vor allem des Schautriebes hin ... Die dem Trinker am nächsten Stehenden, hauptsächlich des eigenen Geschlechtes, zu denen er in besonderer Art, meist ambivalent, affektiv eingestellt ist, erscheinen im Delir in Tiere verwandelt..." Auf die verstärkte homosexuelle Triebkomponente als ätiologisches Element der Trunksucht hat Kielholz bereits früher hingewiesen.[15]

„Zur Psychologie des alkoholischen Beschäftigungdelirs" hat V. Tausk[16] Beobachtungen geliefert; er deutet dort auch den Beschäftigungstraum als Impotenzangsttraum. Narzißmus und unbewußte Homosexualität sind auch nach diesem Autor die Disposition für den Alkoholmißbrauch.

Über „Beschäftigungsträume (Sisyphusträume) und Beschäftigungsdelir" kam H. Christoffel[17] zu dem Resultat, sie seien ein Vorsymptom der Erschöpfungsschlaflosigkeit: Der Patient könne sich nicht mehr vom Tage und seiner Tätigkeit lösen.

Zu meiner kleinen Arbeit aus dem Jahre 1912 „Swedenborgs Paranoia" im Zentralbl. f. Psa. hatte ich Träume Swedenborgs nicht zur Verfügung; ich fand solche erst später im Buch von H. W. Gruhle, „Swedenborgs Träume, ein Beitrag zur Phänomenologie seiner Mystik",[18] woraus die Wandlung der Persönlichkeit Swedenborgs zum religiösen Paranoiker sich klar ableiten läßt. Nehmen wir die endgültige Umwandlung für sein Alter von 57 Jahren an (Visionen!), so sind die Träume aus dem 55. und 56. Jahr uns besonders wichtig. Immer deutlicher wird die passiv-homosexuelle Einstellung, die Abneigung und Angst gegenüber den Frauen, die Kastrationsangst.

Man beachte z. B. den Traum vom 5. August 1744: „*Sah einen Mann mit gezogenen Degen auf mich zukommen; ich glaubte, auch einen Degen mit silbernem Griff zu haben; aber als der Mann kam, hatte ich keinen, sondern eine zerbrochene Scheide. Der Mann legte sich auf meinen Rücken und biß mich in die Hände; ich rief*

---

13) „Die psychol. Beziehungen zwischen Sexualität u. Alkoholismus", Z. f. Sexualwiss., 1908 (Intern. psa. Bibliothek, Bd. X).
14) Int. Ztschr. f. Psa., Bd. XII, 1926.
15) Schweiz. A. f. Neurol. u. Psych., Bd. XVI: „Trunksucht und Psychoanalyse."
16) Int. Ztschr. f. Psa., Bd. III, 1915.
17) Zentrlbl. f. Neurol., 17, 1928.
18) Psychol. Forsch. Berlin, 1925, Bd. 5. — Ausführlicher bei Winterstein: „Swedenborgs mystische Krise und sein Traumtagebuch" (im Erscheinen).

um Hilfe, aber es kam keine." Im Traum vom 18. April ist eine große *Frauens-person Henker, köpft und soll die Stücke dann essen.* Oft träumt er von bissigen Hunden. Am 10. Oktober erschienen ihm Frauen mit Vagina dentata u. dgl. m. Swedenborg erwähnt im Traumtagebuch, daß im Gegensatz zu seiner früheren Sinnlichkeit im Dezember 1743 diese Neigung plötzlich aufhörte, und er keinen Gefallen mehr am weiblichen Geschlecht fand.

Die psychoanalytische Auffassung der Paranoia, wie sie F r e u d am Falle Schreber[19] dargestellt hat, wird durch die Träume Swedenborgs bestätigt.

Von den Beobachtungen über die Halluzinationen bei Amentia ausgehend, betont Paul S c h i l d e r,[20] daß in der Genese des Schlafes und des Traumes ebenso wie in der Genese der Amentia der Faktor toxischer Ermüdungspro-dukte mit eingestellt werden muß. Auf die Halluzinationen bei Intoxikatio-nen (Kokain, Meskalin) hinweisend, spricht S c h i l d e r die Vermutung aus, wir hätten Aussicht von der Pharmakologie her in dieses Problemgebiet noch weiter einzudringen.

In gewissen Richtungen stehe der Traum der Schizophrenie näher als der Amentia. Wie die einzelnen Partien des Ideal-Ichs sich in Traum, Amentia, Schizophrenie verhalten, müßte Gegenstand besonderer Untersuchung sein.

Auch eine Arbeit von H e r s c h m a n n und S c h i l d e r aus dem Jahre 1920 über „T r ä u m e d e r M e l a n c h o l i k e r nebst Bemerkungen zur Pathologie der Melancholie"[21] berücksichtigt nur die manifesten Trauminhalte: In vielen ihrer Träume fühlen sich die Melancholiker glücklich, ganz im Gegensatz zu ihrer Stimmung bei Tage. In anderen Träumen empfindet der Patient zwar kein Glücksgefühl, aber der Inhalt des Traumes führte zu angenehmen und lustbetonten Erlebnissen der Vergangenheit hinüber. Für die allgemeine Psychopathologie ist es von Bedeutung, daß sich die Lustentbindung aus dem vollbewußten Denken in die Träume flüchtet, was mit den sonstigen Erfahrun-gen der Psychoanalyse übereinstimmt. Die Fähigkeit zum lustvollen Erleben ist nicht in Verlust geraten, ist nur gehemmt. Sie wird dem Individuum nur von einem überstrengen Ideal-Ich nicht gestattet. — Hier hätten gründlichere Untersuchungen weitere Vertiefung zu bringen.

Die Beziehungen, welche zwischen seelischen Zuständen und somatischen Krankheiten nachgewiesen sind, lassen auch die T r ä u m e o r g a n i s c h K r a n-k e r in Betracht ziehen. Es folgen hier Angaben neuerer Literatur zum Thema Traum und Organe:

„D e r p h y s i o l o g i s c h - d i a g n o s t i s c h e T r a u m" von E. M i t c h e l l, Ref. Zbl. Neurol., 1923.
„D a s S t u d i u m d e r T r ä u m e a l s M e t h o d e d e r t o p i s c h e n D i a g n o s t i k" von A. G r ü n s t e i n, Ref. Zbl. Neurol., 1923, und ähnlich Zbl. Neurol., 1924.

---

19) Jahrb. f. psa. Forsch., Bd. III, 1911; Ges. Schr., Bd. VIII.
20) „Entwurf einer Psychiatrie auf psychoanalytischer Grundlage", Int. Psa. Verlag, 1925.
21) Ztschr. f. d. ges. Neurol. u. Psych., Bd. 37.

„Fragmente über das Sehen im Traum" von J. Streiff., Z. f. Sinnesphysiol. 1925.
„Träume von leiblicher Herkunft" von F. J. Soesmann, Ref. Zbl. Neurol., 1928.
„Organreizträume" vom selben Autor, am selben Ort.
„Somatisch bedingte Angstträume" von E. Eichenberger, A. f. Psych., 1929.
„Träume bei Labyrinthläsionen" von K. Eisinger und P. Schilder, A. f. Psych., 1929.
„Zusammenhang von Vestibularfunktion, Schlafstellung und Traumleben" von H. Hoff, Mschr. Psych., 1929.
„Träume von Lungenkranken" von H. Hoke, Med. Klinik, 1930.
„Darstellung somatischer Phänomene im Traum", Ref. Zbl. Neurol., 1931.
„Bemerkungen über die Bedeutung des Traumes in der Gynäkologie" von A. Mayer, Ref. Zbl. Neurol., 1932.
„Über das Traumleben der Epileptiker" von L. Göttke, A. f. Psych., 1934.

Im Abschnitt über den inneren organischen Leibreiz als Traumquelle führt Freud an, daß schon Aristoteles es für sehr wohl möglich erklärt, „daß man im Traume auf beginnende Krankheitszustände aufmerksam gemacht würde, von denen man im Wachen noch nichts merkt, und ärztliche Autoren, deren Anschauung es sicherlich fern lag, an eine prophetische Gabe des Traumes zu glauben, haben wenigstens für die Krankheitsankündigung diese Bedeutung des Traumes gelten lassen."

Ganz im Sinne unserer Ausführungen hat Alexander die Bedeutung statistischer Untersuchungen über die Träume scheinbar nur organisch Kranker erkannt und im Chikagoer psychoanalytischen Institut erfolgreich verwertet.

Im Jahresbericht des Institutes 1933—1934 findet sich ein Kapitel statistische Traumstudien an Kranken mit peptischen Geschwüren und Magenneurosen, welche dort psychoanalytischer Behandlung unterzogen werden. Die Analysen an diesen Patienten ergaben ein bemerkenswertes Überwiegen von Träumen und freien Assoziationen über Nahrung, Essen und Trinken (orales Material). Die Annahme, daß an der dauernden Tätigkeit dieser Mägen, auch nachts, seelische Reize schuld seien (oral-rezeptive oder oral-aggressive), wird bestärkt durch die Tatsache, daß in den Träumen Nahrung oder Nahrungsaufnahme halluziniert sind. Ohne daß diese Untersuchung als beendet angesehen werden kann, bestätigt es sich, daß diese Inhalte in den manifesten Träumen recht häufig, besonders bei peptischen Geschwüren erscheinen. Alexander und Wilson haben ihre statistischen Traumstudien natürlich auch auf die im latenten Trauminhalt sich äußernden oralen Tendenzen ausgedehnt.

Die Autoren sind durch diese Traumstudien bestärkt in ihrer Theorie, daß die Unbefriedigung jener oralen Wünsche an der Übertätigkeit und Übersäuerung dieser Mägen, welch letztere sich so oft nachts zeigt, Schuld trägt. Der Einwand, daß etwa diese oralen Träume die Folge der Reizung durch das Geschwür seien, hält nicht stand, da ausgedehnte Beobachtung zur Evidenz erwiesen hat, daß solche orale Träume Ausdruck oral-rezeptiver Wünsche sind, die unabhängig von Geschwüren sind und deren Entwicklung vorausgehen.[22]

Über spezielle Formen von Träumen liegen viele, z. T. noch psychoanalytisch zu vertiefende Publikationen vor; eine auf Vollständigkeit keinen Anspruch machende Reihe sei hier angeführt:

„Der Traum von vergeblichen Anstrengungen" (Gregory, Psyche, Bd. 4, 1923).
„Untersuchungen über Kinderträume" (Raspe, Z. f. pädag. Psychol. u. exp. Pädag., Jg. 25, 1924).
„Über den klassischen Traum der Entjungferung" (Levi-Bianchini, Verh. d. 1. Int. Kongr. f. Sexualforsch., Bd. 3, 1928).
„Die Flugträume" (Levy, J. de Psychol., 25, 1928).
„Über das Bettnässen und die Rolle der Träume in seinem Bilde" (Weißenberg, Z. f. Kinderheilkunde, Bd. 40, 1925).
„Das Traumbild der Blinden" (Deutsch, Psychoan. Review, Bd. 35, 1928).
„Eine Untersuchung der Blindenträume unter bes. Berücksichtigung der Sinne am Aufbau der Traumvorstellungen" (Buttenwieser, Eos, Jg. 19, 1927).
„Bemerkungen zu einigen Träumen einer Normalen" (Sturt, Brit. Journ. of psychol., Bd. 13, 1922).
„Sprachstörungen im Traum" (Saussure, Rev. méd. d. l. Suisse rom., Jg. 43, 1923).
„Die Erklärung des Traumes bei den Primitiven" (Halbwachs, J. de psychol., Jg. 19, 1922).
„Der Traum und die Blinden" (Bolli, J. de psychol., 29, 1932).
„Traum einer frigiden Frau" (Pichon, Rev. franç. Psychoan., 5, 1932).
„Über Häufigkeit der Geschmacks- und Geruchsträume" (Kiesow, A. ital. Psicol., 7, 1929).
„Somatisch bedingte Angstträume" (Eichenberger, A. f. Psych., 87, 1929).
„Der Traum vom Träumen" (Jolowicz, 6. allg. ä. Kongr. f. Psychother., Dresden. 1931).
„Die verschiedenen Träume derselben Nacht" (Löwy, ebenda).
„Der Dynamismus der Dem. praecox. Wovon träumen die Schizophrenen?" Pharmakodynam. Psychoanalyse (Press. méd., 1932).

* * *

Das Kapitel „Symbolik" ist mit Rücksicht auf die zahlreichen Zweifler an der Traumsymbolik ein besonders wichtiges und überdies ein für die Psychoanalyse ruhmreiches. Ist doch die Symbolik auf dem Gebiete der Neurosen und Psychosen geistiges Eigentum der Psychoanalyse, die Symbolik der Träume zum großen Teil.[23]

Dieselben Symbole finden wir bekanntlich in gleicher Bedeutung auch im Mythus, im Witz und im Folklore. Die meisten Symbole, deren Deutung durch die Analyse heftigem Widerspruch begegnet ist, werden hier oft mit bewußter Bedeutungserfassung verwendet. Und es überwiegen hier die Sexualsymbole nicht minder als in Traum und Geistesstörung. Das Bewußtsein der Bedeutung symbolischer Darstellung für die Bildung des Traumes war im vorwissenschaftlichen Denken seit den ältesten Zeiten wohl niemals ganz

---

22) Vgl. auch Alexander, „Über den Einfluß psychischer Faktoren auf gastrointestinale Störungen". Int. Ztschr. f. Psa., Bd. XXI, 1935, H. 2.
23) Wir folgen hier der Darstellung von Heinz Hartmanns „Die Grundlagen der Psychoanalyse", G. Thieme, Leipzig, 1927.

erloschen. Eingang in die Wissenschaft hat aber der Gedanke erst mit Freuds Traumdeutung gewonnen.

Überdies gibt es unter den Symbolen, deren Verständnis sich Freud bei der Analyse der Traumvorgänge erschlossen hat, keines, dessen Bedeutung und dessen psychische Zusammenhänge nicht auch aus der Untersuchung des schizophrenen Denkens bestätigt worden sind.

Die psychoanalytische Symbollehre ist zum Überfluß auch auf experimentellem Wege unmittelbar bestätigt worden. In Versuchen von Schrötter[24] und von Roffenstein[25] wurde den Versuchspersonen in der Hypnose der Auftrag erteilt, ein bestimmtes sexuelles Erlebnis in entstellter Form zu träumen. Es ergaben sich dabei Entstellungen, welche mit den analytischen Traumsymbolen auf das genaueste übereinstimmen. Auch Betlheim und Hartmann,[26] sowie Nachmansohn[27] haben über experimentelle Symbolstudien berichtet.

Schilder sagt in seiner „Medizinischen Psychologie": „Nichts hat so viel Widerspruch erfahren wie die Lehre von der Symbolik, wiewohl sie als absolut gesichert gelten kann." Aber der Traumsymbolik wird noch immer große Skepsis und Abneigung von jenen entgegengebracht, welche nie analysiert oder Träume zu deuten versucht haben. Ursula H. McConnel[28] wendet sich besonders gegen die analytische Deutung des Schlangensymbols und setzt ihr die Vermutung entgegen, daß die Schlange im Traum keine phallische Bedeutung habe bei jenen Primitiven, bei denen die Schlange auch Symbol von etwas Heiligem und Gütigem bedeute.

Daß es sich bei der Symbolik um eine Wissenschaft handelt, welche vom Traumdeuter so herangezogen wird, wie die Bakteriologie vom Internisten, wird noch nicht allgemein verstanden. Wenn ich in meinem ersten Aufsatz hier Beweise aus den Träumen dafür gebracht habe, daß dem hysterischen Erbrechen so regelmäßig Fellatio-Phantasien verdrängt zugrunde liegen, so wird dies zu lesen, gewiß auf viele abstoßend gewirkt haben. Der erste aber, der die Beschäftigung mit dem Zusammenhang der Hysterie mit den Perversionen als „Wühlen im menschlichen Schmutz" bezeichnet hat, war — Freud selbst, vor 35 Jahren, in der ersten Auflage der Traumdeutung. Man muß sich bemühen, den Tatsachen des so häufigen sexuellen Träumens der Neurotiker eben so unerschrocken ins Auge sehen zu können, wie Freud es tat; zu ändern ist an ihnen nichts! Die länglich geformte Speise erscheint übrigens auch in einem experimentellen Traum, von Roffenstein berichtet, als Penissymbol: und zwar die Banane.

Das Kapitel Symbolik in der Psychopathologie der Träume wird neben den

24) Zbl. f. Psa., II, 1912.
25) Ztschr. f. d. ges. Neurol. u. Psych., 87, 1923.
26) Arch. f. Psychiatrie, 72, 1924.
27) Ztschr. f. d. ges. Neurol. u. Psych., 98, 1925.
28) „Die Bedeutung der Schlange im Traum" (Psyche, Jg. 1926).

typischen, erwiesenen Symbolen auch nur plausible, seltene und unsichere aufzuzählen haben. Dazu werden aber immer noch persönliche, fakultative,
originelle kommen.

Hier ist der psychoanalytischen Forschung, aber auch der Symbolforschung
überhaupt, noch ein weitverzweigtes, wichtiges Gebiet eröffnet.

Das sichergestellte Gesetzmäßige der Symbolik aber läßt sich oft aus dem
manifesten Traum bereits mit Eindeutigkeit herauslesen.

* * *

Die Beobachtung auch nur der manifesten Traumbilder, ferner der durch
die Psychoanalyse durchschaubaren Träume oder wie Bleuler einmal sagt,
der „Träume mit auf der Hand liegender Deutung",[29] vor allem aber die
weitere Anwendung der Freudschen Traumdeutung, eröffnen Gebiete neuer
Forschung in der gesamten Psychopathologie und Psychologie.

Wenn es möglich wäre festzustellen, wann bei einem Kinde die naiven
Wunschträume abgelöst werden von Träumen mit Äußerungen des Über-Ichs
als Zensur, also den komplizierten und sich der Symbolik bedienenden
Träumen, so hätten wir damit eine wichtige Tatsache der seelischen Ent-
wicklung des Kindes erfahren. Hier verfließen die Grenzen zwischen
Psychopathologie und Psychologie.

Auch das Gebiet der Charakterologie ist ein Grenzgebiet. Zu der so
bedeutsamen Arbeit von Freud „Über libidinöse Typen" habe ich die Frage
aufgeworfen: Weist solch ein Typus Eigenart in seinem Traumleben auf?[30]
Eine Frage, die sich durch Sammlung zugehöriger Träume leicht positiv beantworten läßt. Man würde daraus gewiß auch erfahren, wieso der eine Typus
erotisch geblieben oder geworden ist, oder wodurch der Zwangstypus, offenbar
schon unter frühen Einflüssen, sein strenges Über-Ich erworben hat.

Hier überall wird das Gesetzmäßige in Traumreihen das Beweisende sein.

Die überaus aufklärende Wirkung von in Patho- oder Psychographien
herangezogenen Träumen, bei denen nur der manifeste Inhalt zur Verfügung
steht, ergibt sich aus fast allen psychoanalytischen biographischen Beiträgen.
Gottfried Keller[31] und Swedenborg erleichterten die Heranziehung ihrer
Träume durch Anlage eines Traumbuches. Laforgue hat in seinem Buch
über Baudelaire[32] einen Traum des Dichters als wichtiges Beweismittel herangezogen. Franz Schubert[33] schrieb einen künstlichen, erfundenen Traum
nieder, der sich aber ebenfalls für eine psychoanalytische Betrachtung als

---

29) Münch. med. W., 1913, Nr. 45.
30) „Freud über Menschentypen", Psa. Bewegung, 1932, H. 3.
31) Hitschmann, „Gottfried Keller. Psychoanalyse des Dichters, seiner Gestalten und
Motive." Int. Psa. Verlag, 1919.
32) „Der gefesselte Baudelaire", Int. Psa. Verlag, 1933.
33) Hitschmann, „Franz Schuberts Schmerz und Liebe", Int. Ztschr. f. Psa., Bd. III,
1915.

bedeutsam erwies. Meine Studien über Goethe wie über Schopenhauer, Eckermann und Hamsun stützten sich gleichfalls auf Träume.[34]

Die Träume des Dichters Dauthendey, wie sie in der wertvollen Traumsammlung von I. Jézower (Rowohlt, Berlin, 1928) zu finden sind, bestätigen mir nachträglich meine Annahmen über die' besondere Vaterfixierung des Dichters.[35] Eigene Träume haben Friedrich Huch und Isolde Kurz gesammelt und veröffentlicht.

Sieht man „Das Buch der Träume" Jézowers durch, so erkennt man den Wert auch ohne jeden Versuch psychoanalytischer Deutung angeführter, nur manifest mitgeteilter Träume, sieht aber mit Bedauern, wieviel Aberglaube und Mystik sich um das Trauminteresse rankt und wieviel wissenschaftliche Menschenkenntnis damit verzögert und verschleudert wurde.

Daß auch die Träume, die von Dichtern geschaffenen und erfundenen Personen im Zusammenhang eines Dichtwerkes beigelegt werden, der psychoanalytischen Traumtheorie entsprechen, hat Freud in „Der Wahn und die Träume in W. Jensens ‚Gradiva'"[36] (1912) erwiesen.

Die Traumbilder sind „die sozusagen physiologischen Wahnschöpfungen des Menschen", sind „harmlose Psychosen einer Nacht".

* * *

Das Thema „Träume während der psychoanalytischen Kur" erfordert eine wesentliche Bereicherung, schon zur Belehrung der Adepten der Psychoanalyse. Das Grundlegende hat Freud in seinem Aufsatz „Bemerkungen zur Theorie und Praxis der Traumdeutung" angegeben; einige bedeutsame Sätze seien hier zitiert: „Die Verwertung in der Analyse ist eine Absicht, die dem Traume ursprünglich ganz ferne liegt. — Die meisten der in der Analyse verwertbaren Träume sind Gefälligkeitsträume und verdanken der Suggestion ihre Entstehung. — Bei hohem Widerstandsdruck sind die Träume wenig aufschlußreich." — Naturreine Träume sind also meist nur außerhalb einer psychoanalytischen Behandlung feststellbar.

Die Technik der psychoanalytischen Behandlung, welche die Bekämpfung der Ich-Widerstände vor allem zu leisten hat, führt natürlich dazu, daß diese Umstände während der Phasen der Kur zu beobachten sind.

So sagt Fenichel: „Der Traum ist ja ein Kommentar zu den Ich-Haltungen des Patienten am Vortage. Unter den latenten Traumgedanken gibt es immer welche, die der bewußten Haltung sehr nahe stehen, aber gerade ein Element mehr enthalten, oder gerade die Haltung in einer Verbindung zeigen, an die der P. aus Verdrängungsgründen nicht gedacht hat. ‚Traumdeuten' muß nicht heißen, dem P. sagen: ‚Sie wollen mit ihrer Mutter schlafen', sondern kann auch heißen, ‚latente Traumgedanken ermitteln und

---

34) Int. Psa. Verlag.
35) „Ein Dichter und sein Vater", Imago, Bd. IV, 1915/16.
36) Ges. Schr., Bd. IX.

mit ihnen dem P. sein gegenwärtiges Verhalten und dessen Absichten zeigen'..."[37]

Damit sind aber nur Andeutungen gegeben für ein Kapitel der „Psychopathologie des Traumes", das die Verwendung der Träume in der Therapie zu behandeln hätte, und Freuds Aufsätze „Die Handhabung der Traumdeutung in der Psychoanalyse" und „Bemerkungen zur Theorie und Praxis der Traumdeutung" als Richtschnur nimmt.[38] Der Traum ist manchmal der erste Zugang zu der „eigentlichen (unbewußten und bewußten) seelischen Wirklichkeit" des Patienten. So berichtet Graber[39] aus einer Kinderanalyse:

In der ersten Sitzung ist Rolf kaum zum Sprechen zu bewegen. Auch auf Fragen antwortet er selten und nur mit Ja oder Nein. Schließlich frage ich ihn nach Träumen. Er staunt. Sein Gesicht hellt sich auf, dann wird es von ticartigen Zuckungen verzerrt. Er spricht erregt: „Jetzt träume ich nicht mehr so viel wie früher." „Nun, von was träumst du denn?" Er stutzt und sieht mich zum erstenmal an, mißtrauisch und verlegen. „Hast Du denn noch niemandem von Deinen Träumen erzählt?" — „Nein. Es kommen darin immer Geister, um mich zu nehmen. Und dann liege ich immer wach, bis es hell wird, damit ich nicht mehr träume. Ich habe immer Angst vor den Geistern. Am Tage sind sie dann im Wald, oder in den Höhlen oder im Keller. An diese Orte gehe ich nicht allein. Ich denke nicht immer an Gespenster, denn wenn man gerade nicht daran denkt, können sie einen nehmen."

Noch nirgends sind Träume zusammengestellt worden, welche den so oft typischen Ausdruck der positiven Übertragung beinhalten. Der Analytiker wird z. B. im Hause des Patienten als Gast empfangen; der Patient sitzt dem Arzt vis-à-vis; der Patient wird trotz vieler anderer Patienten bevorzugt; der Patient trifft Gattin oder Kind des Analytikers und bewundert sie; der Arzt ist mit dem geliebten Elternteil zu einer Mischperson verdichtet, identifiziert u. dgl. m. Ist die Übertragung erotischer Natur, so findet dies oft merkbaren Ausdruck.

Die Todeswünsche, die auf den Arzt übertragen werden, sind ebenso schonungslos bei negativer Übertragung, wie der Ausdruck der Eifersucht auf die Kinder oder Gattin des Analytikers boshaft und mörderisch zum Ausdruck kommen kann. Um die Darstellung der psa. Situation im Traum hat sich M. Steiner bemüht. In Parenthesi: Wer die Serien von Todeswunschträumen von Zwangsneurotikern oder Zwangscharakteren an sich vorüberziehen hat lassen, wird leicht zu überzeugen sein, daß der angebliche telepathische Todestraum nur zufällig, als einer von vielen, mit dem Sterben der Person zusammenfällt.

---

37) O. Fenichel, „Zur Theorie der psa. Technik", Int. Ztschr. f. Psa., Bd. XXI, 1935.
38) Ges. Schr., Bd. VI und Bd. III.
39) „Gespensterangst", Psyche, Jg. 1935, Nr. 2—3.

Wenn ich hier Dinge vorbringe, welche dem geübten Analytiker als Gemeinplätze erscheinen müssen, geschieht es nur, um den Stoff dieser Psychopathologie zu umgrenzen. Anderseits ist manche Entscheidung erst zu fällen. Schon in der ersten Auflage der Traumdeutung berichtet Freud, ein besonders gut gefügter, lückenlos und klar erscheinender Traum hätte ihm den Vorsatz eingegeben, „eine neue Kategorie von Träumen zuzulassen, die nicht dem Mechanismus der Verdichtung und Verschiebung unterlegen waren, sondern als ‚Phantasien während des Schlafens‘ bezeichnet werden durften". Freud ließ diese Kategorie von Träumen jedoch fallen. Dreißig Jahre später, in der 8. Auflage der Traumdeutung (1930), hat Freud hinzugefügt: „Ich weiß heute nicht, ob mit Recht."

* * *

Unsere praktisch-nüchterne Betrachtung des Traumlebens von Seite der Gesetzmäßigkeit her erscheint blaß und akademisch gegenüber der Traumtiefenforschung in Freuds „Traumdeutung", wo jede Seele sozusagen als eine Einzigartigkeit behandelt wird. Trotzdem muß auch diese neue Arbeitsart einmal inauguriert werden, wenn das Traumleben in einer Psychopathologie erfaßt werden soll.

Wie ist das gesamte Traumleben eines Patienten während der Kur[40] zur Beobachtung heranzuziehen? Die Träume eines ganzen Lebens!?

Es wäre möglich, den Versuch zu machen, die Träume von der Kindheit eines Individuums angefangen zu registrieren. Praktisch wird jedoch nur die Frage nach dem „Traumstatus" eines Individuums vorliegen und durch eine Anamnese über frühere, auch kindliche Träume, wiederkehrende sowie typische Träume eingeleitet sein. Die relative Häufigkeit, Lebhaftigkeit, das Festhalten oder Vergessen, die Beteiligung von Sprechen aus dem Schlaf oder gar somnambulem Verhalten im Schlaf werden das Traumleben charakterisieren. Die Traumernte aus der Gegenwart wird von der Aufforderung zum Festhalten, von Übertragung und Widerstand abhängig und ihre Gewinnung z. T. erlernbar, erübbar sein. Wandlungen im gewohnten Träumen werden bedeutsam sein.

Die Wissenschaft, deren Interesse auf typisch Gemeinsames gerichtet ist, wird die Besserung während der Kur auch im Traumleben feststellen wollen, das Zurücktreten von Komplexen usw.

Als Vorarbeit zur Psychopathologie der Träume hat eine erweiterte Traumbeobachtung einzusetzen, von Einzelträumen und Traumserien, auch an Gesunden, an Geheilten, an Primitiven, an Blindgeborenen, an Psychotikern, bei bestimmten Charakteren, auch an organisch Kranken. Wandeln sich die Träume während Hormonbehandlungen? Durch Transplantationen

---

40) Vgl. den Versuch Ranks: „Eine Neurosenanalyse in Träumen", Int. Psa. Verlag, Wien 1924.

von Hoden oder Ovarien? Gibt es pathognomonische Träume? Wie kommt es zu den scheinbar telepathischen? Wie geht ein Wandel der Persönlichkeit, z. B. bei Bekehrungen, in den Träumen vor sich? Wie gleichen einander die Träume bei eineiigen Zwillingen? Sind die verschiedenen Träumertypen der drei „libidinösen Typen" Freuds — auch als Träumertypen von drei verschiedenen Dispositionen: zur Hysterie, Zwangsneurose und Psychose erweisbar?

Die erweiterte Traumbeobachtung eröffnet ein unübersehbares Arbeitsgebiet von größtem Wert.

Auch wird sie den leichtsinnigen Leugnern der psychoanalytischen Wahrheiten den Garaus machen.

*   *   *

Anhang: Disposition für eine Psychopathologie des Traumes

I. Geschichte der vorwissenschaftlichen Auffassungen des Traumes.

II. Die Wissenschaft vom Traume vor Freud.

III. Freuds Traumdeutung 1900. Wesen und Entwicklung der Psychoanalyse.

IV. Die Psychologie des Traumes. Manifestes Bild — latenter Inhalt. Traumzensur. Traumentstellung, Traumarbeit. Symbolik. Wunscherfüllung. Peinliche Träume. Angstträume. Träume von Gesunden. Experimentelle Träume.

V. Die Technik der Traumgewinnung. Die Technik der Traumdeutung. Durchschaubare Träume. — Beispiele.

VI. Phänomenologie des Traumes. Formale Differenzen. Kinderträume, Träume von infantilem Charakter, Bequemlichkeitsträume. Körperliche Beeinflussung. Typische Träume. Traumserien. — Beispiele.

VII. Psychopathologie des Traumes. Die Traumdeutung in der Psychoanalyse. Traumbeeinflussung durch die Psychoanalyse; Widerstands- und Übertragungsträume.

VIII. Psychopathologie des Traumes. Die Träume der Patienten, der Disponierten, der Geheilten. Die Träume von Neurotikern, Perversen, Psychotikern. Pathognomonische Träume. Kastrationsträume. Ödipuskomplexträume. Wandlungen der Träume im Lauf der Behandlung. — Beispiele.

IX. Die Träume der Primitiven, der Verbrecher. Träume bestimmter Charaktere, libidinöser Typen. Die Träume der Produktiven. Traum und allgemeine Psychologie.

X. Die Bedeutung der Träume und ihrer Deutung für die psychoanalytische Neurosenlehre.

XI. Ausblick.

XII. Literaturangaben.

REFERATE

Aus der Literatur der Grenzgebiete

Beiträge zur Charakter- und Persönlichkeitsforschung. Herausgegeben von Dr. Franziska Baumgarten, Privatdozentin an der Universität Bern. Heft 1. FRANZISKA BAUMGARTEN: Die Charaktereigenschaften. Verlag A. Francke AG., Bern.

Frau Baumgarten, bekannt durch ihre Arbeiten über praktische Psychologie und ihre mit Kritik durchgeführte psychotechnische Forschung, stellt, historisch und systematisch geordnet, die verschiedenen Definitionen des Charakters zusammen (Kant, Ribot, Watson, Losskij u. a.). Aus den Unvollkommenheiten der Definitionen schließt die Autorin auf die Unrichtigkeit des Ausgangspunkts von den Manifestationen der Charaktere, sie versucht dagegen von der Untersuchung der Charaktereigenschaften auszugehen. Sie sieht als das Wesen der Charaktereigenschaften an, daß sie eine Bereitschaft oder Hemmung zu besonderem Tun und Verhalten bilden. Vor allem zeigt sie die Unzulänglichkeit, Verhalten und Charaktereigenschaften zu identifizieren, denn zwischen beiden besteht kein eindeutiges Verhältnis. Es wird darauf verwiesen, daß diese Auffassung sich mit der psychoanalytischen Symptomenlehre berührt. „Freud hat auf das mehrdeutige Verhältnis zwischen Charaktereigenschaften und dem Verhalten aufmerksam gemacht, indem er in den Handlungen und Haltungen (ähnlich wie im Traum) eine Symbolik aufgedeckt hat, so daß jede Handlung zum Symptom wird. Nach dieser Auffassung kann jede Haltung, jedes Tun in seiner eigentlichen und symbolischen Bedeutung verstanden werden."

Bei der Auseinandersetzung mit Charakterforschern zeigt die Autorin, wie nahe La Rochefoucauld, der französische Moralist (1705), den tiefenpsychologischen Erkenntnissen des 20. Jahrhunderts war, wenn er meint, unsere Tugenden seien meistens verkappte Laster. Ein besonderes Verdienst erwirbt sich Frau Baumgarten mit der Konfrontierung von Paulhan und Klages. Die Eigenmächtigkeit, mit der Klages bestimmte „elementare" Charaktereigenschaften als „echt" bezeichnet, wie z. B. Vorsicht und Ehrgeiz, wird als wissenschaftlich unmöglich zurückgewiesen, denn echt und unecht sind keine qualitativen Begriffe, jede Charaktereigenschaft kann echt oder unecht sein, je nach der Determinierung. Bei der Gegenüberstellung von Paulhan und Klages wird gezeigt, daß Paulhan sehr viele Definitionen über Form und Elemente des Charakters gegeben hat, die verwandt oder fast gleichlautend sind mit Anschauungen von Klages, ohne dessen Eigenmächtigkeiten vorzugreifen. Bahnsen, dessen Beiträge zur Charakterologie von J. A. Barth, Leipzig 1932, wieder herausgegeben wurden, wird als Vorläufer moderner Charakterforschung gewürdigt.

Als wichtigstes Ergebnis unterstreicht die Autorin die Tatsache der mehrfachen Determinierung der Charaktereigenschaften, „schlechte" Eigenschaften können aus „guten" stammen und umgekehrt, soziales Verhalten kann seine Gründe in egoistischen Tendenzen haben. Sie fordert, daß die gesicherten Ergebnisse der Charakterforschung Allgemeingut der Pädagogen und Berufsberater werden müssen. Ein Anhang gibt – auf 12 Seiten – die erste bisher vorgenommene Aufstellung der in der Sprache festgelegten Bezeichnungen für Charaktereigenschaften, ihre „Inventarisierung", ferner eine tabellenartige Anordnung für die differente Determinierung von Charaktereigenschaften und Verhaltensweisen.

Ein Beispiel: „Edelmut

1. aus angeborner Tendenz, die Rechte des andern zu respektieren,
2. aus einem Desinteressement,
3. aus raffinierter Berechnung (Mittel zum Zweck):

a) um in besserem Lichte zu erscheinen,
b) um ein konkretes Ziel zu erreichen."
„Verschwiegenheit
1. aus Unsozialität, geringem Mitteilungsbedürfnis,
2. aus Klugheit—Unlust viel zu verraten.
3. aus Passivität—Unlust sich zu derangieren,
4. aus Schüchternheit, Scheu oder Angst, wie das Mitgeteilte aufgenommen wird."
Daß eine solche Zusammenstellung ihre Mängel hat, widerspricht nicht der Bedeutung eines Versuchs, Verhaltensweisen auf Grund der Einstellung des Trägers, auch unbewußter, zu ordnen. — Die Publikation ist in knapper Sprache gefaßt, sie läßt die angekündigte Schrift über „Die Deutungsmethoden in der Charakterologie" mit Spannung erwarten.   H. Meng (Basel)

Aus der psychiatrisch-neurologischen Literatur

BENJAMIN, ERICH: Die Krankheit der Zivilisation. 75 S. Verlag Rudolf Müller & Steinicke, München 2 SW. 1934.

Benjamin sieht in der Schwererziehbarkeit des Kindes eines der sinnfälligsten Symptome der Zivilisationskrankheit, verwandt dem Symptom Kinderlosigkeit, Ehezerfall u. ä. Er führt die individuell und sozial bedingte Schwererziehbarkeit auf Schädigungen in der Frühkindheit zurück, ihre Hauptquelle sei falsches Verhalten des Erwachsenen und die seelische Komplikation des Kulturkindes mit dem primitiven Menschen in ihm. Der Autor zieht historische Parallelen zwischen Rom in den Jahrhunderten vor und nach Christi Geburt und dem Heute. Er sieht den Weg zur Vorbeugung der Zivilisationskrankheit in der Sanierung der Familie, vor allem in der Früherziehung des Kindes in Familie, Krippe und Kindergarten bei geeigneten selbsterzogenen Erwachsenen. Er fordert für seelisch kranke und abnorme Kinder psychotherapeutisch durchgebildete Ärzte, ohne dabei allzu große Hoffnung auf sie zu setzen, er meint, daß es „uns Ärzten nicht beschieden ist, bis zu den Quellen des Unheils vorzudringen".

Der Autor erkennt zwar, wie auch in frühern Publikationen, einzelne Verdienste Freuds für die seelische Hygiene an, aber er steht zu Freud in grundsätzlichen Auffassungen der Entwicklungsgeschichte des Kindes in Widerspruch. Er wirft ihm vor, daß er keine Gelegenheit gehabt hätte, durch persönliche Anschauung das Kind genauer kennenzulernen, und daß er durch die Rückerinnerung seiner erwachsenen Patienten ein verzerrtes, unvollständiges, unwahres oder halbwahres Bild gewonnen hätte. Ein fernerer Einwand ist, daß die Psychoanalyse in die Lebensäußerungen des Säuglings und des Kleinkindes sexuelle Tendenzen hineindeute. Bei Besprechung der Trotzphase wird behauptet, daß die Grundlage und die Symptome mißdeutet worden seien. Der Autor weist ferner darauf hin, daß der Ödipuskomplex zunächst keineswegs ein sexuelles Phänomen im Sinne Freuds sei, sondern eine Ausdrucksform einer bestimmten sozialen Strebung. — Wir können aus Raumgründen nur kurz folgendes sagen: Freud und seine Schüler haben seit Veröffentlichung der Krankengeschichte vom „Kleinen Hans" im Jahr 1908 viele unmittelbare Beobachtungen am Kind publiziert. Es dürfte keinem gründlichen Forscher entgehen, daß Freud auf Grund seiner dualistischen Trieblehre den Begriff der Sexualität erweitert hat, und zwar über den Bereich der Funktion der Genitalien und der Fortpflanzung hinaus. Der genetische Gesichtspunkt zwang Freud zu dieser Begriffserweiterung, die er auf induktivem Weg gewonnen hat, wobei er die Vorstadien und Umbildungen der Sexualität (im allgemeinen Sinn) in seinen erweiterten Begriff miteinbezieht. Weder er, noch seine Schule haben die Gleichheit der Erlebnisweisen des Kindes und der Erwachsenen behauptet.

Die gegensätzliche Auffassung des Autors in Fragen der Trotzphase und des Ödipus-

komplexes beruht u. a. darauf: Benjamin nennt unter den Mechanismen, die zur Trotz-
reaktion führen, die Auflehnung, Abwärtswendung und Rückwärtswendung, über die Trieb-
schicksale der Analerotik werden aber keine Angaben gemacht, so daß der Kernpunkt der Freudschen Auffassung nicht Gegenstand einer wissenschaftlichen Untersuchung wurde. Wie auch
in früheren Publikationen wird die Auffassung des Ödipuskomplexes verkannt, vor allem
seine Determinierung durch die Bisexualität. Es ist ja nicht nur die Angst vor dem Vater,
oder die Liebe zur Mutter, die die Ödipussituation schafft, sondern auch die zwiespältige
Einstellung zu beiden Elternteilen oder ihren Ersatzpersonen.

Das Hauptverdienst der Schrift liegt in ihrer Bedeutung für den Kinderarzt: Sein Blick
wird geschärft für die seelische Vorgeschichte jedes Heranwachsenden, und sein Interesse für
eine Psychotherapie vieler Störungen, die früher rein körperlich behandelt wurden, wird
erweckt. Die geschichtlichen Abschnitte sind reichhaltig, vor allem bringen sie viel
Anregungen zum Vergleich der Kindererziehung in der antiken Kultur und in der modernen
Großstadtkultur. Die Krankheit der Zivilisation wird als ein Leiden aufgefaßt, das zum
Erlöschen einer Nation führt und dem man nur vorübergehend Einhalt gebieten kann.

H. Meng (Basel)

HARTMANN, HEINZ: Psychiatrische Zwillingsprobleme. Jahrbücher f. Psych. u. Neuro-
logie. Bd. 50 u. 51.

ROSANOFF, HANDY und PLESSET: The etiology of manic-depressive syndrom with
special reference to their occurrence in twins. Amer. J. Psychiat. 91, 735, 1935.

J. CRONIN: An analysis of the neuroses of identical twins. Psychoanal. Rev. 20, 375.

Die Zwillingsforschung könnte auch dem Analytiker wertvolle Erkenntnisse übermitteln,
wenn in ihr eine Methode gefunden worden wäre, den Aufbau einer Persönlichkeit von
seiner erblichen Bedingtheit zu erkennen. Wichtigkeit und Bedeutung der erbbedingten Anlage sind von der biologisch orientierten Psychoanalyse niemals verkannt worden. Aber
ebensowenig wie eine genetische Psychologie z. B. bei der Erörterung der Abgrenzung zwischen organischer oder psychologischer Genese eines Symptomes jemals eine Alternativfrage
stellen würde, ebensowenig kann eine völlige Trennung von anlagebedingten und umwelt-
bedingten Erscheinungen angestrebt werden. Bedeutungsvoll aber wäre es, in der ererbten
Anlage nicht lediglich einen psychologisch unauflösbaren Rest zu sehen, zu dem man gewissermaßen nur *per exclusionem* gelangt, sondern etwas, das durch eine eigentümliche
wissenschaftliche Methode, nämlich die Zwillingsforschung, erfaßbar ist. Daß die Zwillingsforschung zu dieser Aufgabe geeignet ist, weist H. Hartmann in einer vorwiegend kasuistischen Arbeit, einem ausführlichen Bericht über 10 eineiige Zwillingspaare nach. Drei von
diesen erbgleichen Paaren sind psychotisch erkrankt, und zwar zwei an einer schizophrenen
Psychose, ein weiteres Zwillingspaar an einer atypischen Psychose aus dem manisch-depressiven Formenkreis, während das vierte Zwillingspaar imbezill ist. Im wesentlichen verhielten
sich alle Zwillinge konkordant. Diese sehr eindrucksvoll geschilderten und lebendig dargestellten Fälle werden ergänzt durch die ebenfalls sehr ausführliche Mitteilung über sechs
nicht erkrankte, sondern „normale" eineiige Zwillingspaare. Zum Schluß wird über sehr
wichtige, leider vom Verfasser nicht selbst beobachtete und deshalb nur unvollständig er-
faßte Fälle berichtet, die in der amerikanischen Literatur niedergelegt sind und sich auf
sieben eineiige Zwillingspaare beziehen, die seit frühester Kindheit getrennt aufgewachsen
sind und deren Diskordanz in Eigenschaften, die sonst bei eineiigen Zwillingen konkordant
zu sein pflegen, sehr beträchtlich zu sein schienen. Bei keinem seiner gesunden Zwillinge
— so muß Hartmann konstatieren — fehlt eine kindliche Neurose, was aber schwerlich
in Zusammenhang mit der Zwillingsgeschwisterschaft steht. Die Neurosen zeichnen sich
durch ihre große Diskordanz aus. Die größte Konkordanz wiesen die Merkmale auf, die

man gemeinhin unter Intelligenz und Begabung zusammenfaßt. Unter den Eigenschaften des Charakters und der Temperamente finden sich alle Übergänge von überzeugendster Konkordanz bis zu recht weitgehender Diskordanz. Besonders der analerotische Charakter zeichnet sich durch seine hochgradige Diskordanz aus.

Im Gegensatz zu oder besser in Ergänzung der analytischen, psychologischen, kasuistischen Arbeitsweise von Hartmann steht die mit mehr statistischer Methode arbeitende, ein schon beinahe grotesk anmutendes Material zusammenstellende Veröffentlichung von Rosanoff, Handy und Plesset. Sie berichten über nicht weniger als 90 selbstuntersuchte Zwillingspaare mit Erkrankungen aus dem manisch-depressiven Formenkreis. Von 23 eineiigen Zwillingspaaren erkrankten in nur 16 Fälle beide Partner, in 7 Fällen nur einer von beiden. Bei den 67 zweieiigen Zwillingspaaren war das Häufigkeitsverhältnis von Konkordanz zu Diskordanz umgekehrt wie bei den Eineiigen, in 11 Fällen erkrankten beide Partner, dagegen in 56 nur einer. Der Kontrast im Prozentsatz der Konkordanz bei Eineiigen und Zweieiigen (69% Konkordanz bei Eineiigen, 16% bei Zweieiigen) beweist die entscheidende Bedeutung erblicher Faktoren bei der Entstehung von Erkrankungen aus dem manisch-depressiven Formenkreis. Der hohe Prozentsatz Diskordanz selbst bei den Eineiigen (30%) ist ein Hinweis, daß die Erbverhältnisse wiederum nicht einfach liegen können. Unter den vielen Einzelheiten des mitgeteilten Materials fällt noch auf, daß offenbar die zweieiigen Zwillingsschwestern viel häufiger zur Manifestation der Erkrankung neigen als ihre Zwillingsbrüder. Der Grad der Konkordanz bei Eineiigen ist sehr verschieden, niemals aber wurde beobachtet, daß der Zwilling eines manisch-depressiven Patienten, wenn er überhaupt erkrankt, eine andere Psychose bekam als aus dem manisch-depressiven Formenkreis. Nach Ansicht der Autoren ist der Erbgang manisch-depressiver Erkrankungen nur durch die Annahme zweier verschiedener Gene zu erklären: einem Anlagefaktor und einem „activating factor A" der im X-Chromosom verankert vorgestellt wird. So wird in einleuchtender und ungezwungener Weise der scheinbare Wechsel von dominantem, rezessivem und geschlechtsgebundenem Vorkommen, wie auch die scheinbare verschiedene Erkrankungsbereitschaft erklärt.

Cronin berichtet über die Analyse eines eineiigen Zwillingsbrüderpaars und ihrer gemeinsamen Freundin. Sam und Jim zeigten größte Ähnlichkeit im Äußeren, im Verhalten und in ihrer Intelligenz. Sie galten in der Schule als Musterknaben, verliebten sich mit 8 Jahren in dasselbe Mädchen, mit dem sie ihre ersten, gemeinsamen Liebesabenteuer hatten und mit der sie die Ödipussituation durchlebten. Während des Studiums heiratete Sam seine Freundin Zoe, die auch Jim liebte und beiden den gemeinsamen Haushalt führte, sich von beiden nacheinander schwängern ließ und dann beiden untreu wurde. In dieser Situation gingen dann alle drei zu demselben Analytiker. Aus dem Bericht über den Verlauf der Analyse geht nicht klar hervor, weshalb sich bei erbgleicher Veranlagung, gleichem Milieu und gleichen Erlebnissen zwar in ihrer Intelligenz und in ihrer Reaktionsweise sehr ähnliche, aber in ihrer Affektivität und Erotik so verschiedenartige Menschen entwickelten. Sam wurde durch den glücklichen „Zufall" seiner Heirat zu normalem heterosexuellem Verkehr geführt, während Jim unreif, in der Ödipussituation fixiert, inzestuös gebunden blieb. Er verpaßte den heterosexuellen Anschluß, suchte und fand Befriedigung seiner Homosexualität und seines Masochismus in dem Verhältnis zu der Frau seines Bruders. Die Konstitution Sams ähnelt der seines Bruders, auch er akzeptiert die gemeinsame Ehe. Es werden viel treffende Bemerkungen zur Charakterisierung dieses dreieckigen Verhältnisses mitgeteilt, ohne daß die ungeheueren Möglichkeiten dieser zwei Jahre dauernden Analyse eines eineiigen Zwillingsbrüderpaares erschöpft oder die mannigfaltigen psychologischen Probleme der Zwillingsbrüderschaft dem Verständnis wesentlich nähergebracht worden wären.   M. Grotjahn (Berlin)

KOGERER, HEINRICH: Psychotherapie. Ein Lehrbuch für Ärzte und Studierende. Verlag Wilhelm Maudrich, Wien. 1934.

Der Autor dieses Buches, das dem praktischen Arzt die Suggestivtherapie empfehlen, andererseits ihn darüber aufklären will, „daß auf keinem Gebiet des menschlichen Lebens so viele Irrtümer und Fehler verbreitet sind, wie auf dem der Sexualität", ist sichtlich ausgezogen, um die Seuche der Psychoanalyse endlich auszurotten, allerdings nicht, ohne dabei infiziert worden zu sein. Er zeiht Freud der Überheblichkeit, gibt ihm Belehrung, wirft ihm Übertreibungen und mangelhaft fundierte Hypothesen vor, zeigt aber dabei eine weitgehende Unkenntnis der analytischen Materie. So behauptet Kogerer, Freud sei von zwei Erscheinungen des täglichen Lebens, den Träumen und den Fehlleistungen, der Weg zur analytischen Technik gewiesen worden. „Freud versuchte," heißt es, „die Mechanismen, die er im Traum und in den Fehlleistungen als spontane kennengelernt hatte, willkürlich nachzuahmen. So entstand die Methode der freien Assoziation." Der Weg war natürlich der umgekehrte! (Vgl. Freud, Traumdeutung, IV. Auflage, S. 77: „Es lag nun nahe, den Traum selbst wie ein Symptom zu behandeln und die für letztere ausgearbeitete Methode der Deutung auf ihn anzuwenden.")

Unter „Übertragung" versteht Kogerer nur die positive; die negative hat er offenbar übersehen. Immerhin hat er seine Scheu vor der positiven Übertragung aufgegeben, die er noch 1926 in der Wiener Klin. Wochenschrift abgelehnt hat: „Eine Behandlung, in der geradezu gefordert wird, daß der Patient den Arzt, wenn auch nur vorübergehend, als Liebesobjekt akzeptieren müsse", sei abzulehnen. Inzwischen scheint der Autor mehr Erfahrung gesammelt zu haben, denn er setzt sich mit der positiven Übertragung vernünftig auseinander.

Auf S. 74 scheint der Autor Narzißmus und Masturbation zu verwechseln: Freud bezeichne die schizophrenen Psychosen als narzißtische, weil sie bei der Masturbation verharren (!?); es werde so der Anschein erweckt, als ob die Regression auf eine bestimmte Stufe der Sexualität die Ursache der Erkrankung wäre, während der endogene Faktor dabei bewußt vernachlässigt werde. Daß Kogerer das Verbleiben bei einer sexuellen Übung mit der Rückkehr zu einer Libidoposition, hier dem Narzißmus der Kindheit, verwechselt, ist sonderbar genug. Daß im Jahre 1923 Freud mit seiner Schrift „Das Ich und das Es" die Psychoanalyse durch Erkenntnisse über die verdrängenden Kräfte bereichert, die drei Instanzen des Ichs dargestellt hat usw., wird in dem Lehrbuch Kogerers ganz vernachlässigt. Mißverständnisse finden sich z. B. auch bei der Darstellung der Analerotik, dem Analcharakter und den Zusammenhängen mit der Zwangsneurose: „Aus der grundlegenden Anschauung, daß die Wurzel der Zwangsneurose in der analsadistischen Periode zu suchen sei, sei Freuds Konzeption des Analcharakters hervorgegangen."

Nach diesen Hervorhebungen kann ich mich der Kritik dieses Buches durch Kurt Schneider (München) anschließen, der ihm „jede Originalität" abspricht und die Kasuistik des Buches „von kaum unterbietbarer Dürftigkeit" findet.

Auch von des Autors Statistik aus dem Jahre 1926 und ihrem Optimismus ist jetzt nicht mehr die Rede. Damals wies die Behandlung bei Kranken mit überwiegendem Minderwertigkeitsgefühl, ferner solchen mit sexuellen Konflikten und mit verschiedenen akzidentellen Ursachen Erfolgsziffern auf, „die zwischen 90 und 100% schwanken".

Der Autor ist skeptisch gegen die psychoanalytische Therapie; m. E. mit Unrecht, denn woher sollte er unsere geheilten Fälle kennen? Betrachten wir aber z. B. sämtliche von ihm als Beispiele angeführten Fälle von Hysterie und hysterischer Reaktionsweise, so ergibt sich das Folgende: 1. 5 Monate Behandlung. Eine wesentliche Besserung des Zustandes tritt nicht ein. 2. Keine Angabe über Erfolg. 3. Zur Behandlung erscheint der Kranke nur unregelmäßig. Wegen seines frechen, unbotmäßigen Benehmens wird die Behandlung schließlich abgebrochen. 4. Unlösbarer Ehekonflikt als Hindernis. 5. Die ambulatorische Psychotherapie bleibt erfolglos. 6. P. protestiert ausdrücklich dagegen, für krank gehalten zu werden. 7. P. kommt nur kurze Zeit zur Behandlung und bleibt dann aus. 8. Nach 6 Wochen Behandlung in die Sommerfrische; nach Rückkehr Wohlbefinden. 9. Psychotherapie wird empfohlen, P. erscheint jedoch nicht zur Behandlung. 10. 6 Monate Behandlung. Die Patientin wird psychisch zugänglicher, freilich nur dann, wenn der behandelnde Arzt zum Schein auf ihre Bemächtigungstendenzen eingeht. Ein später unternommener Versuch, sie etwas energischer anzupacken, wird von ihr sofort mit dem Abbruch der Beziehungen beantwortet. Eine nachträgliche Versöhnung erweist sich als nur vorübergehend. 11. In diesem Falle sehen wir deutlich, daß ein ursprünglich hysterisches Zustandsbild auf dem Wege über die Imitation in die Schizophrenie ausgemündet ist. 12. Patientin stellt sich auf jede ihr nicht genehme Bemerkung hin schwer beleidigt. Andererseits hat sie doch wiederum ein starkes Mitteilungs- und Anschlußbedürfnis. Wegen zunehmender Depression und Suizidgefahr wird sie in ein Sanatorium gebracht. — Wenn der Autor nunmehr der Psychosexualität eine so hervorragende Rolle in der Verursachung der Neurosen zuweist, so sehen wir ihn doch z. B. der Behandlung der Frigidität, Homosexualität (Fall 57) u. a. wehrlos gegenüberstehen. Das Buch K o g e r e r s ist so unwillentlich ein Plädoyer g e g e n die Suggestionstherapie geworden, und f ü r eine — aber gründliche — Kenntnis der Psychoanalyse. Ist diese auch nur eine Therapie unter vielen, so ist sie doch eine *prima inter pares* (F r e u d). E. H i t s c h m a n n (Wien)

MAYER, LUDWIG: Der Wandertrieb. Eine Studie auf Grund vorhandener Literatur, eigener Beobachtungen und Untersuchungen. Würzburg, 1934.

Von einer Arbeit, die sich den Wandertrieb, dies Prototyp des triebhaften Verhaltens, zum Gegenstand der Untersuchungen gemacht hat, kann wohl eine Erörterung tiefenpsychologischer Zusammenhänge erwartet werden. Statt dessen gibt der Verfasser eine Materialsammlung, eine erneute Zusammenstellung der Symptomatologie auf Grund der bisherigen psychiatrischen Literatur, ergänzt durch einige eigene Untersuchungen und Beobachtungen. In einem gewissen Gegensatz zur bisherigen psychiatrischen Anschauung, nach der der Wandertrieb lediglich ein psychopathologisches Syndrom ist, werden hier auch Erscheinungsformen des Wandertriebes in die Untersuchung mit hineingezogen, die nach Ansicht des Verfassers noch in das Bereich der Norm gerechnet werden müssen. Anschließend wird ein Versuch unternommen, die Motive des Wanderns aufzudecken: Drang nach Freiheit und Ungebundenheit, Drang nach Bewegung und in die Weite, triebhaftes Verlangen nach Veränderung und Neuem werden angeführt. Gesteigerte Motorik, Fortfall von „Angsthemmungen" und „sexuelle Antriebe" können einen latenten Trieb zu manifesten Handlungen aktivieren.

Eine solche symptomatologische Schilderung wird als Ursachenforschung verkannt, gelegentlich wird noch der alles erklärende Konstitutionsbegriff herangezogen oder auch auf eventuelle soziologische Bedingungen andeutungsweise hingewiesen. So kommt es, daß dem an sich interessanten Material und dem doch wirklich verlockenden Thema keine neuen Seiten oder Erkenntnisse abgewonnen werden. Es fehlt jeder Hinweis auf die unbewußten Motive des normalen und krankhaften Wanderns, nichts wird verständlicher oder verstehbar. Es fehlt jeder Hinweis auf die innere Verwandtschaft des triebhaften Wanderns mit den Zwangshandlungen, oder mehr noch mit der Süchtigkeit, auf die sekundäre Sexualisierung des Wanderns, das ursprünglich Schutz und Flucht vor der Triebgefahr bedeutete. Auch die offenbaren, nunmehr bald auch dem Nichtanalytiker sichtbaren Zusammenhänge zwischen Wandern und einem symbolischen, oft als inzestuös phantasierten Sexualakt, aus dem heraus erst sich die „primäre" Depression, die sehnsuchtsvolle Stimmung, der romantische Drang in die Ferne, die Angst und die Schuldgefühle des Wanderns, seine Einsamkeit und Ausdauer erklären ließen, werden kaum erwähnt. M. G r o t j a h n (Berlin)

SCHÜLLER, ARTHUR und WILDER, JOSEF: **Der Kopfschmerz.** Bücher der ärztlichen Praxis, Band 40. Julius Springer, Berlin und Wien. 1934.

Die Aufgabe des Buches ist es, den als einheitliche Krankheitsbezeichnung unhaltbar gewordenen Begriff „Kopfschmerzen" aufzulösen und an seine Stelle einen neuen Begriff zu setzen, der unter Kopfschmerzen lediglich ein Symptom verschiedenartigster Krankheiten verstehen will. Diesen Bemühungen um immer verfeinerte differentialdiagnostische Genauigkeit stehen fortlaufend praktische Vorschläge zu einer kausalen rationellen, im wesentlichen internistischen Therapie zur Seite. Vom Standpunkt des Praktikers werden klar und sachlich, dabei anschaulich und lebendig die Kopfschmerzen verschiedenartigster Genese dargestellt: bei Schädeltraumen, bei Erkrankungen der Hirnhäute, bei intrakraniellen Neubildungen, bei Gefäßerkrankung, als Folge von neuritischen, allergischen, toxischen, vasomotorischen Prozessen. Die Darstellung des psychogenen Kopfschmerzes und der Migräne ist recht kurz; immerhin werden sie in einem gesonderten Kapitel erwähnt, wobei auf die Möglichkeit der seelischen Verursachung und Behandlung, in schwierigen Fällen sogar durch Psychoanalyse, hingewiesen wird. Es fragt sich, ob eine doch wohl schon einseitige Beschränkung auf Physiologie und Somatologie und ein so weitgehender Verzicht auf die Darstellung tiefenpsychologischer und genetischer Auffassungen bei einem nach beiden Seiten so schwer abzugrenzenden Gebiet, wie es die Kopfschmerzen sind, heute noch berechtigt ist, und ob nicht auch dem Praktiker damit gedient wäre, wenn seine Aufmerksamkeit nicht nur auf die Möglichkeit eines intrakraniellen Neoblastoms hingelenkt würde, sondern vielleicht auch noch auf das, was seinen Patienten aus ganz anderen Gründen im wahrsten Sinne des Wortes „Kopfschmerzen" machen könnte. M. Grotjahn (Berlin)

SPEER, ERNST: **Die Liebesfähigkeit** (Kontaktpsychologie). Lehmanns Verlag, München.

In stark ichbetonter, mehr überzeugter als überzeugender Weise trägt der Verf. seine Ansichten und Meinungen vor, die nicht sonderlich neuartig erscheinen und für deren Berechtigung eigentlich kein neuer Beweisgrund angeführt wird. Im wesentlichen knüpft der Verf. an die Konzeptionen Kretschmers an über den grundsätzlichen Dualismus der Psychosen. Für ihn ist die schizophrene Psychose lediglich die Zuspitzung einer normalpsychologisch erfaßbaren Entwicklung, Endabschnitt einer „Zerfallserscheinung der Seele schlechthin". Die Voraussetzung der Psychose ist das „Sonderlingswesen", ungefähr dem Schizoid Kretschmers entsprechend, das sich durch seine „schizophrene Farbe", die nach Ansicht des Verf. bisher so nirgends beschrieben worden ist, durch die „Kontaktlosigkeit" kennzeichnet. Vom Begriff des kontaktunfähigen Sonderlings aus wird dann der Ödipuskomplex behandelt, der sich nun in einem ganz neuartigen Licht darstellt: die Schwierigkeiten der Ödipussituation sind die typischen Schwierigkeiten des Sonderlings, sind bereits Ausdruck seiner primären Kontaktunfähigkeit, der familiären Umgebung gegenüber. Deshalb erübrigt es sich auch, den Ödipuskomplex zu analysieren, es genügt ein Hinweis auf seine für die Persönlichkeit lediglich symptomatische Bedeutung. Die Ansichten des Verf. über die Psychotherapie des Sonderlings sind schwer zu referieren, denn in ihnen ist alles enthalten, was gut und modern ist. Gegensätze werden durch ein konziliantes „sowohl — als auch" überbrückt: Psychotherapie ist Arbeits- und Erlebnisgemeinschaft, eine wichtige Rolle spielt Glaube, aber auch Skepsis, Pathos und Sachlichkeit, Liebe und Strenge; Analyse, doch keine Symboltüftelei; unter Ausschaltung des ominösen Ödipuskomplexes kann sie angewandt werden; dagegen tut etwas synthetisch-konstruktive Seelenbehandlung immer gute Dienste ebenso wie Priestertum und autogenes Training; der Seelsorge muß die Körpersorge an die Seite gestellt werden. Immer aber muß sich der Psychotherapeut klar sein, daß auch er im Kampf gegen die Entartung steht, indem er „Unartige" wieder zu „Artigen" machen soll.

M. Grotjahn (Berlin)

Aus der psychoanalytischen Literatur

BUNKER, HENRY A.: The Voice as (Female) Phallus. Psa. Quarterly III, 3.

Wir wissen, daß die männlichen Perversionen der unbewußten Absicht dienen, die Kastrationsangst zu leugnen, und zwar meist dadurch, daß sie die Existenz penisloser Wesen zu leugnen versuchen. Der männliche Homosexuelle macht dies, indem er nur Wesen mit Penis lieben kann und deshalb sich selbst mit seinem ursprünglichen Liebesobjekt (seiner Mutter) identifiziert; der Fetischist, indem er in symbolischer Form das Vorhandensein des Penis bei seinem Objekt fordert; der Transvestit, indem er beides zugleich macht: er agiert eine phallische Frau, um sich zu überzeugen, daß er sich femininen Wünschen hingeben darf, ohne sich der Gefahr der Kastration auszusetzen; der „Zopfabschneider", indem er zwar die Kastration selbst zu einem Sexualziel gemacht hat, aber eine reversible Kastration, die ihn von der Existenz des weiblichen Penis überzeugt.

Bunker berichtet ausführlich, klar und überzeugend die analytische Krankengeschichte eines sexuell und auch sonst schwer gehemmten, prägenital fixierten Neurotikers, der, unter der Herrschaft einer schweren Kastrations- (und Todes-) Angst, von all diesen Mechanismen etwas aufwies. Im Vordergrund des Bildes stand seine Identifizierung mit einer phallischen Frau. Das Merkwürdige war nun, daß der „weibliche Penis" in seinen fetischistischen Handlungen — abgesehen von starken haarfetischistischen Neigungen — in zweierlei Weise hervortrat: Er liebte Schuhe und Stiefel — und verhielt sich in dieser Beziehung wie jeder Schuhfetischist (er liebte es aber auch, die bewunderten Stiefel anzuziehen und sich darin sehen zu lassen); aber er liebte und sammelte auch Grammophonplatten mit den Stimmen von Sängerinnen und phantasierte viel von allen großen Sängerinnen und Schauspielerinnen, mit denen er sich, so Schautrieb und Exhibition verdichtend, identifizierte. Die weibliche Stimme war ihm zu einem Fetisch geworden, dem die gleiche Bedeutung zukam wie allen Fetischen: die des mütterlichen Penis, dessen Existenz die Kastrationsangst widerlegen soll. — Die Eigenarten der Kindheitserlebnisse machen viel von dieser Entwicklung verständlich; gerade die sonderbare Verschiebung des Interesses für das weibliche Genitale auf die weibliche Stimme konnten sie nicht genügend aufklären.

An diesen klinischen Teil seiner Arbeit schließt Bunker einen sehr lesenswerten und überzeugenden mythologischen Teil über die Sirenen, jene Mutterfiguren, die mit Hilfe ihrer Stimme verführen. Sie stimmen mit den Sexualobjekten des Patienten darin überein, daß außer der Schönheit ihrer Stimme auch die ihres Haares (Lorelei) betont wird, und deuten auch durch ihre Eigenschaft, halb Frau, halb Tier zu sein (die Sirenen sind Vogelmenschen, die Lorelei ein Fischmädchen), auf die Frage nach ihrem Penisbesitz oder ihrem Kastriertsein hin. — Die Sirenen erweisen sich als eine Gruppe jener zahlreichen mythologischen Schwestern wie die Gorgonen, die Harpyen, die Erinnyen, die Sphinx, die als schön, aber gefährlich, als verführend, aber tod- (kastrations-) bringend geschildert werden und Projektionen der gefürchteten Inzestwünsche der Männer darstellen. Bunker geht den Verzweigungen der verschiedenen Bedeutungen und Symbole dieser Figuren mit reichem mythologischem Wissen nach. (Sie sind u. a. die Seelen Verstorbener = Todesgöttinnen = = Gebärende = Mütter.) Er findet, daß das unbewußt gleichzeitig ersehnte und gefürchtete Verlangen danach, die mütterlichen Genitalien, die dann oft gleichzeitig phallisch und „kastriert" erscheinen (Medusa), zu betrachten, dabei keine geringe Rolle spielt. Wir möchten vielleicht hinzufügen, daß wohl die Penislosigkeit („weibliches Genitale als fressender Rachen") dabei häufig das primärere Moment sein dürfte, die phallische Symbolik dagegen eine Überkompensation, die die Angst widerlegen will, aber das nicht zu leisten vermag. So war es ja auch beim Falle Bunkers gewesen. O. Fenichel (Oslo)

FEIGENBAUM, DORIAN: **Clinical Fragments.** Psa. Quarterly III, 3.

Feigenbaum gibt in dieser Arbeit eine Sammlung von Anekdoten aus der analytischen Praxis, die zum Teil recht interessant und überzeugend sind, zu einem anderen Teil den Wunsch wecken, mehr von der betreffenden Analyse zu hören, um urteilen zu können. Er beginnt mit der Analyse einer aus Kastrationsangst erfolgten überdeterminierten Fehlhandlung; schreibt dann über Lachkrampf als Zeichen unbewußter Aggression, speziell als Anzeichen einer negativen therapeutischen Reaktion, wenn sich das Lachen als Antwort auf eine Deutung einstellt; zwei Fälle von Ejaculatio praecox zeigten stark ausgebildete Mutterleibsphantasien, verbunden mit einer besonderen Neigung zu schweren Enttäuschungsreaktionen in der Übertragung; ein anal fixierter Patient, der die Monatsrechnungen nie pünktlich zu zahlen pflegte, konnte endlich seinen Vorsatz, dennoch pünktlich zu zahlen, erfüllen, träumte aber in der Nacht vorher einen Traum, der eine überraschende Identifizierung mit der Mutter zeigte, entsprechend Überkompensation der Gefühle männlicher Inferiorität; die Angst einer Patientin, ihr zukünftiges Kind werde eine Mißgeburt sein, entsprach ihrem Penisneid, nämlich etwa der Idee, ein kastriertes Wesen könne auch nur ein kastriertes Kind in die Welt setzen; das Material, das Patienten in der letzten Analysestunde vor Beendigung der Kur bringen, pflege dem Analytiker zu zeigen, wie weit die Analyse gewirkt, und welche Einstellung der Patient nun bezogen habe, und so eine Prognose zu ermöglichen; gelegentlich erscheine dabei auch noch gänzlich neues Material; eine Patientin, deren Widerstand die Form einer „passiven Resistenz" anzunehmen pflegte, entdeckte, daß diese Passivität der Abwehr höchst aktiver sadistischer Strebungen diente, daß sie, die Machtlose spielend, in Wahrheit Allmachtsphantasien nachhing.

Die Arbeit Feigenbaums schließt mit einer interessanten und problematischen Kinderbeobachtung: Ein 10 Monate altes Mädchen wurde eines Morgens von der Nurse ins elterliche Schlafzimmer gebracht, und zwar so, daß sie von beiden Eltern, die die Arme nach ihm ausstreckten, ungefähr gleich weit entfernt war. Das Kind blickte abwechselnd zum Vater wie zur Mutter, fühlte sich offenbar von beiden gleich stark angezogen und brach in Schreien aus, das anhielt, bis der Vater seine Arme wegnahm; darauf hörte das Schreien sofort auf und das Kind wandte sich den ausgestreckten Armen der Mutter zu. Offenbar hatte ihm die Situation des Esels zwischen den beiden Heubündeln höchste Unlust bereitet. Welcher Art war diese Unlust? Feigenbaum fragt, ob die durch die Situation hervorgerufene akute Libidostauung direkt „narzißtischen Schmerz" zu verursachen imstande sei, und sagt mit Recht, ein Mensch im Zustande der Ambivalenz sei in einer ähnlichen psychischen Situation wie dieses Kind. — Wir möchten dazu bemerken, daß es einer Grundauffassung der psychoanalytischen Neurosenlehre entspricht, daß Abfuhrhemmung von abfuhrbereiter (nicht durch Gegenbesetzung gebundener) Libido unlustvolle Sensationen macht.

O. Fenichel (Oslo)

HERMANN, IMRE: **Die Psychoanalyse als Methode.** Beihefte zur „Internationalen Zeitschrift für Psychoanalyse" und zur „Imago". Nr. 1, 114 Seiten. Internationaler Psychoanalytischer Verlag. Wien 1934.

Hermanns Buch ist in seiner klaren Besonnenheit eines der erfreulichsten Bücher der analytischen Literatur der letzten Jahre. Es verfolgt systematisch das Ziel, die psychoanalytische Methode darzustellen.

H. macht mit Recht darauf aufmerksam, daß die analytische Technik dem Patienten nicht lediglich vorschreibe, alles auszusagen, was ihm durch den Sinn geht, sondern daß sie vom Patienten auch ein Gerichtetsein, ein Suchen verlangt. Man könnte freilich sagen, daß H. diesen Faktor des Gerichtetseins im freien Einfall doch noch zu wenig betont, und man könnte auch unterstreichen, daß wir vom Patienten in der Analyse wesentlich mehr verlangen als ein passives Sichhingeben an aufsteigende Gedanken.

Es ist interessant, daß H. die freisteigenden Gedanken mit den phantastischen Gesichtserscheinungen Johannes Müllers vergleicht. Er betrachtet diese wie die eidetischen Phänomene als Regressionen. Er deutet so mit Recht auf den inneren Zusammenhang des freien Einfalls und der Phantasie mit Grunderscheinungen der Sinnesphysiologie hin.

Er hat auch klar betont, daß der freie Einfall zwar Affekte hervorlockt, daß aber der Affektautomatismus in die Richtung der Sprache dirigiert werden muß. Am Gedanken und am Worte findet die Objektivierung statt, die für die Analyse so wesentlich ist. Sprache ist sozial. Sprache und Aussprache wirken dem Geheimnis und der Tendenz zur Isolierung entgegen.

Vielleicht wäre es möglich gewesen, das Verhältnis der Sprache zur psychoanalytischen Technik noch eindringender zu behandeln als es H. getan hat. Die Sprache ist ein Werkzeug der Wirklichkeitsbewältigung und nötigt daher zur unmittelbaren Realitätsanpassung. Sprache desillusioniert und zerstört den Affekt. Sie wirkt aber nicht durchaus im Sinne des Abreagierens. Soll Analyse wirksam sein, so muß in der Übertragungssituation vieles auftauchen, was nicht sprachlich formulierbar ist.

H. betont mit Recht, daß der Analytiker niemals vollkommen passiv sein soll und kann. Die Diskussion des Widerstandes ist sorgfältig und durch eine Tabelle veranschaulicht.

H. besteht mit Freud und Ferenczi auf dem Unterschied zwischen Übertragungsliebe und der Liebe des Alltags und betrachtet nicht jede Affektäußerung in der Analyse als Übertragung.

Interessante Ausführungen weisen darauf hin, daß Erlebnisse in verschiedenen Niveaus gleichzeitig ablaufen können. Die Formulierung, daß im Es wirbelartige Kräfte wirksam werden und daß die Triebe Wirbelkräfte sind, ist jedoch schwer zu verstehen.

Die Ausführungen über Sinn, seelische Kontinuität und Determinismus kulminieren in der treffenden Formulierung, der Sinn eines Erlebnisses bestehe darin, daß er in das Lebenskontinuum eingeordnet werden könne. Nach H. ist die Seele aufzufassen als ein dem Bewußtsein fremdes eigenartiges Kontinuum, in dem der Teil das Ganze enthält, wo Anfang und Ende nicht anzugeben sind und die Kontinuität ins Unendliche verläuft.

Ich habe den Eindruck, daß diese Formulierungen weit mehr von den üblichen analytischen Formulierungen abweichen, als es der Autor zu erkennen gibt. Ich gehe jedoch hier in den wesentlichen Punkten mit dem Autor und folge ihm auch, wenn er schreibt, daß es meistens keinen echten Sinn hat zu fragen, ob die nach außen oder innen gerichtete Aggression früher da war; ja ich bin geneigt, auch auf das „meistens" zu verzichten.

H. will die seelische Kausalität der Psychoanalyse zu sehr als Sonderereignis sehen und von anderer Kausalität abtrennen. Ich glaube, daß das auf eine ungenügende Analyse des Sinnbegriffes zurückzuführen ist. Ich kann hier nicht im einzelnen beweisen, daß Sinn letzten Endes Handlungsmöglichkeit und Handeln „bedeutet" und damit durchaus in den Bereich objektiver Beobachtung gerät. H. weist mit Recht darauf hin, daß es methodisch nicht so einfach ist, die Psychogenese organischer Krankheiten zu „beweisen", und betont mit Recht die Bedeutung „des Zufalls", oder wie man auch sagen könnte, des Schicksals. Es ist erfreulich, daß H. gegenüber „den Aufstellungen Hollós'" über Telepathie skeptisch bleibt. H. sieht natürlich das Seelenkontinuum nicht im Bewußtsein allein — er folgt hier der üblichen analytischen Anschauung.

Es spricht für die zweifelhafte Stellung der Metapsychologie in der Psychoanalyse, daß H. glaubt, daß in ihr das Seelisch-Sinnvolle ausgeschaltet sei und die „eigentliche" Kausalität zur vollen Geltung gelange. Die Unterscheidung zwischen eigentlicher und uneigentlicher Kausalität scheint mir ebenso unzulässig wie die Behauptung, die Aktualneurose habe keinen analytischen Sinn. Doch kann sich H. in diesem letztgenannten Punkte auf die Autorität Freuds berufen.

Die Formulierung, daß es im Seelenkontinuum keine Abstrakta gebe, halte ich vom praktischen Gesichtspunkt aus für sehr glücklich. Ich halte es für weniger glücklich, wenn H. von einem Sinnorgan spricht. Doch sind seine Beschreibungen des Urtraumas, der Transponierung sehr klar und eindringlich.

Am Beispiele der Analerotik und der Schlagephantasie erörtert H. treffend den analytischen Forschungsweg.

Ausgezeichnet sind auch H.s Ausführungen über männlich und weiblich, aktiv und passiv. Begriffskontrolle ist hier besonders nötig. Auch die Begriffe Über-Ich, Kastrationskomplex, Identifizierung bedürfen einer scharfen Formulierung. Die Hauptschwierigkeit der analytischen Begriffsbildungen scheint dem Ref. darin zu liegen, daß sie sehr häufig allzufrüh vom Erfahrungsboden losgerissen werden und dann gleichsam als Spuk ohne Substanz herumlaufen. Über-Ich und Ich werden dann sehr häufig Gegenstand einer scholastischen Wortanalyse.

Die Schlußausführungen H.s beschäftigen sich mit der Kontrolle analytischer Forschungsarbeit.

Das Referat hat nur einige Punkte hervorheben können. Das Buch könnte sehr wohl die Grundlage für eine eingehende Diskussion der psychoanalytischen Grundfragen abgeben. Die Vertrautheit des Verf. mit den Problemen der Philosophie und Psychologie hat seinen Blick in mancher Hinsicht geschärft. Er steht den begrifflichen Problemen der Psychoanalyse mit erheblicher Selbständigkeit des Denkens gegenüber, die ihm zu glücklichen und scharfen Formulierungen und Einsichten verhilft.

Ich bin der Ansicht, daß jeder ernsthafte Psychoanalytiker dieses Buch gründlich studieren sollte.   P. Schilder (New York)

KUBIE, LAWRENCE S.: Body Symbolization and the Development of Language. Psa. Quarterly III, 3.

Kubie teilt eine Anzahl verblüffender Beispiele für das „symbolische Denken" bei Kindern und naiven Erwachsenen mit. Es ist auffallend, daß die Symbole, mit denen Hilfe körperliche Sehnsüchte und Funktionen ausgedrückt werden, oft von einem Kind ausschließlich aus der Sphäre etwa der Haushaltdinge, von einem anderen aus der der Kleidung, von einem dritten aus der Welt der Tiere, von einem vierten aus der der Maschinen genommen wird. — Kubie erklärt das symbolische Denken überhaupt für verständlich aus einer Tatsache, die für das Sprechenlernen des Kindes von grundlegender Bedeutung sei: Es sind körperliche Bedürfnisse (Zustände der Unbefriedigung), die das Kind veranlassen, sich ausdrücken zu wollen. Jedes neue Faktum, das das Kind aufnimmt, müsse irgendwie mit Körperlichem verknüpft sein, aber natürlich müsse eine solche Verknüpfung nicht direkt sein. „Es gibt" daher „zunächst eine lange Periode, in der die Begriffe vage, weit und sich überschneidend sind; und erst mit dem Fortschreiten der Jahre werden sie mehr diskret und unterschieden", was auch mit den Forschungen von Piaget übereinstimme.

O. Fenichel (Oslo)

PARRY, ALBERT: Tattooing Among Prostitutes and Perverts. Psa. Quarterly III, 3.

Parry ist der Autor eines Buches über das Tätowieren in den Vereinigten Staaten, das im gleichen Heft des Psa. Quarterly von Susanne S. Haigh referiert wird. Im Anschluß an dieses Referat teilt er einiges weitere Material zu diesem Thema mit, das er in sein Buch nicht aufnehmen konnte. Wir erfahren überraschende, aber leider nicht analytisch geklärte Einzelheiten über die Beziehungen zwischen dem Brauch des Tätowierens und der Sexualpathologie, besonders über obszöne und sonstige exhibitionistische Tätowierungen, über Tätowieren als masochistischen Genuß, über die Häufigkeit des Tätowierens bei männlichen Homosexuellen u. dgl.   O. Fenichel (Oslo)

128

ZILBOORG, GREGORY: The Problem of Constitution in Psychopathology. Psa. Quarterly III, 3.

Zilboorg erörtert einleitend breit die Geschichte und Tradition des Konstitutions-begriffs in der Psychiatrie — in der Auffassung, Geisteskrankheiten wären Gehirnkrankheiten, in der humoralen Denkweise, in der Kraepelinschen Nosologie, in der psychiatrischen Erblichkeitsforschung. Überall lege die tradierte Denkweise eine therapeutisch-nihilistische Auffassung nahe. Demgegenüber fragt Zilboorg, was für Beiträge die Psychoanalyse der Konstitutionsforschung leisten könne. Sie schränke zunächst diesen Begriff durch ihre Erkenntnisse über die individuell historische Bedingtheit der Neurosen und Psychopathien und über die Identifizierungen, die Heredität vortäuschen, ein. Gewiß bleibe trotzdem die Wirksamkeit eines konstitutionellen Faktors, der mit den Erlebnisfaktoren zusammen eine „Ergänzungsreihe" bilde. Es sei wahrscheinlich, daß jener Faktor sich auf die „Sexualkonstitution", auf die relative Betonung der einzelnen Partialtriebe bzw. erogenen Zonen, beschränkt. Ein Fall von Depression, dessen Einzelsymptome weitgehend historisch bedingt waren (Identifizierung mit einer toten Frau), gibt den Eindruck: „Was ererbt zu sein scheint, ist nicht eine Krankheit oder der besondere Typ von Krankheit, den sie hatte, sondern ihre intensive Oralität", die aber auch noch zum Teil erlebnismäßig bedingt ist durch den postnatalen Einfluß der Oralität der Mutter. Ebenso stammten bei einer auf analer Fixierung beruhenden Psychopathie mit Perversionen die Einzelzüge des Krankheitsbildes aus der Kindheitsgeschichte; die hervorragende Analität aber war deutlich eine durch Generationen anhaltende Familieneigentümlichkeit. — Vermutlich bestehe also in dieser Beziehung zwischen Neurose und Psychose kein prinzipieller Gegensatz und müsse die übliche statistische Methode der psychiatrischen Erblichkeitsforschung nach psychoanalytischen Einsichten ergänzt werden.   O. Fenichel (Oslo)

KORRESPONDENZBLATT

DER

INTERNATIONALEN PSYCHOANALYTISCHEN VEREINIGUNG

———

Redigiert vom Zentralsekretär Edward Glover

———

I. Vierländertagung

⟨Österreich, Ungarn, Italien, Tschechoslovakei⟩

Die Wiener Psychoanalytische Vereinigung, die Magyarországi Pszichoanalitikai Egyesület, die Società Psicoanalitica Italiana und die Psychoanalytická kupina v Č. S. R. veranstalteten zu Pfingsten (8.—10. Juni 1935) in Wien eine gemeinsame Tagung. Die beiden letztgenannten Gesellschaften gehören nicht der I. P. V. an, doch ist die tschechoslowakische Gesellschaft als Arbeitsgemeinschaft der Wiener Vereinigung angeschlossen, die Società Psicoanalitica Italiana ist eine vollständig unabhängige Organisation, von deren Mitgliedern jedoch vier (zum Teil seit Jahrzehnten) der Wiener Vereinigung angehören. An der Tagung waren nicht nur die Mitglieder der vier einladenden Gesellschaften, sondern darüber hinaus alle Mitglieder der der International Psychoanalytical Association angehörenden Zweigvereinigungen sowie die von den Gruppenvorsitzenden eingeführten Gäste teilnahmsberechtigt. Die Veranstaltung nahm den nachfolgenden Verlauf:

Samstag, 8. Juni.

20 Uhr Empfang der Teilnehmer.

21,15 Uhr Geschäftssitzung (nur für solche Teilnehmer, die Mitglieder einer der der International Psychoanalytical Association angeschlossenen Zweigvereinigungen sind). Gegenstand: **Die didaktische Analyse und die Analysenkontrolle.** Vorsitz: Dr. Paul Federn.

Federn begrüßt die Teilnehmer an der Tagung; ein Begrüßungstelegramm vom Präsidenten der International Psychoanalytic Association, Dr. Ernest Jones, sowie ein Schreiben von Frau Dr. Helene Deutsch, die ihre durch Gesundheitsrücksichten notwendig gewordene Abwesenheit von der Tagung entschuldigt und den Beratungen vollen Erfolg wünscht, werden verlesen.

Hierauf verliest Dr. Imre Hermann das einleitende Referat, in dem der Standpunkt einiger Lehrer der ungarischen Gruppe in Ausbildungsfragen dargelegt wird; Anna Freud verliest sodann das Referat von Dr. Helene Deutsch über Grundsätze und Praxis der Wiener Gruppe zum gleichen Gegenstand.

An der folgenden sehr regen Aussprache nehmen (zum größten Teil mit mehreren Diskussionsbemerkungen) teil: Deri, R. Sterba, Burlingham, W. Hoffer, Anna Freud, Federn, J. Lampl-de Groot, B. Bornstein, M. Bálint, Hermann, E. Weiß, E. Bibring, A. Bálint, G. Bibring, H. Lampl, R. Wälder, Hollós, Gyömröi.

130

Sonntag, 9. Juni.

9 Uhr Erstes wissenschaftliches Symposion. Vorsitz: Dr. István Hollós. Thema: Todestrieb und Masochismus.

Federn teilt mit, daß die Leitung der Tagung Begrüßungstelegramme an Prof. Sigm. Freud, Dr. Jones und Dr. Eitingon sowie ein Danktelegramm an die Wirtschaftliche Organisation der Ärzte Wiens abgesandt hat, in deren Räumlichkeiten die Tagung stattfindet.

Dr. Edoardo Weiß erstattet das Referat.

Leitlinien:

Unzulänglichkeit der theoretischen Begründung des Todestriebes, Erscheinungen, die zugunsten seiner Existenz sprechen: Wirkungen einer nichtlibidinösen Energie mit destruktiver (aggressiver) Funktion; deren Verwendung zur Verteidigung und Erhaltung des Ichs (Extroversion, Ich-Funktionen). Die Rolle dieser Energie — Mortido (Federn), Destrudo (Weiß) — bei der Entstehung der Angst (neurotische und Realangst) und des seelischen Traumas; die Destrudo gibt den wirklichen Anlaß zur Verdrängung (Ich-Schutz).

Der supponierte Todestrieb und der Geltungsbereich des Lust-Unlustprinzips. Revision der ökonomischen Vorstellung über die Lust- und Unlustempfindungen im allgemeinen.

Begriffsbestimmung des Sadismus und Masochismus in bezug auf die Äußerungen der Libido und Destrudo und deren Beziehung zum Lustprinzip. Der Masochismus setzt die Existenz von destruktiver Triebenergie (Destrudo) voraus, welche aber nicht unbedingt als Ausdruck eines „Todestriebes" angesehen werden darf, wie wahrscheinlich dies auch sein mag. Stellungnahme zur Radoschen Angsttheorie.

Hierauf leitet Dr. Imre Hermann die Diskussion ein.

Leitlinien:

1. Gesichtspunkte der Fragestellung. 2. Ferenczis Gedanken über Heilungstendenz. 3. Selbstverstümmelungstendenz und deren Deutung: Anklammerungsdrang als Partialtrieb der Libido; Konflikt der Trennung. 4. Kritik des Destruktionstriebes. Eine Wirbeltheorie der Triebe. 5. Schmerz und Orgasmus vom Standpunkt derselben Triebtheorie.

Diskussion: Hartmann, Eidelberg, Federn, M. Bálint, R. Wälder; Schlußwort: Weiß.

15,30 Uhr Zweites wissenschaftliches Symposion. Vorsitz Dr. Edoardo Weiß. Thema: Das psychische Trauma und die Handhabung der Übertragung.

Dr. Richard Sterba erstattet das erste Referat (Leitlinien hierüber waren nicht vorgelegt); anschließend trägt Dr. Alice Bálint ihr Referat vor.

Leitlinien:

Die Rolle der Persönlichkeit des Analytikers bei der Handhabung der Übertragung.

Der Charakter des Analytikers ist ein wesentlicher Faktor der analytischen Situation, der bei bestem Willen nicht auszuschalten ist. Die aus dieser Quelle stammenden Störungen der Übertragungssituation können nur dadurch unschädlich gemacht werden, daß ihnen eine gesteigerte Aufmerksamkeit zugewendet wird.

Bei einer solchen Einstellung zum Patienten entpuppt sich manche vermeintliche Projektion als reale Einfühlung in den Analytiker, wobei jedoch die außerordentlich gesteigerte Sensibilität des Patienten in bezug auf den Analytiker das Wiederaufleben einer infantilen Fähigkeit bedeutet.

Die Auflösung der so erkannten analytischen Situation erfordert in erster Linie jene Aktivität des Analytikers, die in dem Ausdruck „Handhabung der Übertragung" inbegriffen ist.

Diskussion: G. Bibring, Stengel, J. Lampl-de Groot, Anna Freud, A. Reich, M. Bálint, E. Bibring, Hermann, E. Weiß; Schlußwort: A. Bálint.

Montag, 10. Juni.

9 Uhr Drittes wissenschaftliches Symposion. Vorsitz: Francis Deri. Thema: Problematik der Ichpsychologie. Dr. Robert Wälder erstattet das Referat.

Leitlinien:

Thema des Referats ist ein Überblick über den heutigen Stand der Ich-Psychologie und ihrer Probleme.

Die Ablehnung der Psychoanalyse in der Außenwelt war und ist auf der Ablehnung der Es-Psychologie begründet; dasselbe gilt von den ersten Abfallsbewegungen. Die heutigen Meinungsverschiedenheiten innerhalb der Psychoanalyse beruhen zum großen Teil darauf, daß die Ich-Psychologie der Analyse vielfach nicht assimiliert wurde, bzw. auf andern Konzeptionen auf dem Gebiete der Ich-Psychologie.

Beispiele für Probleme der Ich-Psychologie sind etwa: 1. Art und Systematik und zeitliche Lokalisation der Abwehrformen; 2. Unbewußtheit von Abwehrformen und ihre Folgen für die Technik; Technik der Deutung der Abwehrformen und ihr Verhältnis zur Deutung der Wünsche; 3. Formen der Magie, ihre Grundlagen, ihr allmählicher Abbau und dessen Mechanismen, Verhältnis des Magischen zur jeweiligen Realitätsprüfung; 4. Aufbau der Realitätsprüfung und Mechanismen ihrer Störung (Psychosenproblem); 5. das Problem der Ich-Stärke, ihre Bedingungen und die Wege ihrer pädagogischen und therapeutischen Förderung; 6. die von Federn behandelten von der Phänomenologie des Depersonalisationserlebens ausgehenden ökonomischen Probleme.

Unzulänglichkeit jeder psychoanalytischen Erklärung ohne Ich-Psychologie.

Voranalytische und analytische Ich-Psychologie.

Eine Systematik der Ich-Psychologie ergibt: Die Funktionen des Ichs sind: 1. Kontakt mit der Außenwelt; 2. die Antizipation des Künftigen (Denken, Angst); 3. die Verarbeitung der Aufgaben und Konflikte. Die Verarbeitungsmethoden: Das Ich steht vor den Aufgaben, die ihm von außen (1. Es, 2. Außenwelt, 3. Über-Ich) gestellt werden, und 4. der Aufgabe der Beherrschung dieser Instanzen, die es sich selbst stellt. Dem Ich obliegt es, Lösungsmethoden für diese Aufgaben zu finden. Da die Aufgaben untereinander widerspruchsvoll sind, sind gleich glückliche Lösungen der vier Aufgabengruppen nicht möglich. Die Lösungsmethoden („Mechanismen") sind durch die Aufgabenstruktur bestimmt. Drei Typen von Lösungsmethoden: 1. Mittelwege (es wird teils dieser, teils jener Forderung Genüge getan); 2. Vereinigungen auf höherer Ebene (Integration); 3. Abwehrmethoden. Die Abwehrmechanismen können angreifen: 1. an der Außenwelt (motorische Aktion, Ablehnung oder Modifikation einer Wahrnehmung); 2. am Es (Triebabwehr); 3. am Über-Ich und 4. an der Angst.

Je nachdem, wie weit die vierte Aufgabe, die das Ich sich selber stellt (Beherrschung von Es, Über-Ich und Außenwelt durch das Ich), gelöst wird, ist die Freiheit des Ichs größer, das Ich „stärker". Problem der Ich-Stärke. Alle höheren Ich-Funktionen nur vom Es und Über-Ich her „asymptomisch" zu bestimmen. Ich-Stärke ist starke Objektivierung des eigenen Seelenlebens (Über-Ich-Komponente) bei äußerster Plastizität des Trieblebens (Es-Seite).

Die Plastizität der Triebe ist schon von jeher (vor der Begründung der Ich-Psychologie) als Grundlage der Gesundheit bekannt gewesen. Alle Gesetze des Trieblebens kehren in der Ich-Psychologie auf gleichsam höherer Stufe wieder.

Ich-Stärke ist Fähigkeit, von der Realität her gesteuert zu werden (Realitätsanpassung).
Problematik des Begriffs der Realitätsanpassung.

Realitätsanpassung ist grundsätzlich Anpassung nicht an die Realität von heute, sondern
an die von morgen, die eine Funktion der Realität von heute und meines heutigen Han-
delns ist. Für die meisten Menschen ist dieser Faktor freilich zu vernachlässigen.

Realität teils gegeben, teils aufgegeben.

Pathologische Erscheinungen Fehllösungen des Prozesses der Realitätsanpassung. Ausblick
auf die Neurosentheorien innerhalb der Analyse; Unzulänglichkeit des (aus der Psychiatrie,
nicht der Analyse) stammenden Begriffs der „Neurose".

Wann sind Voraussagen über menschliches Verhalten mit hinreichender Wahrscheinlichkeit möglich? Wenn die höheren Schichten des Ichs ausgeschaltet sind (Reduktion auf die
Gesetzmäßigkeiten des Trieblebens und der primitiven Ich-Mechanismen), oder wenn das Ich
alleinherrschend ist (Steuerung vom Gegenstande her, Reduktion auf die Sachstruktur).

Ich-Stärke als pädagogisches Ziel. Die Regel „Versagung nur bei Anbot einer anderen
Befriedigung als Kompensation" ist auch ichpsychologisch begründet (als Training für die
Plastizität der Triebe).

Die Förderung der Ichstärke in der Pädagogik: Lohn und Strafe sind die Methoden, die
nicht die Stärke des Ichs voraussetzen; Appell an die Vernunft ist die Methode, die zum Ich
spricht. Es gilt, die vorhandene Ich-Stärke des Kindes voll zu belasten, nicht überzu-
belasten. Es ist immer der Appell an die Vernunft bis aufs äußerste dessen anzuwenden, als
die Vernunft des Kindes schon reicht. Demnach ein Maximum an Liebe und ein Maximum
der Beanspruchung der Vernunft.

Diskussion der ichpsychologischen Differenzen innerhalb der Analyse.

Diskussion: E. Bibring, E. Kris, Hartmann, Hermann, A. Reich, Federn, M. Bálint,
E. Weiß, Hollós, Stengel, A. Bálint. Schlußwort: R. Wälder.

Federn schlägt unter allgemeinem Beifall vor, die Tagung so bald wie möglich zu
wiederholen.   Das Komitee.

II. Berichte der Zweigvereinigungen

The American Psychoanalytic Association

Tagungsbericht

Die American Psychoanalytic Association tagte in gemeinsamer Sitzung mit der
Sektion für Psychoanalyse der American Psychiatric Association Mittwoch, den
15. Mai 1935, vormittag, im Hotel Mayflower, Washington, D. C.; Dr. A. A. Brill,
Vorsitzender der Sektion für Psychoanalyse und Präsident der American Psychoanalytic Association führte den Vorsitz. Es gelangte folgendes Programm zur Ab-
wicklung:

Dr. A. A. Brill: Anticipations and Corroborations of the Freudian Concepts from
Non-Analytic Sources.

Obwohl Freud die Psychoanalyse als eine spezielle wissenschaftliche Methode entdeckt und entwickelt hat, machte er doch selbst auf die Tatsache aufmerksam, daß
eine Anzahl seiner Erkenntnisse von anderen entweder vorweggenommen oder unabhängig von ihm gefunden worden ist. Dies trifft zum Teil auch für seine Auffassungen über den Traum zu. Viele Stellen und Hinweise in der klassischen und
modernen Literatur zeigen eine bemerkenswerte Ähnlichkeit mit den Freudschen

Gedankengängen; am merkwürdigsten ist aber die kürzlich gemachte Feststellung, daß Hippokrates, der Vater der Medizin, in derselben Art wie Freud Psychoanalyse betrieben hat, und zwar durch Analyse der Träume und durch die Untersuchung der Vergangenheit des Individuums. Auf diese Weise gelang es ihm, einen Psychoneurotiker auf dem Königsthron zu heilen, nachdem sich sein ärztlicher Gegner vergeblich gemüht hatte, durch Diät und Medikamente einen Erfolg zu erzielen. Es folgt eine Schilderung dieser Kur.

Dr. Clarence P. Oberndorf: The Feeling of Unreality.

Das Gefühl der Unwirklichkeit, das sich in vielen Neurosen und leichten Depressionen vorfindet, ist verbunden mit einem Konflikt zwischen männlichen und weiblichen Identifizierungen, die sich vorwiegend auf intellektuelle Tätigkeit beziehen. Unwirklichkeitsgefühl tritt häufiger bei Frauen auf, die „Denken" als männliche Qualität auffassen. Es folgt an Hand klinischen Materials die Beschreibung einer Periode von Unwirklichkeitsgefühl bei einem jungen Mann während seiner Studienjahre, die durch eine gemischte Identifizierung mit den Eltern bedingt war.

Dr. Bernard Glueck: The Application of Psychoanalysis to Psychiatric Problems.

Der Vortragende hatte einige Jahre früher auf der gemeinsamen Tagung der American Psychoanalytic und der American Psychiatric Association in einer vorläufigen Mitteilung die Möglichkeiten und Grenzen der Anwendung der psychoanalytischen Technik bei psychotischen Patienten dargestellt. Einige Jahre neuerlicher Erfahrungen ergaben neue Modifikationen dieser Technik und brachten so ein tieferes Verständnis — und damit eine verfeinerte Technik —, wodurch weitere Anwendungsmöglichkeiten der psychoanalytischen Erkenntnisse auf dem Gebiete der Psychiatrie ermöglicht werden. Der Vortragende belegt seinen detaillierten Bericht über die Entwicklung und den gegenwärtigen Stand dieser Technik mit ausführlichem Krankenmaterial.

Dr. Smith Ely Jelliffe: The Bodily Organs and Psychopathology.

Der menschliche Organismus stellt den Höhepunkt der Entwicklung und die Verdichtung einer Welterfahrung von Äonen dar. Er ist mit allem Vergangenen zeitlich verbunden, und jene sowohl inneren wie äußeren Modelle seines Verhaltens, die bleibenden Wert hatten, wurden fast so unabänderlich wie der Lauf der Gestirne. Die Ursachen vieler organischer Erkrankungen werden in Übereinstimmung mit der Auffassung gedeutet, daß infantile Fixierungen erotischer Befriedigung zu einer Störung der Systeme der Intuition, des Instinkts und der Selbstheilung führen. In dem Ausmaß, in dem diese Fixierungen auf frühen organischen Ursachen beruhen und stark mit Libido besetzt sind, entstehen Konversionen, die in ihrer reversiblen und verhältnismäßig harmlosen Form überwiegend als hysterisch bezeichnet werden, in ihrer mehr malignen Form jedoch gewisse Komponenten einer organischen Erkrankung bilden. Diese Gesichtspunkte werden auf Hautkrankheiten, Blutdruckveränderungen, Nephrosen und Störungen des innersekretorischen Systems, sowie auf respiratorische, gastrisch und muskuläre Vorgänge angewendet.

*

Die 34. Tagung der American Psychoanalytic Association fand Mittwoch, den 15. Mai 1935, nachmittags, im Hotel Mayflower, Washington, statt. Folgende Vorträge wurden vorgelegt und fanden eingehende Diskussion, an der sich Drs. Glueck, Kaufman, Jelliffe, Lorand und Sullivan beteiligten.

31*

Dr. William V. Silverberg: Towards a Theory of the Instincts.

Der Vortragende leitet das Thema durch einen Hinweis auf Briffaults Behandlung des Triebproblems in „The Mothers" ein und schlägt versuchsweise vor, auf dieser Grundlage eine Trieblehre zu formulieren sowie den Begriff der biologischen Gesundheit auf der Basis der Triebe zu konzipieren. Es folgt eine Kritik der heutigen Freudschen Trieblehre mit besonderer Berücksichtigung der Frage, ob der sogenannte Todestrieb als Trieb zu gelten habe. Weiters werden Wachstum und Reproduktion, insbesondere bei den Protozoen, als Triebmanifestationen aufgefaßt. Die Sexualität wird nach ihrem Verhältnis zu den Trieben bewertet. In einem kurzen Überblick wird der Vorgang beschrieben, durch welchen sich eine Hypothese wie die vorliegende entwickelte, unterstützt durch einige der klinischen Daten, die die Grundlage dieser Hypothese bilden.

Dr. Karen Horney: Certain Reservations to the Concept of Psychic Bisexuality.

Männlichkeitswünsche bei Frauen und Weiblichkeitswünsche bei Männern werden in der psychoanalytischen Literatur entweder als direkter Ausdruck innewohnender psychischer Bisexualität oder als Resultat eines psychischen Konfliktes, der auf dieser Grundlage irgendwie entstanden ist, aufgefaßt. Ohne die angenommene Existenz einer naturgegebenen psychischen Bisexualität in Frage zu stellen, lenkt die Vortragende die Aufmerksamkeit auf die Unsicherheit hinsichtlich der Reichweite und genauen Funktion dieser bisexuellen Faktoren. Man kann in vielen Fällen beobachten, daß Charakteristika und Haltungen des anderen Geschlechts als Deckmantel für sadomasochistische Tendenzen angenommen werden. Bei diesen Patienten sind nicht die bisexuellen Wünsche, sondern die ihnen zugrunde liegenden sado-masochistischen Vorgänge das dynamische Prinzip. Hier sollten therapeutische Bemühungen einsetzen, da die Betonung der bisexuellen Haltungen das Durcharbeiten des zugrundeliegenden Sado-Masochismus gefährdet.

Dr. Fritz Wittels: A Type of Woman with a Threefold Love Life.

Der Vortragende stellt fest, daß Frauen in dreifacher Weise auf die Anforderungen ihres Geschlechtes reagieren: 1. durch ihre Verleugnung, 2. durch Umstellung auf herausfordernde Männlichkeit, 3. durch die normale Haltung der Fügsamkeit gegen sie. Es gibt Frauen, die alle drei Reaktionsformen — manchmal fast gleichzeitig, manchmal in verschiedenen Lebensabschnitten — in ihrem Leben realisieren. Diese dreifache Haltung gegenüber dem Mann und seinen Forderungen zeigt ein kompliziertes und verworrenes Bild. Aus der Analyse einiger Fälle dieser Art werden Belege zu diesen Beobachtungen angeführt. Es scheint klar, daß diese Frauen dem hysterischen Typus angehören.

Dr. Franz Alexander und Dr. George W. Wilson: Quantitative Dream Studies (A Methodological Attempt of a Quantitative Evaluation of Psychoanalytic Material).

Der Vortrag behandelt eine quantitative Studie über das Traummaterial aus verschiedenen analytischen Behandlungsgeschichten. Die Träume wurden nach den wesentlichen dynamischen Tendenzen, die sie zum Ausdruck bringen, eingeteilt. Die verhältnismäßige Intensität dieser elementaren dynamischen Tendenzen wurde nach der Häufigkeit, mit der sie im Traumleben des Patienten auftraten, eingeschätzt. Das Vorherrschen oral-rezeptiver und aggressiver Tendenzen ließ sich bei gewissen Typen von gastro-intestinalen Neurosen feststellen. In anderen wieder waren anale und retentive Tendenzen vorherrschend. Diese Unterschiede, die durch die dargestellte

Methode quantitativ ausgedrückt wurden, gestatteten die Ausarbeitung quantitativer Beziehungen, die für bestimmte Krankheiten typisch sind. Ferner wurde eine quantitative Wiedergabe des Verlaufs der psychoanalytischen Behandlung in individuellen Fällen durch eine quantitative Bewertung des Wechsels der dynamischen Tendenzen, wie sie sich in den Träumen des Patienten während der Analyse ausdrückten, versucht.

Der gegenwärtige Vorstand: Dr. A. A. Brill, Permanent President; Dr. William A. White, Vice-President, und Dr. Ernest E. Hadley, Secretary-Treasurer, wird wiedergewählt.

Ernest E. Hadley,
Sekretär

Boston Psychoanalytic Society

I. und II. Quartal 1935

5. Februar: Außerordentliche Sitzung zum Gedächtnis Dr. William Hermans, dessen plötzlicher Tod für die Vereinigung einen schweren Schlag bedeutete. Die Gedenkrede hielt der Präsident der Vereinigung Dr. Martin W. Peck.

24. Februar: Außerordentliche Sitzung: Dr. Gregory Zilboorg, New York: Some Side-lights on the Psychology of Murderers.

17. März: Dr. John M. Murray, Vorsitzender des Komitees zur Institutsgründung, berichtet über die Arbeiten des Komitees und die Satzungen des in Aussicht genommenen Institutes.

Dr. I. H. Coriat wird an Stelle des verstorbenen Dr. Herman zum Mitglied des Lehrkomitees gewählt.

Bericht über die Schaffung des Hanns-Sachs-Fonds in der Schweiz zur Förderung des Unterrichtes künftiger Kandidaten und emigrierter Lehranalytiker.

23. April: Ordentliche geschäftliche Sitzung der Vereinigung.

27. Mai: Jahresversammlung: Bericht des Lehrkomitees, des Kassenwartes und des Komitees zur Institutsgründung. Dessen Vorsitzender wird bevollmächtigt, das Institut den Vorschriften des Staates Massachusetts gemäß behördlich eintragen zu lassen und an der Organisation des Institutes, das im Herbst 1935 eröffnet werden soll, weiterzuarbeiten.

Die Verfassung und die Statuten der Boston Psychoanalytic Society werden einstimmig angenommen.

Einstimmige Wiederwahl des Vorstandes: Dr. Martin W. Peck, Präsident; Doktor John M. Murray, Vizepräsident; Dr. M. Ralph Kaufman, Sekretär-Kassenwart; Dr. Hanns Sachs und Dr. I. H. Coriat werden für drei Jahre in das Lehrkomitee gewählt; die Wahl von Dr. John M. Murray und Dr. Martin W. Peck wird bis zum Jahre 1938 verlängert. Infolge ihrer Mitgliedschaft beim Lehrkomitee werden Drs. I. H. Coriat, John M. Murray, Martin W. Peck und M. Ralph Kaufman automatisch Sachwalter des Institutes. Drs. Ives Hendrick, William Healy, Henry Murray jr. werden einstimmig gewählt. Dr. Hanns Sachs wird zum Vorsitzenden der Beratungsstelle des Institutes gewählt. Drs. I. H. Coriat, Ives Hendrick, John M. Murray, Hanns Sachs und M. Ralph Kaufman werden auf Empfehlung des Lehrkomitees als Lehranalytiker für das kommende akademische Jahr bestätigt.

M. Ralph Kaufmann,
Sekreätr

Chicago Psychoanalytic Society

I. und II. Quartal 1935

12. Januar: Dr. Robert K n i g h t: Theoretical and Practical Considerations in the Analysis of a Minister. Diskussion über die Frage, ob religiöse Vorstellungen durch die analytische Technik abgebaut werden: Drs. B l i t z s t e n, F r e n c h, S a u l und E i s l e r.

26. Januar: Dr. Thomas R a t l i f f: Case of Schizophrenia.

Diskussion mehrerer Mitglieder der Vereinigung über das von Dr. R a t l i f f vorgelegte Deutungsmaterial und über die Beziehung zwischen dem akuten schizophrenen Ausbruch und der analytischen Behandlung.

9. Februar: Geschäftliche Sitzung: Diskussion über die Frage außerordentlicher Sitzungen, zu denen ein ausgewählter Kreis von Psychiatern und Ärzten eingeladen werden könnte.

Wissenschaftliche Sitzung: Dr. Ives H e n d r i c k (Boston): Defect in Ego Development and Character Neurosis.

23. Februar: Dr. Catherine B a c o n: Conflicts Related to the Feminine Role in a case of Constipation and Bulemia.

Dem Vortrag liegt die Krankengeschichte einer 40jährigen Patientin zugrunde, deren Bulimie und Obstipation den Wunsch, alles für sich zu haben und nichts dafür zu geben, repräsentiert. Ein Orgasmus bedeutet für sie weibliches Geben, das ihrer Angst vor analem Geben parallel läuft. Menstruieren bedeutet ebenfalls Geben wider Willen. Die weibliche Rolle bedeutet für sie zu geben, wann es erwartet wird. Ihr Wunsch ist es, nur in männlicher Weise zu geben. Die Diskussion erörtert das Problem des „Gebens".

9. März: Geschäftliche Sitzung: Dr. F r e n c h berichtet über den gegenwärtigen Stand der Arbeiten des Statutenausschusses der American Psychoanalytic Association. Die Frage der Erfordernisse zur außerordentlichen und ordentlichen Mitgliedschaft bei der Chicago Psychoanalytic Society und für Lehranalytiker wird dem Lehrkomitee zur weiteren Behandlung zugewiesen.

Wissenschaftliche Sitzung: Dr. George J. M o h r: Psychotherapy in Childhood.

Außer einer Beschreibung der Technik werden die Vorteile und Nachteile der Kinderanalyse dargelegt. Die Diskussion befaßt sich hauptsächlich mit den verschiedenen Indikationen und Kontraindikationen für die Analyse am Kinde.

23. März: Geschäftliche Sitzung. Das Lehrkomitee legt eine revidierte Fassung der Vorschriften für Lehranalytiker vor, in der auf die wissenschaftliche Ausbildung und klinische Befähigung besonderer Nachdruck gelegt wird.

Wissenschaftliche Sitzung. Dr. Leon J. S a u l: A Note on the Psychogenesis of Organic Symptoms.

Organische Symptome sind entweder direkte Gefühls- oder Konfliktsäußerungen oder indirekte, bzw. zufällige mechanische Endresultate einer direkten psychischen Gefühlsäußerung. Das vorliegende Material zeigt, daß organische Symptome, obwohl sie zu Gefühlskonflikten in Beziehung stehen, nicht deren Symbolisierung sein müssen, sondern auch nur zufällige Endeffekte von Gefühlsäußerungen sein können. Die Erkenntnis dieses Mechanismus nimmt dem Sprung vom Psychischen ins Körperliche seine Rätselhaftigkeit. In der nachfolgenden Diskussion belegen mehrere Mitglieder die Auffassung des Vortragenden durch Krankengeschichten.

27. April: Geschäftliche Sitzung. Diskussion über die vorgeschlagenen Statuten der American Psychoanalytic Association.

25. Mai: Dr. Hyman Lippmann (St. Paul): A Case of Obsessional Neurosis.

8. Juni: Dr. Maurice Levine: Notes on the Acting Out of Incest Urges.

Statistische Daten über 26 Fälle aus der sozialen Arbeit, in denen Inzest zwischen Vater und Tochter, Bruder und Schwester, Mutter und Sohn vorkommen, werden in der Reihenfolge ihrer Häufigkeit angeführt. Mehrere Mitglieder unterziehen den Vortrag vom statistischen Gesichtspunkt aus einer Kritik.

Dr. Maurice Levine: Interpretation of the Panic Reaction.

Der Vortragende schlägt vor, die Schreckreaktionen als ein Überwältigtwerden des Ichs durch Angst angesichts einer Gefahr von seiten der Außenwelt, des Über-Ichs und des Es zu formulieren. Es wird die Beziehung zwischen Schreckreaktionen und Kastrationsangst angedeutet und schließlich eine Analogie zwischen Schreckzuständen und Alpdrücken erwähnt.

22. Juni: Geschäftliche Sitzung: Dr. Robert Knight wird zum außerordentlichen Mitglied gewählt. Der Präsident, Vizepräsident und Sekretär werden für das kommende Jahr wiedergewählt.

Helen Vicent McLean,
Sekretärin

The New York Psychoanalytic Society
I. und II. Quartal 1935

29. Januar: Wahl des Vorstandes: Dr. A. A. Brill, Präsident; Dr. Bertram D. Lewin, Vizepräsident; Dr. George E. Daniels, Sekretär; Dr. Monroe A. Meyer, Kassenwart; Drs. Blumgart, Oberndorf und Stern, Vorstandsmitglieder. Von den sechs vom Präsidenten nominierten Personen werden Drs. Amsden, Jelliffe, Lehrman und Oberndorf zusammen mit den bei der Gründung vorgesehenen ex-officio-Mitgliedern in das Lehrkomitee gewählt. Bei der ersten Sitzung werden Dr. Jelliffe zum Vorsitzenden und Dr. Lehrman zum geschäftsführenden Sekretär gewählt. Dr. Meyer kündigt als Leiter des Institutes die Veröffentlichung eines Berichtes über die Arbeit des Institutes während der drei Jahre seines Bestehens an.

Wissenschaftliche Sitzung: Dr. Fritz Wittels: Existence Philosophy and Psycho-Analysis. — Dr. Robert Fliess: Material Projection.

26. Februar: Dr. O. Spurgen English: The Need for an Analytic Background in Prison Psychiatry.

12. März: Außerordentliche Sitzung: Diskussion über den neuen Satzungsentwurf für die American Psychoanalytic Association. Dr. Oberndorf legt als Vertreter der New York Society den Entwurf vor, der von den Mitgliedern Punkt für Punkt erörtert wird. Zur endgültigen Beschlußfassung wird noch eine eigene Sitzung einberufen werden.

26. März: Dr. Hermann Nunberg: Homosexuality and Aggression.

30. April: Ordentliche Sitzung. Dr. Ives Hendrick: The Sexualization of Hostile

Trends in Dream Resistance and in Schizophrenia. Diskussion: Drs. Feigenbaum, Nunberg, Lorand, Lewin und Schimenti.

21. Mai: Wissenschaftliche Sitzung: Zwei Vorträge zum Thema „Lactation in a Virgin": Dr. Walter Briehl (als Gast) behandelt die psychischen, Dr. Ernest W. Kulka (als Gast) die somatischen Aspekte des vorliegenden Falles. An der von Dr. Max Mayer eröffneten Diskussion beteiligen sich Drs. Feigenbaum, Jelliffe, Nunberg, Rado und Lehrman.

Während der Berichtsperiode wurden Dr. Karen Horney (von der Chicago Society), Dr. Simon Rothenberg und Dr. William J. Spring zu ordentlichen Mitgliedern gewählt.

George E. Daniels,
Sekretär

The Washington-Baltimore Psychoanalytic Society
I. Quartal 1935

12. Januar: Dr. Lucile Dooley: Notes on the Development of Psychological Sex Differences.

Geschäftliche Sitzung: Bericht von Dr. William V. Silverberg, Vertreter der Vereinigung beim Statutenkomitee der American Psychoanalytic Association. Wahl des Vorstandes: Dr. Lewis B. Hill, Präsident; Dr. Clara Thompson, Vizepräsident; Dr. Bernard S. Robbins, Sekretär-Kassenwart; Dr. Lucile Dooley, Vorstandsmitglied.

9. Februar: Dr. Karen Horney (New York City, als Gast der Vereinigung): Notes on the Problem of Masochism.

9. März: Dr. Harry Stack Sullivan: Specific Restrictions to Personal Awareness. Geschäftliche Sitzung. Diskussion über die neuen Statuten der American Psychoanalytic Association.

Dr. Bernard S. Robbins,
Sekretär

Finnisch-Schwedische Psychoanalytische Vereinigung
II. Quartal 1935
I. Sitzungen

18. April: Satzungen, Mitgliedergebühren. — Dr. Kulovesi: Zur Symbolik. — Dr. Kulovesi: Ein Fall mit Erythrophobie und psychogenen Hautveränderungen. (Diskussion.)

18. Juni: Dr. Sandström. Autoreferat ihres neuerschienenen Buches „En psykoanalytisk kvinnostudie". Ernst Ahlgren—Victoria Benedictsson. (Eine psa. Frauenstudie.)

Geschäftliches: Zum ordentlichen Mitglied wurde nachträglich gewählt: Dr. phil. Tora Sandström.

II. Referierabende

5. April: Ekman: Neueres zum Angstproblem.

2. Mai: N. Bratt: Melanie Kleins „Psychoanalyse des Kindes".

III. Kontrollseminare

25. April, 7. Mai, 4., 11. und 13. Juni: Referenten: Nielsen, Ekman, Nycander, Nielsen.

IV. Vorträge

für Mediziner, Pädagogen u. a. im Stockholmer Krankenhaus „Serafienerlasarettet". (Etwa 50 Zuhörer.)

1. April: G. Lundberg: Erziehungsprobleme.
15. April: Dr. Tamm: Intellektuelle Hemmungen.

Alfhild Tamm

Indian Psycho-Analytical Society

I. Quartal 1935

27. Januar: Jahresversammlung. Wahl des Vorstandes: Dr. G. Bose, Präsident; Lt.-Col.Berkeley Hill und Mr.H.P.Maiti, Vorstandsmitglieder; Mr.M.N.Banerji, Sekretär; ferner Dr. S. C. Mitra, Bibliothekar, Mr. M. N. Samanta, Bibliothekarstellvertreter; S. K. Bose, Stellvertretender Sekretär. Weiters wurde beschlossen, Dr. Laha angesichts der Häufung dringlicher Arbeiten als stellvertretenden Geschäftsführer für das laufende Jahr zu bestellen.

Ausschuß des Indian Psycho-Analytical Institute (für 1935 bis 1937): Dr.G.Bose (Präsident), Lt.-Col. Berkeley Hill, Mr. M. P. Maiti, Dr. B. C. Ghosh, Mr.Gopeswar Pal und Mr. M. N. Banerji (Sekretär).

Dr. Surendra Chandra Laha wurde (im März 1934) zum Mitglied gewählt.

7. Februar: Tagung des Indian Psycho-Analytical Institute. Alle in Kalkutta lebenden ordentlichen und außerordentlichen Mitglieder wurden zur Teilnahme an der Tagung des Instituts eingeladen, bei der eine Zusammenkunft mit Lt.-Col. C. D. Daly stattfand, der nach seiner Rückkehr aus Europa nach Kalkutta versetzt worden war. Dr. Bose stellte ihn den Mitgliedern der Vereinigung vor. Die Mitglieder des Instituts besprachen eine Anregung des Sekretärs, monatlich an zwei Abenden zur Diskussion wissenschaftlicher Themen, insbesondere solcher, die im „Journal of PsA." erörtert werden, zusammenzukommen. Diese Zusammenkünfte sollen den ordentlichen und außerordentlichen Mitgliedern sowie den Lehrkandidaten zugänglich sein. Der Vorschlag wurde angenommen; vorläufig wurde der erste Mittwoch jedes Monats zur Abhaltung solcher Abende bestimmt.

6. März: Mr. Banerji: A synopsis of Laforgues paper „Resistances at the Conclusion of Analytic Treatment" (siehe Journ. of PsA., Oktober 1934).

Lt.-Col. Berkeley Hill beschreibt verschiedene Methoden zur Hervorrufung von Träumen (indem z. B. eine Flasche oder ein „Kukri" unter das Kopfkissen gelegt wird oder die Beine vor dem Schlafengehen mit einer Schnur zusammengebunden werden) unter Berücksichtigung der Eigenart und des Verlaufes des einzelnen Falles.

27. März: Lt.-Col. Daly: One Aspect of the Mother Complex. Der Vortragende ist der Ansicht, daß der Geruch und der Anblick der Menstrualblutung der Mutter die Ursache der Kastrationsangst und der Entwicklung des Ödipuskomplexes bilden, und führt Krankengeschichten, Träume usw. zur Unterstützung seiner Auffassung an.

3. April: Lt.-Col. Berkeley Hill: Some Reactionary Tendencies in Psycho-Analysis.

Der Vortragende bespricht die gegen die Psychoanalyse erhobenen Vorwürfe, daß
sie einen Faktor der Zersetzung bilde und die Kulturideale gefährde.

M. N. Banerji,

Sekretär

Chewra Psychoanalytith b'Erez=Israel

I. Quartal 1935

12. Januar (Jerusalem): Frau Peller-Roubiczek: „Realitätsannäherung als Aufgabe der Erziehung."

9. März (Jerusalem): Frau Obernik-Reiner: „Die psychoanalytische Individual-
beobachtung innerhalb der Kindergruppe und ihr Wert für den Aufbau der Gemein-
schaftserziehung."

Geschäftliche Sitzung. Wiederwahl des Vorstandes: Dr. M. Eitingon, Vorsitzender; Dr. I. Schalit, Sekretär-Kassenwart.

Bericht über die Arbeit der einzelnen Mitglieder und ihre Eingliederung in die
Ärzteschaft des Landes sowie über die Zusammenarbeit mit den Pädagogen.

Frau Peller-Roubiczek (bisher außerordentliches Mitglied der Wiener Psychoanalytischen Vereinigung) wird als außerordentliches Mitglied aufgenommen.

Dr. I. Schalit,

Sekretär

Société Psychanalytique de Paris

II. Quartal 1935

6. April: Vorsitz: Dr. Pichon.

Dr. Spitz: „Le rôle des facteurs sociaux dans la typologie des névroses."
Diskussion: Dr. Odier, Mme. Marie Bonaparte, Mme. Morgenstern, Mme.
Codet, MM. Schiff, Pichon und Spitz.

In dieser Sitzung werden zu außerordentlichen Mitgliedern gewählt:

Herr Dr. J. L. Pierre, 39, Avenue Charles Floquet, Paris VII.

Prinz Peter von Griechenland, 6, rue Adolphe Yvon, Paris XVI.

18. Mai: Vorsitz: Dr. Pichon.

Dr. Pizarro Crespo: „Le rôle des facteurs psychiques dans le domaine de la
clinique."

Diskussion: MM. Laforgue, Codet, Parcheminey, Mme. Marie Bonaparte,
MM. Schiff, Leuba, Dalbiez, Pizarro.

In dieser Sitzung werden die Herren Dr. Laforgue und Dr. Leuba zu Bericht-
erstattern für die „Neuvième conference des psychanalystes de langue française" bestimmt. Berichtsthema: „La famille névrotique et la névrose familiale."

18. Juni: Vorsitz: Dr. Pichon.

Dr. Odette Codet: „A propos de trois cas d'anorexie mentale."

Diskussion: Mme. Marie Bonaparte, MM. Leuba, Borel, Mme. Morgenstern, MM. Löwenstein, Laforgue, Codet, Odier, Parcheminey, Spitz,
Lacan, Chentrier, Pichon, Mme. Codet.

Mademoiselle G u e x, 9, Florimont, in Lausanne (Schweiz), wird einstimmig zum außerordentlichen Mitglied gewählt.

Dr. C o d e t und Dr. René S p i t z werden zu ordentlichen Mitgliedern gewählt.

Das Datum der „Neuvième conférence des psychanalystes de langue française" wird für Ostern 1936 festgesetzt. Sie wird über Vorschlag des Herrn Dr. d e S a u s s u r e, der die Kongreßteilnehmer einlädt, in Morges (Schweiz) stattfinden.

Die Sitzung im Juli fällt wegen der Sommerurlaube aus.

Dr. J. Leuba,
Sekretär

Schweizerische Gesellschaft für Psychoanalyse

I. Quartal 1935

19. Januar (Zürich). Dir. Dr. med. A. K i e l h o z, Königsfelden: „Über Garderobediebstähle." Es werden zwei Fälle referiert, die von Gerichtsbehörden zur psa. Begutachtung und Beobachtung in die Pflegeanstalt Königsfelden eingeliefert wurden. Ref. zieht Parallelen zur Pseudologie, zum Fetischismus und zu den symbolischen Diebstählen, weist hin auf die psychotherapeutischen Möglichkeiten bei mehr neurotischen und bei mehr psychopathischen Garderobedieben. Das Problem der Zurechnungsfähigkeit wird diskutiert.

Diskussion: Bally, Boß, Kielholz, Pfister, Sarasin, Steiner, Zulliger.

In einer kurzen geschäftlichen Sitzung wird gewünscht, daß ein welschschweizerisches Mitglied den Vorstand ergänze.

9. Februar (Zürich). Generalversammlung. Hans Z u l l i g e r, Ittigen: „Zur Psychologie des narzißtisch-triebhaften Charakters." (Wird zusammen mit Korreferat M e n g und eventuellen Diskussionsbeiträgen in der „Zeitschrift f. psa. Pädagogik" abgedruckt.) Korreferat und Diskussion auf eine besondere Sitzung verlegt.

Geschäftliche Sitzung: Jahresbericht, Kassabericht, Bericht der U. K., des Bibliothekars werden genehmigt, der alte Vorstand entlastet. Der alte Vorstand wird, ergänzt durch Privatdozent Dr. med. Hry. F l o u r n o y, Genf, wiedergewählt (S a r a s i n, F l o u r n o y, B l u m, P f i s t e r, Z u l l i g e r), er amtiert unter der Leitung von B l u m, Bern, zugleich als Unterrichtskommission. Rechnungsrevisoren 1935: B o ß und S t e i n e r. Jahresbeitrag inkl. Zeitschriftabonnements Frs. 75.—.

M e n g referiert über seine Tätigkeit als Volkshochschuldozent in Basel vor 150 bis 250 Hörern. Er hielt auch Vorträge und Kurse über Psa.-Pädagogik vor Lehrerorganisationen, die von Behördemitgliedern offiziell besucht und freundlich aufgenommen wurden. Die Gästeliste wird ergänzt.

2. März (Zürich). Dr. med. H. M e n g, Basel: „Korreferat zum Vortrag Zulliger vom 9. Februar." (Wird zusammen mit dem Vortrag Zulliger in der Zeitschrift f. psa. Pädagogik" publiziert.)

Diskussion: Frau Behn-Eschenburg, Bally, Kielholz, Meng, Frl. Sachs (a. G.), Busch (a. G.), Sarasin, Steiner, Zulliger.

Geschäftliche Sitzung: M e n g, Basel, wird einstimmig als ordentliches Mitglied aufgenommen.

30. März (Bern). Dr. med. E. B l u m, Bern: „Zur Psychologie und Psychopathologie

der Arbeit." Vergleiche zwischen der ursprünglich-primitiven und der modernen Maschinenarbeit, Rückwirkungen auf die Psyche des Arbeiters. (Wird publiziert.)

Diskussion: Bally, Boß, Blum, Frau Dr. Blum, Frau Behn-Eschenburg, Kasser (a. G.), Kielholz, Mariasch (a. G.), Pfenninger, Frl. Sachs (a. G.), Sarasin, Steiner, Zulliger, alle in mehreren Voten.

Zulliger hielt zwei psychoanalytisch orientierte Vorträge am Radio Bern, einen Vortrag über psa. Erziehungshilfe vor dem kantonalbernischen Handarbeitslehrerinnenverein im Rathaus, Bern, und ein Referat vor dem Ausschuß für das Schweiz. Jugendschriftenwerk.

Hans Zulliger,
Sekretär

III. Mitteilung

In dem als Beilage zu Heft 1 dieses Jahrganges erschienenen Mitgliederverzeichnis der Internationalen Psychoanalytischen Vereinigung wurde auf Seite 11 als Adresse des Zentral-Präsidenten der I. P. V. und Präsidenten der British Psycho-Analytical Society, Dr. Ernest Jones, fälschlich 42 York Terrace, London N. W. angegeben. Es soll richtig heißen: 81 Harley Street, London W. 1.